Publisher
Lloyd J. Short

Associate Publisher
Tim Huddleston

Acquisitions Manager
Cheri Robinson

Managing Editor
Matthew Morrill

Marketing Manager
Gregg Bushyeager

Acquisitions Editor
Rob Tidrow

Product Director
Rob Tidrow

Senior Editor
Nancy E. Sixsmith

Production Coordinator
Lisa Wagner

Production Editors
Patrice Hartmann, John Kane

Editors
Jo Anna Arnott, Jill Bond, Chuck Hutchinson,
Steve Weiss, Lisa Wilson, Phil Worthington

Technical Editor
Robert Waring

Acquisitions Coordinator
Stacey Beheler

Editorial Assistant
Karen Opal

Publishing Assistant
Melissa Lynch

Book Design
Roger Morgan, Mathew Morrill

Production
Nick Anderson, Angela Bannan, Ayrika Bryant, Charlotte Clapp, Lisa Daugherty, Terri Edwards,
Mitzi Foster Gianakos, Dennis Clay Hager, Stephanie McComb, Sean Medlock, Mike Mucha, Wendy Ott,
Linda Quigley, Angela Pozdol, Beth Rago, Tonya Simpson, Dennis Wesner, Donna Winter, Lillian Yates, Alyssa Yesh

Indexed by
Suzanne Snyder

About the Author

Jim Boyce is a Contributing Editor to *Windows Magazine*, and a regular contributor to *CADENCE Magazine* and other computer publications. He has been involved with computers since the late seventies, and has used computers in one way or another as a structural designer, production planner, systems manager, programmer, and college instructor. He has a wide range of experience in the DOS, Windows, and UNIX environments. Jim is the author of the best-selling books *Maximizing Windows 3.1* and *Windows for Non-Nerds*, both from New Riders Publishing. Jim has authored and coauthored a number of other books, including the following titles:

- *Windows for Non-Nerds*
- *Maximizing Windows 3.1*
- *Inside Windows for Workgroups*
- *Inside Windows 3.1*
- *Windows 3.1 Networking*
- *Maximizing Windows 3.0*
- *Maximizing MS-DOS 5*
- *AutoCAD for Beginners*
- *Inside AutoCAD*
- *Inside AutoCAD for Windows*
- *Maximizing AutoCAD Volume 1*

Jim is a transplanted Texan living in Minnesota. You can contact Jim via his CompuServe ID, 76516,3403, or on the Internet at the address 76516.3403@compuserve.com.

Mike Buckingham, who took the photographs for this book, was born in Fargo, North Dakota, and was raised in Fergus Falls, Minnesota. He became interested in photography while in the military in the 1960s. Mike began taking formal classes in photography in the mid 1970s. By the late 1970s Mike was working in the electronic repair field and teaching adult education classes in photography.

Mike started his current career in the photo retail industry in the early 1980s. He now is living in Grand Forks, North Dakota, with his family and their cat.

Dedication

This book is dedicated with great affection to Lee Langford, "the Old Man," who always beats the system. Special thanks also go to Ruth Langford, who has the difficult task of keeping that old Irishman in line.

Acknowledgments

Many people helped in the creation of this book in one way or another. I offer my wholehearted thanks to:

Mike Buckingham, for the outstanding job of setting up and shooting the photographs for the book. Besides being a super guy, he's also a terrific brother-in-law.

Cheri Robinson and Rob Tidrow, for developing and coordinating this project, and for handling the headaches that always go with a new book project. Rob, please tell Cheri to take a vacation.

Lloyd Short, for agreeing to take on the book. Besides, he's the President and I have to butter him up some.

Stacey Beheler, for her invaluable help in arranging for equipment and slides, for helping coordinate the project, and for always being a pleasure to talk to on the phone.

Fred Howland and JDR Microdevices, for great support over the years and for helping provide the majority of the equipment for the book. JDR Microdevices can be reached at 2233 Samaritan Drive, San Jose, CA 95124; or by phone at (800) 538-5000.

Patrice Hartmann, for her superb editing and other contributions to the book.

Matthew Morrill, for the terrific job editing the artwork.

Jo Anna Arnott, Jill Bond, Chuck Hutchinson, John Kane, Steve Weiss, Lisa Wilson, and Phil Worthington, for their editing prowess.

The Production department of Prentice Hall Computer Publishing, for turning text and photos into a real book.

John Schmitt, because I seem to have this compulsion to see his name in print in my books. I don't understand it.

Snerdly T. Whipplefoot, for saving the Universe from destruction, although no one knew it was in any danger, least of all Snerdly.

Mike Buckingham wishes to thank:

Jim Boyce, for thinking of me and giving me the opportunity to photograph this book.

Jim's family, for allowing me to turn their basement into a studio.

Michelle, Evin, and Spot the cat, for taking care of everything at home during the photography sessions.

New Riders Publishing

The staff of New Riders Publishing is committed to bringing you the very best in computer reference material. Each New Riders book is the result of months of work by authors and staff, who research and refine the information contained within its covers.

As part of this commitment to you, the NRP reader, New Riders invites your input. Please let us know if you enjoy this book, if you have trouble with the information and examples presented, or if you have a suggestion for the next edition.

Please note, however, that the New Riders staff cannot serve as a technical resource for DOS or DOS application-related questions, including hardware- or software-related problems. Refer to the documentation that accompanies your DOS or DOS application package for help with specific problems.

If you have a question or comment about any New Riders book, please write to NRP at the following address. We will respond to as many readers as we can. Your name, address, or phone number will never become part of a mailing list or be used for any other purpose than to help us continue to bring you the best books possible.

New Riders Publishing
Paramount Publishing
Attn: Associate Publisher
201 West 103rd Street
Indianapolis, IN 46290

If you prefer, you can fax New Riders Publishing at the following number:

(317) 581-4670

We welcome your electronic mail to our CompuServe ID:

70031,2231

Thank you for selecting *Keeping Your PC Alive!*

Contents at a Glance

Part 1: Fiddling and Tweaking Your Computer

Part 2: Adding New Stuff to Your Computer

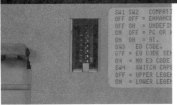

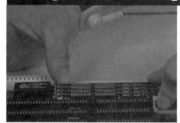

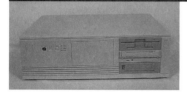

Part 4: Appendix

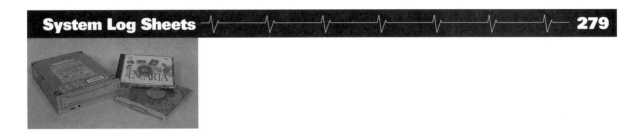

Contents

Part 1 Fiddling and Tweaking Your Computer

3   Tweak Your System Files 33

4   All You Need To Know
      about Memory 53

5 Hard Disk Tweaking: Cleaning, Packing, and Compressing 71

Part 2   Adding New Stuff
to Your Computer

10   Floppy Disk Drives 133

11   CD-ROM Drives 143

Part 3 Healing Your Computer

23   The System Runs, But Not Without Complaining 245

Read Me First

Few people ever read the introduction of a book, particularly in a computer book. Instead of an introduction, I've included material that would go in an introduction in this chapter. The chapter also covers some basic concepts about the way a PC works so that you can get ready to begin improving your computer.

This chapter covers the following topics:

- How this book can help you

- How this book is structured, including conventions

- How to use some of the programs on your PC to view and change your PC's configuration

- How some of the parts of the computer's operating system work (and work together) to make the computer a useful tool

Getting Started with Your PC

I began to use personal computers in the late seventies, when the IBM PC was just a gleam in IBM's eye. Back then, personal computers were a big deal—you had to be a card-carrying member of the techno-geek union to use them. Personal computers were difficult to learn, often poorly documented, and usually required someone with enough patience to spend hours and hours puzzling over the most trivial thing.

Hmm…doesn't sound much different from today, does it?

Okay, things have changed some. Personal computers are no longer a big deal. They're just tools for doing jobs faster and better (hopefully). And to be fair, there's no lack of documentation about today's PCs. The booming computer book business is proof of that.

The last ten years have brought PCs to the masses (you and me), just like the Volkswagen helped bring cheap transportation to the masses. You no longer have to understand the way an electron orbits a nucleus to write a letter with your computer, any more than you have to know the way the fuel injection system in your car works to be able to drive it.

But this PC proliferation also means that a large number of computer users aren't technically knowledgeable. They don't know how a hard disk works, or the way the modem enables a computer to talk to someone else's computer. But that's fine—after all, we still haven't figured out that fuel-injection bit, have we?

Great—now we've established a car/computer analogy. What happens when your PC breaks down and you can't (or won't) spend a couple hundred bucks to have someone *maybe* fix it? What if you want to give it a do-it-yourself tune-up to keep it useful for another year or two? What if you need to install a new gadget in it? What if you pulled a bonehead stunt such as pouring a cup of coffee on your keyboard? Use *Keeping Your PC Alive*.

What This Book Is All About

Back in the sixties, John Muir wrote a book called *How to Keep Your Volkswagen Alive*, and billed it as a manual of

step-by-step procedures for the complete idiot. Using John's book, *anybody* with a few tools and a little self-confidence could fix whatever ailed a VW.

I'm proof—I used John's book to completely rebuild engines, replace brakes, and do all sorts of other mischief to the car. I couldn't afford to pay someone else to fix it for me, even though I knew absolutely nothing about auto-mechanics. As I gained experience, it became a matter of refusing to pay someone to do something I was perfectly capable of doing. (By the way, if you're a VW sort of person, John's book is still in print, updated for the very latest VW stuff.)

Why should fixing or tuning up a computer be different from tuning-up or fixing a car? They're both just machines. There really isn't that much to computers, and they are *a lot* easier to repair than a car. Take my word—I've done a lot of both.

Do-It-Yourself Repairs?

So that's part of what *Keeping Your PC Alive* is about. If something goes kaput in your PC, *Keeping Your PC Alive* helps you figure out what went bad, find it, and fix it. You don't have to do arcane stuff like solder chips onto a circuit board—you just need to be able to flip some switches, replace a few easily replaceable parts, and be capable of using a screwdriver. Best of all, you don't have to shell out a bundle of money to have someone fix it for you.

How about Tune-Ups?

Keeping your PC alive means more than just fixing it when it implodes into a smoldering pool of molten goo. It also means fiddling with your PC's configuration files, adding memory, making more hard disk space available, and doing all sorts of other things that make your PC run just a little faster, a little better, and a little longer. In short, it means making your PC useful for a few more months or years until it's time for a new one.

Keeping Your PC Alive will help you squeeze the extra performance out of your PC that will help keep it a useful tool. You don't know what configuration files are, or how your system's memory works? No problem. I'll tell you what you need to know, what to do, and how to do it. Whether you're a Windows user or a DOS user, *Keeping Your PC Alive* will help you make your system run better.

I Want To Install One of Those Cool Whatsits

Let's face it—all sorts of cool gadgets, gizmos, and whizmos are available that you can put in your PC. Sound cards, CD-ROM drives, TV cards…you name it. There also are a lot of mundane things such as hard drives, floppy drives, and I/O cards that you can install yourself. Most gadgets take less than 30 minutes to install and get working. In a little longer session you even can replace your PC's motherboard (explained in Chapter 16, "Motherboards,"), and upgrade it to be as fast and powerful as the latest technology.

Keeping Your PC Alive gives you step-by-step procedures for configuring, installing, and testing a wide range of computer gadgets. Best of all, you don't have to know the way a gadget works to install it in your PC. When you do need some background on the way a gadget works to install it and get it running, I give you an explanation that makes sense, not one that makes you reach for a dictionary or computer glossary.

Poking Around in Your PC

The first part of this book provides general background information about the way your PC works. All you need to know about your computer to begin fine-tuning it is how to turn it on, start programs, and start and use Windows (if you use Windows).

But what about when it comes time to open up your PC and poke around in its innards? That has to be complicated, right? Wrong! You just need the right information, presented in a way that's easy for you to understand. In short, you need a good book.

Keeping Your PC Alive is not the only book on the market that covers computer hardware or upgrading and repairing PCs. Books that cover the ins and outs of the way computer hardware works in mind-numbing detail are out there, but they don't explain how to diagnose and fix a problem.

Other books explain how to fix a problem, but they expect you to know what is wrong in the first place. Few books explain the way to configure and install *specific* types of hardware in any detail.

If you use *Keeping Your PC Alive*, you don't need to know anything about the way a specific piece of equipment works to install, diagnose, or fix it. Any technical information you need is included in the book, where you need it, and in terms that make sense.

I promise not to overexplain a bunch of technical stuff you probably don't want to know anyway. I expect you to say, "Who really cares what the pinouts are on the cables from the power supply to the motherboard? Just tell me which plug to plug where, and I'll be happy."

Which leads me to the tone of the book. I promise to avoid technical jargon and long-winded explanations as much as possible. Why say something in three paragraphs when you can say it in one sentence?

When it's time to begin poking inside your computer, you don't need a lot of tools or mechanical inclination. You can do at least 99 percent of the upgrade/repair tasks on your computer with one Phillips-head screwdriver. (It's the only tool I keep in my office.) You might need a few other tools along the way, but that screwdriver is a big start.

How the Book Is Put Together

Keeping Your PC Alive is separated into three main sections. Part 1, "Fiddling and Tweaking Your Computer," covers the types of things you can do to improve your PC's performance with little or no fiddling around inside the machine. The only hands-on topics are adding memory and adding a new hard disk. The rest of the chapters explain changes you can easily make to your operating environment software.

Part 2, "Adding New Stuff to Your Computer," explains ways to configure, install, and test a wide range of computer hardware, from fundamental components, such as the power supply and motherboard, to neat stuff, such as sound cards, video cards, and add-in chips. The procedures in Part 2 explain step-by-step the way to set up the new gadget, install it, test it, and troubleshoot any problems that might crop up. Because it is impossible to cover every brand and model of each type of item, the procedures are written to be generic so that they cover most types. Many of the chapters include tips on using your new gadget in Windows.

Part 3, "Healing Your Computer," helps you figure out what is wrong when your computer goes haywire, and explains what you need to do to fix it. With the exception of memory and hard disk troubleshooting and repair, Part 3 is arranged by symptom, not by hardware. In other words, all you need to know is how your PC is acting, not which piece of equipment is on the blink. If you get an error message, you might have no idea what part of the computer is causing it. Turn to Section 3, look for the error message or symptom, and begin tracking down the problem.

Procedures

Much of *Keeping Your PC Alive* includes step-by-step procedures to help you diagnose problems and install equipment. The procedures typically have an explanation at the beginning of the procedure, followed by a list of steps to perform. Here's a sample procedure:

Procedure:
Becoming a Computer Nerd

Explanation: This procedure gives you the steps you need to become a computer know-it-all nerd. Don't follow this procedure unless you're wearing your pocket protector.

1. Spend every waking moment reading technical manuals. Don't stop until your eyebrows begin to smoke.

2. Disassemble a PC down to the component level, then put it back together again. You get bonus points if it still works.

3. Say "I am not a hacker, I am a human being" 53 times while sitting in the lotus position under a full moon.

Special Characters and Stuff

Throughout *Keeping Your PC Alive*, certain conventions are used to help you distinguish typed commands, things the computer displays, and special key combinations. The following is a list of the conventions used in this book:

- On-screen, all Windows programs and many DOS programs underline a letter in some menu names, menu items, and other control options. The File menu, for example, is displayed on-screen as File. The underlined letter is the letter you can type to choose that command or option. In this book, these *hot keys* are displayed in bold, underlined type: **F**ile.

- Keyboard key combinations appear throughout the book, and appear in the following formats:

  Key1-Key2: When you see a hyphen (-) between two key names, hold down the first key, press the second key, then release both keys. Text example: "Press Alt-Tab to switch to full-screen mode."

  Key1,Key2: When you see a comma (,) between two key names, press the first key, release it, then press and release the second key. Text example: "Press Alt,F to open the File menu."

- Shortcut keys normally are found in the text. Shortcut keys are special keyboard combinations that appear to the right of a menu option. You can press the shortcut keys to choose the associated menu item. A common example is Ctrl-V, the shortcut key for the Paste command in many Windows programs.

- Information you type is in **boldface**. This applies to individual letters, numbers, and text strings. It doesn't apply to special keys, such as Enter, Esc, Alt, or Ctrl.

- New terms appear in *italics*.

- Text displayed on-screen but not part of Windows or a Windows program—such as DOS prompts and messages—appears in a `special typeface`.

- Directory names and file names appear in uppercase letters, along with their file extensions: C:\WINDOWS\SYSTEM.INI.

- DOS commands and other text you type at the DOS command prompt appear in uppercase: **MSD**.

- Whenever you see an instruction to type some text, it means to type the text using the keyboard, but do not press Enter. If you see an instruction to *enter* some text, it means you should type the text and press Enter.

Things To Watch Out For

Chapter 2, "Basic Stuff To Get Started," details safety and other important concepts, but two potential problems bear mentioning here; safety first.

You can get hurt working underneath a car or under its hood while the motor is running. You also can get hurt working on a computer, but in different ways. Aside from getting scratched on some sharp component, your biggest concern is electrocution. That can ruin your whole day. As long as the computer is unplugged when you begin digging around in it, and as long as you don't open up the power supply, you're safe.

Don't take shortcuts—**turn the PC off and unplug it before you even open it up!** And don't forget that even if you don't get hurt working inside a running computer, you can drop a screwdriver, short something out, and fry your PC's guts. That ruins the computer's whole day.

Another thing to watch out for is static electricity. Chapter 2 covers the problem in detail. For now, understand that your body builds up static electrical charges that can zap and destroy some of the tender electronic components inside your PC, rendering the PC useless except as a doorstop until you replace the thing you zapped. Read Chapter 2 before you begin opening up your computer or handling the new add-in boards you just bought.

Making the Most of Windows and DOS

If you haven't done so, upgrade your PC to MS-DOS 6. DOS 6 includes many new features that improve your PC's performance. It includes a new utility called DoubleSpace, which effectively doubles the apparent capacity of the disk by compressing the data on your hard disk.

MS-DOS 6 also includes a new utility called MemMaker to help you configure your system for optimum use of memory. MS-DOS 6 includes utilities for hard disk backup, virus checking and repair, and disk optimization. And, MS-DOS 6 enables you to create multiple system configurations that you can choose from a menu when you start up the PC.

Upgrade to Windows 3.1 if you are using an earlier version. Windows 3.1 is much more stable than Windows 3.0, offers better support for MS-DOS applications, and is considerably faster. In addition, many Windows applications no longer support Windows 3.0.

Using Software Tools You Already Have

You're probably beginning to wonder when we're going to get down to the business of fiddling with the computer. The time is now. This section of the chapter explains some of the software tools already on your computer, and which you can use to begin exploring and fine-tuning your system.

Modifying Files with Edit

For DOS users, the Edit program included with DOS 5 and DOS 6 provides a simple text editor to modify system files (including CONFIG.SYS, AUTOEXEC.BAT, and others). You also can use it to modify Windows initialization files from DOS, useful if you can't get Windows to run and need to modify your Windows INI files to get it running again.

To launch Edit, enter **EDIT** at the DOS command line. You see the program screen shown in figure 1.1. Edit is in your DOS directory as EDIT.COM. If Edit doesn't appear when you type EDIT and press Enter, it probably means that the DOS directory is not part of your system's path (the list of directories the system searches for program files). To overcome this problem, first change to the DOS directory (enter **CD \DOS**) and then try to start Edit.

Figure 1.1: The Edit program with its start-up dialog box displayed.

When Edit first starts and the Welcome to the MS-DOS Editor dialog box appears, you can press Enter for a quick tutorial on using the program. Rather than launch into a big discussion of how to use Edit, I'll just point you to the tutorial.

If you want to get right into the Edit program, press the Esc key when Edit displays its opening dialog box. To load a file for viewing or editing, press Alt,F to open the **F**ile menu, then press O to display the **O**pen dialog box. In the File **N**ame box, enter the name of the file you want to open. If the file is in a different directory, include the path to the file, such as C:\WINDOWS\WIN.INI.

Edit is really just a simple text editor. You can load your system and Windows configuration files into Edit, make changes, and save them. Or, you can view the file and exit Edit without making any changes. You also can create and save new files with Edit. Figure 1.2 shows a typical CONFIG.SYS file loaded into Edit. (CONFIG.SYS is one of the PC's main system configuration files—you learn more about it later in this chapter.)

Figure 1.2: CONFIG.SYS loaded into Edit to view and modify.

Mangling (and Editing) Files with Edlin

Another DOS text editor is the Edlin program (*Edlin*, in a convoluted sort of way, stands for LINe EDitor). You can use Edlin to view and modify a file, just as you can use Edit. Like Edit, Edlin is in your DOS directory as the file EDLIN.EXE.

To start Edlin, you must supply the name of the file you want to edit. To load CONFIG.SYS for editing, for example, enter **EDLIN CONFIG.SYS** on the DOS command line. All you see when Edlin starts is the following:

```
End of input file
*
```

The asterisk (*) is a prompt character, meaning that Edlin is waiting for you to enter a command. Here are some commands you can use:

- **L.** Displays a line or a group of lines. If you want to display the lines beginning at the current cursor location, just enter **L**. To view a range of lines, enter the start and stop lines before the **L**. For example, to display lines 10 through 20, enter **10,20L**.

- ***nnn.*** Where *nnn* is a number, causes Edlin to display that particular line number. To display line 3 for example, just enter **3**.

- **P.** Displays the file a page at a time. Pressing P a second time displays the next page of the file.

- **E.** Exits Edlin and saves the file, including any changes you have made.

- **Q.** Quits Edlin without saving the file.

Edlin has a lot of other command-line options. Edlin is a real headache to use, so I recommend you use Edit. Only use Edlin if you don't have Edit for some reason. If you need help using Edlin, check your DOS manual.

MSD

The Microsoft Diagnostic program, or MSD, probably is on your PC's hard disk in at least one place. Microsoft includes MSD with many of its software products, including MS-DOS and Windows. If you have a number of Microsoft products on your system, you might have more than one copy of MSD floating around (which isn't a problem). The latest version is version 2.01, which is included with MS-DOS 6.

MSD is designed to let Microsoft Technical Support technicians get information from you about your system when you call them about a problem. MSD provides information about your system's memory and other hardware, operating system, software, and much more. It is a useful tool for finding out the way your PC's hardware is configured and for troubleshooting problems.

To start MSD, enter **MSD** at the DOS prompt (see fig. 1.3).

If you receive the error Bad command or file name, MSD is not located in a directory on the specified path. Try changing to the DOS directory, then starting MSD. If that doesn't work, look for MSD in your Windows directory.

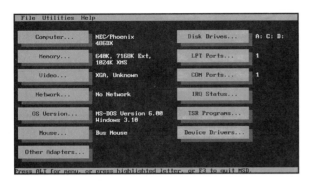

Figure 1.3: The MSD start-up screen displays information about your system.

If you run MSD under Windows, MSD detects Windows running and a dialog box appears (see fig. 1.4). The values reported by MSD when it runs under Windows might be different from those it reports when it runs under DOS. In general, run MSD from DOS to get the most accurate information about your system. The exception is when you want to determine if Windows is changing something from the way it is in DOS.

Viewing Hardware and Software Items

MSD provides information about 13 different items, including your PC hardware, operating system software, programs, and device drivers. To view information about a particular item, press the keyboard key that corresponds to the highlighted letter on the item's bar (such as p for Com**p**uter). MSD then displays a dialog box that contains additional information about the selected item. Figure 1.4 shows an example of the dialog box displayed by the Com**p**uter item.

To activate MSD's menu, press the Alt key. Press F for File, U for Utilities, or H for Help.

Using the File Menu

The **F**ile menu enables you to select from your system's configuration and initialization files. The **F**ile menu also provides a **F**ind File command, which enables you to search your system's disks for a particular file (great when you need to locate a file but don't know where it is on the disk). The **P**rint Report command enables you to create a customized report of your PC's hardware and software configuration (useful when you need to make a hard copy—or

printout—for troubleshooting a problem or installing a new gadget).

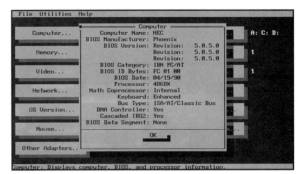

Figure 1.4: The Computer dialog box, which appears when you choose Com**p**uter in MSD.

Using the Utilities Menu

The **U**tilities menu enables you to access two screens that display information about your PC's memory. These two memory screens enable you to view the way your PC's memory is being used by various programs and devices (covered in more detail in Chapter 4, "All You Need To Know about Memory").

The **U**tilities menu also includes **I**nsert Command. This command enables you to insert a line in a configuration or initialization file without having to open up a text editor such as Edit or Notepad (Notepad is discussed later).

For example, you might be using MSD to view your PC's memory so that you can decide which area of memory to use for a new gadget you are installing. Perhaps you need to add a line to CONFIG.SYS that installs a device driver for the gadget, and you need to specify the memory range for it as part of the line. You can insert the line in CONFIG.SYS without having to exit MSD by using **I**nsert Command.

To insert a line into a file with MSD, select **U**tilities, then choose **I**nsert Command (see fig. 1.5).

The dialog box includes three typical configuration lines that you can add to two of your PC's standard configuration files. If you want to add one that is displayed, select it with the cursor keys and press Enter (or choose OK). If you want to add a line not shown in the list, press Enter or choose OK with any one of the three lines selected. After you press Enter, MSD displays a new dialog box (see fig. 1.6) that you can use to specify the **C**ommand, **S**ection, and **F**ile.

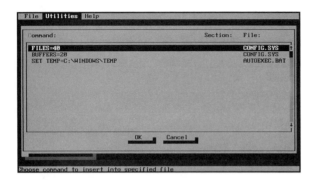

Figure 1.5: Three typical configuration lines that MSD displays for **I**nsert Command.

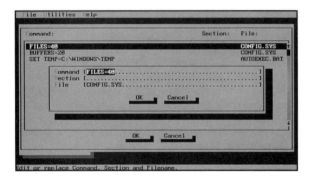

Figure 1.6: Use this dialog box to specify the section and file for the command.

The **C**ommand entry is the actual command line that you want to add to the file. Press Tab until the **C**ommand field is highlighted, or press Alt-C to move the cursor to the **C**ommand field. Type the line as you want it to appear in the file.

The **S**ection field specifies the section of the file where you want the command line added. For example, Windows INI files are separated into sections labeled with a word inside square brackets, such as [386Enh]. Type the section where you want to add the command (include the brackets if applicable).

The **F**ile field specifies the file where you want the command added. Type the name of the file. If it is in a different directory from your current directory, specify the full path, such as C:\WINDOWS\SYSTEM.INI.

After you set the three fields properly, press Enter or choose OK. MSD searches the specified section and file for

a similar entry. If it finds one, it displays two options: ADD LINE, and REPLACE (line), where (line) is the existing copy of the command. Select the appropriate response for your situation, then press Enter or choose OK.

Testing a Printer

The **U**tilities menu includes a command labeled **T**est Printer. The **T**est Printer command is a great way to test whether your printer and computer are communicating properly. If you select the **T**est Printer command, a dialog box appears (see fig. 1.7).

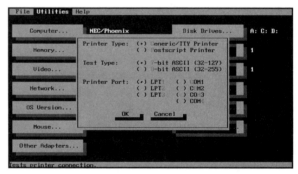

Figure 1.7: This dialog box enables you to specify options for testing a printer.

The **T**est Printer options are explained in detail in Chapter 13, "Printers."

Notepad

If you use Windows, Notepad is a useful program for viewing and editing configuration and initialization files. Notepad is in the Windows directory as NOTEPAD.EXE. It's program icon is in the Accessories group in Program Manager. Figure 1.8 shows Notepad with the file WIN.INI loaded for viewing and editing.

Notepad is a simple program. To open, save, or print a file, select the **F**ile menu. To cut and paste data to and from the Clipboard, select the **E**dit menu. To find a specific string of text in a file, select the **S**earch menu. To get help on using Notepad, select the **H**elp menu.

Figure 1.8: WIN.INI loaded into Notepad for viewing and editing.

SysEdit

The System Configuration Editor, SysEdit for short, is a seldom-documented program that comes with Windows. SysEdit provides the easiest way to view and edit your PC's AUTOEXEC.BAT, CONFIG.SYS, WIN.INI, and SYSTEM.INI files (see fig. 1.9). SysEdit is in your Windows System directory as the file SYSEDIT.EXE (such as \WINDOWS\SYSTEM\SYSEDIT.EXE).

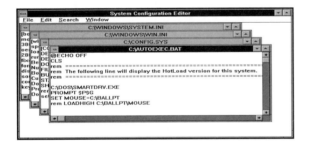

Figure 1.9: SysEdit displays CONFIG.SYS, AUTOEXEC.BAT, WIN.INI, and SYSTEM.INI in separate windows.

SysEdit displays each of the four files in a separate window. The SysEdit window is called the *parent window*. Each of the four other windows is called a *document window*, or *child window*. To view and edit one of the four files, click on its document window or press Ctrl-Tab to cycle through the windows. When the correct window appears, scroll through it and make changes to the file as in any other text editor. After you complete your changes, select **F**ile, then **S**ave to save the current file. Selecting **F**ile, **S**ave does not save all the files—it only saves the file displayed in the active document window.

Now that you are familiar with some of the programs you can use to fine-tune and fix software problems on your PC, you're ready to learn some basic concepts about the way your PC works. The next section explains the operating system (DOS), the BIOS, the system boot process, and the way Windows and applications relate to the operating system.

Some Basic Concepts about Your Computer

Although you don't have to know the way your car works to drive it, you do have to understand some basics about the way it works to fix it. The same is true for computers. You need to understand some basic concepts to give your PC a tune-up, install new gadgets, and troubleshoot problems.

Hardware Versus Software

You probably already know the difference between hardware and software, but it doesn't hurt to mention it here. *Hardware* refers to the physical parts of your computer, such as the keyboard, monitor (display), the printer, the system unit (where the actual computer part of the system lives), and all the gadgets inside the system unit, such as your disk drives.

Software refers to the programs that run on your PC. Basically, software is just a set of instructions programmed into the computer in one way or another that make the PC's hardware do the things it does. When it isn't being used, software usually lives on your hard disk, floppy disks, or CD-ROM (compact discs). When it is being used (the software is *running*), software lives in the PC's memory. (You learn about memory in Chapter 4.)

Software includes DOS, Windows, and programs such as word processors, spreadsheets, drawing programs, and so on. Software also includes other programs that work "behind the scenes."

Are hardware and software clear in your mind? Next, you need to learn about the BIOS.

Understanding the BIOS

BIOS stands for Basic Input/Output System. The BIOS is a set of software instructions that enable the PC's software to communicate with and control the PC's hardware. Generally, the BIOS is contained in a small microchip on the PC's *motherboard*, the main circuit board inside the PC. The BIOS is software stored in a chip. This type of software-in-hardware combination is often called *firmware*. It's not *hard*ware, and it's not *soft*ware…it's somewhere in between. Get it? Figure 1.10 shows the BIOS chips on a motherboard.

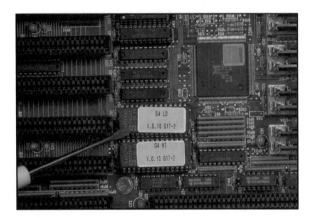

Figure 1.10: The BIOS is contained in one or more microchips on the PC's motherboard.

You can install lots of types of devices in a PC. One brand and model of device often is different from another in the way the computer must control it, even if the two perform the same type of function. With so many different devices to support, the operating system (DOS) would have to be a massive collection of programs to know how to communicate with each device. Also, DOS would have to be revised every time a new device comes on the market.

The BIOS overcomes these problems. The BIOS contains program code that performs system diagnostic testing when the PC is first turned on. The BIOS also contains standard functions that perform common tasks such as putting characters on the screen, reading keystrokes from the keyboard, writing data to a file, and so on. The PC's operating system (DOS) usually doesn't directly access a piece of hardware. Instead, it passes a request to the BIOS. The BIOS then accesses the hardware for DOS.

In addition to the system BIOS, many adapters in a PC include BIOS chips. *Adapters* are circuit cards that plug into your PC internally and perform special tasks. A video adapter generates the images you see on the monitor. A hard disk controller is an adapter that enables the PC to communicate with the hard disk. The BIOS routines on these adapters extend the BIOS to support devices that are contained on or connected to the adapters. These extended BIOS routines enable the operating system to access these devices.

DOS: What It Is and What It's Good For

Another item that makes the PC a functional system is the operating system, which is called *DOS* (*Disk Operating System*). Similar to the way the BIOS serves as an intermediary between software and hardware, DOS often serves as an intermediary between programs and the BIOS. If a program needs to access a piece of hardware, it passes a request to DOS. DOS then passes the request to the BIOS, which actually accesses the hardware.

DOS also serves as an intermediary between you (the user) and the system's hardware. DOS includes commands and programs that you can use to read and write files, create directories on a disk, send information to the printer, and perform other common tasks.

Some of the commands included with DOS are internal commands. *Internal commands* load into the PC's memory when the computer is on. Because they are in memory, you can almost always use these commands. You don't have to make the DOS directory active, for example, to use them. A few of the common internal DOS commands are DIR, DEL, COPY, and CD.

Other DOS commands are stored in the DOS directory in various files. These are *external commands.* Examples of some external commands are FDISK, FORMAT, DISKCOPY, and FIND. To use these external commands, you must change to the directory where they're located, or that directory must be on the system's path.

Today, a PC needs DOS to run DOS programs and to run Windows. When Windows 4 becomes available in 1994, it will work as a complete operating system in its own right, and you won't need DOS. DOS will be available for users who don't run Windows. In fact, DOS 7 will incorporate some of the new features provided by Windows 4.

In addition to DOS, you can use other operating systems on a PC. These include UNIX, OS/2, Windows NT, and a few others. These other operating systems perform the same function as DOS—they act as an intermediary between programs and the system's BIOS and hardware—but provide more powerful performance. For the average user, though, DOS is the most common.

The Boot Process

Now that you have an inkling of what the BIOS and DOS are and the way they are related, you are ready to learn about the PC's boot process. The *boot process* is the process the computer goes through when you turn it on or reset it. Understanding the boot process helps if you have to troubleshoot a problem that is preventing the computer from starting properly.

IO.SYS and MSDOS.SYS

When you first turn on the computer, the BIOS performs some very basic system-level diagnostics called the *POST* (*Power-On Self Test*). The BIOS checks the PC's memory, hard disk, floppy disk drives, keyboard, and adapters. If it runs into an error, the BIOS displays an error message. If it can't display an error message, it emits coded beeps that identify the problem (assuming you know what the beeps mean).

After the BIOS finishes the POST, it begins to search for an operating system. Because DOS is the most common operating system for PCs, I deal just with it (specifically, with MS-DOS). First, the BIOS routines check for an operating system on the first floppy disk, drive A. If drive A doesn't have a disk, the BIOS looks for an operating system (DOS) on the hard drive.

When the BIOS finds DOS, it loads a hidden file called IO.SYS, which is located in the root directory of the boot disk. If your PC is booting from the hard drive, IO.SYS is located in C:\. If you don't believe me, enter the following command from DOS:

```
DIR C:\*.SYS /A
```

You see a directory listing for IO.SYS, possibly along with other SYS files (if the root directory of the disk has others). If you use a version of DOS from a manufacturer other than Microsoft, IO.SYS might have a different name, but you probably can spot the right one. (You don't mess with

IO.SYS anyway, so it doesn't really matter if you can't find it—if your PC boots, you have the necessary file, somewhere.)

Great! But what is IO.SYS? Essentially, *IO.SYS* is a software extension of the BIOS, providing basic I/O functions that DOS and programs that run on top of DOS use to access the PC's hardware. Think of it as just containing more BIOS routines to supplement or replace some of the BIOS routines contained in the PC's BIOS chips.

After IO.SYS is read, another hidden file, MSDOS.SYS, is also read from the disk. Like IO.SYS, MSDOS.SYS is a hidden file in the boot disk's root directory. If you are using a version of DOS other than MS-DOS, the file might have a different name. MSDOS.SYS contains program routines that support basic functions such as reading and writing to a file, accepting and processing keyboard input, displaying data on the screen, sending information to the printer, and so on. These are the low-level functions that DOS uses to translate requests from programs down to the BIOS level for servicing. These functions comprise the *DOS kernel*.

CONFIG.SYS

After MSDOS.SYS is loaded, the file CONFIG.SYS is read and processed from the root directory of the boot disk. CONFIG.SYS is one of the files you fiddle with to tune-up your computer. CONFIG.SYS usually contains commands that specify options for the way the PC runs, and commands that load device drivers. *Device drivers* are programs that enable DOS to communicate with devices not directly supported by the BIOS.

AUTOEXEC.BAT

After CONFIG.SYS is processed, a batch file named AUTOEXEC.BAT is processed. AUTOEXEC.BAT usually contains a PATH statement to set the system's path, and other commands that launch a few optional programs (which vary according to your system—your system might use none). You can add commands to AUTOEXEC.BAT to have them executed automatically when the system is booted.

COMMAND.COM

After AUTOEXEC.BAT is processed, control is turned over to a program called COMMAND.COM, a command processor. COMMAND.COM is what is responsible for the

DOS prompt (such as the C:> on the monitor after the PC finishes booting). COMMAND.COM is the part of DOS that enables you to enter commands at the DOS prompt.

Remember those internal DOS commands such as DIR and COPY you read about earlier? Those commands are contained in COMMAND.COM. COMMAND.COM interprets what you type at the DOS prompt, and if the input is an internal DOS command, it executes the command. If what you type isn't an internal command, COMMAND.COM checks the current directory and then the path for a file that matches what you typed. If it finds a file with an EXE, COM, or BAT extension, COMMAND.COM executes (runs) the file. If it doesn't find a matching file of the right type, COMMAND.COM issues that familiar Bad command or file name error message.

So, COMMAND.COM is an intermediary between you and the rest of DOS. Now you're familiar with the different levels of the PC's operating system. You also should understand the way Windows and your programs fit into the picture.

Windows

Windows currently is not a complete operating system in itself. (Windows 4, when it is released in 1994, *will* be an operating system in its own right, and will not require DOS.) Instead, Windows is an *operating environment*, which means it provides an environment in which other programs run. But, so does DOS—DOS also provides an environment in which other programs run. So, what's the difference?

The difference is that Windows does not provide the same complete hardware-level access as DOS. Windows can provide some file and print services without DOS, but in general, it isn't a complete operating system because it doesn't support all of the PC's hardware directly. Instead, it has to go through DOS to get at the hardware.

Where does Windows fit in? It adds yet another layer to the PC's software. At the bottom you have the BIOS and IO.SYS. Then comes the kernel (MSDOS.SYS) and COMMAND.COM. On top is Windows.

Application Software

What about application software? The term *application* is another word for program. So, applications are programs. Often, the word application refers to a group of individual programs that work together. You might have a word

processing application, for example, that includes a word processing program, a spell-checking program, a thesaurus program, and so on. Whenever I mention the word *program* in this book, it is synonymous with *application*.

How do programs fit in with all of the other software running on your PC? Programs run on top of DOS, on top of Windows, or both. DOS programs can run on top of DOS or on top of Windows. And Windows programs can only run on top of Windows.

Part 1

Fiddling and Tweaking Your Computer

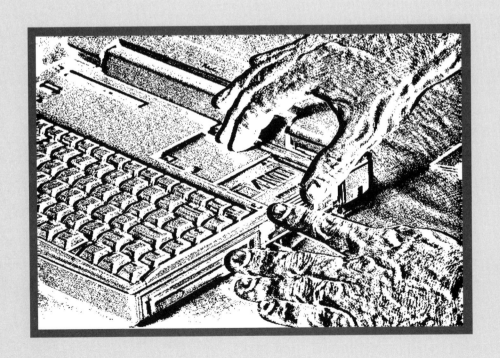

2

Basic Stuff To Get Started

Every task includes some preparation work that you need to accomplish before you dive into the main job. This chapter, which is about exactly that—preparation work—covers the following topics:

- How to create a bootable (system) disk in DOS and Windows

- Basic tools

- **Important safety tips!**

- Procedures for opening and closing your computer

- Your PC's main hardware components

Before you begin fiddling with your PC (with its configuration files or with the hardware inside it), you need to make a system disk. The next section explains why and how.

Make That Bootable (System) Disk Now!

A bootable disk, or *system disk*, is a floppy disk that contains enough of the disk operating system to boot the computer. Remember the files IO.SYS, MSDOS.SYS, and COMMAND.COM discussed in Chapter 1, "Read Me First"? Those are the parts of DOS that enable the computer to boot. Normally, your PC boots from its hard disk. But, it also can boot from a floppy disk that has been inserted in drive A.

Why Do You Need a System Disk?

You need a system disk to prevent calamity, disaster, and distress. Think of your system disk as an emergency disk. The following are some important reasons why every PC user should have a system disk tucked away somewhere safe:

- Changes you make to your configuration files (namely, CONFIG.SYS), if not correct, can prevent your system from booting from the hard disk. Having a system disk enables you to boot the computer, change the offending lines in CONFIG.SYS, and once again boot from the hard disk.

- Your hard disk might suddenly suffer a catastrophe of some kind. Without a system disk handy, you won't be able to boot your computer to try to fix the problem.

- You might do something really stupid, such as accidentally erasing all of the files in the root directory of your hard disk (I've done it a couple of times). The system disk you create will have copies of the important stuff from your hard disk's root directory.

- You might do an incredibly stupid thing, such as accidentally format your hard disk, wiping out everything on it. The system disk that you create will have a few commands that you will need to recover all that lost information.

I cannot stress strongly enough how important it is that you make a system disk. Even if you put this book down now and never pick it up again, create that system disk immediately.

What's on a System Disk?

A system disk is a regular floppy disk that contains four basic things:

- **A boot sector.** The storage space on a disk is separated into areas called *sectors*. The first sector on a system disk is called the *boot sector*. It contains some program code that enables the BIOS to load IO.SYS, MSDOS.SYS, and COMMAND.COM. On a floppy disk that hasn't been formatted as a system disk, the first sector doesn't contain this program code, so the disk cannot be used to boot DOS.

- **IO.SYS.** This was discussed in Chapter 1. IO.SYS is a hidden file that contains software extensions to the PC's BIOS. (Hidden files don't show up with a regular DIR command—you must add the /A switch to DIR to see them.)

- **MSDOS.SYS.** This hidden file contains the DOS kernel, which is a set of software routines that form the core functions that make up DOS. These include functions for reading and writing to a disk, accepting keyboard entry, displaying information on the monitor, and more.

- **COMMAND.COM.** This is the DOS command interpreter, which is responsible for placing the DOS prompt on the display. COMMAND.COM also contains internal DOS commands, such as COPY, DIR, and DELETE. COMMAND.COM enables you to enter DOS commands and start programs from the DOS command prompt.

A system disk often contains two other files, CONFIG.SYS and AUTOEXEC.BAT. The system disk that you create contains these two files, as well as a few others.

You can make a system disk three different ways. The following procedures explain each of these three methods. If you prefer to use DOS commands, use the first procedure. If you have Windows on your PC, and you are not very comfortable using DOS commands, use the second procedure. I don't recommend that you use the third procedure, although I've included it because it might be useful to you in the future.

Also, a system disk can boot the computer only from drive A. You cannot boot the computer from drive B. If your PC contains two different floppy drive types, such as a 5 1/4-inch and a 3 1/2-inch drive, I recommend that you create two system disks, one of each type.

Why should you go to the trouble of creating two system disks? It's quite simple. Sometime in the future you might say, "Gee, I'd like to have this 3 1/2-inch drive as drive A instead of the 5 1/4-inch drive." Or, maybe you will want it to be the other way around.

The trouble with the preceding scenario is that you might swap the drives and forget to make a new system disk for the new drive A. If a problem crops up and you have to boot from the floppy, you have to swap the floppy drives again before you can boot the system. With both types of system disks handy, it won't matter—you'll have whichever one you need.

Procedure:

Creating a
System Disk in DOS

Explanation: This procedure helps you create a system disk using commands that you enter at the DOS prompt. You can perform the steps directly from DOS, or from a DOS session running from within Windows.

1. Place a new, unused floppy disk in drive A. If the drive is a 5 1/4-inch disk drive, engage the drive latch (3 1/2-inch drives engage automatically). Usually, the drive latch is a little lever gadget on the front of the drive.

2. At the DOS prompt, enter **CD \DOS**. If your DOS files are located in a different directory from \DOS, specify the appropriate directory.

3. At the DOS prompt, enter **FORMAT A: /S /U**.

Make sure that you include the A: in the FORMAT command shown in step 3. Otherwise, you run the risk of formatting the wrong disk (such as your hard disk). Formatting the hard disk is not something you want to do, unless you want to lose everything on the disk! If you make a mistake, press Ctrl-C to cancel the FORMAT command.

Step 3 causes the FORMAT command to format the disk in drive A. The /S switch directs FORMAT to add the boot record, IO.SYS, MSDOS.SYS, and COMMAND.COM to the disk. The /U switch causes FORMAT to perform an unconditional format of the disk, erasing anything that might be on it.

4. FORMAT prompts you to insert a new disk in drive A. The disk is already there (step 1), so just press Enter.

   After the disk has been formatted, FORMAT prompts you to enter a volume label, which is just a name for the disk that is stored electronically on it.

5. A volume label is optional, so just press Enter to bypass the volume label entry.

   When the FORMAT command has finished formatting the disk, the system asks you if you want to format another disk.

6. Press N to end the FORMAT command.

   If drive B is a different size format from drive A, you should make a system disk in drive B also. If you have only one floppy drive, or both drives are the same size format, skip to step 10 now. Otherwise, continue with the following steps.

7. Insert a new, unused disk in drive B.

8. At the DOS prompt, enter **FORMAT B: /S /U**. Make sure that you use B: (and no other drive letter) in the FORMAT command.

9. Repeat steps 4, 5, and 6 for the system floppy in drive B.

You cannot boot from drive B. Having a system disk for your current drive B will be useful if you ever swap drive B and drive A.

10. Write the words "System Disk" on a sticky disk label, along with the version of DOS you are using. Example: "System Disk, MS-DOS 6.0." Place the label on the disk. Repeat for the second system disk, if you made one.

Procedure:

Creating a System Disk in Windows

Explanation: The following procedure helps you create a system disk by using the File Manager in Windows. Use this procedure if you are a Windows user and are not comfortable using DOS commands.

1. Locate the File Manager icon in the Main program group and double-click on it to start File Manager. Or, use your favorite method to run the program WINFILE.EXE, which is located in the Windows directory.

2. In File Manager, choose the **D**isk menu.

3. From the **D**isk menu, choose **F**ormat Disk.

   The Format Disk dialog box, which is shown in figure 2.1, appears on the Windows desktop.

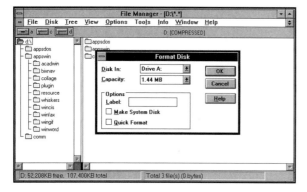

Figure 2.1: The Format Disk dialog box enables you to create a system disk in Windows.

4. From the **D**isk In drop-down list, choose Drive A:. (Drive A might already be selected.)

5. From the **C**apacity drop-down list, choose the highest capacity possible for your drive A. (It might already be selected.)

6. Click on the **M**ake System Disk check box to place a check in it.

7. Click on OK.

   A dialog box appears, warning you that formatting will erase all data from the disk. Check the last sentence of the warning to make sure it's referring to the correct disk (drive A or drive B, as appropriate).

8. If everything is fine, click on **Y**es. If you're not sure, click on **N**o, then return to step 4.

   After File Manager finishes formatting the disk, a dialog box appears with information about the new disk. You then are asked if you want to format another disk.

9. Click on **N**o.

10. Repeat steps 2 through 9, creating a system disk for drive B instead of drive A.

11. Write the words "System Disk" on a sticky disk label, along with the version of DOS you are using. "System Disk, MS-DOS 6.0," for example. Place the label on the disk. Repeat for the second system disk, if you make one.

Making an Existing Disk Bootable

If you have a disk that already has been formatted as a regular data disk, and you want to make it a system disk, you can do so with just one command.

As an example, assume that you formatted a disk and added all your configuration files to it as explained in some upcoming procedures. You forgot, however, to add the /S switch to the FORMAT command, or you forgot to check the **M**ake System Disk check box in File Manager. Your disk is formatted, but it doesn't have the system files on it. That means that the disk isn't bootable. But don't panic! The following procedures add the system files to an existing, already-formatted disk, and modify the boot sector to make the disk bootable.

Adding System Files to a Disk (DOS)

1. Insert the formatted disk in the appropriate floppy drive.

2. At the DOS command prompt, type **SYS A:** to add the system files to the floppy disk in drive A, or **SYS B:** to add the system files to the floppy disk in drive B.

   After a few moments, DOS displays a message indicating that the system has been transferred to the disk.

   If you have files on the disk when you issue the SYS command, they will be unaffected. So, if you already have added CONFIG.SYS, AUTOEXEC.BAT, or other files to the disk, they will be intact after the system has been transferred to the disk.

Adding System Files to a Disk (Windows)

1. Open File Manager, then from the **D**isk menu, choose **M**ake System Disk.

   The Make System Disk dialog box shown in figure 2.2 appears on the Windows desktop.

Figure 2.2: The Make System Disk dialog box is used to add system files to an existing disk.

2. From the drop-down list in the dialog box, choose the floppy disk to which you want to add the system files.

Procedure:

Testing the New System Disk

Explanation: Everything probably worked when you created the system disk, but you should test it to make sure. It would be a shame to suddenly need a working system disk, only to discover that yours doesn't work. Use the following steps for DOS and Windows systems:

1. If you are running Windows, exit Windows and return to DOS.

2. Insert your new system disk in drive A.

3. At the DOS prompt, with Windows no longer running, press Ctrl-Alt-Del.

   The system will attempt to reboot from drive A. If the system boots properly, you will receive a DOS prompt similar to A:>. If there is a problem, you will receive the error message Non-system disk or disk error. This message means that the system files were not properly installed on the system disk. If you receive this error, repeat the procedure you used to create the system disk.

Procedure:

Adding Files to the System Disk

Explanation: You can use your new system disk as is without putting any additional files on it. But this system disk will be used mainly when you have a problem with your PC. You should add some useful files to the disk so that you have them available in the event of a PC crisis. Also, you should set up the system disk so that it loads your PC's device drivers and other start-up programs, just like when you boot from the hard disk.

The files to add to the system disk include your PC's main configuration files, CONFIG.SYS, and AUTOEXEC.BAT, as well as your Windows initialization files and some useful utilities.

1. Place the system disk in the appropriate drive.

2. **DOS users:** Use the DOS COPY command to copy the files listed in table 2.1 to the floppy disk. Example: COPY C:\CONFIG.SYS A:\.

3. **Windows users:** Open File Manager and use it to copy the files listed in table 2.1 to the floppy disk.

The files listed in the following table total roughly 766K.

Table 2.1
Files To Include on the System Disk

File Name	Where To Find It	Purpose of File
CONFIG.SYS	C:\	PC's main configuration file
AUTOEXEC.BAT	C:\	PC's other main configuration file
WIN.INI	Windows directory	Windows initialization file
SYSTEM.INI	Windows directory	Windows initialization file
CHKDSK.EXE	DOS directory	Hard disk repair/cleanup utility
DEFRAG.EXE	DOS directory	Hard disk optimizer (MS-DOS 6 only)
EDIT.COM	DOS directory	Text editor
EMM386.EXE	DOS directory or Windows directory	DOS memory manager
FDISK.EXE	DOS directory	Hard disk partition utility
FORMAT.COM	DOS directory	Format disks
HIMEM.SYS	DOS directory or Windows directory	DOS memory manager
INTERLNK.EXE	DOS directory	Enables file transfer between two computers via a null-modem cable
INTERSRV.EXE	DOS directory	See INTERLNK.EXE
MSD.EXE	DOS directory or Windows directory	Microsoft Diagnostic utility for viewing system configuration
QBASIC.EXE	DOS directory	Enables you to run BASIC programs, required for EDIT.COM
SETVER.EXE	DOS directory	Helps fool programs into thinking they're running on a different version of DOS—required for some programs and device drivers
SMARTDRV.EXE	DOS directory	DOS disk caching program (speeds disk access)
SYS.COM	DOS directory	Transfers system files to a formatted disk
UNDELETE.EXE	DOS directory	Enables you to recover a deleted file
UNFORMAT.EXE	DOS directory	Enables you to unformat a disk, recovering the data that was lost
XCOPY.EXE	DOS directory	Enables you to copy multiple files from one disk to another with a single command

Note: The Windows directory usually is C:\WINDOWS or C:\WIN, and the DOS directory usually is C:\DOS.

This means that they will not fit on a 720K 3 1/2-inch floppy disk, but they will fit on a 1.2M or 1.44M floppy without any problem. If you have to boot from a 720K floppy (or 360K floppy), put the excess files onto another disk. The second disk doesn't have to be bootable (you don't have to put the system files on it).

What To Do If You Don't Have a System Disk

Don't tell me! You suddenly have discovered that your PC won't boot properly, and you forgot to make a system disk. Or, you swapped out your two floppies, and don't have a system disk for your new drive A. Don't panic—at least not yet.

Situation: You Can't Boot Your System

If you are using MS-DOS 6, try pressing the F5 key when you see the "Starting MS-DOS" message on the display. Doing so should bypass your configuration files and boot DOS. If you never see the "Starting MS-DOS" message (MS-DOS 6 only), the problem is not with your configuration files, and you need a system disk. Ask the nice salesperson at your favorite computer store or a friend who has a PC and is using MS-DOS 6, to *please, please, please* make a system disk for you.

If you are using a version of DOS other than MS-DOS 6, you need a system disk. Follow the previous advice to find someone who can make one for you.

Situation: Your System Will Boot from the Hard Disk

If your system still boots from the hard disk, you probably need a system disk because you forgot to make one and for some reason have just realized that you should have one. As long as the FORMAT command is still accessible on the hard disk, you can create a system disk. Run through the procedure "Creating a System Disk in DOS."

If you don't have access to the FORMAT command, you probably have erased some files or something has screwed up your hard disk. See the advice in "You Can't Boot Your System" to get a new system disk.

Basic Tools, Safety, and Work Habits

You're almost ready to begin opening up your computer to have a tour around its guts. First, though, you need to learn about safety, your toolkit, and some important habits to have and to avoid. Safety is the most important topic, so it's first.

Your Safety First!

Working inside a computer is a lot safer than working inside a TV or inside a car's engine. But, there are some things you should watch out for to ensure your own safety at all times.

You can receive an electrical shock if you work inside a computer that is plugged in and turned on. The chance of actually getting hurt is pretty remote, because 5 to 12 volts is the most used by any of the devices in the computer. But you can still receive a shock, so you should unplug the computer before opening the case.

WARNING

Don't work inside the PC when it's turned on unless, a) you have a death wish, or b) you want to screw up your PC. Always turn it off.

You don't have to unplug the PC from the wall—instead, you can unplug the power cord from the back of the PC. Sometimes that's easier than trying to get to the outlet if the outlet is behind a desk or something.

Your only source of real danger is the computer's power supply. The *power supply* is a metal box inside the computer that contains a bunch of components that convert the alternating current (AC) that comes out of the wall receptable to the direct current (DC) that the computer uses. The power supply has some big capacitors in it; the capacitors are electronic components that store electrical charges.

The danger in these capacitors is that they store these charges even when the computer is turned off and unplugged. This means that if you open the power supply, even with the computer unplugged, you can get a really nasty shock. That's why power supplies have profuse warnings on them such as "Do not remove this power supply cover under any circumstances," and "There are no service-able components inside. Serious shock hazards are present inside this power supply." The power supply manufacturer doesn't want to be sued because you opened it up and got fried.

 **NOTE** *I don't want to be sued, either, so I recommend that you do not open the power supply. The only thing you can replace inside the power supply is the cooling fan. I've done that type of repair, but I mention it only so that you know it's possible to replace the fan without buying a new power supply. I still, however, do not recommend that you open the power supply.*

Next, the Computer's Safety

The main reason for not working inside a running PC is to keep from damaging the PC, not to keep from damaging yourself. If you try to remove or install an adapter in the PC while it is running, you stand a good chance of damaging the adapter, the PC, or both. Don't try it.

Also, you probably will be using a screwdriver or some other tool inside the PC. What happens when you drop it? You stand a good chance of shorting something out and damaging the PC or one of its adapters. Take my advice and never, never, never work inside a running PC. There's no problem running the PC with the cover off for testing, but turn it off before you start working inside the case again.

Your Basic Toolkit

There are very few tools you'll need to perform the majority of your PC upgrade/repair tasks. The only tool I use the majority of the time is a single Phillips-head screwdriver. Figure 2.3 shows a shade-tree PC mechanic's toolbox. Table 2.2 describes the tools.

Some of the tools are optional. The multitester, also called a *Volt-Ohm meter*, costs about $10 to $12 if you get an analog one (has a meter for its readout). You can get a digital VOM with an LCD display for about $25. That's what I have. You might never need the VOM, so don't buy

Table 2.2
Your PC Fiddling Toolkit

Tool	Comments
Medium Phillips screwdriver	Use this to remove the screws that hold the cover on the case
Small Phillips screwdriver	This one is good for the screws that hold the adapters in place
Small flat-bladed screwdriver	Useful for cable securing screws and prying chips out of their sockets
Cordless screwdriver	Great for case and adapter screws
Double-ended screwdriver	My favorite tool, used for flipping tortillas, pointing, and generally separating me from the average chimpanzee (also great as a screwdriver)
IC extractor	You can use one of these to extract ICs (chips), but a small flat-bladed screwdriver actually works better (not shown)
A long Phillips bit	Used in the cordless screwdriver; a long one can reach the adapter screws without having to stick the screwdriver into the case
A multitester (VOM)	For checking the power supply and checking cables; LCD digital types are nicer, but a little more expensive
Some paper clips	I use these with the multitester when checking cables (see Chapter 26)
A nut driver	You can use it on the case screws instead of using a screwdriver

one until you need it for testing the power supply or cables, unless you want to have one around to check batteries before you throw them out.

Figure 2.3: A basic set of tools for upgrading and fixing a PC.

The cordless screwdriver also is a luxury. You can just as easily use the nut driver or screwdriver in its place. The cordless screwdriver is just faster, and preferable for a lazy person like me.

Item 5, the double-ended screwdriver, has a small Phillips head on one end and a flat-bladed screwdriver on the other. I got mine from JDR Microdevices for about 80 cents. I use it for most of the work I do inside the PC.

Good and Bad Habits To Keep in Mind

The worst thing you can do when working inside the PC is to end up with spare parts. Usually, that means extra screws. A missing screw here and there probably won't hurt anything, but if you're going to do the job, you might as well do it right. The following are some tips to help you get organized as you begin your foray into the inner workings of your PC.

- Keep track of what you take out, and put it back when the time comes. Use a small cup or other container to hold screws and little parts so that they don't get lost.

- If necessary, draw diagrams that will help you remember where things go, or how cables are connected. If you're not very good at drawing, consider using a floppy disk label or other stick-backed label to label parts, cable ends, and so on.

- Better still, use an instamatic camera to take pictures before you start disassembling anything. There aren't that many parts inside the PC, so it's unlikely that you'll have trouble remembering where things go. If you feel confused by the gadgets and cables, use diagrams or photographs until you become familiar with the inside of the PC.

NOTE *Don't leave the adapter hole covers in the back of the case uncovered. These are the holes where the adapter cards stick out the back of the PC. The empty sockets will have a small metal bracket screwed into the case that covers the hole.*

If you leave the the adapter hole covers uncovered, you reduce the efficiency of the cooling fan in the power supply, and also allow extra dust to get into the system.

- Write down all of the changes you make to your system. Spend an hour or so performing an inventory of your system, writing down the settings and memory locations used by each adapter. If you're not familiar enough with your PC yet to do that, follow through the procedures in the upcoming chapters for each of the devices in your PC.

Each time you add a new device to your PC or change the settings on an existing device, write those changes in a log. Having a system log makes it much simpler to install new devices—you won't have to spend a lot of time checking your system to find settings for the new device that won't conflict with the rest of the PC. You can look in the log and quickly find settings that will work.

Appendix A contains log sheets you can use for tracking the settings used by the devices in your PC. Take my word for it—the best habit you can develop is to keep track of your PC's equipment in this way.

Getting Comfortable Inside Your PC

You're probably chomping at the bit to open up your computer and start fiddling with it. Your wait is over. The rest of this chapter explains how to open your PC, remove and install adapters, and reassemble the PC. The procedures don't focus on actually making any changes. Instead, the focus is on becoming comfortable working inside the PC and on learning about each of the main parts of your PC.

Even if you don't have any new gadgets to install in the PC right now, you might want to open it up anyway and have a look inside it to become familiar with its parts. The first step, then, is to open up the computer.

Opening and Disassembling the Desktop

Desktop systems are those which sit on top of a desk (duh...). Usually, the monitor sits on top of the computer case. Sometimes, you'll find a desktop system standing on its side in a special holder beside the desktop. You can spot these by the fact that their floppy drives are mounted vertically, rather than horizontally (you have to hold the floppy vertical to insert it).

1. Unplug the monitor, either at the rear of the monitor or at the wall receptacle (optional, but a good idea).

2. Move the monitor off the case and set it on the desk or floor where it won't get knocked over or kicked. You'd really hate it if you knocked if off the desk.

3. Unplug the power cord from the back of the PC! If you prefer, unplug the power cord from the wall receptacle instead.

Most desktop cases have five screws at the rear of the case that hold the cover in place. Check each of the four corners of the case for a screw. The fifth usually is located near the top center of the case. After the screws are removed, the cover will slide forward (toward the front of the PC).

4. Remove the cover screws from the back of the PC and put them in a safe place where they won't get lost.

5. Carefully slide the cover forward to expose the inside of the PC. With some cases, you have to slide the cover *backward* instead of forward. These types of covers have narrow flanges that bend around the back of the PC's chassis.

The screw retainer for the top-center cover screw sometimes will get snagged on cables inside the PC as you slide the cover forward. Keep it free of cables if necessary. Also, the cover sometimes will get stuck. If you can't seem to slide it forward, slip a flat screwdriver between the chassis (the metal part that the cover is covering) and the cover, and gently pry the cover forward. If it won't budge, quit prying and check for a screw you may have missed.

6. Pull the cover free of the PC and set it aside.

Opening and Disassembling the Tower

Tower cases usually sit on the floor beside the desk. Such cases provide more room for devices such as tape drives, CD-ROM drives, and hard disks. You can spot a tower case by the labels on the front—they will be readable horizontally, rather than vertically. Also, the disk drives will be mounted horizontally.

Some tower cases have a plastic cover that snaps into place in back to cover the screws and metal chassis. This usually just pops off. There generally are six screws that hold the cover to the chassis, three on each side of the PC, located at the corners and middle of the chassis. The metal cover usually slides toward the back of the PC an inch or so, and then lifts straight up and off.

1. Make sure that the monitor is safe from being bumped around.

2. Unplug the power cord from the back of the PC.

3. If the case has a plastic cover in back covering the screws, remove it. If there are no retaining screws visible, the cover just pops off. Slip a flat screwdriver

between the cover and the metal chassis and gently pry off the cover. If it won't come off, look for hidden screws or catches. If you see retaining screws, remove them.

You might need to disconnect some cables from the PC before removing the plastic cover. The plastic cover will have holes in it where the cables pass through and connect to the adapters sticking out the back of the chassis. Most of the time you can simply slide the cover back, letting the cables pass through it and remain connected to the PC. If a cable gets hung up on the cover, disconnect it (write down where it goes if you think you're going to forget).

4. Remove the cover screws from the back of the PC and put them in a safe place where they won't get lost.

5. Carefully slide the cover about an inch toward the back of the PC.

6. Lift the cover straight up and off, then set it aside.

After the cover is removed, there are three ways to work inside the tower system: lie down on the floor, stand the PC up on a table, or rest it on its side so it looks roughly like a desktop PC (so that the adapters pull straight up for removal). For small jobs, the easiest thing to do is to lie down on the floor to work on it. If you're going to be doing any extensive monkeying around inside the PC, consider setting it on its side—it will be easier to work on.

A hard disk generally can be mounted vertically or horizontally in a case, but it should be operated only in the same position in which it was formatted. If you turn a tower case on its side to work on it, don't turn the PC on again until you place it upright. Running it on its side could cause loss of data on the hard disk.

Removing Adapters

Adapters are the circuit cards that plug into sockets in the PC's motherboard (the main circuit board inside the PC).

Cables usually connect to the adapters through the back of the PC's chassis from devices such as the monitor, printer, mouse, and so on. Most of the new devices you add to your PC will either be adapters or will include adapters.

Common adapters in a typical PC include the video adapter, I/O adapter (where gadgets such as printers, modems, and mice connect), and hard disk controller. Knowing how to remove and install adapters is a necessary and important skill.

Ribbon cables are flat, thin cables made up of many insulated wires stuck together side-by-side, forming a sort of ribbon. Ribbon cables often are used to connect a device to an adapter, such as connecting a hard disk to your IDE or SCSI adapter. Sometimes the connectors on either end of a ribbon cable are keyed so that they only go into or on their respective connections one way. At other times, you have to keep track of which edge of the cable goes where.

Take a look at a ribbon cable and you'll see that the wire on one edge is colored, sometimes faintly, in red or blue (usually it's one of those two colors). The color strip indicates the wire that's supposed to connect to Pin 1 on the adapter's connector. If you know which pin on the adapter is Pin 1, the colored wire tells you how the cable should be connected to the adapter. The cable should be connected so that the edge with the colored stripe hooks up on the Pin 1 side of the connector.

Figure 2.4: The location of Pin 1 usually is marked on a connector and on a cable.

1. Open the PC using the proper opening procedure as a guide.

2. Touch the metal part of the PC's chassis to discharge any static electricity that has built up in your body. Do this often if you're working on a carpeted floor. See the following note for an explanation.

WARNING

Avoid touching the edge connector, connector pins, or any chips on an adapter. If you've built up a static charge, you could discharge it into the adapter, zapping a sensitive component. That would really make you mad. Handle the card by its edges whenever possible (but not by the edge connector).

3. Locate the adapters. In a desktop system, the adapters will be installed vertically in the PC starting at the left-rear quarter of the case. In a tower case, they are located toward the bottom-rear of the case (viewed upright).

The following steps tell you how to remove the video adapter so that you can examine it.

4. Follow the cable from the monitor to the computer to locate the video adapter.

5. Disconnect the monitor cable from the video adapter. The cable will either have small thumbscrews or regular screws.

NOTE

Your video adapter may include a feature connector, which is an edge connector at the top edge of the card. An edge connector is a portion of a printed circuit card to which a ribbon cable is connected, or which is inserted into a socket. The connector part of an adapter that plugs into each of the PC's bus sockets is an edge connector. But, back to that feature connector.

A feature connector is used on some video adapters to connect it to another device inside the PC, such as to a video capture board. If there is a ribbon cable connected to your PC's video adapter, make a note (mental or otherwise) of the location of the colored stripe on the ribbon cable. Then, gently pull the ribbon cable off the adapter.

6. With a screwdriver or nut driver, remove the screw that secures the video adapter to the PC's chassis.

7. Discharge your static again, then grab the adapter with both hands, trying to keep from touching any chips if at all possible. Pull straight up (or out, for tower systems) to remove the adapter from its socket. You may have to wiggle it some (front to back) to get it out.

8. Set the adapter somewhere safe where you won't sit on it, step on it, or otherwise abuse it.

Installing Adapters

Installation essentially is the reverse of removal, if you just went through the removal procedure. There are a few things to watch out for when installing an adapter that you don't have to concern yourself with when removing one. These things are mentioned in the following procedure. One item that bears mentioning here, though, is the difference between 8-bit cards and 16-bit cards ("card" and "adapter" mean the same thing).

An *8-bit adapter* has a single edge connector that slides into one of the PC's bus sockets (on the motherboard). A *16-bit adapter* has two edge connectors that slide into two sockets in the motherboard. Many PCs have some 8-bit sockets and some 16-bit sockets. Others have only 16-bit sockets.

An 8-bit card can be installed either in an 8-bit slot or in a 16-bit slot. Some 16-bit cards are designed to operate in 8-bit mode or in 16-bit mode, and these types of adapters can be installed in either an 8-bit or a 16-bit socket. (The 16-bit part of the edge connector doesn't get inserted into anything if you install the adapter in an 8-bit socket.)

Usually, you want to install a 16-bit card in a 16-bit socket to get the best performance from it. If you have run out of 16-bit sockets, check the adapter's documentation to see if it can be used in an 8-bit slot, and what the performance penalties will be if you do so. Or, try to move a less important adapter from a 16-bit slot to an 8-bit slot to make room for the new adapter.

Jumpers and DIP Switches

Many adapters require configuration before you install them in the PC. The configuration process includes setting small switches, called DIP (Dual In-line Package) switches. Figure 2.5 shows a typical DIP switch.

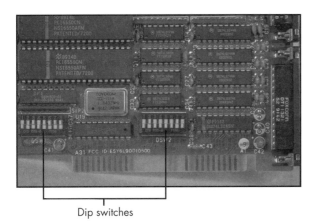

Dip switches

Figure 2.5: Typical DIP switches on an adapter.

A DIP switch has two positions, on and off. The on position often is marked on the switch by a 1. The off position often is marked by a 0. Usually, you need to set a selection of switches on the adapter to configure various options. Just use the tip of a ballpoint pen (or something similar) to flip the little switches into the position required by the device.

Many adapters also include jumpers. A *jumper* really is nothing more than a rectangular plug that you install on a couple of pins. When the jumper is installed on the pins, it makes an electrical connection between the two pins. To install a jumper, just slide the jumper onto the pins. To remove a jumper, just slide it off and store it somewhere (you might need one someday). If the jumper is in a crowded location on the adapter, you may need to use a small flat screwdriver to carefully pry it up.

Procedure:
Installing an Adapter

1. Set any jumpers or switch settings required on the adapter (these are explained in more detail in later chapters).

2. Locate a free slot in which to install the adapter (see earlier explanation about 8-bit and 16-bit slots).

3. If a bracket is installed in the chassis covering the hole for the socket you've selected, remove the screw holding the bracket in place and remove the bracket. Set it aside in a place you'll remember—you may need it to cover another slot's holes.

4. Line up the adapter's edge connector with the slot, then slide the adapter firmly into the socket, making sure any connectors that stick out the back of the adapter fit through the hole in the back of the chassis. If you're installing a full-length adapter, read the following note before inserting the adapter.

 *If you are installing a full-length adapter, there are guides for the front end of the adapter mounted near the front of the PC. Make sure that you slide the front edge of the adapter into the proper guide (the one that's aligned with the slot in which you're installing the adapter).*

5. Check the installation to make sure that the adapter is seated securely in its socket, and that you haven't pinched any cables or wires with the adapter.

6. Install a screw in the adapter's bracket to secure it to the PC's chassis.

Connecting Cables

Most adapters connect to devices by ribbon cables (inside the PC) or by various other types of cables (connected to the back of the adapter at the back of the PC). External connectors that connect to the adapter at the back of the PC are keyed in one way or another so they can be inserted in only one way. They almost always include some type of screw to secure the cable to the adapter.

Ribbon cables, though, often are not physically keyed. With ribbon cables, you must pay attention to the location of Pin 1 on the connector and match the colored strip on the ribbon cable with Pin 1 on the connector.

Reassembling and Closing the Desktop

After you have finished fiddling inside the PC, it's time to put the cover back on. That's what the following procedure is all about.

If you haven't spent any time looking around inside your PC and exploring its components, don't close it up yet. Run through the next section of the chapter to take a guided tour of your PC's parts.

1. Check your installation/modification one last time to make sure you haven't left out any screws or forgotten to connect a cable.

2. Slide the cover back onto the chassis, making sure that you don't catch any cables or wires while sliding it into place.

3. Reinstall the screws that hold the cover in place.

4. If you're ready to begin testing the PC, reconnect all cables, the power cord, and the monitor.

Reassembling and Closing the Tower

1. Check your installation/modification one last time to make sure that you haven't left out any screws or forgotten to connect a cable.

2. Slide the cover back down onto the chassis, making sure that you don't catch any cables or wires while sliding it into place.

3. Slide it forward into place, if necessary.

4. Reinstall the screws that hold the cover in place.

5. If the case uses a plastic cover in back, snap it back into place (or screw it in place if it uses screws).

6. If you're ready to begin testing the PC, reconnect all cables, the power cord, and the monitor.

A Tour Around Your Computer

This section of the chapter takes you on a guided tour of your PC's hardware. It isn't meant to give you an in-depth look at how the PC's hardware works. Instead, it helps you become familiar with where each of the primary components is located and what function each one performs.

The System Unit

The *system unit* is the box that contains the majority of the PC's components (more about these later). The keyboard, mouse, monitor, printer, and other devices connect to the back of the system unit. Often, the system unit is called the PC's CPU, but that isn't correct. The CPU (central processing unit) is the PC's primary microprocessor (microchip) inside the system unit.

In a desktop PC, the system unit generally sits on top of the desk, and the monitor sits on top of the system unit. Figure 2.6 shows an example of a desktop system unit. Sometimes a desktop system unit is placed on the floor in a special stand. The system unit rests on its side in the stand.

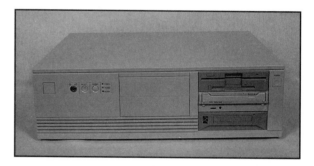

Figure 2.6: A desktop system unit, as its name implies, usually sits on top of a desk.

In a tower PC, the system unit generally sits beside the desk, standing vertically beside it. Tower system units often have more room for expansion, such as offering more slots for additional disk drives (called *drive bays*). That's why network servers often are configured in tower cases. Like a desktop system unit, the keyboard, mouse, and other devices connect to the back of the unit. Figure 2.7 shows a tower system unit.

Other than the fact that a tower case generally provides more room for expanding the system with additional drives, desktop and tower units are functionally the same.

The Motherboard

The *motherboard* is the PC's main printed circuit board, and it's located inside the system unit. Figure 2.8 shows a typical PC motherboard. On the motherboard lives the CPU, which is where all the computing actually takes place in the

PC. The motherboard contains a lot of support circuitry and all manner of electronic components. The system's memory also is usually installed on the motherboard.

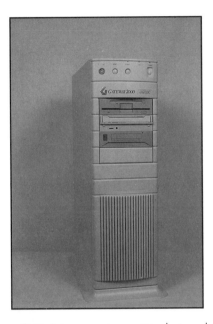

Figure 2.7: A tower system unit is designed to stand vertically.

Figure 2.8: A typical PC motherboard. This one is a 486-based motherboard.

The motherboard includes sockets in which the system's adapters are installed. These sockets are called *bus slots*, because they connect adapters to the PC's bus. The *bus* provides an electronic pathway by which the adapters communicate with the CPU, and vice versa.

In some newer motherboards, many functions are built into the motherboard rather than being added with external adapters that plug into the bus slots. These types of motherboards often incorporate the PC's video, I/O (COM and LPT) ports, IDE adapter, and other devices on the motherboard, eliminating the need to install adapters to support these functions. Depending on the motherboard's design, you often can disable these on-board devices and install external adapters that provide better performance or special features.

Memory

The PC contains two types of memory: RAM and ROM. *RAM* stands for random-access memory. The PC's RAM is where the operating system, programs, and data are located when the PC is running (that is, programs that are running at the time). RAM is volatile, meaning that if you turn off the PC or reboot it, the contents of RAM are lost. If you've got a document loaded into a program and haven't saved it, and then turn off the PC, you'll lose any changes you've made to the document since the last time it was saved to disk.

RAM comprises the majority of the PC's memory. Today's typical PC has at least 4M (megabytes) of RAM, with higher-performance systems including 8M, 12M, or more. Megabytes and memory capacity are explained in Chapter 4, "All You Need To Know about Memory." Figure 2.9 shows the memory installed on a typical PC motherboard.

Figure 2.9: Memory installed on a PC motherboard.

The second type of memory is ROM. *ROM* stands for read-only memory. The name says it all: the contents of ROM can be read, but not written to (at least, not without a special program to do so and the right type of ROM chip). ROM is used to store the PC's configuration, the BIOS, and other data that is static (unchanging). Accessing data in ROM usually is slower than accessing data in RAM. Figure 2.10 shows the ROM BIOS chips on a typical PC's motherboard.

Figure 2.10: Typical ROM chips on a PC's motherboard.

Data Storage (Disk Drives)

The PC's disk drives are used for long-term storage of data. A typical PC usually includes at least one floppy disk drive and one hard disk drive. A *floppy disk drive* is most often used for installing software onto the system and making backup copies of programs and data. Floppy drives provide an easy means of moving data between two PCs without a network.

A *hard disk* has a much higher storage capacity and operates much faster than a floppy disk. Hard disks usually are used for storing applications and data, and are the main long-term storage media used in today's PCs.

Figure 2.11 shows a floppy disk drive and a hard disk drive.

Many PCs also now include CD-ROM drives. *CD-ROM drives* enable the PC to read CDs (compact discs). A CD holds about 680M, which is the equivalent of about 472 high-density 3 1/2-inch floppy disks. Many software developers are making their software available on CD because of the high capacity and relatively cheap reproduction cost of the CD compared to floppy disk reproduction.

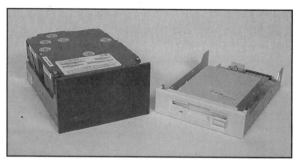

Figure 2.11: A floppy disk drive and a hard disk drive.

With the right software, CD-ROM drives also can be used on a PC to play audio CDs (the same CDs you play in your stereo CD player). CD-ROM drives are available in two types: internal and external. Internal CD-ROM drives are installed in the PC's system unit. External CD-ROM drives sit on the desk and connect to the back of the PC. Figure 2.12 shows an internal CD-ROM drive.

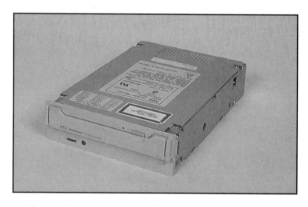

Figure 2.12: An internal CD-ROM drive.

Video Stuff

The PC's *video adapter* is the device that generates the image you see on the monitor. In most PCs, the video adapter is a separate card that plugs into one of the PC's bus slots. In some PCs, the video adapter is integrated into the motherboard (there's no separate adapter card). The video adapter connects to the PC's monitor (the display) by a cable. Figure 2.13 shows a typical video adapter.

Figure 2.13: A typical video adapter.

The Keyboard and Mouse

The *keyboard* and *mouse* are the PC's primary input devices. Although you now can get a special device that enables you to control the PC with voice commands, the technology available today is still a bit crude. The voice recognition capability of the computer on "Star Trek: The Next Generation" is still a few years away (but not very many). So, the keyboard and mouse remain the primary form of input for PCs, especially because they offer a relatively private way of entering data into the computer. Figure 2.14 shows a keyboard and mouse.

Figure 2.14: A typical keyboard and mouse.

The Printer

The printer is sometimes the most maligned piece of PC equipment because it's often the most difficult piece of equipment to get working properly. Basically, all the printer does is give you a hard copy (printout) of a document. Common printer types in use today include dot-matrix printers, laser printers, and inkjet printers. Figure 2.15 shows a typical laser printer.

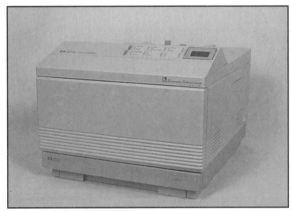

Figure 2.15: A typical laser printer.

Other Hardware

Besides the devices described above, a PC often comprises other types of hardware. These other hardware items include audio adapters that give the PC the capability to reproduce sounds, special video adapters for capturing video and manipulating images, tape drives for backing up data, modems and fax-modems for connecting to other computers, and more. Many of these hardware items are described elsewhere in this book.

3

Tweak Your System Files

You can do a lot to your PC to improve its performance without opening its case or even picking up a screwdriver. By making simple changes to a handful of files, you can fix hardware and software compatibility problems that might crop up, make the system run faster, and make more memory available in your PC.

This chapter explains many of the changes you can make to CONFIG.SYS, AUTOEXEC.BAT, WIN.INI, SYSTEM.INI, and other Windows INI files. The chapter covers the following topics:

- Keeping track of changes
- Making changes to CONFIG.SYS
- Making changes to AUTOEXEC.BAT
- Using MS-DOS 6's multiple-boot feature
- Making changes to primary Windows INI files SYSTEM.INI and WIN.INI
- Making changes to other Windows INI files (PROGMAN.INI and WINFILE.INI)

As mentioned in Chapter 2, "Basic Stuff To Get Started," one of the most important habits you should acquire is that of using comments and log files to keep track of the changes you make.

Using Comments and Logs

Before even explaining the how or why of changing your system's configuration files, you need to learn why it's important to keep track of any changes you make. If you make a change to a file, the change might not be correct. In fact, some changes can prevent your PC from booting normally (that's why you should make a system disk, if you haven't already done so).

To avoid the possibility of making a change that you'll have a hard time undoing, make a comment out of the line you're changing, then insert a new line that includes the changes you want to make. If you have a problem booting the system, you can restore the original line (the commented line) or use it as a basis to change the other entry. I'll give you an example shortly.

You also should get in the habit of adding comments to your configuration files that explain what you changed and why you changed it. With the comments in the file, you can look at the file six months or a year from now and remember what you changed and why you changed it.

To place comments in CONFIG.SYS or AUTOEXEC.BAT, preface the line in the file with REM (which stands for REMarks). DOS ignores the lines when it processes CONFIG.SYS and AUTOEXEC.BAT during system boot. Here's an example of some comments you might put in AUTOEXEC.BAT:

```
REM    The following line loads the mouse software
REM    into upper memory:
REM    C:\MOUSE\MOUSE.COM  (This was the old line)
LH C:\MOUSE\MOUSE.COM
```

You need only one space between the REM statement and the comment, but you can put in as many as you like.

In Windows files, use a semicolon (;) rather than the REM statement to indicate a comment. Windows will ignore the line when it reads the file. Just place the semicolon at the beginning of the line:

```
;    ------ I added the the following setting -------
;         to eliminate DOS prompt instruction
DOSPromptExitInstruc=0
;    -----------------------------------------------
```

Notice that the third line in the example isn't prefaced with a semicolon—it's an example of a configuration setting for Windows.

It's also a good idea to use asterisks (*) or hyphens (-) above and below the line to set your changes apart from the rest of the INI file. Just make sure to include the semicolon on each line that you add as a comment, including the * and - separator lines.

CONFIG.SYS Changes

You learned a little bit about the PC's CONFIG.SYS file in Chapters 1 and 2. The system reads CONFIG.SYS when it boots, and CONFIG.SYS generally contains statements that configure the PC's hardware, load device drivers, and specify operating system options. Don't worry if you're not familiar with all these topics—they are explained later in this chapter.

You'll find a handful of common settings in a typical CONFIG.SYS file. By changing these settings, you can speed up disk access, conserve memory, specify the location of COMMAND.COM, and change the way device drivers load. CONFIG.SYS is where you should begin optimizing your system.

Modifying CONFIG.SYS

There are a couple of ways to modify CONFIG.SYS. If you prefer to edit the file from DOS, the DOS Edit program works well. In Windows, you can use Notepad, SysEdit, or any other word processor that can edit text files. If you're not sure how to use any of these editors, have a look at Chapter 1, "Read Me First."

WARNING Whenever you edit CONFIG.SYS, always make a backup copy before making any changes to the file. If you make a mistake or somehow lose the file, you can restore the backup copy. In DOS, use the COPY command to make a backup of the file. In Windows, you can use File Manager. You should make the backup copy on a floppy disk, rather than on the hard disk.

If you make an error editing CONFIG.SYS, you can prevent the system from booting normally. After you boot the PC with your system disk, you can copy the backup CONFIG.SYS file to the hard drive, then reboot from the hard drive.

Although you can place the backup copy of CONFIG.SYS on your system disk, it's a good idea to leave the CONFIG.SYS file on the system disk unchanged. Never making changes to it will ensure that you will always be able to boot the PC.

Changes that you make to CONFIG.SYS do not become effective until the PC is rebooted. After making changes to CONFIG.SYS, press Ctrl-Alt-Del to reboot the system and make the changes take effect.

FILES: Make It Possible To Open More Files

The first of the settings in CONFIG.SYS that you might want to change is FILES. The FILES setting specifies the number of files the PC can have open at one time. Here's a typical FILES statement in CONFIG.SYS:

```
FILES=30
```

FILES can be set to any integer (whole number) from 8 to 255. The default is 8. When you increase the setting, you cause more memory to be allocated for keeping track of open files, but the amount of memory is minimal. If you receive an error message such as `Not enough file handles` or `Too many files open`, you need to increase your FILES setting.

In Windows, start with a setting of 30. If you run a lot of applications at once, bump the number up to 50 or so. On a DOS-only system, 30 should cover most situations.

BUFFERS: Improve Disk Performance

The BUFFERS statement in CONFIG.SYS specifies the number of file transfer buffers that DOS creates. A *file transfer buffer* is an area of memory that DOS sets aside to temporarily store data while that data is being transferred to or from the disk. Buffers can improve disk performance, because the data can rest in the buffer until the system isn't busy, then be transferred to the disk.

MS-DOS includes a program called SmartDrive that acts as a *disk cache manager.* Essentially, it can take the place of the DOS buffers that are provided by the BUFFERS command.

If you're using SmartDrive, you can omit the BUFFERS statement entirely from CONFIG.SYS. Or, you might prefer to reduce the number of buffers to 10. The following is a BUFFERS statement that sets the number of file buffers in CONFIG.SYS:

```
FILES=10
```

The FILES setting can have a value from 1 to 99. Allocate no more than 10 if you're using SmartDrive (recommended). To determine if you're using SmartDrive, check your AUTOEXEC.BAT file for a statement that references the file SMARTDRV.EXE. There also might be a statement for SMARTDRV.EXE in CONFIG.SYS if you have a SCSI drive (this is explained later in this chapter). If you're using an older version of MS-DOS, the file may be named SMARTDRV.SYS.

LASTDRIVE: Setting the Last Useable Drive ID

The LASTDRIVE setting in CONFIG.SYS specifies the last available logical drive letter. This is the last letter that can be used to identify a disk drive on the system. By default, LASTDRIVE is set to one letter higher than your last logical disk. If you have one hard disk that is recognized as drive C, for example, LASTDRIVE will be set to D. If you have a hard drive that is partitioned into drives C, D, and E, LASTDRIVE is set to F.

You can use the LASTDRIVE setting in CONFIG.SYS to explictly specify the highest drive ID that the system will be able to use. LASTDRIVE can be set to any letter from A to Z. To enable your system to access the maximum number of drives, you can use the following statement in CONFIG.SYS:

```
LASTDRIVE=Z
```

MS-DOS sets up a data structure in memory to keep track of each possible logical drive. So, increasing the setting for LASTDRIVE increases the system's use of memory. Rather than using LASTDRIVE to make the maximum number of logical drive IDs available, you should use it to limit the number of available drives, and thereby conserve memory.

If your system is not connected to a network, leave the LASTDRIVE setting out of CONFIG.SYS; doing so allows only one additional available drive ID. If you are on a network and do not expect to connect to any additional remote drives across the network, set LASTDRIVE equal to one letter higher than your current highest drive ID.

If you connect and disconnect periodically from additional remote drives on the network, set LASTDRIVE to accommodate the maximum number of drives to which your system will be connected at any one time.

SHELL: Configuring COMMAND.COM

The SHELL statement in CONFIG.SYS specifies the command interpreter used on your system. By default, this command interpreter is COMMAND.COM. Although you can use the SHELL statement to specify a command interpreter other than COMMAND.COM, I've never met anyone who used anything other than COMMAND.COM (which is the only command interpreter included with MS-DOS).

The primary use of the SHELL statement for normal users such as you and me is to specify a different location for COMMAND.COM than the root directory, or to change the environment size used by COMMAND.COM.

Changing COMMAND.COM's Location

Normally, COMMAND.COM is located in the root directory of drive C (drive A if you boot from a floppy). You might want to move it to a different directory to make your root directory as sparse as possible (purely an aesthetic move), or to hide it for safety (like if you're worried that you or someone else will accidentally erase it from your root directory).

To place COMMAND.COM in a location other than the root directory, use the MOVE command (MS-DOS 6 only) or COPY command to place COMMAND.COM into its new directory. Then, add (or change) an entry in CONFIG.SYS for the SHELL statement. The following example specifies that COMMAND.COM is located in the directory C:\DOS:

```
SHELL=C:\DOS\COMMAND.COM /P
```

The first parameter in the example, C:\DOS\COMMAND.COM, specifies the location of COMMAND.COM. This parameter is used to set an environment variable named COMSPEC, which DOS uses to keep track of the location of COMMAND.COM whenever DOS needs to access it. (Environment variables are explained in the next section.) The second parameter, /P, makes permanent the instance of COMMAND.COM that

is loaded by CONFIG.SYS. If the /P is omitted, COMMAND.COM will drop out of memory after it executes AUTOEXEC.BAT, leaving the PC basically lifeless. So, always include the /P parameter at the end of the SHELL statement.

Changing Environment Size

DOS uses *environment variables* to help it get its job done. The system's PATH is an example of an environment variable, and so is COMSPEC (mentioned in the last section). Programs also sometimes use environment variables to keep track of the location of driver files or other information. When you run a lot of applications that each use different environment variables, it's possible to run out of space to contain all of those needed variables.

You can add a setting to the SHELL statement in CONFIG.SYS to control the size of the DOS environment. Doing so means that you can increase the environment size to accommodate many applications that use environment variables, or reduce the environment size if your applications don't use environment variables. If you have a problem with the PATH being truncated, or receive the error message Out of environment space, increase the DOS environment size.

The /E switch is added to the SHELL statement to specify the environment size. By default, the environment size is 256 bytes, but you can set the environment size to any size between 160 bytes and 32,768 bytes (32K). The following example increases the environment size to 512 bytes:

```
SHELL=C:\DOS\COMMAND.COM /E:512 /P
```

Remember that you must add the /P switch to keep COMMAND.COM in memory.

The /E and /P switches are not parameters of the SHELL statement. The SHELL statement does not recognize any switches or optional parameters. The /E and /P switches are switches for COMMAND.COM, not for the SHELL statement. If you are using a command interpreter other than COMMAND.COM (highly unlikely), the switches might be different.

NOTE You can control the DOS environment size for DOS sessions under Windows separately from the global environment size for COMMAND.COM outside of Windows. You can specify an environment size of 1024

bytes for COMMAND.COM outside of Windows, for example, but specify that DOS sessions in Windows use only 256 bytes. This is accomplished with the CommandEnvSize setting in SYSTEM.INI. Chapter 4, "All You Need To Know about Memory," explains this setting.

STACKS: Setting Aside Some Memory for Interrupts

A *stack* is a block of memory used to keep track of dynamic data (data that changes). A *hardware interrupt* is an event that is caused by various types of hardware activity (such as keys being pressed on the keyboard). Generally, DOS needs a stack to keep track of data generated by the interrupt, so MS-DOS allocates one stack from a reserved pool each time an interrupt occurs.

On most systems, MS-DOS allocates nine stacks of 128 bytes each. The exceptions are the original IBM PC, PC/XT, and PC Portable, on which DOS allocates no stacks. On some computers, allocating zero stacks can cause the system to behave erratically. If you receive the errors `Stack Overflow` or `Exception error 12`, you don't have enough stacks allocated and you need to increase their number. You do so with the STACKS statement in CONFIG.SYS. The following example allocates nine stacks of 256 bytes each:

```
STACKS=9,256
```

No tried-and-true formula exists to help you determine how many stacks you need on your system, because the number varies with program activity and the level of hardware interrupts that are generated on the system. If you experience a problem, start with a setting of 9,256, and increase the setting if you still have problems. (Increase the number of stacks, and leave the stack size at 256 bytes.)

Fooling Applications with SETVER.EXE

Most programs work fine regardless of the version of DOS under which they run. Some programs, however, check the version of DOS that's running on the system before they start. If they find the wrong version of DOS, the programs won't run.

The SETVER.EXE program enables you to work around that problem. SETVER maintains a version table that contains program names and the DOS version under which each program in the table will run. When a program that's listed in the table queries DOS to determine on which version of DOS it's running, SETVER intercepts the query and returns the version number that the program wants to see. This enables a program that is expecting DOS version 4.1, for example, to run under DOS 6.0. SETVER tells the program that it is running under 4.1, when the program is really running under 6.0.

The chances are good that you won't need to use SETVER. If you want to view the default version table provided by SETVER, enter the following at the DOS prompt:

```
SETVER | MORE
```

The preceding command redirects the output of the SETVER command to the MORE command, which displays the output one page at a time, so that the output doesn't scroll past too quickly to read.

NOTE *If you have a problem finding the | character on the keyboard, it's located on the same key as the \ character, usually above the Enter key.*

The output consists of two columns of data; the first column shows the names of program files, and the second shows the DOS version that SETVER reports to these programs to enable them to run under the current version of DOS.

If you have a problem running a program under your version of DOS, you can install SETVER and add an entry to its version table for your program. First, install SETVER in CONFIG.SYS by adding the following line to your CONFIG.SYS file:

```
DEVICE=C:\DOS\SETVER.EXE
```

If SETVER is located in a directory other than C:\DOS, specify the correct directory. (Don't reboot the system yet, because you have one more change to make.)

Next, you need to add an entry to the version table for your program. Assume you have a program named FRED.EXE that expects to be running under MS-DOS 4.1. At the DOS prompt, enter the following command to add FRED.EXE to SETVER's version table:

```
SETVER FRED.EXE 4.1
```

You receive a prompt to reboot the system to make the change take effect. If you don't have any more changes, go ahead and reboot the system.

If you need to change an entry that's already in the version table, you first need to delete it. To delete FRED.EXE from the version table, type the following command at the DOS prompt:

```
SETVER /D FRED.EXE
```

If you're just deleting the entry, you're done. If you're changing an entry, use the SETVER command again to add a new entry for the program to the version table.

You might be able to get by without ever using SETVER. It may be installed in your CONFIG.SYS file, even though you've never added it there. There's no harm in having SETVER installed if you don't need it, except that it takes up a little bit of memory. If you like, add a REM to the beginning of the SETVER line to make it a comment and try running your programs. If all your programs still start properly, you can leave the SETVER line commented, or you can delete it altogether.

Controlling Devices with Drivers

One major function of CONFIG.SYS is to install device drivers. A *device driver* is a program that enables the PC to communicate with a device that's installed in or connected to the PC. You might have a device driver that controls a CD-ROM drive in the system, for example, or a device driver that enables the PC to read input from the mouse.

Device drivers are usually installed by a DEVICE= or DEVICEHIGH= statement in CONFIG.SYS. The DEVICE= statement loads the device driver into conventional memory (below 640K), and the DEVICEHIGH= statement loads a device driver into upper memory (640K to 1023K). Conventional and upper memory are explained in Chapter 4.

If you're not familiar with those two different types of memory, just understand for now that you should place device drivers in upper memory instead of conventional memory. Doing so makes more conventional memory available for your applications. Loading a device driver with the DEVICEHIGH= statement usually is preferable to loading it with the DEVICE= statement.

Another bit of CONFIG.SYS tweaking you might want to do is to change some of the DEVICE= entries in the file to DEVICEHIGH= entries. But wait! If you're using MS-DOS 6, you can make use of a better way to optimize your CONFIG.SYS file and device drivers than muddling around with the file yourself. Proceed directly to Chapter 4 to learn about MemMaker, which is a program for optimizing CONFIG.SYS that's included with MS-DOS 6.

If you aren't using MS-DOS 6, then you don't have MemMaker. This means that you will have to change the device drivers in CONFIG.SYS manually by editing the file and changing DEVICE= entries to DEVICEHIGH= entries wherever appropriate.

The problem is that not all device drivers can be loaded into upper memory. Doing so prevents them from working properly, and can even lead to you losing some data. Check the manuals that came with the device driver to see if the manual mentions loading the device driver into upper memory. If the manual doesn't mention loading the device driver into upper memory, contact the company's technical support department and ask the technician if the device driver can be loaded into upper memory with the DEVICEHIGH= setting.

In general, most device drivers work properly when loaded into upper memory, but some don't. You should avoid loading network drivers and hard disk device drivers into upper memory unless the documentation you have for them specifically indicates that you can load them into upper memory.

If you are using SmartDrive and have an entry in CONFIG.SYS for SMARTDRV.EXE, your hard disk requires double buffering (explained later in this chapter and in Chapter 5, "Hard Disk Tweaking: Cleaning, Packing, and Compressing"). You can't load the double-buffer portion of SMARTDRV.EXE into upper memory—it must be loaded into conventional memory with the DEVICE= statement.

The following is a list of a few of the device drivers you should not load into upper memory:

> aspi4dos
>
> netbios
>
> protman
>
> smartdrv
>
> sswap
>
> vdefend

Speeding Up Disk Access with SmartDrive

SmartDrive is a *disk cache* program that can speed up disk access considerably on your PC (speeding up disk access is what a disk cache is for). SmartDrive is explained in detail in Chapter 5. In this chapter, I'll just explain why SMARTDRV might appear in both your CONFIG.SYS and AUTOEXEC.BAT files (you might have seen it in both places and are wondering why it's there).

The portion of SmartDrive that provides disk caching is loaded with an entry for SMARTDRV.EXE in AUTOEXEC.BAT. If your system includes an entry for SMARTDRV.EXE in CONFIG.SYS, that is because your hard disk probably requires double buffering (I say probably because it actually might not need it). Put simply, *double buffering* is a technique that SmartDrive uses to ensure that the disk is read correctly. Double buffering is installed by an entry in CONFIG.SYS for SmartDrive. Therefore, the entry in AUTOEXEC.BAT loads the disk cache, and the entry in CONFIG.SYS sets up double buffering.

Some SCSI hard disks commonly require double buffering. There is no harm in using double buffering even with disks that don't require it. The only drawback to doing such a thing is that double buffering uses up some memory that could be used by your applications.

If you have an entry in CONFIG.SYS for SmartDrive, but don't have a SCSI hard disk, check with the manufacturer of the hard disk controller to find out why your PC is using double buffering. If your system does use a SCSI disk and you're one of those people who has to know everything there is to know about your PC, contact the hard disk controller manufacturer to find out if double buffering really is required with your hard disk.

AUTOEXEC.BAT Changes

The other system configuration file that your PC probably uses is AUTOEXEC.BAT. Whereas CONFIG.SYS is used generally to configure the PC's hardware, *AUTOEXEC.BAT* often is used to configure the PC's software environment. AUTOEXEC.BAT also is used to load device drivers.

AUTOEXEC.BAT is a batch file. A *batch file* is a special file that contains a list of commands that typically are executed sequentially. COMMAND.COM has the built-in capability to execute a batch file. That means that it executes each of the commands in the batch file, one after the other. AUTOEXEC.BAT is unique in that it is automatically executed when the system boots.

As with CONFIG.SYS, you can make a handful of changes to AUTOEXEC.BAT to make your system more useful. This section of the chapter covers the most common changes you might want to make to AUTOEXEC.BAT.

Modifying AUTOEXEC.BAT

Like CONFIG.SYS, the AUTOEXEC.BAT file is a text file that you can edit with the DOS EDIT program in DOS or with the Notepad or SysEdit programs in Windows. Check back in Chapter 1 if you're not sure how to use these programs to edit a file.

WARNING Whenever you edit AUTOEXEC.BAT, always make a backup copy before making any changes to the file. If you make a mistake or somehow lose the file, you can restore the backup copy. In DOS, use the COPY command to make a backup of the file. In Windows, you can use File Manager.

Editing AUTOEXEC.BAT is not as dangerous as editing CONFIG.SYS, because an incorrect change to AUTOEXEC.BAT will not prevent your PC from booting.

Changes that you make to AUTOEXEC.BAT do not become effective until AUTOEXEC.BAT is executed. You can enter **AUTOEXEC.BAT** at the DOS prompt to execute the commands in AUTOEXEC.BAT, but you might want to reboot the system instead (which will cause AUTOEXEC.BAT to be executed). After you've finished making changes to AUTOEXEC.BAT, press Ctrl-Alt-Del to reboot the system.

 **NOTE** *Although you can place the backup copy of AUTOEXEC.BAT on your system disk, it's a good idea to leave the AUTOEXEC.BAT file on the system disk unchanged. If you never make changes to it, you ensure that the original AUTOEXEC.BAT file for your PC is always intact.*

Modifying the DOS Prompt

Unless Windows starts automatically on your system when the PC is booted and you've never used anything else but Windows, you're probably familiar with the DOS prompt. It's that ubiquitous prompt on the DOS command line that usually reads C:>, or something very similar.

DOS nerds love to fiddle with the DOS prompt to make it display all sorts of information beyond just the C:\> business. For example, you can set the prompt to display the name of the current directory as well as the current drive. Or, maybe you want the prompt to include the current time and date. Whatever you want the prompt to be, it's a simple matter to change it—just specify a PROMPT statement in AUTOEXEC.BAT.

 **NOTE** *You also can enter a PROMPT statement from the DOS command line, but AUTOEXEC.BAT is where the prompt generally is set. Including the PROMPT statement in AUTOEXEC.BAT causes the PROMPT to be set automatically when the system boots.*

Here's an example of a PROMPT statement that causes the DOS prompt to include the current drive and directory, followed by a greater than sign (>):

```
PROMPT=$P$G
```

If you are using the preceding prompt, and you change to the Windows directory, the following command prompt appears:

```
C:\WINDOWS>
```

What are the $P and $G characters? They are special characters used with the PROMPT statement to display specific information with the DOS prompt. *$P* represents the current drive and path, and *$G* represents the > character. The following is a list of the special codes you can use with the PROMPT statement to display various types of data on the DOS command line as part of the DOS prompt:

- **$Q**   = (equal sign)
- **$$** $ (dollar sign)
- **$T**   Current time
- **$D**   Current date
- **$P**   Current drive and path
- **$V**   MS-DOS version number
- **$N**   Current drive
- **$G**   > (greater-than sign)
- **$L**   < (less-than sign)
- **$B**   ¦ (pipe)
- **$_**   ENTER-LINEFEED
- **$E**   ASCII escape code (code 27)
- **$H**   Backspace (to delete a character that has been written to the prompt command line)

Using the PATH Statement

The PATH statement is used to set a system path, which is stored in the PATH environment variable. The *path* is the selection of directories through which DOS will search for applications.

If you enter the name of an EXE, COM, or BAT file at the DOS prompt, for example, COMMAND.COM first looks in the current directory for the specified file. If it doesn't locate the file, COMMAND.COM then begins searching through the directories specified in the path until it finds the file (or has searched through the entire path without finding the file).

By adding a particular directory to your system path, you eliminate the need to switch to that directory to start progams that are located in it. You can add a PATH statement to your AUTOEXEC.BAT file to automatically set the system path when the PC boots (your system probably already has a PATH statement in AUTOEXEC.BAT).

Generally, you should keep the PATH to a reasonable minimum, such as no more than 80 characters, to conserve environment space. The maximum length for the PATH variable is 127 characters. A good rule of thumb is to include the root directory of drive C, your DOS directory, and your Windows directory on the path, along with the directories of any DOS applications that you use frequently (Windows programs generally don't have to be included on the path). Here's an example of a PATH statement that might appear in AUTOEXEC.BAT:

PATH=C:\;C:\DOS;C:\WINDOWS;C:\UTILITY

Each directory in the PATH statement is separated from the next by a semicolon (;).

If you want to view the current path, just enter **PATH** at the DOS prompt with no other characters on the line. To clear the PATH variable, enter the following:

PATH;

Doing so reduces the path to include only the current directory.

The TEMP Environment Variable

The TEMP environment variable is used to tell Windows where to store temporary files, such as the files that Print Manager creates when you print a document in Windows. Typically, the TEMP directory is C:\TEMP. You should specify a directory that isn't used for anything else, but you can use any directory for the TEMP directory.

Organize Directory Listings with DIRCMD

Another feature in MS-DOS 6 is the DIRCMD environment variable. *DIRCMD* gives you a means to preset command-line options for the DIR command, and have them used automatically whenever you use the DIR command.

The /W switch, for example, can be used with DIR to produce a wide listing of the directory that fills the width of the screen. If you set the DIRCMD environment variable to /W, entering DIR at the DOS prompt produces the equivalent output of entering DIR /W. Setting DIRCMD to /W saves you the trouble of adding the /W switch each time you enter the DIR command.

Perhaps more useful is the fact that you can set DIRCMD to sort your directory listings. For example, you might prefer to see all directories displayed first, then files, and all in alphabetical order. The following is the DIR command line that would achieve that, followed by a sample output:

```
C:\>DIR /OGN
 Volume in drive C is MS-DOS_6
 Volume Serial Number is 3464-12D7
 Directory of C:\

BALLPT       <DIR>        05-12-93   11:21a
DOC          <DIR>        05-21-93    5:10p
DOS          <DIR>        05-12-93   11:14a
NECUTILS     <DIR>        05-12-93   11:16a
PCMCIA       <DIR>        05-12-93   11:21a
SAFE         <DIR>        05-19-93    2:28p
TEMP         <DIR>        05-12-93   11:21a
UTIL         <DIR>        05-21-93    3:41p
WINDOWS      <DIR>        05-12-93   11:16a
AUTOEXEC BAT         1373 05-30-93   12:39p
COMMAND  COM        52925 03-10-93    6:00a
CONFIG   SYS         2397 05-31-93   11:28a
TEST     JNL         4939 05-19-93    2:42p
TEST     LOG         5535 05-19-93    2:54p
VERSION                53 04-15-93   10:03a
WINA20   386         9349 11-18-92    9:00a
        16 file(s)      76571 bytes
                     10395648 bytes free
```

Do you want your DIR output sorted the same way? Just set the DIRCMD, and each time you enter DIR at the DOS prompt, the correct options will be applied automatically. To set the DIRCMD environment variable, either enter the following line at the DOS prompt or add it to AUTOEXEC.BAT to have it executed automatically:

SET DIRCMD=/OGN

For a list of the switches that you can use with the DIR command, enter **HELP DIR** at the DOS prompt.

Storing Commands with DOSKEY.COM

If you work at the DOS command line frequently, you will want to begin using DOSKEY (if you aren't already). *DOSKEY* is a utility included with DOS that keeps track of the commands you enter on the DOS command line.

With DOSKEY installed, you can use the arrow keys to retrieve, edit, and reuse commands you entered earlier. Pressing the up-arrow key cycles back through the commands you've entered, and pressing the down-arrow key cycles forward through them. You can use the left- and right-arrow keys to position the cursor within a retrieved command, then type over portions of it to change the command.

To insert text in a command string, press the Ins key, then type the text you want inserted at the cursor location. When the command reads the way you want it, press Enter to execute it (with the cursor at any location in the command). If you use the same commands frequently, DOSKEY saves you a lot of typing.

To use DOSKEY, just start the DOSKEY.COM program by entering **DOSKEY** at the DOS prompt. Better still, add a line for DOSKEY to your AUTOEXEC.BAT file so that DOSKEY will start automatically when your system starts. You also can load DOSKEY into upper memory. Use the following command in AUTOEXEC.BAT to have DOSKEY.COM load into upper memory each time the PC is booted:

```
LOADHIGH C:\DOS\DOSKEY.COM
```

If DOSKEY.COM is in a directory other than C:\DOS on your PC, substitute the proper directory.

Using Multiple Configurations with MS-DOS 6

If you're one of those users who switches often between different hardware or software configurations, you'll love MS-DOS 6. Until now, you've had to manually edit your CONFIG.SYS and AUTOEXEC.BAT files and reboot the system, or use a utility program that automated the process for you.

With MS-DOS 6, you can create a menu system that appears when your system boots. By selecting different menu options, you can control how your PC boots.

Here's an example: Say your PC is on a network, but you use the network only occasionally. The majority of the time you prefer not to load the network drivers, and instead load a utility called FRED.COM that for reasons beyond your control is not compatible with your network software. Wouldn't it be great if, when the system booted, you could select from a menu that let you control whether or not the network drivers loaded? With MS-DOS 6, you can.

Understanding the Multiple-Boot Feature

MS-DOS 6 adds new commands that you can add to CONFIG.SYS to create a menu that appears when the system boots. You can associate specific sections of CONFIG.SYS to each menu item. Selecting a particular menu item causes the lines in CONFIG.SYS that are associated with the menu item to be executed. You also can control which portions of AUTOEXEC.BAT execute based on your boot menu selection.

Here's how the preceding scenario works: In CONFIG.SYS, you can add configuration blocks. A *configuration block* is a portion of CONFIG.SYS that has a special header line enclosed in square brackets that names the configuration block. The following is an example of a configuration block named [COMMON] from a typical CONFIG.SYS file:

```
[COMMON]
DEVICE=C:\DOS\HIMEM.SYS
DEVICE=C:\DOS\EMM386.EXE NOEMS X=D000-DFFF
DOS=HIGH,UMB
FILES=30
BUFFERS=10
STACKS=9,256
SHELL=C:\DOS\COMMAND.COM /P
```

In addition to configuration blocks, CONFIG.SYS can include menu blocks. The menu block labeled [MENU] is used to define the menu options that appear when the PC boots. Here's an example of a [MENU] configuration block with two menu items defined—one for a network configuration and one without the network:

```
[MENU]
MENUITEM=YESNET, Run Network Drivers
MENUITEM=NONET, No Network
```

The YESNET and NONET entries specify the names of configuration blocks that will be executed when either of the menu items is selected. The strings "Run Network Drivers" and "No Network" are the text that appears beside each of the two menu items when the menu is displayed. If you select "Run Network Drivers" from the boot menu, for example, DOS executes the commands contained in the YESNET configuration block in CONFIG.SYS.

Great! Now we need to bring everything together and create the YESNET and NONET configuration blocks. Here's the completed CONFIG.SYS file, with comments:

```
[COMMON]
REM ------- Execute this section all the time
REM ------- for both configurations, net and no-net
DEVICE=C:\DOS\HIMEM.SYS
DEVICE=C:\DOS\EMM386.EXE NOEMS X=D000-DFFF
DOS=HIGH,UMB
FILES=30
BUFFERS=10
STACKS=9,256
SHELL=C:\DOS\COMMAND.COM /P

[MENU]
REM ------- Define two menu selections
MENUITEM=YESNET, Run Network Drivers
MENUITEM=NONET, No Network
MENUDEFAULT=NONET,10
MENUCOLOR=15,0

[YESNET]
REM ------- Execute this section if the user
REM ------- selects the option "Run Network
REM ------- Drivers" from the menu
DEVICE=C:\WINDOWS\PROTMAN.DOS /I:C:\WINDOWS
DEVICE=C:\WINDOWS\WORKGRP.SYS
DEVICE=C:\WINDOWS\SMCMAC.DOS

[NONET]
DEVICE=C:\UTILITY\FRED.COM

[COMMON]
REM ------- This additional COMMON section is
REM ------- here for applications that modify
REM ------- CONFIG.SYS to add settings or device
REM ------- drivers. The new settings will be
REM ------- appended to the CONFIG.SYS file,
REM ------- which means they'll be added to
REM ------- this section.
```

Here's how the preceding CONFIG.SYS file works: when the system boots, the commands in the first [COMMON] group are executed. The [MENU] block then causes a menu of two items to be displayed. The MENUDEFAULT setting specifies that if the user does nothing, the NONET block will be executed after ten seconds, making it the default menu selection. The MENUCOLOR line sets the text color for the menu to bright white (color 15) and the background to black (color 0).

If the user picks the first menu item before the ten-second time limit is up, the statements in the [YESNET] block are executed. If the user selects the second menu item, the [NONET] block is executed. After either block is executed, any statements contained in the second [COMMON] block are executed.

What about AUTOEXEC.BAT?

Wait! We forgot that we also need to run a program called BARNEY.EXE from AUTOEXEC.BAT whenever the FRED.COM utility is running. That means we need to run BARNEY.EXE whenever the [NONET] menu item is selected. No problem!

When a menu item is selected, its menu name is stored in the environment variable CONFIG. You can check the CONFIG environment variable in AUTOEXEC.BAT and execute statements in AUTOEXEC.BAT based on the value of the CONFIG variable. How do you do it? You use the IF and GOTO commands. Here's an example:

```
C:\DOS\SMARTDRV.EXE
PROMPT $P$G
PATH C:\WINDOWS;C:\DOS;C:\NECUTILS;c:\util
SET TEMP=C:\TEMP
LOADHIGH C:\DOS\DOSKEY.COM

GOTO %CONFIG%

:YESNET
REM ------- In this section, add any commands that
REM ------- you want executed when the YESNET menu
REM ------- item is selected at boot.
:NONET
REM ------- In this section, add any commands
REM ------- that  you want executed when the NONET
REM ------- menu item is selected at boot (like
REM ------- BARNEY.EXE in this example).
C:\UTILITY\BARNEY.EXE
```

When the user selects the YESNET menu item at boot, the CONFIG environment variable is set to YESNET. When the user selects NONET, the CONFIG environment variable is set to NONET. When AUTOEXEC.BAT is executed, the line GOTO %CONFIG% evaluates either to GOTO YESNET or GOTO NONET, depending on which menu item was selected.

I Want More!

You now have enough background on MS-DOS 6's multiple-boot feature to create a boot menu. If you need more than one menu, you can create submenus in CONFIG.SYS. For an explanation of how to do that, enter **HELP SUBMENU** at the DOS prompt. For a listing of the different colors you can use for the menu, enter **HELP MENUCOLOR** at the DOS prompt. For additional information of menu items, enter **HELP MENUITEM** or **HELP MENUDEFAULT** at the DOS prompt.

Tweaking Your Windows Files

The first half of this chapter explained changes you can make to CONFIG.SYS and AUTOEXEC.BAT to make your PC more useful or make it function better. The following part of the chapter explains changes that you can make to your Windows initialization files so that you can fine-tune the way Windows runs.

Why Make Changes to INI Files?

Windows uses *initialization files* to store various settings that control the way Windows runs. These initialization files are text files that have a file extension of INI, and they usually are referred to as INI files. INI files are separated into sections, with each section having a label enclosed in square brackets. Here is a sample section from WIN.INI:

```
[Desktop]
Pattern=(None)
Wallpaper=(None)
GridGranularity=0
IconSpacing=75
TileWallPaper=0
```

Two primary Windows INI files control Windows globally. WIN.INI contains settings that define the Windows software environment, and SYSTEM.INI contains settings that generally determine your Windows hardware configuration. WIN.INI sets options for display colors and other operating parameters, for example, and SYSTEM.INI loads device drivers and specifies how Windows functions in its different operating modes.

In addition to WIN.INI and SYSTEM.INI, many Windows programs use their own INI files to store operating settings. Program Manager uses the file PROGMAN.INI to store its settings. File Manager stores its settings in WINFILE.INI. Control Panel uses CONTROL.INI, and Microsoft Mail uses MSMAIL.INI for its settings.

Many of the settings in the various INI files (that are used by Windows and your Windows programs) are set automatically when you use Control Panel or set options within a program. When you set the options in Program Manager's **O**ptions menu, for example, some of the settings in PROGMAN.INI are changed automatically. If these changes happen automatically, why would you want to make changes to the file manually?

Some of the settings in the Windows INI files are not set automatically. The only way to add certain features or change certain options is to edit the INI files manually and add or change settings.

The following sections of the chapter cover the most common of the INI settings that have to be set manually. Settings that can be set with Control Panel or with an application's menu and commands are not covered. If you're interested in these additional settings, pick up a copy of *Maximizing Windows 3.1*, from New Riders Publishing.

Modifying an INI File

Because INI files are standard text files, you can edit them from DOS with EDIT, or you can edit them in Windows with Notepad. SysEdit is designed to enable you to edit SYSTEM.INI and WIN.INI. If you want to edit any of the other Windows INI files besides these two, use Notepad. Just load the INI file into Notepad (or Edit), make your changes, then resave the file.

Some changes to INI files take effect immediately. Other changes require that you restart Windows for the change to take effect. There's no hard-and-fast rule, so if you're in doubt, just restart Windows after changing the file if the change doesn't seem to be having any effect.

When editing an INI file, you should always make a backup copy of the file. If you're editing SYSTEM.INI, for example, copy or save it to a file called SYSOLD.INI. If the changes you then make to SYSTEM.INI prevent Windows from running properly, you can copy SYSOLD.INI to SYSTEM.INI and eliminate the problem.

About the INI File Settings

The following sections do not go into a lot of unnecessary detail about the settings described in them. Instead, I've just listed the settings, explained where they go in each INI file, and described in brief what they do. That should give you enough information to decide whether you want to add or change the settings.

The values that can be assigned to an INI file setting depend on the setting. Some are assigned *integer* values (whole numbers such as 1 through 256, for example). Here's an example:

```
IconVerticalSpacing=70
```

Other settings store boolean values. *Boolean* values represent On/Off, True/False, and Yes/No conditions, which to a computer all mean basically the same thing. With most boolean settings in Windows INI files, you can use On, True, Yes, or 1 for a true condition. You can use Off, False, No, or 0 for a false condition. The following is an example of a boolean setting:

```
MouseInDOSBox=False
```

Still other INI settings contain strings, or text. The following is an example of this type of setting:

```
SystemStart=tada.wav, Windows Start
```

INI settings also can be *quoted strings*, which are strings enclosed in quotes. Whether you need the quotes or not depends on the setting. The following is an example of a quoted string:

```
SlimeyGreenFrogs="Really slippery and disgusting"
```

In each of the following examples, I've included the type of value required by the setting. If a particular setting doesn't appear in its INI file, the default value for the setting applies. You won't see the setting MenuDropAlignment, for example, in WIN.INI unless you add it yourself, so the MenuDropAlignment value of 0 is in effect until you add the setting and set it to 1 (the other possible value for that setting).

WIN.INI Changes

WIN.INI is one of Windows' primary INI files. *WIN.INI* primarily controls the software environment in Windows. It specifies settings that control colors, the screen saver, printer port definitions, and so on. You can think of WIN.INI as the file you change when you want to control how Windows appears and control some of the options available to you in Windows.

The following sections separate the WIN.INI file settings by section. Bear in mind that not all of the possible settings are included here, even if they are ones that must be set manually. Some settings are so obscure that almost no one has any use for them.

Settings for the [Windows] Section

- **DoubleClickHeight=***integer.* Defines the vertical distance, in pixels, that the screen pointer can move between the two clicks in a double-click event (a *pixel* is one of the tiny dots that make up the image on your display). If the screen pointer moves more than the specified number of pixels, the two clicks are treated as separate single-clicks. The default is 4. Raise the number if you can't keep the mouse stationary during a double-click (which sometimes is difficult with a trackball). Example: DoubleClickHeight=10.

- **DoubleClickWidth=***integer.* Defines the horizontal distance, in pixels, that the screen pointer can move between the two clicks in a double-click event. This is basically the same as the DoubleClickHeight setting (preceding), except that it is for horizontal movement. The default is 4. If you change DoubleClickHeight, you probably want to set DoubleClickWidth equal to DoubleClickHeight. Example: DoubleClickWidth=10.

● **MenuDropAlignment=*0* or *1*.** This one's purely for aesthetics. If set to 0 (the default), menus drop down left-aligned with their menu names. If set to 1, this setting causes menus to drop down with their right edges aligned with their menu names in the menu bar.

I can't think of a reason to change this setting, but you're welcome to fiddle with it if you want to. Example: MenuDropAlignment=1.

● **MouseTrails=*integer*.** This one actually can be set from the Mouse icon in Control Panel most of the time. This setting controls how many "ghost images" of the screen pointer will follow it around on the display when you move the mouse. MouseTrails only works if you're using the EGA, VGA, or Super VGA driver for Windows, or a third-party driver that has been written to provide support for mouse trails.

This one is useful on a computer with an LCD display if you have a hard time finding the mouse. With MouseTrails set to 4, for example, you'll see four images of the screen pointer as you move the mouse. Example: MouseTrails=6.

Settings for the [Desktop] Section

● **IconTitleFaceName=*string*.** This setting specifies the name of the font used for the descriptions under icons. You might want to specify a TrueType font to get a different look for your Windows desktop. Example: IconTitleFaceName=Times New Roman.´

● **IconTitleSize=*integer*.** Specifies the point size of the font used for icon descriptions (see IconTitleFaceName). The default is 8. Increase the setting on a high-resolution display in order to read the icon titles more clearly. Example: IconTitleSize=12.

● **IconTitleStyle=*0* or *1*.** Specifies whether the icon title text is normal or bold. Set it to 0 for normal (the default) or 1 for bold. Example: IconTitleStyle=1.

● **IconVerticalSpacing=*integer*.** Specifies the vertical distance, in pixels, between rows of icons on the desktop (and in program groups) when you use the Arrange Icon command to arrange icons. Example: IconVerticalSpacing=70.

● **WallpaperOriginX=*integer*.** Specifies the horizontal pixel location (relative to 0 at the upper-left corner of the Windows desktop) offset where the wallpaper image will appear on the desktop. Use this setting in conjunction with the WallpaperOriginY setting to center a wallpaper image that otherwise would be off-center (or to cause a wallpaper tile to be centered on the desktop). Example: WallpaperOriginX=20.

● **WallpaperOriginY=*integer*.** Specifies the vertical pixel location (relative to 0 at the upper left corner of the desktop) where the wallpaper image will appear. Use this setting in conjunction with WallpaperOriginX (see preceding). Example: WallpaperOriginY=15.

Settings for the [Ports] Section

● **LPT*x*.*string*=.** This one doesn't actually get a value. The *x* is replaced with a number from 1 to 3 to specify one of the system's LPT ports. The *string* entry is just a unique string that identifies the port, and it can be set to anything you wish. You can add entries to the [Ports] section to maintain multiple printer driver configurations for the same port.

For example, you can create entries for LPT1.Portrait and LPT1.Landscape, then configure your printer for portrait and landscape modes, respectively. Select the Printers icon in Control Panel, then use the **C**onnect button to associate the printer driver with a port entry (the LPT*x*.*whatever* entries will appear in the Connect dialog box). Example: LPT1.Portrait=.

Settings for the [Windows Help] Section

● **JumpColor=*red green blue*.** Specifies the color used in Windows Help to identify topic strings (which appear as solid underlined text in a Help topic page). Clicking on a topic string causes Help to jump to a new topic page that's associated with the underlined phrase. Each of the red, green, and blue values can be an integer from 0 to 255.

Mix different amounts of each color to get your final jump text color. A value of 0 means none of that color, and 255 means the maximum amount of the color. Example for turquoise (equal amounts of green and blue with no red): JumpColor=0 128 128.

● **PopupColor=*red green blue*.** Specifies the color used in Windows Help to identify popup definitions (which appear as dashed-underlined text). Clicking on a popup causes Help to display a description or definition of the selected word or phrase. Mix red, green, and blue values to come up with your final popup color. Example for purple (equal amounts of red and blue with no green): PopupColor=128 0 128.

● **MacroColor=*red green blue*.** Specifies the color used in Windows Help to identify text that, when selected, executes a Help macro. Example: MacroColor=255 255 0.

● **IFJumpColor=*red green blue*.** Similar to the JumpColor setting, except that this setting specifies the color of text that, when selected, causes Help to display a topic page that is contained in a different Help file. Example: IFJumpColor=128 255 128.

● **IFPopupColor=*red green blue*.** Similar to the PopupColor setting, except that this setting specifies the color of text that, when selected, causes Help to display a popup panel that is contained in a different Help file. Example: IFPopupColor=0 90 230.

Making SYSTEM.INI Changes

While WIN.INI generally controls the Windows user software environment, SYSTEM.INI controls Windows' hardware environment and system-level options. The settings in the SYSTEM.INI file load device drivers, specify operating parameters for 386 Enhanced mode and for Standard mode, specify fonts used by Windows, and define other system-level operating parameters.

You can make a log of changes to SYSTEM.INI to change the way Windows functions, but it's particularly important that you make a backup copy of SYSTEM.INI before editing the file. An incorrect change to SYSTEM.INI can prevent Windows from starting until the problem in SYSTEM.INI has been corrected.

The following are the most common of the settings that you must manually edit SYSTEM.INI to add or change.

Settings for the [Boot] Section

● **Shell=*EXE filename*.** Specifies the name of the program that functions as the Windows shell. By default, Program Manager is the Windows shell. You can use almost any Windows program as your shell. If you prefer to use File Manager instead of Program Manager, for example, specify WINFILE.EXE as the value of Shell=. Example: Shell=C:\EXCEL\EXCEL.EXE.

● **TaskMan.Exe=*EXE filename*.** Specifies the name of the program that functions as the Windows task switcher. By default, Task Manager is the Windows task switcher.

If you're not sure what Task Manager is, double-click on an empty space on the Windows desktop or press Ctrl-Esc. The dialog box that pops up is the Task Manager, and it enables you to switch among whichever programs are running. The Task Manager also enables you to organize windows and icons. Example: TaskMan.Exe=FRED.EXE.

Settings for the [NonWindowsApp] Section

● **CommandEnvSize=*bytes*.** Specifies the environment size of DOS virtual machines (DOS sessions) that are started under Windows' 386 Enhanced mode. This is similar to the /E parameter of COMMAND.COM, except that it overrides the environment size that is set outside of Windows, either by default, or with the /E parameter of the SHELL statement in CONFIG.SYS. Example to set the environment to 512 bytes: CommandEnvSize=512.

● **DisablePositionSave=*0* or *1*.** When set to 0 (the default), Windows keeps track of the position on the desktop of windowed DOS programs and the fonts they use from session to session. Set DisablePositionSave to 1 if you don't want Windows to keep track of any position or font changes that occur when you use a DOS program.

● **ScreenLines=*integer*.** Specifies the number of screen lines that DOS programs that are run under Windows will use. If you want a DOS prompt with 50 lines instead of the default 25, for example, set ScreenLines=50. Many DOS programs override this setting. You can't force a word processor program to display 50 lines, for example, when it normally displays only 25. Example: ScreenLines=50.

Settings for the [386Enh] Section

● **COMBoostTime=***milliseconds.* This setting specifies the amount of time in milliseconds that a DOS session will have to process a COM port interrupt. If you have a DOS communications program that loses keyboard characters, increase this setting from its default of 2. Example: COMBoostTime=10.

NOTE *There are a lot of other settings for the [386Enh] section that control the PC's COM ports. Read the file SYSINI.WRI that's located in your Windows directory for more information on these settings.*

● **DOSPromptExitInstruc=***boolean.* If enabled (set to Yes, On, True, or 1), Windows displays an initial message when you open a DOS session under 386 Enhanced mode. The message appears at the top of the DOS session's window, and it explains how to get out of the DOS session and back to Windows. I already know how to get out of the DOS session, so I like to turn off the message. Just specify a setting of 0 if you don't want to see the message anymore. Example: DOSPromptExitInstruc=0.

● **FileSysChange=***boolean.* If this setting is enabled, File Manager keeps track of all file changes by DOS programs and updates its display accordingly. This can really slow down the system's performance. Instead, you can just press the F5 key in File Manager to update its display when necessary. To prevent File Manager from updating each time a DOS program changes a file, specify a setting of Off. Example: FileSysChange=Off.

● **LocalLoadHigh=***boolean.* If enabled (the default), Windows will use all available upper memory blocks

(UMBs) for itself, making none available for DOS sessions that you run under Windows. To make UMBs available to DOS sessions in Windows, disable this setting with Off, 0, No, or False. Example: LocalLoadHigh=False.

● **LocalReboot=***On* or *Off.* If this setting is On (the default), pressing Ctrl-Alt-Del when a program is running under Windows will cause Windows to attempt to kill the program without rebooting the system. If set to Off, pressing Ctrl-Alt-Del immediately reboots the system. Example: LocalReboot=Off.

● **MessageBackColor=***color value.* Specifies the background color of full-screen messages, such as the ones that appear when you press Ctrl-Alt-Del anywhere in Windows or press Alt-Tab in a full-screen DOS application. Valid values are 0 through 9 and A through F. Table 3.1 shows the colors and their values. Example for a black background: MessageBackColor=0.

● **MessageTextColor=***color value.* Specifies the text color of full-screen messages (see MessageBackColor). Use the values in Table 3.1 to specify a color. Example for yellow: MessageTextColor=E.

Table 3.1
Color Values for MessageBackColor and MessageTextColor

Value	Color	Value	Color
0	Black	8	Gray
1	Blue	9	Bright blue
2	Green	A	Bright green
3	Cyan	B	Bright cyan
4	Red	C	Bright red
5	Magenta	D	Bright magenta
6	Brown	E	Yellow
7	White	F	Bright white

There are a ton of other settings for SYSTEM.INI, particularly for the [386Enh] section. For more information on these settings, check *Maximizing Windows 3.1*, or the files SYSINI.WRI and WININI.WRI in your Windows directory.

Using PROGMAN.INI Settings

There are a handful of settings you can add to Program Manager's INI file, PROGMAN.INI, to control the way Program Manager works. These settings are useful if you are responsible for setting up and maintaining Windows for other users, because the settings prevent users from accessing certain Program Manager functions.

These settings also can be useful on a home system that your children use, because you can use them to prevent the children from making any changes to your program groups and items (like deleting all the icons in a group).

PROGMAN.INI can contain three sections labeled [settings], [groups], and [restrictions]. The settings in the [settings] and [groups], sections are set by manipulating the Program Manager window or setting options using the Program Manager menu.

The [restrictions] section is optional. It's the section in which you add settings to disable certain Program Manager features. To add or make changes to the [restrictions] section, you have to manually edit PROGMAN.INI.

Here's a list of the settings that can be added to the [restrictions] section of PROGMAN.INI to disable certain Program Manager features:

- **NoRun=.** Disables the **R**un command in Program Manager's **F**ile menu. If NoRun is set to 1, the **R**un command is dimmed and cannot be accessed. When NoRun is set to 0 (the default), the **R**un command is available.

- **NoClose=.** Disables the E**x**it Windows command in Program Manager's **F**ile menu. When this setting is set to 1, the E**x**it Windows command is dimmed. When this setting is 0, the E**x**it Windows command is available.

- **NoSaveSettings=.** This setting disables the **S**ave Settings on Exit command in Program Manager's **O**ptions menu. If set to 1, NoSaveSettings causes the **S**ave Settings on Exit command to be dimmed, making it unavailable. Specifying a setting of 0 causes the command to be available as normal.

- **NoFileMenu=.** When set to 1, this setting removes the **F**ile menu from Program Manager's menu bar. Removing the **F**ile menu makes its commands unavailable. A setting of 0 makes the **F**ile command available as usual.

- **EditLevel=.** This setting can have a value from 0 to 4. These different values for EditLevel control the user's ability to modify items in the Program Manager environment. These settings are described in detail a little later in this section.

Disabling the Run Command

If you add the setting NoRun=1 to the [restrictions] section of a user's PROGMAN.INI file, the **R**un command still appears in Program Manager's **F**ile menu, but the menu item is dimmed and cannot be selected. This prevents the user from executing a program using the **R**un command, and helps restrict the user to executing only those programs that are contained in program groups on the user's desktop.

Even with the **R**un command dimmed, the user still can use the **R**un command in File Manager or double-click on program files in File Manager to execute applications. The user also can add the program to a program group and execute it.

If File Manager is available to the user, the NoRun= setting in the [restrictions] section therefore provides only limited security against the user executing restricted programs. To ensure better security, place applications in shared remote directories that are protected by passwords.

Figure 3.1: The **R**un command dimmed in Program Manager's menu.

Preventing Exit from Windows

The NoClose= setting in the [restrictions] section of PROGMAN.INI enables you to prevent a user from exiting the Windows environment (assuming Program Manager is the user's shell). When set to 1, NoClose= disables the E**x**it Windows command in the **F**ile menu (see fig. 3.2), the **C**lose command in Program Manager's control menu, and the Alt-F4 shortcut key for closing Program Manager. This setting effectively prevents the user from exiting Windows, short of rebooting with Ctrl-Alt-Del or cycling power on the workstation.

Figure 3.2: The E**x**it Windows command dimmed.

Disabling Ability To Change Program Manager

The setting NoSaveSettings=1 in the [restrictions] section disables the **S**ave Settings on Exit command in Program Manager's **O**ptions menu. This prevents the user from saving any changes that have been made to the Windows desktop during the current session. This includes such changes as moving group windows or changing the iconic/windowed state of a group.

This setting is most useful for preventing inexperienced users from making accidental changes to their Program Manager environment.

Restricting Group and Program Item Features

In addition to controlling the functions that a user has to some of the menu items in Program Manager, you also can control the user's ability to create and edit program groups and program items. These abilities are controlled by the value of the EditLevel setting in the [restrictions] section of PROGMAN.INI.

The following list explains the possible values for EditLevel:

- **0.** This is the default value. The user can make any change to the desktop, including creating and deleting program groups and items.

- **1.** This setting disables the user's ability to create, delete, and rename groups. This setting dims the **N**ew, **M**ove, **C**opy, and **D**elete items from the **F**ile menu when a group is selected. A setting of EditLevel=1 does not affect the user's ability to perform these same types of functions on program items within a group. This setting also disables shortcut methods for deleting groups, such as pressing Del when a group icon is selected.

- **2.** This setting incorporates the same restriction level as a setting of 1, but also prevents the user from creating or deleting program items (icons in a program group). This setting dims the **N**ew, **M**ove, **C**opy, and **D**elete menu items in the **F**ile menu at all times. Shortcut methods for corresponding commands also are disabled.

- **3.** Includes all restrictions present in level 2, and also prevents the user from changing a program's **C**ommand Line entry property. The user still can view the item's properties by selecting the item's icon, then choosing **P**roperties from the **F**ile menu or by pressing Alt-Enter. All other properties, including the item's **D**escription, still can be edited by the user.

- **4.** Includes all of the restrictions of level 3, but prevents the user from making any changes to a program item's properties. The user still can view the item's properties, but all fields in the Program Item Properties dialog box are read-only.

Changing the WINFILE.INI

There aren't a lot of changes to WINFILE.INI that have to be made manually. If you're running Windows for Workgroups and want to disable the capability to share additional disk resources, there is one setting you can add to WINFILE.INI in a [Restrictions] section.

The setting NoShareCommands=1, if added to a [Restrictions] section in WINFILE.INI, disables the commands in File Manager that enable you to share local disk resources with other users on the network. This prevents another user from sitting down at your PC while you're away and sharing some of your disk resources.

You can add a *NoShareCommands=1* setting to the [Spooler] section of WIN.INI to disable the capability to share any additional local printers with remote users.

Adding the NoShareCommands=1 setting to either WINFILE.INI or to the [Spooler] section of WIN.INI does not affect existing shared resources. These existing shared resources still can be accessed by remote users. Only the capability to share *additional* resources is disabled.

4

All You Need To Know about Memory

In the earlier chapters, you read about changes you can make to your system without picking up a screwdriver or opening up the system. This chapter is the first in which you actually might need to open your PC to make some changes to it. I say *might* because some of the changes you can make to the system to optimize its memory just require modifying a few settings in CONFIG.SYS and AUTOEXEC.BAT.

This chapter is all about your PC's most important resource—its memory—and covers the following topics:

- What the PC's memory is and what it does

- Types of memory and how they're packaged

- Memory managers and optimizing memory for DOS and Windows

- Adding memory to your PC

- Troubleshooting memory problems

Before monkeying around with your system's memory, you need some background information.

Basic Information about Memory

Memory in the PC is a little like your own memory. Just as you use your memory to keep track of information, the PC uses its memory to store information. While the PC's disks are used for *long-term storage*, the PC's memory essentially is used for *short-term storage*.

When you load a program, some or all of the program goes into the PC's memory. When you're working on a document, the data that makes up the document is stored in the PC's memory. When you save a document, the program you're using copies the document into a file on disk. When you close the document, the file is cleared from the PC's memory and makes room for something else, such as another program or document.

The most important point about memory is this: the more your system has, the better, particularly if you are running Windows. If you don't run Windows, the amount of memory in your system isn't as important as how you manage the memory it does have. (There are exceptions—some DOS programs require a large amount of memory to run well.) Later in this chapter you will learn about techniques to help optimize your PC's memory with DOS and with Windows.

RAM and ROM

The average PC contains two main types of memory. The first type is *random-access memory*, or *RAM*. RAM is dynamic, meaning that its contents can change. Information can be stored in RAM, read, and erased, and new data can then be stored in it. RAM consists of microchips of one sort or another that usually are installed on the PC's motherboard. Sometimes, RAM is added on an adapter card that plugs into one of the motherboard's bus sockets.

NOTE When you talk about how much memory your PC has, you're actually referring to how much RAM it has. RAM is where your programs and data reside in the PC when you're using them.

The other type of memory is *read-only memory*, or *ROM*. Information can be stored in ROM and read back; however, in a PC you usually can't write new information to ROM. That is why it's called *read-only*. The ROM chips are programmed before being installed in the system, usually with special hardware designed just for programming ROM chips.

The BIOS in a PC is a good example of ROM. In most PCs, you can't reprogram the BIOS yourself. In some newer PCs, however, you can upgrade the BIOS by running an upgrade program that reprograms the chip.

NOTE The important points to understand about ROM are that usually you can't change it, and you don't need to concern yourself with how much is in the system, how fast it is, and so on. It doesn't matter to you as a user.

Bits, Bytes, Kilobytes, and Megabytes

Confused by all the talk about bits, bytes, kilobytes, and megabytes? Don't be—there's really nothing complicated about it. They all are just measurements of memory capacity.

A *bit* represents the smallest unit of data. A *byte* is eight bits, and is enough to store, for example, a single character, such as the letter R or the number 3. But wait a minute! Why does it take eight bits to store a single character? Take a look at figure 4.1.

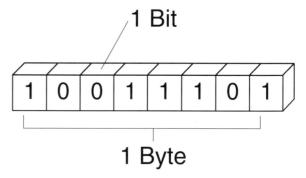

Figure 4.1: Eight bits make up one byte of data.

Figure 4.1 shows a representation of a byte, which is made up of eight bits. Each of the bits is either a one (1) or a zero (0). In fact, ones and zeros are all that a digital computer such as today's PCs can understand.

So how do the bits translate into a byte that means something? It's the *pattern* of the bits in the byte that the PC recognizes. The bits form a *binary number* made up of ones and zeros. The computer is programmed to recognize specific binary numbers as different characters. That's a simplistic explanation, but it's good enough for now. Let's get back to kilobytes.

A *kilobyte* is 1024 bytes, or enough space to store 1024 characters. That's equal to about one page in a document. Usually, kilobytes is abbreviated with a K; 32 kilobytes, for example, is abbreviated as 32K.

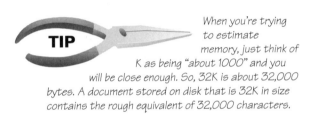

TIP

When you're trying to estimate memory, just think of K as being "about 1000" and you will be close enough. So, 32K is about 32,000 bytes. A document stored on disk that is 32K in size contains the rough equivalent of 32,000 characters.

A *megabyte* is 1024 kilobytes. Megabyte usually is abbreviated with an M, so 200 megabytes would be abbreviated as 200M. 200M is a lot of storage space—it will hold the equivalent of about 209,715,200 characters. That is 1024 bytes (1K), times 1024K in a megabyte, times 200 megabytes.

Great! How can we apply that seemingly useless information to the topic of memory? The amount of RAM in a PC generally is measured in megabytes. A typical PC has from 2M to 8M of RAM, and systems that are running high-powered applications sometimes have as much as 16M to 32M.

You also are going to run into situations in which you're measuring a block of memory in kilobytes. You may, for example, need to allocate a 16K block of memory in the UMA (I'll tell you how to do that). All you need at this point is a vague understanding of how much memory 16K represents.

Memory Addresses

When you're reminiscing about the good old days, do you think about where in your brain you're pulling those faded childhood memories from? No—it just happens. (We have pretty poor control over our brains, don't we?) A computer has to exercise a little better control over its memory. The PC has to know *where* in memory a particular piece of information is located. Otherwise, it would never be able to find it.

Think of memory as a big array of holes in which you can store information. Each one of those holes represents a byte. If your PC has 4M of RAM, it has 4,194,304 of those holes in which to store data. How does the PC locate a specific memory location out of all of those possibilities? It does it by assigning an address to each location. It then locates each memory location by its address, just like you locate a house by its street address.

Unfortunately, you need to understand memory addresses in a little more detail than the previous analogy describes to optimize your PC's memory. In particular, you need to understand how those memory addresses are labeled.

A memory address is represented by a hexadecimal value or hex value. A *hex value* is a base 16 number composed of the digits 0 through 9 and the letters A through F. Think of it this way: you start at 0, count up to 9, and then start using letters—use A for 10, B for 11, and so on up to the letter F. Here's the base 16 number set:

`0,1,2,3,4,5,6,7,8,9,A,B,C,D,E,F`

Each hex digit represents a four-digit binary number. The hex digit 0h, for example, represents the binary number 0000. The hex digit 9h equals binary 1001. Following is an example that may make more sense to you: convert the hex value for 640K back into a decimal number.

The value 640K is A0000 in hexadecimal; 20 binary digits are needed to express the value 640K. In a hexadecimal number, the first digit to the right represents 16^0, and the digits to the left represent 16^1, 16^2, 16^3, and so on. Now, look at figure 4.2. With A (which represents the value 10) in the fifth place, multiply 10×16^4 and you get 655,360, which is a value in bytes. Divide that by 1024 bytes per kilobyte, and the result is 640K (655,360 / 1024 = 640). 640K, therefore, is the *decimal*, or base 10, equivalent of A0000.

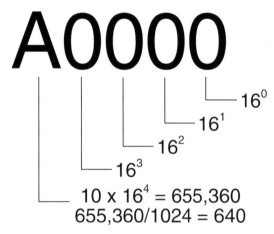

Figure 4.2: A0000 is the hex equivalent of the decimal value 640K.

I know that is confusing, but I inserted it in this book for those of you who feel compelled to understand everything you touch. I never try to convert memory addresses—that would be too much like work. Instead, I use a *memory map* that shows the hex and decimal equivalents for particular ranges of memory. Figure 4.3 shows that memory map. (You usually need to deal with memory addresses only between 640K and 1M, so that is the range included in the map.)

The first column of the map shows the hex addresses. The second column shows the decimal equivalents. The third column explains how the memory typically is used. When you're dealing with a memory address, don't try to convert it—just look at the memory map.

NOTE

By convention, the last digit in a hex memory address often is dropped. The address C8000, for example, usually is referred to as C800, or "C-eight hundred." The address D0000 becomes D000, or "D-thousand." The "hundred" and "thousand" designations are slang—they don't really represent a hundred or a thousand anything.

Figure 4.3: A memory map for addresses between 640K and 1M.

Types of Memory

The RAM in your PC is used in different ways according to the range of addresses in which it falls. Generally no physical difference in the memory exists; only the way it is allocated and used by the system differs. The exception is virtual memory, which you will read about later. This section of the chapter explains the five primary categories of memory classification in the typical PC, beginning with conventional memory.

Conventional Memory

The original IBM PC could address a maximum of only 1M of memory. This was a limitation of the Intel 8088 CPU (central processing unit) that was used in the IBM PC. DOS originally was written specifically for the IBM PC, so DOS was constrained to use only 1M of memory.

The reason the 8088 CPU is capable of addressing only 1M of memory is because of the number of physical address lines it contains (limited by the number of pins sticking out of the chip). Later CPUs, such as the 80486, can address 1G (1 gigabyte, which is 1024M) of memory because they have more address lines than the 8088 (more pins sticking out of the chip).

The first 1M of RAM in the PC is called *conventional memory*. The first 640K of RAM is set aside, by convention, for programs and data. The range of memory from 640K to 1023K is reserved for use by peripherals and device drivers. Because of that separation, the PC industry has generally come to regard only the first 640K of RAM as belonging to conventional memory. The upper 384K from 640K to 1023K is now referred to as *upper memory*.

Upper Memory

Upper memory is the memory in the PC between the addresses 640K and 1023K (A000 through FFFF), and often is referred to as the *UMA*, which stands for *Upper Memory Area*. Blocks of memory in the UMA are called *Upper Memory Blocks*, or *UMBs*.

One use for the UMA is to provide memory for device drivers. These device drivers use the UMA for their program code and data. Certain devices have standard memory ranges allocated to them. If you look at your UMA map (fig. 4.3), you will see that the range A000–AFFF is allocated to the EGA and VGA video adapter. In fact, a typical video adapter uses memory from A000–BFFF, and some use a little additional memory.

Another use for the UMA is to map ROM into RAM. On many PCs, for example, the system's ROM BIOS is mapped into the memory range F000–FFFF. This means that this range of memory addresses is assigned (mapped) to the ROM BIOS. This doesn't necessarily mean that the contents of the BIOS are copied into the physical RAM located at the addresses between F000 and FFFF. It just means that the BIOS chip has been assigned those addresses.

The BIOS isn't the only ROM allocated a range of RAM addresses. Some hard disk controllers also require that a range of UMBs be mapped to the BIOS chips contained on the controller. In addition, most network interface cards (NICs) require that a range of UMBs be allocated for use by the network card.

It's important to note that there is no difference between conventional memory and upper memory. Programs can run in upper memory just as well as in conventional memory. The only difference is that the industry has adopted a standard for using the memory, and DOS programmers generally don't let their programs and data use any memory above 640K. This standard prevents a program from accidentally using the same area of memory as one of the PC's peripherals, which might lock up the system.

You learn more about using upper memory a little later in this chapter. Next, you learn about extended memory.

Extended Memory

The memory in a PC above 1023K is called *extended memory*. If your PC has a total of 8M of RAM, typically that means it has 1M of conventional memory and 7M of extended memory.

DOS by itself can't address memory above 1M, so it can't directly access extended memory; a *memory manager* is used to provide access to extended memory. The HIMEM.SYS driver is the standard MS-DOS extended memory manager.

A DOS program written specifically to access extended memory can do so by requesting it from the memory manager. The memory manager takes care of allocating the extended memory to the DOS program and returning it to the pool of available memory when the program has finished using it.

If a DOS program hasn't been written to take advantage of extended memory, it never will use it—HIMEM.SYS will not provide extended memory to a program unless the program requests it. With these types of programs, you can have 8M of RAM in the PC, but the program will not use more than the first 640K—a real waste of resources.

What's so great about extended memory? Programs can access it *linearly*. That means that if a program needs to have 4M of RAM in which to store its data, it can request a 4M block of extended memory, and use all of it to store its data. If it needs to read the data, it can start at the beginning of that 4M block and read all the way to the end. That might not sound like such a big deal—until you read about expanded memory.

Expanded Memory

If your PC contains *expanded memory*, it's probably an older system. Newer systems use extended memory because it offers better performance than expanded memory. To understand why extended memory is better, you need to understand how expanded memory works.

Expanded memory was developed to overcome the DOS limitation of addressing only 1M of RAM (before extended memory came along). Expanded memory does not directly enable DOS to access more than 1M of RAM. Instead, an expanded memory manager (a memory driver program) is used to set up an *expanded memory page frame* in the UMA. The page frame is a 64K block of memory. Figure 4.4 helps illustrate how expanded memory works.

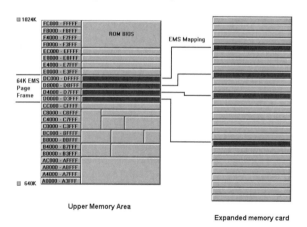

Figure 4.4: Expanded memory maps a block of memory on the memory adapter to a page frame in the UMA.

The actual expanded memory generally resides on an expansion card. The expanded memory manager dynamically remaps memory addresses on the expanded memory card to those of the page frame, essentially swapping 64K blocks of memory on the expanded memory card into the

page frame. The expanded memory card may have 2M of RAM on it, for example, but DOS can address only 64K of it at a time (the amount that can be mapped into the page frame). This enables DOS to access more than 1M of RAM, although only 64K at a time.

NOTE

Even with expanded memory, DOS still can't access memory addresses above 1M. Because the expanded memory page frame is located in the UMA, the memory addresses of the expanded memory are always below 1M (and always within the allocated page frame). A DOS program doesn't "know" that the memory in the page frame really is located on an expansion card—it "thinks" the memory is located in the UMA at the addresses allocated to the page frame.

You need to understand two main points about expanded memory. Because of the need to remap (swap) memory constantly into the page frame, expanded memory provides slower performance than extended memory, which doesn't require page frame swapping. The second point about expanded memory is this: If you want to add memory to your system, add extended memory—don't add expanded memory.

Virtual Memory

The fifth category of memory is *virtual memory*. In computer jargon, *virtual* refers to something that really doesn't exist, but which is simulated. Virtual memory is just what its name implies—it is *simulated* memory.

If you run Windows in Enhanced mode, Windows can use a portion of your hard disk as virtual memory. Windows creates a permanent swap file on the disk, and uses it as if it were RAM. When the PC begins to run low on available memory, Windows *swaps* (copies) a portion of whatever is in physical memory to the swap file, making some physical memory available. When the data that was swapped to disk is needed again, Windows swaps something else to disk to make room for the data, and then moves the data from the swap file back into physical memory.

Virtual memory enables Windows to function as if your system has much more physical memory than it really has. If you use a 12M swap file, for example, and your PC has

8M of physical RAM installed in it, Windows can function as if there were 20M of RAM in the system. This enables you to run more programs concurrently or work with very large data files.

Getting Physical about Memory

Memory in today's PCs is fairly standard. This section of the chapter describes the different types of physical packaging used for memory, beginning with a quick look at DRAMs, SIMs, and SIPs.

DRAMs, SIMs, and SIPs

DRAM stands for *dynamic RAM*. DRAM chips were used in early PCs for the system's primary memory, and are still found in many current systems, if only as secondary memory on adapters (such as video memory on a video adapter). DRAMs are microchips that plug into sockets on an adapter or on a system's motherboard (see fig. 4.5).

Figure 4.5: DRAM chips installed on an adapter.

Another type of memory packaging (currently the most popular) is the SIM. *SIM* stands for *single in-line module*. Sometimes SIMs are referred to as *SIMMs*, which stands for *single in-line memory module*. A SIM is a small, standard-sized printed circuit card on which some memory chips and support components are mounted (see fig. 4.6). The SIM plugs into a socket on the motherboard or adapter on which it is used.

Figure 4.6: SIMs.

The main advantage to SIMs is the ease with which you can install them. SIMs are so common that you now can buy them at discount retailers such as Wal-Mart.

Another type of memory packaging is the SIP. *SIP* stands for *single in-line package*, and SIPs are very similar to SIMs. The only real difference between a SIM and a SIP is that the SIP has small pins sticking out of it that connect to a different type of socket from those used by SIMs (see fig. 4.7). A disadvantage to SIPs is that the connector pins can become bent.

Figure 4.7: A SIP memory module.

Memory on the Motherboard

In most of the PCs manufactured today, the system's primary memory is installed directly on the motherboard. Usually, this memory takes the form of SIMs. SIMs are available in 256K, 1M, and 4M capacities, meaning that a single SIM will have either 256K, 1M, or 4M of RAM on it. Usually, there isn't any reason for adding 256K SIMs (you might as well add a respectable amount if you're going to add RAM), so I'm going to disregard the 256K SIMs for now.

A typical new motherboard contains eight SIM sockets, which can accommodate from 8M to 32M of RAM (eight of the 1M SIMs or eight of the 4M SIMs). Some of the more expensive systems—designed for use as file servers and high-performance workstations—have additional sockets that can accommodate as much as 64M of RAM, and in select systems, even more.

 **NOTE** *The early PCs also had the main memory installed on the motherboard, but these systems used DRAMs rather than SIMs. Typically, the motherboards for these systems had four rows of sockets called banks, with each bank capable of holding nine DRAM chips.*

Figure 4.8: A 16-bit memory card, useful for adding memory to a 286 system.

Memory Cards

When 386-based motherboards first came out, many of them did not include sockets on the motherboard for memory. Instead, these motherboards had a special 32-bit bus socket that accommodated a special 32-bit memory adapter called a *memory card*. Depending on the design, the memory adapter used DRAMs or SIMs. The memory was installed on this special memory adapter, and the adapter plugged into the 32-bit bus socket, just like the other adapters plugged into the 8-bit and 16-bit bus sockets. If you have one of the earlier 386s, this may be how the memory is installed in your PC.

In addition to these special 32-bit memory cards, you also can buy 16-bit memory cards that plug into one of the PC's regular bus sockets. DRAMs or SIMs are installed on the memory card just as they are with a 32-bit memory card. The main difference is that these 16-bit memory cards can be used in 286 PCs as well as 386 and 486 systems. In fact, their main use is in 286 PCs. Installing a 16-bit memory card in a 386 or 486 can actually slow the system down, because the 16-bit memory becomes a bottleneck to the fast 386 and 486 processors. Memory cards are fine for 286 systems, because the 286 is a 16-bit CPU. Figure 4.8 shows a 16-bit memory card.

Memory in Other Places

The system's primary RAM is not the only place you will find memory in a PC. Some adapters also include their own memory, and often you can add more memory to these adapters to improve performance. Video adapters are a good example of a type of adapter that often includes its own memory.

Video Memory

Virtually all VGA and Super VGA video adapters have at least some memory installed on the adapter. The more memory the adapter contains, the more colors it can display and the higher its best resolution.

These adapters often are preconfigured with a minimum amount of RAM to keep the initial cost down, and you can add more memory to the adapter yourself. Going from 512K to 1024K on a video adapter, for example, generally improves the color capability from 16 colors to 256 colors and the resolution from 800×600 to at least 1024×768. Chapter 8, "Video Adapters and Monitors," explains video adapters in more detail.

Cache Memory

Your PC also might contain some cache memory. *Cache memory* essentially is used as buffer memory for the CPU or for disk I/O (input/output). The 486 CPU, for example, includes 8K of internal cache memory, but many 486 motherboards also include an external cache of 32K or more.

This cache memory serves as a buffer for the CPU's I/O, improving its performance. In some systems, the size of the cache is fixed. In others, you can add more CPU cache memory. My opinion is that in most cases, the amount of CPU cache memory that came with the system is sufficient, and that adding more probably will not improve the system's performance enough to be worth the time, trouble, or money involved in adding more.

The CPU cache, however, is not the only place in the PC that you might find cache memory. Your system might have, or you can add to it, a *caching disk controller*. A *caching disk controller* is just like any other disk controller with the exception that it has its own cache memory installed on the controller. The cache memory serves essentially the same function as a software disk cache such as SmartDrive, which is covered briefly in Chapter 3, "Tweak Your System Files."

A disk cache, whether software or hardware, provides a buffer for disk I/O and speeds up disk performance. The only difference is this: a caching disk controller includes RAM that is dedicated to the disk cache, and a software cache such as SmartDrive uses some of the PC's primary memory for the cache.

TIP If you want to make as much memory as possible available to your applications, but don't want to give up your disk cache, you might consider replacing your existing disk controller with a caching controller and reduce or eliminate your software disk cache. If you already have a caching disk controller, adding more memory to it may improve the system's performance even further.

Memory Managers

Your PC probably uses at least one memory manager. A *memory manager* is a program responsible for managing the PC's memory and allocating memory to programs when they need it. Understanding how to optimize your PC's use of memory requires that you understand a little bit about these memory managers. One of the standard memory managers included with MS-DOS is HIMEM.SYS.

HIMEM.SYS

HIMEM.SYS (which I'm going to call Himem from now on) is a memory device driver included with MS-DOS. Himem's primary function is to provide access by programs to your PC's extended memory. Himem is installed through your PC's CONFIG.SYS file.

When the PC boots and Himem is executed, Himem takes control of all the PC's extended memory. When a program needs some extended memory, Himem gives control of some of the extended memory to the program. When the program finishes using it, Himem takes control again and places the memory back in its pool of available memory.

You can use several switches with Himem to control the way it functions on certain types of hardware and with certain hardware configurations. The vast majority of users don't have any need for the Himem switches. If you want to know what they are, consult your DOS manual or type **HELP HIMEM** at the DOS prompt.

EMM386.EXE

EMM386.EXE also is a memory manager supplied with MS-DOS (with earlier versions of DOS, this memory manager was EMM386.SYS). Because you probably will be working with some of EMM386's switches, it requires a little deeper explanation than Himem.

EMM386 performs two main functions: it manages the memory in the UMA, and it simulates expanded memory using some of the system's extended memory. By managing the UMA, EMM386 enables device drivers to be installed into the UMA rather than in conventional memory. Because DOS programs run in conventional memory, installing device drivers in the UMA rather than conventional memory makes more memory available for your programs.

The other function that EMM386 can perform—simulating expanded memory—is far less useful. Few programs today use expanded memory rather than extended memory; thus, very few users have any need to waste extended memory to simulate expanded memory. So, this section on EMM386 explains how to turn *off* expanded memory emulation by EMM386, and explains how you can use EMM386 to manage the UMA.

Disabling EMS Support with EMM386

The EMM386.EXE device driver is installed in CONFIG.SYS. Although you can install it without any switches, you probably will want to add a few if they aren't already included in your CONFIG.SYS file.

The first switch to consider is the NOEMS switch. If you include the NOEMS switch, EMM386 will not allocate any memory in the UMA for the expanded memory page frame. If you don't need expanded memory, why waste 64K of RAM in the UMA for the page frame? You can put it to better use for a device driver. To install EMM386 in CONFIG.SYS with the NOEMS switch, type **DEVICE=C:\DOS\EMM386.EXE NOEMS**.

Including and Excluding Ranges of Memory

Normally, EMM386 takes control of most of the memory in the UMA (as much as it detects as being available). There are situations in which you need to configure EMM386 to exclude a range of memory from use. If you have a network adapter, sound adapter, or video adapter that uses a particular range of memory in the UMA, for example, you need to prevent EMM386 from also trying to use that same block of memory. If a device is using a range of memory and EMM386 makes it available to another device or program, the devices using the overlapping memory range will not work properly.

The X switch (which stands for eXclude) causes EMM386 to not use a specified range of memory. If you have a network card that is using the range D000–DFFF, for example, you need to make sure EMM386 will not try to use that same memory range. Following is an example of the switches you need to add to EMM386 in CONFIG.SYS:

```
DEVICE=C:\DOS\EMM386.EXE NOEMS X=D000-DFFF
```

If you need to provide expanded memory emulation, omit the NOEMS switch from the preceding example.

That covers excluding a range of memory, but can you also *include* a range of memory? You bet you can! Just use the I switch with EMM386. If you have a range of memory available in your system, but, for some reason EMM386 is detecting it as being in use, you can direct EMM386 to include that range specifically. If you want EMM386 to manage the area E000–EFFF, for example, use the following switch:

```
DEVICE=C:\DOS\EMM386.EXE NOEMS I=E000-EFFF
```

If you need to include and exclude ranges of memory, just add the appropriate switches to the EMM386 command line in CONFIG.SYS, as in the following example:

```
DEVICE=C:\DOS\EMM386.EXE  NOEMS  X=D000-DFFF  I=E000-
➥EFFF
```

Understanding how to include and exclude UMA memory ranges will be important when you begin adding certain types of devices to your system. In the upcoming chapters, the hardware installation procedures include instructions for including and excluding memory ranges whenever appropriate.

Tweaking Memory: Management and Optimization

Now that you have some background information on memory, you're ready to start tweaking your system to make more memory available and make the system perform better. How you optimize your PC's memory depends on whether you primarily use DOS or Windows. The next two sections explain which memory issues are important to DOS and to Windows.

What's Important for DOS

If you don't run Windows, or you run it very seldom, it's important to make as much conventional memory available in your system as possible. This is because DOS programs run only in conventional memory (with the exception of DOS programs that are designed to use extended memory). The more conventional memory is available, the better your DOS programs will run.

How do you make more conventional memory available? You move as many device drivers and TSRs (terminate-and-stay-resident utility programs) as possible from conventional memory into the UMA. *Device drivers* are programs that enable the PC to use certain types of devices. You need a special device driver, for example, to control a CD-ROM drive.

TSRs are utility programs that load into memory and "hang around" unseen until you need them. Usually, you activate a TSR by pressing a special sequence of keys. DOSKEY is a good example of a TSR (see Chapter 3 for an explanation of DOSKEY, or enter **HELP DOSKEY** at the DOS prompt).

NOTE *Because DOS programs don't use the UMA, loading it up with device drivers and TSRs will not bother your DOS programs one bit. You move TSRs and device drivers from conventional memory into the UMA by using the DEVICEHIGH and LOADHIGH commands in CONFIG.SYS and AUTOEXEC.BAT.*

Using DEVICEHIGH

Device drivers usually are installed by a DEVICE= or DEVICEHIGH= statement in CONFIG.SYS. The DEVICE= statement loads the device driver into conventional memory, and the DEVICEHIGH= statement loads a device driver into upper memory.

If you're not familiar with those two different types of memory, just understand for now that it's usually better to place device drivers in upper memory rather than conventional memory because doing so makes more conventional memory available for your applications; thus, loading a device driver with the DEVICEHIGH= statement usually is preferable to loading it with the DEVICE= statement.

This means that another bit of CONFIG.SYS tweaking you might want to do is to change some of the DEVICE= entries in the file to DEVICEHIGH= entries. But wait! If you're using MS-DOS 6, there is a better way to optimize your CONFIG.SYS file and device drivers than muddling around with the file yourself. Proceed directly to the section in this chapter about MemMaker, which is an MS-DOS utility program for optimizing CONFIG.SYS.

If you aren't using MS-DOS 6, you don't have MemMaker. This means that you will need to change the device drivers in CONFIG.SYS manually by editing the file and changing DEVICE= entries to DEVICEHIGH= entries wherever appropriate. (Or, use this as an excuse to upgrade to MS-DOS 6.)

The problem is that not all device drivers can be loaded in upper memory. Doing so prevents them from working properly, and can even lead to you losing some data. Check the manuals that came with the device driver to see if it mentions loading the device driver into upper memory. If it doesn't, contact the company's technical support department and ask the technician if the device driver can be loaded into upper memory with the DEVICEHIGH= setting.

NOTE *In general, most device drivers will work properly when loaded into upper memory; however, some will not. Avoid loading network drivers and hard disk device drivers into upper memory unless the documentation you have for them indicates specifically that you can load them into upper memory.*

If you are using SmartDrive and have an entry in CONFIG.SYS for SMARTDRV.EXE, it indicates that your hard disk requires double buffering (explained later in this chapter and in Chapter 5, "Hard Disk Tweaking: Cleaning, Packing, and Comparing"). You can't load the double-buffer portion of SMARTDRV.EXE into upper memory—it must be loaded into conventional memory with the DEVICE= statement.

The following is a list of a few of the device drivers you should not load into upper memory:

aspi4dos

netbios

protman

smartdrv

sswap

vdefend

Using LOADHIGH or LH

Usually, TSRs are loaded by adding an entry for the TSR in AUTOEXEC.BAT. Some device drivers also are installed with a statement in AUTOEXEC.BAT. A TSR or device driver installed through AUTOEXEC.BAT usually is installed with a statement that specifies its executable file. To load DOSKEY.COM from the C:\DOS directory, for example, add the following to AUTOEXEC.BAT:

```
C:\DOS\DOSKEY.COM
```

The AUTOEXEC.BAT file has its equivalent to the DEVICEHIGH= statement that enables you to load device drivers and TSRs into the UMA rather than conventional memory. The command is LOADHIGH, or LH. Making DOSKEY.COM load into the UMA is simple—just add a LOADHIGH or LH command in front of its name, as in the following example:

```
LOADHIGH C:\DOS\DOSKEY.COM
```

As with device drivers and the DEVICEHIGH= statement in CONFIG.SYS, you should make sure that the TSRs and device drivers you are loading into the UMA actually can operate in the UMA without any problems. Check the documentation for the device driver / TSR, or check with the tech support staff for the company that publishes it.

Reducing TSRs

Another thing you should do to make more memory available is eliminate any TSRs you don't use, as well as those you use infrequently. If they are loaded by a statement in AUTOEXEC.BAT, you can just as easily load them only when you need them. Eliminate the entry in AUTOEXEC.BAT for the TSR to keep it from loading whenever the system boots. When you need to use the TSR, load it from the DOS command line by entering the same command that previously was used in AUTOEXEC.BAT to load it.

What's Important for Windows

If Windows is your primary operating environment and you run few, if any, DOS programs, conserving conventional memory isn't very important. Windows makes extensive use of your system's extended memory, and also uses the memory in the UMA if any is available. In fact, Windows takes control of *all* the available memory in the UMA. If you're a Windows-intensive person, therefore, it's probably not worth the trouble to fiddle with your CONFIG.SYS and AUTOEXEC.BAT files to free up a considerable amount of conventional memory.

If you run DOS programs under Windows, however, you still may want to optimize your system's memory to make available a large amount of conventional memory. This is why: Each DOS program you run in Windows inherits the DOS environment that exists before Windows starts. If a large amount of available conventional memory exists before Windows starts, each DOS program you run under Windows will have plenty of conventional memory with which to work. Making available large amounts of conventional memory makes your DOS programs run better under Windows.

If Windows is your primary environment, what can you do memory-wise to make it run better? You can add lots of extended memory. With 1M SIMs selling for about $40,

you can add a substantial amount of memory to your system without going into debt to do it.

Using MemMaker

If you have upgraded to MS-DOS 6, you can use its memory optimization program, called *MemMaker*, to fine-tune your system's use of memory. MemMaker evaluates your CONFIG.SYS and AUTOEXEC.BAT files, examines the device drivers and programs you are starting from both files, and then makes use of new features of the DEVICEHIGH and LOADHIGH commands to rearrange these device drivers and programs into specific memory blocks in the UMA. This makes better use of the UMA and usually results in more free memory below 640K.

To use MemMaker, exit Windows and type **MEMMAKER** at the DOS prompt. MemMaker will run three times to configure and test your system's memory, rebating the system after each time. The first time MemMaker runs, you specify options for how MemMaker will optimize your system's memory. (You have to start MemMaker only the first time—MemMaker will reboot the system and start itself automatically the second and third times.)

When the first MemMaker window appears, press Enter to access the first configuration screen. MemMaker then displays a succession of screens that prompt you to specify options. To switch between options on-screen, press the space bar. The following lists the options to select to optimize your system's memory:

- **Express Setup or Custom Setup.** Choose Custom Setup to set special options for Windows.

- **Do you use any programs that need expanded memory (EMS).** Choose No, unless you have DOS programs that require expanded memory, and you run those DOS programs outside of Windows. If you run those programs inside of Windows, choose No. Windows will simulate expanded memory if needed.

- **Specify which drivers and TSRs to include in optimization.** Choose No, unless you have a driver that you specifically know cannot be loaded into the UMA.

- **Scan the upper memory area aggressively.** Choose Yes to instruct MemMaker to scan the range of addresses between F000 through F7FF for free UMBs. If your system shadows the system BIOS in the memory range F000 through F7FF, leave this setting at No.

- **Optimize upper memory for use with Windows.** Choose Yes if you run DOS programs in Windows. Choose No if you do not run DOS programs in Windows (or run very few).

- **Use monochrome region (B000–B7FF) for running programs.** Choose No, unless your video adapter does not use this range of memory (many EGA and VGA adapters do not use this memory range, but some do).

- **Keep current EMM386 memory exclusions and inclusions.** Choose Yes, unless you know that some of the inclusions or exclusions are not necessary, or you want MemMaker to rescan and respecify your inclusions and exclusions.

- **Move Extended BIOS Data Area from conventional to upper memory.** Choose No. Setting it to Yes will gain only 1K of conventional memory.

After setting the preceding options, press Enter. MemMaker prompts you to enter the directory in which Windows is located, if applicable. Specify the directory, and then press Enter. To complete the optimization process, follow the prompts MemMaker provides.

Adding Memory

Before you rush out and buy some additional memory to install in your PC, read this section. You especially need to be sure that you get the type of memory required by your system. Following are points to check before buying additional memory.

Packaging

What type of physical packaging does your PC use? Do you need DRAMs, SIMs, or SIPs? You also should determine whether your system requires installation of RAM on the motherboard or uses a memory card.

Speed

Memory is available in different speeds, which is measured in *nanoseconds* (ns). Typical speeds are 60ns, 70ns, 80ns, and 100ns, with other speeds also available. Check your system's manual to see what speed of memory it uses. It's fine to install faster memory than what is required, but don't install

slower memory. Don't put in 100ns SIMs, for example, if your system manual calls for 70ns SIMs. Also, if you're installing DRAMs, be sure that all the DRAMs in a particular memory bank are the same speed and vendor. Don't mix and match.

Replace or Add?

Check the memory currently in your system to determine if your system has some available sockets for more memory. If sockets are available, check the manual to determine which capacity of memory you can add to the system.

If your PC doesn't contain any free memory sockets, you have two options: replace some of the existing RAM with greater capacity RAM, or add a 16-bit memory card to the system. If your system is a 286, add a memory card and populate (fill up) the memory card with as much RAM as you can.

You actually have a third option. My recommendation for a 286 is to replace the motherboard and upgrade the system to a 386 or 486. You can buy a 386SX motherboard with 4M of RAM for as little as $300, and a 486SX with 4M of RAM for about $500.

If your PC is a 386 or 486, don't add a 16-bit memory card to the system—doing so creates a bottleneck that slows down the system. Instead, consider replacing some of the existing RAM with greater capacity RAM. If your system has eight SIM sockets that are filled with 1M SIMs, consider replacing four of those SIMs with 4M SIMs. Doing so increases your RAM capacity from 8M to 20M. If your system is filled with 256K SIMs (giving you a current capacity of 2M), replace four of the SIMs with 1M or 4M SIMs, giving your PC a capacity of either 6M or 18M. If you're made of money, replace all of the SIMs with 4M SIMs, giving the PC a total capacity of 32M.

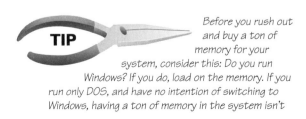

Before you rush out and buy a ton of memory for your system, consider this: Do you run Windows? If you do, load on the memory. If you run only DOS, and have no intention of switching to Windows, having a ton of memory in the system isn't

going to do you a whole lot of good. The exception is if you have an application that uses (and needs) lots of extended memory to perform well. My recommendation: switch to Windows.

Before buying additional memory for your PC, read through the manuals for your system to determine all your options for adding memory, including which types of memory you need and whether you must add or replace memory.

Don't Handle It!

When you do purchase extra memory for your system, handle it as little as possible. Keep the memory chips or modules in their packaging until you have the PC open and you're ready to install the memory. Then, before touching the chips, be sure to discharge your body's static (touch the metal part of the PC's chassis).

When handling the chips be sure that you don't touch the chips or connectors at all, if possible. With DRAMs, this is impossible—you need to touch the chip. Hold the chips at either end and try not to touch the connectors. With SIMs and SIPs, hold the module by either end of the module, and try not to touch the chips on the module or the pins or edge connectors.

Removing and Installing DRAMs

Explanation: If your system uses DRAMs, you may need to remove some in order to install greater capacity chips. Even though you probably will not be using the chips in your system again, take care when removing them because you may be able to sell them to someone else or use them on an adapter card.

You also may be installing additional DRAMs in a system, either on the motherboard or on an adapter card.

Procedure:
Removing DRAMs

1. Disconnect and open the system.

2. If necessary, remove the motherboard in order to gain easy access to the chips. (For more information

regarding removing the motherboard, see Chapter 16, "Motherboards.") If you're removing DRAMs from an adapter, just remove the adapter from the system.

3. To determine which chips you need to remove, consult the system manuals.

4. Use a small, flat-bladed screwdriver to *carefully* pry the chips from their sockets. Insert the screwdriver between the chip and the socket at one end of the chip and gently twist the blade to lift the chip from its socket (see fig. 4.9). Alternate each end of the chip, prying a little each time until the chip comes free of the socket. Take care not to bend the pins on the chip, if possible.

Figure 4.9: You can remove a DRAM chip by carefully prying it out with a small screwdriver.

5. If you have a static-free bag, place the chips in the bag. Otherwise, place the chips in the container in which the new chips were supplied.

Procedure:
Adding DRAM

Explanation: This procedure is the same for motherboards, memory cards, and other types of adapters that use DRAM chips. It also is the same for other chips, including BIOS chips. Following are the keys to successful installation:

● Be sure that the chips are properly oriented in their sockets.

- Be sure that each of the pins is properly inserted in its corresponding hole in the socket.

- Be sure that each DRAM is firmly and fully seated into its socket.

   1. Check the system manual and board to determine the sockets to which the DRAMs will be added.

   2. Discharge your body's static.

   3. Examine the chip—you will find a semicircle or small notch on top of the chip at one end. Looking at the chip from the top with the notch facing up, pin 1 on the chip is located at the upper left corner of the chip (see fig 4.10).

Figure 4.10: Chips and sockets have a notch at one end to indicate the location of pin 1 and provide a visual key for proper insertion.

   4. Examine the board—you should find an indicator on the board at one end of each socket to define how the chip will be installed. Often, an outline of the chip is painted on the board, and a semicircle or notch indicator is painted on one end. If the board doesn't include these indicators, examine the socket. The socket will have a notch at one end, similar to the chip (see fig. 4.10).

   5. Discharge the static from your body again, and then examine the chip and gently straighten any pins that are bent.

   6. Orient the chip to the socket—the end of the chip with the notch goes into the end of the socket that contains a notch indicator.

   7. With the chip at an angle, rest one edge of pins on the chip in their respective socket holes. Then, rotate the chip down toward the socket and insert the other pins on the other edge of the chip into the socket.

   8. Check to be sure that all the pins are lined up properly with the right holes and that none of the pins are bent under the chip.

   9. Place your thumbs at either end of the chip and press it firmly into place.

   10. Check the system manual to determine which jumpers or DIP switch settings must be changed to correctly specify the amount of installed RAM on the board. Then, set the jumpers or DIP switches accordingly.

Removing and Installing SIMs

Explanation: You may need to remove SIMs from your system in order to replace them with greater capacity modules, thus increasing the memory capacity of the system or adding additional cache RAM to the system. *Patience* and *care* are the two most important words in these procedures. Take your time and be gentle so that you don't damage the SIM socket or the SIM.

The SIM socket has a tab at each end that holds the SIM in place. It also contains a round plastic pin that goes into a hole in the SIM to keep it from pulling up and out of the socket. SIMs don't so much insert as they tilt into the socket and snap into place. The component side of the SIM generally faces the side of the socket in which the round plastic pins are located (but check your system manual to get the proper orientation before installing the SIM, just to be sure).

The SIM sockets generally are very close together. Because the SIMs tilt and snap into place during installation, and tilt out during removal, the order in which you install or remove SIMs from a socket is important. When removing SIMs, first remove the SIM that tilts away from the other, and then remove the second SIM. When installing SIMs, first install the SIM that tilts into place away from the other SIM. Then, install the other SIM (that tilts into place toward the one that already is in place).

A final word of caution: *Be very careful with the tabs and the SIMS!* If you break a tab, the SIM may not stay seated properly. The only solution is to replace the socket, something you probably will not be able to do. You will have to pay to have someone else do it.

If you do break a tab and have a problem with the SIM remaining in place, try to wedge a piece of foam rubber or a nonconducting substance (such as a chunk of rubber eraser) between the damaged SIM and the SIM directly behind it. The idea is that the rubber wedge will help keep the SIM firmly in place. It's a flaky repair, but if it saves you some money, it's worth trying. Just be careful you don't screw up something else in the process.

Procedure:
Removing SIMs

1. Examine the system manual and the sockets to determine which SIMs need to be removed.

2. Discharge your static.

3. With your finger or a small screwdriver, carefully pull the tab away from the SIM far enough to enable you to tilt that corner of the SIM slightly past the tab with your index finger (see fig. 4.11).

Figure 4.11: Release one tab first and tilt the SIM slightly away from the socket.

Be careful not to break the tab! Always release one side of the SIM at a time to prevent damaging the socket.

4. Still holding the free edge of the SIM, release the other tab. With your thumb or another finger, tilt the other edge of the SIM away from the socket.

5. Tilt the SIM away from the socket, and then lift the SIM free of the socket. Store it in a static-free bag or in the packaging that came with your new SIMs.

Procedure:
Adding SIMs

Explanation: This procedure covers adding SIMs to any device, whether the device is a motherboard or adapter, such as a caching disk controller. The primary difference is that you usually need to set jumpers or DIP switches on a motherboard to set the amount of memory on the board. Many adapters do not require jumper or DIP switches to specify installed RAM.

1. Check the system manual and board to determine in which sockets the SIMs are to be installed, and to determine the proper orientation of the SIMs.

2. Discharge your static.

3. While being careful to avoid touching the SIM's connector pins or the chips, insert the SIM into the socket at an angle as shown in figure 4.12.

4. Gently press the SIM down into the socket as far as you can, and then tilt the SIM fully into the socket. It will snap into place.

5. Set any DIP switches or jumpers on the board as necessary to accommodate the new SIMs (check your system or adapter manual for the necessary settings).

Figure 4.12: Insert the SIM into the socket at an angle, and then press it down and tilt it forward to snap into place.

Removing and Installing SIPs

Explanation: The same criteria applies for removing and adding SIPs that apply to SIMs. You may be adding additional SIPs to your system to increase its main or cache RAM.

Procedure:
Removing SIPs

1. Examine the system manual and the sockets to determine which SIPs need to be removed.

2. Discharge your static.

3. Grasp the SIP at each end and pull straight up to remove the SIP from its socket; be careful not to bend the pins.

4. Place the SIP in a static-free bag or in the packaging that came with your new SIPs.

Procedure:
Adding SIPs

1. Examine the manual to determine the proper sockets and the proper orientation of the SIPs in the sockets.

2. Discharge your static.

3. Carefully align the pins on the SIP with the holes in the socket.

4. After checking to ensure the alignment of the pins, gently but firmly push the SIP into place, taking care not to bend the pins.

Adding Memory to the System with Memory Cards

Some 386 and 486 systems have memory sockets on the motherboard, as well as an optional 32-bit memory card that you can install in the system to add even more memory to the PC. You can install 16-bit memory cards into a 286 system to add more memory to it, as well.

Adding memory by adding a memory card is less common these days than adding or changing memory on the motherboard. Also, the same procedures for installing DRAMs, SIMs, and SIPs on a motherboard apply to installing RAM on a memory card. Because of this, I'm not going to devote a procedure to installing RAM cards. Just check the documentation that comes with the card (and your system) to determine the types of memory you need, how much, and what jumper and switch settings you need to use after you install the board. Use the memory installation procedure (given previously) that best fits your situation.

5

Hard Disk Tweaking: Cleaning, Packing, and Compressing

Your PC's most important resource is its memory. Its next most important resource is hard disk space. Having plenty of free disk space gives you room to add new programs and data, but free disk space is particularly important to Windows users. Having as much free disk space as possible enables you to create a large permanent swap file for Windows' enhanced mode, which makes Windows perform better.

This chapter covers techniques you can use to make the most of your PC's disk space, including the following topics:

- Weeding out old files
- Defragmenting a hard disk
- Using and optimizing SmartDrive
- Using DoubleSpace and Stacker for disk compression
- Backup strategies
- Adding a new disk controller and hard drive

Before peeling your system open and dropping in a new hard disk (at significant expense), you should analyze your disk to see if there is anything you can do to make more space available. The disk might be getting full, but that doesn't mean it's full of *useful* stuff. Maybe it's time for some spring cleaning on your hard disk.

Disk Maintenance

A new 120M hard disk sells for about $250 nowadays. Higher capacity drives cost more, naturally. The point is that adding a second hard disk to your system, although certainly a good way to get more free disk space, isn't cheap. That's why it's important to perform regular maintenance on your hard disk to weed out files you no longer need, compact the drive, and so on. This is the approach taken in the first half of this chapter.

A handful of steps to optimize your hard disk follows:

1. Delete any files no longer needed.

2. Check the file structure on the disk to find any lost but potentially available disk space.

3. If you're going to resize your permanent Windows swap file, delete it.

4. Defragment the drive to make all the free disk space available in a single contiguous (continuous) block on the disk.

5. Re-create your Windows swap file, if you want to resize it.

6. If you're going to add disk compression, do it now.

Now we are going to do a little "file gardening."

Weeding Out Files

On a regular basis (every month or two, for example), you should take an hour or so and examine your hard disk for files that have become obsolete. If you use Windows, File Manager offers a good tool for scanning your disk for files. In DOS, you use the familiar DIR command. In File Manager, you use the Del key or the **File D**elete command to delete files. In DOS, you use the DEL or ERASE commands (functionally identical). File Manager is best, because it enables you to select and delete numerous files simultaneously (see fig. 5.1).

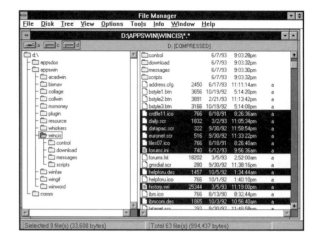

Figure 5.1: With File Manager, you can easily select multiple files to delete.

Scan your disk for these types of files for possible deletion or archiving:

- **BAK files.** Many applications create backup files when you resave a document. The backup file, which often has a file extension of BAK, contains the previous version of the file. It's a good idea to periodically erase these backup files to recover the space they are using.

- **Old programs.** Does your disk contain programs you don't use anymore? Maybe you installed some shareware to try out and decided you didn't like it, but never got around to deleting it. If you think you might want these old programs at some time in the future, back them up on a floppy disk or tape, and then delete them from your hard disk.

- **Old documents.** You probably want to archive rather than delete documents you no longer need or are no longer current. Back them up on floppy disk or tape, then delete them from the system.

- **Extra drivers.** When I first got my notebook computer, it had an extra subdirectory in the Windows directory that contained all the drivers that ship with Windows. The directory took up quite a bit of disk space that I needed, so I deleted the directory and the files in it. Check your system for extra driver files that don't apply to your hardware configuration. The driver files probably are on the distribution disks for the program with which they shipped, so you don't need to keep them on your hard disk. Don't, however, delete any driver files your system *does* use.

WARNING *If you delete a driver file that Windows requires, Windows might not be able to run. At the very least, the feature provided by the driver will not be available until you restore the driver.*

● **Log files.** Some types of programs keep log files that track various types of activity with the program. The communications program I use to connect to CompuServe, for example, logs each communication session to disk. Other programs also maintain activity logs. If you don't need the activity logs, delete them. Also check to see whether the program enables you to turn off logging to disk.

After you clear out all the files you possibly can, you should check the file structure of the disk.

Checking Disk Integrity

The space on the PC's hard disk is segregated into clusters. Without going into detail now, a *cluster* is a small but spe=cific amount of storage space on the disk. Normally, the clusters on a disk are allocated to a file or marked as available. Occasionally, clusters end up in a state of limbo—neither allocated to a file nor marked as free. These clusters are *lost*.

The DOS CHKDSK command enables you to recover lost clusters. CHKDSK converts the clusters to files so that you can examine them, or adds the clusters back into the pool of available clusters, giving you more available storage space on the disk.

WARNING *Never run CHKDSK from inside Windows. Doing so results in a loss of data on the disk. Instead, always exit Windows before running CHKDSK. If you run CHKDSK outside of Windows, your data is safe.*

Procedure:

Running CHKDSK To Recover Lost Clusters

1. Exit Windows, if Windows is running.

2. At the DOS prompt, enter **CHKDSK /F**.

3. If CHKDSK finds any lost clusters, it prompts you to specify whether you want the lost clusters converted to files or returned to the pool of free clusters. If you want the clusters converted to files, choose **Y**. Otherwise, choose **N**.

If you direct CHKDSK to convert the lost clusters to files, CHKDSK creates files in the root directory of the disk with the file name FILE*nnnn*.CHK, where *nnnn* is a number, such as 0001. You can view the contents of the files to see if you still need them.

NOTE *The files created by CHKDSK from lost clusters retain their original file format. If the file was an Excel document originally, you need to open it in Excel to view its contents. After you examine the files, copy them into an appropriate directory if you're going to keep them, or delete them if you don't need them.*

If you answer No to CHKDSK's prompt, CHKDSK marks the lost clusters as available, which increases the amount of free space on the disk.

After checking the disk with CHKDSK, consider whether you need to resize your Windows swap file.

Deleting and Re-Creating a Windows Swap File

If you run Windows on your PC in enhanced mode, Windows can create a *permanent swap file* on your disk to improve Windows' performance. The permanent swap file remains on your system all the time, even when you are not running Windows. Windows uses the permanent swap file as virtual memory (see Chapter 4, "All You Need To Know about Memory").

A permanent swap file is created from *contiguous sectors*, which are sectors that reside on a disk side-by-side. What's the big deal about contiguous sectors? If a file is contained in contiguous sectors, the system can read it much more quickly than if the system had to jump all around the disk to find all the pieces of the file. Windows creates the permanent swap file from contiguous sectors to provide the best possible performance.

Deciding on Swap File Size

By default, Windows creates a permanent swap file based on the amount of free contiguous space on the disk and the amount of RAM installed in your system. The more RAM you have, the smaller the swap file can be. The less RAM your system contains, the larger the swap file should be. The types of programs you run, the number you try to run simultaneously, and the size of the documents you work with also have a bearing on how large the swap file should be. Unless you're running a program that suggests a specific minimum size for your permanent swap file, see table 5.1 for my suggestions based on the amount of RAM in the system.

Table 5.1
Recommended Swap File Sizes

RAM Installed	Swap File Size
4M	8M to 12M
6M	12M
8M	16M
12M	12M
16M	8M
20M	4M
20M+	2M

As the amount of physical RAM increases, you can decrease the swap file size. Even with a large amount of memory in the system, you still should have a minimum 2M swap file. Windows *wants* to swap to disk, even when the system contains a large amount of memory.

Deleting a Permanent Swap File

If you decide that you need to change the size of your swap file, you first should delete the existing swap file, defragment the disk, and then create a new swap file. Defragmenting the disk between the two swap file operations ensures that the hard disk has the greatest possible contiguous free space for the new swap file.

Procedure:
Deleting a Permanent Swap File

1. Start Windows and open the Control Panel (look in the Main group for the Control Panel icon).

2. Select the 386 Enhanced icon from the Control Panel.

3. In the 386 Enhanced dialog box, select the **V**irtual Memory button. The Virtual Memory dialog box appears. (see fig. 5.2).

4. In the Virtual Memory dialog box, select the **C**hange button.

5. In the New Settings group box, click on the **T**ype drop-down list, and then choose None.

6. When your settings are correct, choose the OK button.

7. The Control Panel prompts you to continue working in Windows or restart Windows. Choose the Continue button.

8. Exit Windows.

Creating a Permanent Swap File

After you delete your existing swap file in preparing to resize it, you should defragment the hard disk to place all free space into contiguous sectors (see the following section "Defragmenting a Disk"). After you defragment the drive, you're ready to re-create the permanent swap file at its new size.

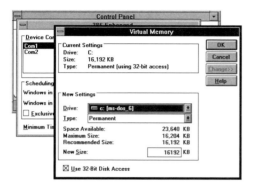

Figure 5.2: The Virtual Memory dialog box enables you to change swap file size.

Procedure:
Creating a Permanent Swap File

1. Defragment the drive (see the following section).

2. Launch Windows and open the Control Panel.

3. Choose the 386 Enhanced icon, then select the **V**irtual Memory button.

4. Select the **C**hange button.

5. From the **D**isk drop-down list, choose the disk on which you want the permanent swap file to be created (it must be a noncompressed disk).

6. Choose Permanent from the **T**ype drop-down list.

7. In the New **S**ize edit box, enter the size you want the new swap file to be, based on the recommendations in table 5.1. Enter the value in kilobytes. For a 16M swap file, for example, enter **16,192**.

8. Choose OK, and when prompted, instruct Control Panel to restart Windows so that the change takes effect.

Defragmenting a Disk

The system, by default, tries to store files in contiguous sectors on the disk for best performance. Because the

system can read the file straight through without moving the disk read heads around the disk to hunt for the different parts of the file, performance improves.

As files are erased and rewritten, the contiguous free space on the disk becomes used up and files begin to become *fragmented*, or scattered into noncontiguous sectors. Because the system is perfectly capable of locating all the "pieces" of a file and reading them to re-create a whole file, this doesn't pose a real problem. Jumping around on the disk to read a fragmented file, however, imposes a performance penalty because it takes additional time to move the read heads from one sector to another.

You should defragment your PC's hard disk periodically. *Defragmenting* rearranges the free space on the disk into contiguous sectors and also arranges the files on the disk into contiguous sectors to enable faster access to them (see fig. 5.3). This is important not only if you want to create a permanent Windows swap file, but it also improves program performance and speeds access to your documents.

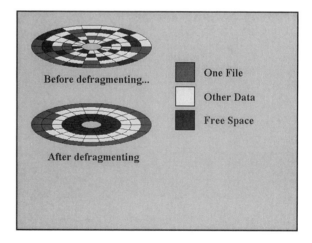

Figure 5.3: A disk before and after defragmention.

You need a special utility program to defragment your disk. Many third-party utilities such as Norton Utilities, PC Tools, and others that include disk defragmenting programs exist. If you are using MS-DOS 6, you don't need to buy another utility program to defragment the disk—MS-DOS 6 includes its own defragmenting utility called Microsoft Defrag.

Procedure:

Defragmenting a Disk with Microsoft Defrag (MS-DOS 6)

1. If Windows is running, exit Windows.

2. At the DOS prompt, enter **DEFRAG**.

3. After the Defrag program examines your system's hard disk, select the Configure button when it appears.

4. Choose **O**ptimization Method from the Optimize menu.

5. Select Full Optimization and then choose OK.

6. Select **B**egin Optimization from the Optimization menu.

Figure 5.4 shows Microsoft Defrag in operation.

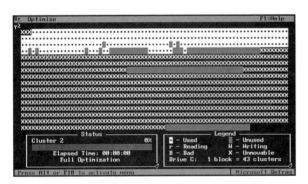

Figure 5.4: The Microsoft Defrag program defragments the system's hard disk.

After you defragment the hard disk, re-create your Windows swap file as described in the preceding section. If you are not resizing your Windows swap file, you do not need to re-create it (defragmenting the disk does not alter the swap file if it exists).

Using SmartDrive

Windows and DOS include a software disk cache program called SmartDrive. A *disk cache* is an area of memory used to buffer disk accesses. Here's how it works: When some data is read from the disk, a cache manager program (SmartDrive in this example) copies the data from the disk into the cache memory. Then, the cache manager passes the data on to the application that requested it. When a new request for data comes through, the cache manager first checks the cache to see if the requested data already is in the cache. If it is, the cache manager retrieves it from the cache and passes it on to the program that requested it. If the data isn't in the cache, the cache manager retrieves it from the disk. A disk cache speeds up system performance because accessing RAM (which is where the cache is located) is much faster than accessing the hard disk.

If you aren't already using a disk cache, such as SmartDrive, adding one to the system speeds up its performance. This is true for DOS programs as well as the Windows environment.

Installing SmartDrive

If SmartDrive is not yet installed, adding a few entries to your CONFIG.SYS and AUTOEXEC.BAT files installs it so that it runs each time you boot the system. If your system contains an RLL, MFM, ESDI, or IDE hard disk, you probably need only an entry in AUTOEXEC.BAT to install SmartDrive. Following is a sample entry for AUTOEXEC.BAT:

```
C:\DOS\SMARTDRV.EXE
```

But wait! Unless you specify otherwise, SmartDrive creates a default-sized cache to use outside Windows and automatically reduces the cache size by a certain amount when you launch Windows. This gives Windows more memory. The sizes of the standard cache and the cache in Windows are based on the amount of RAM in the system. Table 5.2 shows the default cache sizes created by SmartDrive.

Table 5.2

Default Cache Sizes for SmartDrive

Installed RAM	Cache Size	Windows Cache Size
Up to 1M	All extended	Zero (no caching) memory
Up to 2M	1M	256K
Up to 4M	1M	512K
Up to 6M	2M	1M
6 M or more	2M	2M

The default values typically work well, but you might want to change the cache sizes to try to improve overall system performance. If you have much RAM in the system, for example, you might want to try increasing the cache sizes to see if it improves performance. Or, you might have a DOS program you run outside of Windows that would benefit from a larger cache, but you don't want to use the larger cache when running Windows.

To specify cache sizes for SmartDrive, just add two additional parameters on the SmartDrive command line in AUTOEXEC.BAT. The first parameter is the size of the cache outside of Windows, and the second parameter is the cache size when Windows is running. An example follows of a statement for AUTOEXEC.BAT that specifies a starting cache size of 4M and a Windows cache size of 3M:

```
C:\DOS\SMARTDRV.EXE 4096 3072
```

What about CONFIG.SYS?

If you use EMM386.EXE to provide access to the UMA, or run Windows in enhanced mode, you might need to add an entry for SmartDrive in CONFIG.SYS in addition to the entry in AUTOEXEC.BAT. Some SCSI, ESDI, and MCA-based disk controllers require that you use SmartDrive's double-buffering capability. The entry in CONFIG.SYS for SmartDrive enables double buffering.

Some disk controllers have a problem with the memory provided by EMM386 and Windows running in enhanced mode. This sometimes creates the problem of cluster numbers used by SmartDrive not matching the physical cluster numbers on the disk, which leads to garbled data. So, SmartDrive has an optional component that maintains a separate buffer for cluster numbers so that the cluster numbers SmartDrive uses always match the physical cluster numbers on the disk. This is called *double buffering*.

Do you need double buffering on your system? If you have a SCSI disk, it increases the chance that you need to use double buffering, but it's not a sure bet. A procedure to determine if your system requires double buffering follows.

Procedure:

Determining Whether Your System Needs Double Buffering

1. Place the following command in CONFIG.SYS (substitute the correct directory if SmartDrive is not located in the DOS directory):

    ```
    DEVICE=C:\DOS\SMARTDRV.EXE /DOUBLE_BUFFER
    ```

2. Enter the following command in AUTOEXEC.BAT if it isn't already there:

    ```
    C:\DOS\SMARTDRV.EXE
    ```

3. Reboot the system.

4. At the DOS prompt, enter **SMARTDRV /S**.

5. After SmartDrive displays the status of the disk cache, examine the column labeled Buffering. If any of the lines in the display read Yes, your system requires double buffering. If all the lines read No, your system does not require double buffering. If any of the lines include the - (hyphen) character, SmartDrive can't determine whether your system requires double buffering.

NOTE If SmartDrive determines that your system requires double buffering, you don't need to do anything else at this point—you have already installed double buffering by adding the SmartDrive settings to CONFIG.SYS. If SmartDrive determines that your system does not require double buffering, remove the SmartDrive entry from CONFIG.SYS (but leave the entry in AUTOEXEC.BAT), and then reboot the system. If SmartDrive is unable to determine if your system requires double buffering, contact the technical support department for the manufacturer of your *hard disk controller to find out if you need to use double buffering.*

The SmartDrive disk cache, which is loaded through AUTOEXEC.BAT, loads into the UMA automatically if upper memory is available. You do not need to use the LOADHIGH or LH commands to load it into the UMA. You can't, however, load the double-buffering portion of SmartDrive into the UMA. Therefore, to load it, use the DEVICE= setting in CONFIG.SYS rather than the DEVICEHIGH= setting . Also, if you are using double buffering and your system seems to be running slowly, try adding the /L switch to the SmartDrive command in AUTOEXEC.BAT. The /L switch prevents SmartDrive from loading into the UMA, which can cause poor performance in some situations when double buffering is used.

Using DoubleSpace (MS-DOS 6)

If you use MS-DOS 6, you potentially can double your hard disk storage space without having to buy a new hard disk, open up your system, or even buy any new software. MS-DOS 6 includes a utility called *DoubleSpace* that compresses the data on your disk, making it fit into less disk space. Depending on the types of files on your disk, you often can get a compression ratio of as much as 2:1, which means you can turn a 120M disk into a 240M disk. Sounds pretty good considering you don't have to buy anything else, doesn't it?

DoubleSpace enables you to compress your entire existing hard disk, or use some or all the free space on it to create a new compressed drive. The new drive contains twice the capacity of the free space used to create it. You can leave your existing data in an uncompressed drive C, for example, and create a new logical drive D from the remaining free space.

NOTE   *Here is how I set up my systems: I leave Windows and the Windows swap file on an uncompressed drive C. I leave enough space on drive C for my data files, DOS, and any utility programs, such as drivers. I then*

create a compressed drive D to contain all my applications. On a 120M drive, for example, leave 60M uncompressed, then compress the rest into drive D.

If your system doesn't contain enough free space to create a large compressed drive because all your applications are located on drive C, consider backing up your applications and removing them from drive C. Defragment the drive and create a compressed drive from the remaining free space. Then, restore your applications onto the new compressed drive.

Installing DoubleSpace

DoubleSpace includes a setup program that configures DoubleSpace on your PC with only a little input from you. To compress all the data on your hard disk, follow these steps to set up DoubleSpace on your MS-DOS 6 PC:

1. Back up your hard disk. Even though DoubleSpace compresses your hard disk safely, and compression can be suspended and restarted, it's still a good idea to back up any important data.

2. If you are running Windows, exit Windows.

3. Enter **DBLSPACE** at the DOS prompt. The DoubleSpace Setup program starts. When the first screen appears, press Enter to begin configuring DoubleSpace.

4. To compress your existing drive and enable DoubleSpace to set all parameters automatically for you, choose Express Setup. DoubleSpace Setup will compress all your existing data and set all operating parameters for the new compressed drive.

WARNING   *If you're using a permanent Windows swap file, you shouldn't compress your entire disk. The swap file must reside on an uncompressed drive—you can't place it on a drive that has been DoubleSpaced.*

The Custom Setup option enables you to specify which drive you want to compress, and also enables you to create a new compressed drive using the free space on your PC's hard disk. This is the technique I prefer to use. If you still have plenty of free space on a drive and don't want to compress some or all the existing data, use the following steps to install and configure DoubleSpace:

1. Back up your hard disk.

2. Enter **DBLSPACE** at the DOS prompt.

3. Select the Custom Setup option.

4. Select the Create a new empty compressed drive option.

5. From the list of available drives supplied by DoubleSpace Setup, select the drive containing the free space from which you want to create a new compressed logical drive.

6. DoubleSpace Setup then prompts for three parameters:

   ```
   Amount of free space to leave on the drive

   Compression ratio

   Drive letter to be assigned to the drive
   ```

   Specify the amount of free space you want to leave on the existing drive and specify which drive ID to assign to the new drive. Changing the compression ratio value affects only the way DoubleSpace estimates free space on the new disk; it doesn't actually change the amount of storage space on the compressed drive. Leave it at the default of 2.0.

7. Follow the remainder of DoubleSpace Setup's prompts to create the new compressed drive.

DoubleSpace Setup creates a new hidden file to contain the new compressed disk. It also adds a device driver line in CONFIG.SYS for the DoubleSpace device driver.

Using Your DoubleSpace Drive

After you create a compressed drive using DoubleSpace, you can use that drive like any other uncompressed drive. It appears to your system to be a typical drive represented by a drive letter. You can install applications on it, store files on it, and use any commands and utilities you would otherwise use on a regular disk.

After you save a file to a compressed drive, for example, DoubleSpace intercepts the file operation, compresses the document, and places it in a hidden file that comprises the compressed logical drive. When you access a file on the drive, DoubleSpace intercepts the file operation, expands the file, and passes it to your application.

In Windows, the File Manager provides a new feature that enables you to monitor your DoubleSpace disk. In File Manager, first select a compressed drive. Select **T**ools, then **D**oubleSpace Info. File Manager displays the DoubleSpace Info dialog box (see fig. 5.5).

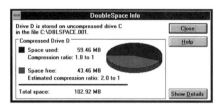

Figure 5.5: The DoubleSpace Info dialog box provides summary information about compressed drives.

The DoubleSpace Info dialog box provides information about the compressed drive, including the amount of compressed free space on the disk, amount of space used, and estimated compression ratio. Select the Show **D**etails button to expand the dialog box to provide information about specific files on the compressed drive (see fig. 5.6).

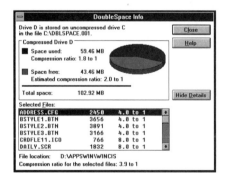

Figure 5.6: The Show Details button displays information about specific files in the compressed drive.

Using FastDisk

Windows 3.1 has a feature called *FastDisk* that can improve disk performance for Windows when Windows runs in enhanced mode. FastDisk enables Windows to bypass the BIOS and communicate directly with the system's hard disk controller.

FastDisk works with any disk subsystem that is 100 percent compatible with the Western Digital 1003 controller. These disk subsystems include ST506-type controllers (for more information about disk controller types, see "Hard Disks, Controllers, and Host Adapters," later in this chapter). Most hard disk controllers, including IDE host adapters, are compatible with FastDisk. Generally, only ESDI and SCSI drives are not compatible with FastDisk.

Speeding Up Disk Access with FastDisk

Without FastDisk, the system must switch a number of times between protected mode and virtual mode to handle disk I/O. FastDisk enables Windows to process disk I/O through virtual device drivers in protected mode, which reduces the number of times the system must switch modes. Because mode-switching takes time, using FastDisk can speed up disk access.

NOTE *The 80386 and newer processors can operate in one of three modes: real mode, protected mode, and virtual mode. Real mode provides compatibility with older CPUs, such as 8088/8086 and 80286, and is limited to addressing 1M of RAM. Protected mode first appeared in the 80286 CPU. In protected mode, the CPU can address up to 4G (gigabytes) of RAM. In virtual mode, the CPU can create an almost unlimited number of "virtual machines," which are simulated 8086-based computers. Virtual mode is what enables Windows to multitask DOS programs in enhanced mode.*

FastDisk's Device Drivers

FastDisk consists of the following four virtual device drivers built into the file WIN386.EXE:

- **WDCtrl.** This supports WD1003 and ST506 controllers. Setup installs this device driver in SYSTEM.INI only if it detects that your PC's hard disk is compatible with FastDisk.

- **Int13.** This traps and handles INT 13h BIOS calls that are otherwise processed by the system BIOS. Int13 is installed in SYSTEM.INI by Setup only if Setup detects that your disk is compatible with FastDisk.

- **BlockDev.** This device driver serves as an interface between FastDisk and devices that request block I/O services. Setup always installs this device driver in SYSTEM.INI.

- **PageFile.** This device driver handles the virtual memory paging file. Setup always installs this device driver in SYSTEM.INI.

Installing FastDisk

Setup does not turn on FastDisk support by default because of the potential loss of data when you use FastDisk on a noncompatible system. To turn on FastDisk, first make sure that your system's hard disk is compatible with FastDisk. Then, use the following procedure to enable FastDisk.

TIP *As long as your PC doesn't use a SCSI or ESDI hard disk, FastDisk probably works on your system. If you use FastDisk on a system that isn't 100 percent compatible with the WD1003 controller standard, a potential for loss of data exists. If you're not sure if FastDisk will work properly on your system, contact the technical support department for your PC vendor (or the disk controller vendor if you purchased it separately) to find out its compatibility. You also might want to make sure you have a current backup of the hard drive.*

Procedure:
Enabling FastDisk

1. Launch Windows, open the Control Panel, and choose the 386 Enhanced icon.

2. From the 386 Enhanced dialog box, select the **V**irtual Memory button. The Virtual Memory dialog box appears.

3. From the Virtual Memory dialog box, select the **C**hange button.

4. To enable FastDisk, click on the **U**se 32-bit Disk Access check box in the bottom left corner of the dialog box. If the box is already checked, your system already is using FastDisk.

5. To ensure that you don't modify the current settings of the system's swap file, from the **D**rive drop-down list, select the same drive you're currently using for your swap file. (If you are unsure, look in the Current Settings group box.)

6. From the **T**ype drop-down list, select the same type of swap file you currently are using (such as Permanent).

7. Choose OK and restart Windows to make the change take effect.

When you turn on FastDisk, Control Panel modifies SYSTEM.INI to include the following lines in the [386Enh] section:

```
device=*int13
device=*wdctrl
32BitDiskAccess=On
```

Turning Off FastDisk

If you're having problems with disk access after you install FastDisk, your hard disk might not be 100 percent compatible with it. To troubleshoot the problem, turn off FastDisk and restart Windows to see if the problem persists.

You can disable FastDisk in the following three ways:

● **Use the Virtual Memory dialog box.** Open Control Panel and double-click on the 386 Enhanced icon. Select the **V**irtual Memory button, then the **C**hange button. Clear the **U**se 32-bit Disk Access check box, choose OK, and restart Windows.

● **Edit the 32BitDiskAccess= setting.** Open Notepad or SysEdit to edit SYSTEM.INI. Find the setting `32BitDiskAccess=On` in the [386Enh] section of SYSTEM.INI and switch it to Off. Save the file and restart Windows.

● **Use the /D:F switch to start Windows.** Exit Windows, and then start Windows again by entering **WIN /D:F** at the DOS prompt, which starts Windows with FastDisk disabled.

This section completes the software-related techniques for improving hard disk performance and increasing free space on the disk. The rest of the chapter focuses on adding hard disk controllers and disk drives to the system.

Hard Disks, Controllers, and Host Adapters

To install a new hard disk or disk controller in your PC, you should have a little bit of background about hard disks and controllers. Rather than go into detail here, the majority of the disk-related technical information is in Chapter 23, "The System Runs, But Not Without Complaining," which covers troubleshooting. You don't need as much background information about disks to install them as you do to troubleshoot a problem with one.

First, you need to learn about hard disk subsystems in general.

Disk Controllers

The PC can't use a hard disk directly. Instead, it requires a *disk controller* to act as an intermediary between the PC and the disk. Typically, the BIOS passes hard disk requests to the hard disk controller, and the controller accesses the disk.

With older drives, the controller is a separate adapter that plugs into the PC's bus. With newer types of hard disks, including IDE and SCSI disks, the controller circuitry is included on a card that's mounted onto the disk (types of hard disks are explained later in this section). A host adapter is used in these systems to connect the disk drive to the PC's bus. The host adapter plugs into the PC's bus just like a disk controller. In some systems, the host adapter is built onto the motherboard, and the disk plugs into the motherboard, not into a separate host adapter.

Many controllers and host adapters include circuitry to support the PC's floppy disk drives. The floppy drives and hard drives then can connect to the same adapter. Also, many tape drives are designed to connect to the system's disk controller or host adapter, so it's not uncommon to see one or two hard disks, a couple of floppy drives, and a tape drive all connected to the same adapter.

Types of Hard Disk Subsystems

Today's PCs use five common types of hard disks. The following list provides a little background information about each type:

- **MFM (Modified Frequency Modulation).** In an MFM disk subsystem, the controller resides on the adapter rather than on the disk. MFM systems use two cables to connect the controller and the hard disk. MFM drives represent old technology and the slowest performance.

- **RLL (Run Length Limited).** RLL drives are a variation of the original MFM drives, and pack data on the disk more densely than do MFM drives (which provides for greater storage capacity with the same size of disk and same number of disk platters). As with MFM drives, RLL drive controllers are separate adapters.

- **ESDI (Enhanced Small Disk Interface).** ESDI drives provide increased speed over MFM and RLL drives. Although technically better than MFM and RLL drives, ESDI drives have never been a big commercial success.

- **IDE (Integrated Drive Electronics).** The hard disk controller circuitry in IDE drives resides on the drive assembly. An IDE host adapter is installed in the PC's bus to connect the hard disk to the system. IDE drives provide excellent performance, and are by far the most common type of drive installed in today's PCs. Some PCs have the IDE host adapter built into the motherboard, which eliminates the need for the host adapter. The disk connects to the adapter by a single cable.

- **SCSI (Small Computer System Interface).** As do IDE drives, SCSI drives have the controller circuitry built onto the disk assembly and use a host adapter to connect the disk to the PC. SCSI actually is a sub-bus to which you can connect up to eight devices. The host adapter counts as one device, and the other seven can be hard disks, tape drives, CD-ROM drives, scanners, and other types of hardware.

The actual hard disk in each of the five types of disk subsystems is very similar physically; only the way the data is organized on the disk is different. The important point is that IDE and SCSI subsystems provide the best perfor-

mance. If you're adding a new disk, consider an IDE or SCSI disk (but read the next section before you rush out and buy one).

Choosing a New Disk

If you're looking at the possibility of adding a new hard disk to your system to increase your PC's storage capacity, you need to consider a couple issues. The first point to consider is what type of drive the system has now, and the second is whether you have the room for another drive.

What Type of Drive Should You Add?

What type of disk does your system have currently? It often makes sense to add another disk like the first one, connecting it to your existing disk controller or host adapter. If you have an IDE, ESDI, or SCSI hard disk in your system, for example, consider installing another drive of the same type.

If you have an older system with an MFM or RLL drive, you probably don't want to add another disk of that type. They're becoming harder to find, the performance isn't as good as that of the newer types, and they cost more per megabyte than IDE and SCSI drives. Does that mean you need to throw out your existing disk? No, it just means you need to look at an alternative.

That alternative is to install an IDE or SCSI host adapter in the system, as well as an IDE or SCSI hard disk. The existing drive remains in the system and serves as your primary disk drive (drive C, for example). The new drive is assigned the next available drive ID, such as drive D.

I recommend you add a SCSI adapter and SCSI hard disk to your system, because some IDE adapters don't coexist with another disk controller. To install an IDE drive in a system with another disk, the IDE controller must be configured as a secondary controller. Some IDE adapters can be configured this way, so why take SCSI over IDE?

Here are my reasons for adding a SCSI subsystem:

- A SCSI disk provides faster performance than the IDE drive.

- Adding a SCSI adapter enables you to add a CD-ROM drive and other SCSI devices. You pay a little more for the drive, but not enough to make SCSI an unattractive alternative.

- Best of all, the SCSI subsystem is compatible with your existing disk subsystem, even if the existing disk is an IDE drive, because the SCSI disk isn't referenced in your system's CMOS setup like the other types of drives. It configures itself using its own BIOS after the system boots.

TIP
When you shop for a SCSI adapter and drive, make sure that you get SCSI-2 compatible components. Older SCSI adapters and drives are referenced simply as SCSI or SCSI-1. SCSI-2 offers improved performance over SCSI-1 systems.

Do You Have Room for Another Drive?

To determine if you actually have room for another hard drive, you need to open your system. You probably have a free slot for the adapter if one is required, but you might not have room for the drive itself. Check whether the system contains an unused drive bay, and make sure that the drive you buy fits into the bay. Half-height and 1-inch drives fit into half of a full-height drive bay, but a full-height drive requires a full bay. If yours is a tower system, check above the floppy drives for an empty bay, which is where many tower systems provide room for a hard disk. Figure 5.7 shows an example of this type of drive bay.

Figure 5.7: A drive bay located above the floppy drives on a tower system.

If you don't have room, but don't want to give up your existing disk, consider adding a SCSI adapter and an external SCSI disk. You might need to buy the case for the disk separately, but they are available (JDR Microdevices has them).

If you don't have room for the new drive, and don't want to add an external drive, your only option is to remove the existing drive and replace it with one that has a greater capacity.

Do You Need Any Special Mounting Hardware?

A special mounting bracket is required to enable 3 1/2-inch form-factor drives to mount into a standard drive bay. If you're buying a 3 1/2-inch drive, ask the salesperson if the drive comes with the necessary mounting hardware. If it doesn't, be sure to order it. Figure 5.8 shows the bracket required for a 3 1/2-inch form-factor drive.

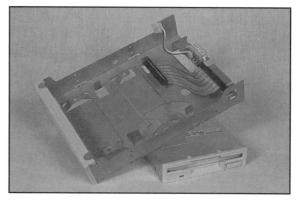

Figure 5.8: A 3 1/2-inch form-factor drive requires a special bracket for installation.

Depending on your PC's chassis design, you might need *mounting rails*. These are two plastic rails that mount to both sides of the drive. The rails slide into tracks in either side of the drive bay, just like drawer rollers slide into the hanger hardware on either side of a kitchen drawer. Check your drive bays to see if they have a track on either side. If they do, you need the mounting rails. Figure 5.9 shows a set of mounting rails attached to a hard drive.

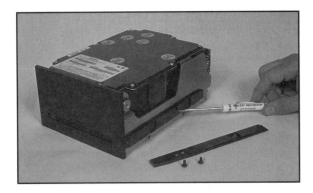

Figure 5.9: A set of mounting rails attached to a hard drive.

Backup before You Add a Disk

If you install a disk controller and a hard drive, usually it's easiest to install the hard drive first, connect the cables to the host adapter, and then install the adapter. Because the other boards can make it difficult to connect the cables after the host adapter is in place, this is particularly true when boards are installed on either side of the slot where the adapter is being installed. This is why I'm covering disk installation before adapter installation.

The first thing to think about is backing up your existing drive.

System Backup

Before installing a new drive, you need to consider whether you need to back up the existing hard disk, if the system has one. If you add a new drive and don't take out the old one, you should not need to back up the existing drive (although it's a good idea to always have a fairly recent backup of your drive).

If you're removing the existing drive and replacing it with the new one, you might need to back up the system. If the new adapter can't coexist in the system with the existing drive subsystem, you definitely need to back up the existing drive, remove the old drive and install the new one, and then restore the files to the new drive.

If you decide that you should back up your hard drive, you should use a backup utility. Although DOS includes a couple of commands that create and restore archives, a backup utility does a much better job and can help you avoid problems with the backup process. For this reason, I won't even tell you what the DOS backup-related commands are.

If you use MS-DOS 6, you already have a backup utility you can use to back up your hard disk to floppy disks. The utility is called *Microsoft Backup*, and it's a subset of a utility from Symantec called Norton Backup. The Microsoft version doesn't support tape drives, but the Symantec version does. (The Microsoft version is free; you have to pay for Norton Backup.) MS-DOS 6 includes a DOS version and a Windows version of Microsoft Backup. Figure 5.10 shows Microsoft Backup for DOS, and figure 5.11 shows Microsoft Backup for Windows.

Figure 5.10: Microsoft Backup for DOS.

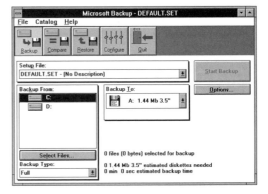

Figure 5.11: Microsoft Backup for Windows.

Because Microsoft Backup is simple to use, I will not go into detail on how to use it. Just remember to back up the entire disk, unless you intend to reinstall some or all of your software from their original distribution disks.

Microsoft Backup compresses the data as it backs it up, using a compression ratio of about 2:1. To calculate how many disks you need, divide the total amount to be backed up by the capacity of the type of disks you will be using.

Other Backup Options

If you replace a high capacity hard disk, it is much easier to back up the disk to tape. If you don't have a tape drive and can afford to buy one, consider doing so. Backing up to tape is much easier and faster than backing up to disk. It's also much easier to restore files from tape.

Microsoft Backup isn't the only software solution. Norton Backup, Central Point Backup, and other utilities do a fine job of backing up your system. If you buy a tape drive, the drive probably comes with its own backup software, so you probably don't need to buy any additional software.

Backup Tips

If the new disk you install can coexist with the existing drive, it might be simpler to leave the current drive in the system until you install the new drive. You then can copy the files from the old drive to the new one without worrying about messing with tape or floppy backups. After you copy the files, you can reconfigure the new drive to be the master drive and remove the old drive.

When does this procedure make sense? Maybe you're selling your old drive to a friend and replacing it with a new one. Or, perhaps you want to place the old drive in another PC that you have. In any case, you can use this direct-copy trick even if there is room in the system for only one of the drives. How is that so? You don't need to install the new drive physically in the system to use it. With a little care, you can connect its host adapter, format it, and use it while it's still outside of the system unit (see fig 5.12).

I don't recommend trying this unless you're very careful. If any electronics on the drive contact any metal or other conductor while the system is on, the drive and the adapter could get ruined. If you do try this method, be sure to place the drive on a rubber mat of some kind that is larger than the drive itself. Or place the drive on the desktop with a

mouse pad or other insulator between it and the PC. A power extension works well to give you a long enough cable to connect from the power supply to the drive.

Figure 5.12: With care, you can connect and use the new drive before installing it.

 Be sure to format the disk in the same orientation in which it will be installed permanently. If the drive will be mounted on its side, be sure that the disk is on its side when you format it. Formatting a disk in one position and running it in another can cause misalignment of the heads.

After you connect the new drive, format it as a bootable system disk (described in a later procedure). Then use File Manager in Windows or the XCOPY command in DOS to copy all the files from one disk to another.

 XCOPY does not copy hidden files. File Manager only copies hidden files if they appear in the files window. To display hidden files in File Manager, select By File Type from the View menu, and then choose the item. Check the Show Hidden/System Files check box.

Then, There's the Network

If your system is connected to a network, see if you can back up the disk to a remote network drive. Although this is somewhat slower than copying directly from disk to disk, it's much easier and safer. Be sure to make the backup when the network is light-loaded, such as after hours. After installing the new drive, you must be able to start the network and connect to the remote drive to restore your files to the new disk. If possible, create a bootable floppy disk that contains your network drivers and will enable you to load your network software. You can boot from the floppy disk, connect to the remote node, and then restore your files.

Adding a Hard Disk

After you back up your files, you are ready to install the new drive. The first procedure involves configuring the drive for your system. Because IDE and SCSI drives are the only types I recommend installing in a system, these are the procedures covered.

Procedure:
Drive Configuration, Dual IDE Drives Only

Explanation: You can install more than one IDE drive in a PC. The first IDE drive is called the *master*, and the second IDE drive is called the *slave*. If you are installing a second IDE drive in a system that currently contains an IDE drive, you must reconfigure the existing drive as the master drive, and configure the new drive as the slave drive. Drive configuration is accomplished by setting a jumper on the disk. Consult your disk manual to determine the correct jumper position for master and slave designation.

NOTE   *Some earlier IDE drives do not contain an option to configure them as master or slave drives. If one of these is installed in your system and you are adding a new IDE drive to increase the system's storage capacity, you may not be able to leave the old drive in the system. Check the manual of the old drive or contact the vendor to find out if you can use both drives in the system simultaneously.*

If you're installing an IDE drive in a system that contains another type of drive such as an MFM drive, you don't need to configure the IDE drive as master or slave. (This assumes that the IDE host adapter you install is compatible with the other disk controller.)

1. Discharge your static, and avoid touching any of the metal components of the drives other than the mounting brackets. Try to handle the drives only by the sides. Avoid touching the electronics or edge connectors.

2. If you install a second IDE drive in a system that already contains an IDE drive, configure the existing drive as the master drive.

   Try to accomplish this step without removing the drive. If you can't reach the jumper, remove the screws on either side of the drive that hold it in place (see fig. 5.13). You should see two screws on either side of the drive. Slide the drive back, if possible, and set the jumper. Otherwise, slide the drive forward and out of the chassis far enough to set the jumper. You might need to remove the power cable and interface cable from the drive.

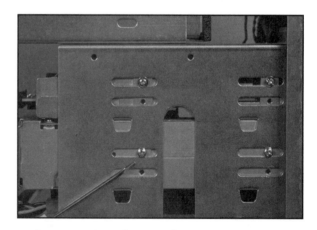

Figure 5.13: A drive usually contains two screws on either side that hold it in place.

3. If you have removed the first drive, discharge yourself, and then reinstall it after you configure it as the master drive.

4. Discharge yourself again before picking up the new drive. Be careful not to bump or drop it.

5. Configure the new drive as the slave drive by setting the appropriate jumper on the drive.

Procedure:

Drive Configuration, Single IDE Drive with Existing Non-IDE Drive

1. Verify that your IDE host adapter is compatible with the existing drive controller.

2. Discharge your static.

3. Configure the IDE drive for single drive use. (This can vary; check the host adapter manual for different instructions for configuring the drive.)

Procedure:

Drive Configuration, Single IDE Drive as the Only Drive

1. Discharge your static.

2. Configure the drive for single drive use by setting the appropriate jumper on the drive.

Procedure:

Drive Configuration, SCSI Drives, All Situations

Explanation: Configuring a SCSI drive requires a few more steps than configuring an IDE drive. Because you can connect up to seven devices to the SCSI bus, you must configure the hard drive to use one of seven address numbers. Each device must be assigned a unique address. The first SCSI hard disk in the system should be at SCSI address 0. The next SCSI drive, if one is present, usually is set to address 1.

The address of a SCSI disk typically is configured by setting a jumper. Check your disk's manual to determine the correct jumper setting for the SCSI bus address you need to assign to the disk. The bus address of the host adapter often is controlled by the adapter's BIOS; sometimes it's controlled by a jumper on the adapter.

In addition to configuring the address, you need to worry about termination (it's not as bad as it sounds). The device at each end of the SCSI bus must be *terminated*, which means that it must have a resistor pack installed on it. To put it in lay person's terms, the terminating resistors soak up excess current flowing through the bus and prevent signals from reflecting back down the cable. That keeps the circuits from getting fried and reduces transmission errors. Figure 5.14 shows the terminating resistor packs on a SCSI hard disk. Figure 5.15 shows the terminating resistor packs on a Future Domain SCSI host adapter.

Figure 5.14: Terminating resistor packs on a SCSI hard disk.

Figure 5.15: Terminating resistor packs on a SCSI adapter.

Because the SCSI host adapter usually is the first device on the bus, it is terminated by default. If, for some reason, the host adapter is *not* the first device on the bus, you need to remove the terminator from the host adapter. If you have internal SCSI devices and external SCSI devices connected to the host adapter, the host adapter is sitting between the devices. So, it isn't at the end of the bus. This means that you need to remove the terminators from the host adapter.

If the disk you install is the only SCSI device in the system, it must be terminated by installing a resistor pack in the appropriate place on the disk. The host adapter also must be terminated. If you just bought the disk, the resistor pack already should be in place. Check the disk's manual to locate the terminating resistor pack and ensure that it's in place.

If you install more than one SCSI device in the system, or another SCSI device already is installed in the system, make sure that only the device at each end of the bus is terminated. If two internal SCSI devices are connected to the host adapter by a single cable, for example, the device at the *end* of the cable requires termination, and so does the host adapter. If you have one internal device and one external device, the two devices must be terminated; the host adapter must not. If there are two internal devices and one external device, the internal device at the end of the cable and the external device are the only ones that should be terminated. I'm sure you get the idea—only the devices at each end of the bus must be terminated.

1. Check the disk's manual to locate the jumpers on the disk that configure the disk's bus address.

2. Decide which bus address should be assigned to the disk. If it's the first SCSI disk, assign it address 0. If it's the second SCSI disk, assign it address 1. If your system contains other SCSI devices, assign their addresses to higher bus numbers than the disks.

3. Discharge your static.

4. Set the jumper on the disk to configure the disk's bus address (see fig. 5.16).

5. Determine whether the disk must be terminated. If the disk should be terminated, verify that the terminating resistors are in place.

6. If other SCSI devices are on the bus, check their termination. Only the devices at each end of the bus must be terminated. Remove the terminating resistors from any devices not located at either end of the bus.

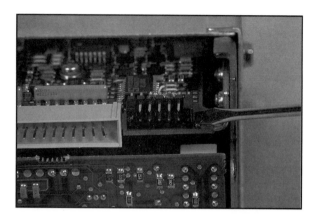

Figure 5.16: Jumpers on a SCSI drive that set its bus address.

Procedure:

Drive Configuration, SCSI Drive with Existing MFM, RLL, or ESDI Drive

Explanation: When installing a SCSI drive in a system with an existing MFM, RLL, or ESDI drive, the existing drive must remain the primary drive (the boot drive). The new SCSI drive is a secondary drive. In this situation, you do not need to change the configuration of the existing drive, nor do you need to change any drive settings in your PC's setup program. Configure the SCSI drive as described in the previous procedure.

Procedure:

Drive Installation, All IDE and SCSI Drives

1. If your new drive requires a mounting bracket or mounting rails, attach them to the disk (see figs. 5.8 and 5.9).

2. Carefully slide the new drive into place (see fig. 5.17).

Figure 5.17: Slide the drive into place to the depth required by step 3.

3. If the drive face is visible through the front of the PC's case, align the face of the hard drive with the face of the floppy drive(s). If the drive is fully concealed within the case, push it back far enough to allow the case to slide fully into place.

4. Secure the drive to the chassis with four mounting screws.

NOTE

If you install a hard drive in a tower case above the floppy drives, you might need to remove the power supply from the system to get the drive into place. You also might need to remove the drive bay brackets, mount the drive in the brackets, and mount the drive and brackets into the chassis as an assembled unit. Remember to reinstall the power supply when you finish installing the drive—it makes the computer much more useful.

Procedure:
Connecting Cables

Explanation: After you configure and install the hard disk, it's usually easiest to connect the cables between the adapter and the drive before you install the adapter. IDE and SCSI

drives both use a single data interface cable to connect the drive and the adapter. This means that two cables connect to the drive—the power cable from the power supply and the interface cable.

The interface cable for IDE drives usually isn't keyed so that it installs in the correct position. Instead, there's a colored stripe on the side of the cable where pin 1 is located. When you connect the cable to the drive and to the adapter, examine the pins on the connectors to locate pin 1 (it is clearly marked). Make sure that the cable plugs into the connectors so that the stripe on the cable is oriented with pin 1 on the connectors (see fig. 5.18).

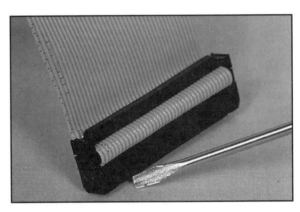

Figure 5.18: IDE cables are color-coded for pin 1 and have a key notch.

SCSI interface cables usually have a key on them that prevents them from being installed incorrectly. The key is a bump at the center of one side of the connector that fits into a slot in the connector (see fig. 5.19). Even if the cable isn't keyed, it will have a colored stripe to indicate pin 1. Check the connectors and the manuals to locate pin 1, and connect the cable accordingly.

1. Locate a free power supply cable and connect it to the back of the drive. The power connector is keyed so that it will install correctly. If the cable isn't long enough to reach the back of the drive, you can purchase a power extension cable that will make the cable long enough (see fig. 5.20).

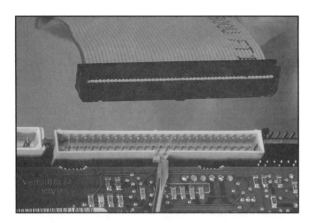

Figure 5.19: SCSI interface cables often are keyed for proper insertion.

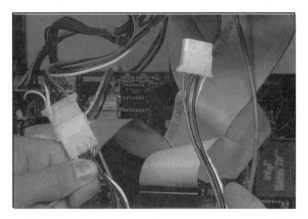

Figure 5.20: You can add a power extension cable if the cable from the power supply isn't long enough to reach the disk.

2. Connect the interface cable to the back of the hard disk, taking care to orient the cable properly. Make sure that the cable is firmly seated on its connector.

3. Connect the interface cable to the host adapter.

4. If the host adapter controls the floppy drives, connect the floppy drive cable to the appropriate header on the adapter (check the adapter's manual for this).

5. Continue with the host adapter installation procedure.

Adding a Hard Disk Controller

This section includes procedures that help you configure and install IDE and SCSI host adapters in a PC. As with the hard disk procedures, I have included only these two types because they are by far the most common, and because I don't recommend installing any other type of new disk subsystem for performance reasons.

Adding an IDE Host Adapter

The configuration process for an IDE host adapter often is complicated by the fact that sometimes the IDE host adapter does more than just provide a connection for the hard disk(s). Many IDE host adapters also control the floppy drives. In addition, many IDE host adapters also serve as the system's I/O card, containing the serial and parallel ports. When you install an IDE host adapter, you must take the following points into account:

● **Floppy support.** If the IDE adapter is used to control the floppy drives, you can remove the existing floppy controller from the system. If the floppy controller is built into an existing disk controller in the system, and you won't be removing that existing disk, there's no need to connect the floppy drives to the new IDE controller. Instead, you must disable the IDE adapter's floppy support. This is accomplished by setting jumpers on the IDE adapter.

● **I/O ports.** If the IDE adapter provides serial and parallel ports, and is being installed in a system that already has an existing I/O adapter, you need to configure the I/O ports on the IDE adapter accordingly. If the system already contains the full complement of ports (four COM ports and three LPT ports), you must disable the IDE adapter's I/O ports. If the system contains only two COM ports and a single LPT port, configure the IDE adapter's COM ports as COM3 and COM4. Configure its LPT port as LPT2 or LPT3, according to the number of LPT ports already in the system.

Procedure:

Configuring the IDE Host Adapter

1. Determine whether you need to configure the host adapter's COM and LPT ports, if it has them. Check your system logs to determine which ports already are installed in the PC. Follow the installation manual for the IDE adapter to configure the COM and LPT ports accordingly. Usually, I/O port configuration requires only that you set a few jumpers on the adapter. The manual for the adapter has the necessary instructions for setting the jumpers.

2. Determine whether you will be using the IDE host adapter's floppy support, if the adapter provides such support. If the existing floppy controller is a stand-alone unit (it's not part of an existing hard disk controller and it doesn't do anything else except control the floppy drives), remove it from the system and use the new IDE adapter to control the floppy drives. Removing the existing floppy controller makes another slot available for a device you might decide to add later (such as a sound card). If the existing floppy controller is part of an existing hard disk controller that remains in the system, disable the IDE adapter's floppy support. Consult the manual for the host adapter for the jumper settings that disable floppy support.

3. In your system log, mark down the settings for the new host adapter. You also might want to write them in the IDE host adapter's manual.

4. After setting I/O and floppy options on the IDE host adapter, locate an available slot. Choose a 16-bit slot for a 16-bit host adapter, and an 8-bit or 16-bit slot for an 8-bit host adapter.

5. Remove the slot cover for the selected bus slot.

6. Connect cables to the host adapter as required.

7. Insert the IDE host adapter into its slot, firmly pushing it into place (see fig. 5.21). Install the retaining screw in the adapter's bracket.

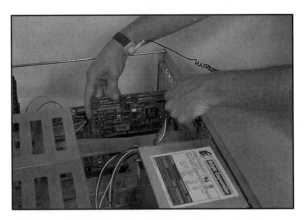

Figure 5.21: Installing the host adapter in a bus slot.

Adding a SCSI Host Adapter

Some of the same configuration issues that relate to IDE host adapters also relate to SCSI adapters. Many SCSI host adapters include built-in support for floppy drives. When you configure your SCSI host adapter, you need to take into account whether you are going to use an existing floppy disk controller or the SCSI adapter's floppy support.

Another issue that surrounds SCSI host adapters is the fact that the adapter generally requires that its BIOS be mapped to a block of memory in the UMA. You need to determine if the default memory address used by the adapter is available. If the memory address range already is in use by another device, you must change the adapter's address or the address of the other device so that they do not conflict. The memory address will be set by jumpers or switches on the host adapter, as well as on the conflicting device.

You also might need to specify an interrupt line number (IRQ) for the host adapter. This varies among the different brands and models of adapters. The IRQ setting, if required, is controlled by jumpers on the host adapter.

Procedure:
Configuring a SCSI Host Adapter, No Other SCSI Adapters Present

1. Check the host adapter's manual to determine if your SCSI adapter requires selection of a memory address in the UMA for the adapter. If it requires a memory address, determine whether the default address for the adapter is available. If the address is not available, discharge yourself, then change the address of the host adapter or the conflicting device.

2. If the SCSI host adapter is not at one end of the SCSI bus (if you have internal and external SCSI devices connected to it), remove its terminating resistors. If you have external devices only or internal devices only, leave the terminating resistors in place.

3. Check the manual for the adapter to see if your SCSI adapter must have an IRQ assignment. If it does, determine a free IRQ (use MSD). I recommend IRQ14 if it's available. Set the adapter's IRQ according to the instructions in its manual.

4. If you install the SCSI adapter in a system that has another SCSI adapter installed, check the adapter's manual to determine how to set the new adapter as the *secondary adapter*.

5. Enable or disable the SCSI host adapter's floppy support, if required.

6. Check the manual for any other settings required by your particular brand and model of adapter.

7. Locate an appropriate bus slot in which to install the adapter and remove the slot cover.

8. Connect the hard disk interface cable and floppy cables (if required) to the host adapter.

9. Install the host adapter in its bus slot. Secure it with a screw.

10. If you are using the UMA for device drivers, edit CONFIG.SYS and exclude the range of memory used by the SCSI host adapter. If you use EMM386 to manage the UMA, use the X= switch on the EMM386 command line to exclude the range of memory used by the host adapter. Following is an example, assuming the host adapter uses the memory range CA000–CBFFF:

```
DEVICE=C:\DOS\EMM386.EXE X=CA00-CBFF
```

Disk Setup, Preparation, and Formatting

After you install your new adapter and hard disk, the disk must be prepared to use. Earlier types of drives, including MFM, RLL, and ESDI drives, require low-level formatting. This low-level formatting marks out, among other things, the tracks and sectors on the disk.

You can't, don't want to, and shouldn't try to low-level format an IDE or SCSI drive. Doing so will screw up the drive. The drives are preformatted when they are manufactured. What's left if you don't have to perform a low-level format? There's enough work left to keep you busy for another hour or so, at least.

Following is a basic checklist of what you need to do to make a disk usable after you install it:

- Configure it in the PC's system configuration setup program (not required for SCSI drives).
- Partition the hard disk.
- Format the hard disk.
- Install DOS on the hard disk (primary hard drive only).
- Restore files to the hard disk (only when replacing an existing drive).

Partitioning

At this point, I'll just tell you that partitioning a disk sets up a logical structure on the disk that's compatible with the operating system. If you use DOS, you need to create a DOS partition. If you use UNIX, you need to create a UNIX partition, and so on. You must partition a disk before you can use it. DOS includes a program called FDISK that enables you to create, view, and delete partition information for a disk.

After you create a DOS partition, you use FDISK to create *logical drives* in the partition. A logical drive is an area in the partition that DOS recognizes by a unique drive ID, like C:, D:, E:, and so on.

DOS partitions created with DOS versions 3.*x* can be a maximum of only 32M in size. If you have a 200M hard disk, this means you must create six 32M logical drives and one

8M logical drive in the partition to use up the whole 200M with DOS 3.*x*. Starting with DOS 4.0, the 32M limitation became obsolete, and you can create a single logical drive that uses all the space in the partition. That's just one of the reasons why you should upgrade to the latest version of DOS if you have been holding out.

Deciding How To Partition the Drive

Should you create a single logical drive that uses the whole partition? Should you break up the partition into multiple logical drives? How do you decide?

Following are some guidelines I recommend:

- **The new drive complements an existing drive.** If you add the disk to a system that already has a disk in it, create a single logical drive that uses all the space in the partition. If you want to segregate your programs and data onto different drives, you can leave the programs on the existing drive and put your documents on the new drive (or vice versa).

- **The new drive is the only drive in the system.** Consider creating two logical drives: one to contain your programs and a second for your documents. How you size each one depends on how many programs you use versus how much document space you need. Here's the exception: If you plan to use Stacker, DoubleSpace, or some other disk compression option, create a single logical drive. Then, use part of that drive to create a new, compressed drive with the compression software. This gives you two drives; one uncompressed and one compressed. You then can segregate your programs and data on these two drives.

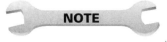

NOTE *Why do I recommend separating programs and data onto different disks? It makes system backup much easier. After you install your programs, you can back it up once and probably never need to back it up again. Your documents, on the other hand, should be backed up regularly. If they are on a drive of their own, just back up that entire drive, and all your documents are backed up.*

The easiest way to partition a disk is to run the MS-DOS Setup program to install DOS on the drive, and let Setup partition it for you. If you boot the system from a floppy disk that contains the FDISK program, you can use FDISK to partition the drive.

If you add a second drive to the system, FDISK will be in the DOS directory of your primary hard disk. Just change to that directory and run FDISK to partition the new drive.

Formatting

After the disk is partitioned, it must be high-level formatted with the DOS FORMAT command. FORMAT sets up some things on the disk called the File Allocation Tables (FATs), Boot Record, and Root Directory. The FORMAT command also can enable you to make the disk bootable.

Sometimes with SCSI drives, you might need to use special software that comes with the host adapter to format the drive. You also might need to use some special drivers that come with the host adapter. The host adapter manual covers the installation and use of those programs.

As with partitioning, the easiest method is to run MS-DOS Setup on the disk to format it. If you add a second drive, the FORMAT command is in the DOS directory of your primary hard drive. Change to that directory and run FORMAT. You also can run FORMAT from a floppy disk.

Setting Up IDE Drives

IDE drives require configuration in the PC's system setup (usually called the *CMOS setup*). You need to tell the PC things such as how many cylinders, heads, and sectors the drive has, as well as a few other items of information about the drive. These items of information are included with the disk's manual.

You specify these settings to the PC by running the PC's setup program. How you get into the PC's setup program depends on the PC. With some, you press Del or another key when the system is booting. The PC's boot message prompts you what to press. Other systems, such as my Gateway system, for example, require you to press Ctrl-Alt-Esc or some other keystroke to start the setup program. Check the manual for your PC to find out how to run its setup program if you don't already know.

In addition to specifying the types of hard drives connected to the system, the system configuration setup program also is where you define the types of floppy drives connected to the system and other hardware information.

You can configure up to two hard drives in the PC's setup screen. Drive 1 is the boot drive, and Drive 2 is a secondary drive. If you install only one IDE drive in the system, and no other drives are installed, the IDE drive will be Drive 1. If you install an IDE drive in a system that already has a hard disk installed, the new IDE drive will be Drive 2.

After you run the PC's setup program and configure the hard disk information, exit the setup program. The system reboots to make the changes take effect.

Setting Up SCSI Drives

The SCSI host adapter contains its own BIOS that enables it to read and write to a disk. SCSI drives are not configured in the PC's setup program. If you have only SCSI hard drives in the system, your PC's setup indicates No Drive Installed. As the system boots and the SCSI adapter's BIOS goes to work, the SCSI BIOS takes on the task of recognizing the disk and making it available to DOS.

This simplifies setup of a SCSI drive. After physically installing the drive, configuring the adapter, and rebooting the system, all that's left to do is partition and format the drive.

Procedure:
Partitioning and Formatting a Disk, Only One Hard Disk in the System

Explanation: The easiest method for preparing the disk and installing DOS is to run the DOS Setup program. Setup partitions the hard disk, formats it, and installs DOS on the drive.

1. After drive installation, run the PC's setup program to configure the drive parameters for the newly installed drive (IDE drives only). Then, reboot the system.

2. Place the MS-DOS 6 disk 1 in drive A: and reboot the system.

3. Follow the directions provided by Setup to partition and format the disk. Setup installs DOS for you.

Alternative method: Boot the PC from a floppy disk that contains the FDISK and FORMAT programs. After the system is booted, run to partition the disk, and then run FORMAT to format the disk. See the following procedures for guidelines on how to use FDISK and FORMAT.

Procedure:
Partitioning a Disk with FDISK, Multiple Hard Drive Systems, or Booting from a Floppy

Explanation: If you're partitioning a disk in a system that already contains a bootable hard drive, this procedure helps you partition it using the FDISK command. This procedure also covers partitioning the disk using a bootable floppy disk that contains the FDISK program.

1. After drive installation, run the PC's setup program to configure the drive parameters for the newly installed drive (IDE drives only). Reboot the system.

2. If you run FDISK from an existing hard disk, make the existing disk active, then change to the DOS directory.

3. If you booted DOS from a floppy that contains FDISK, make the floppy drive active, and change to the directory on the floppy disk that contains FDISK.

4. Enter **FDISK** at the DOS prompt.

5. Follow the prompts provided by FDISK to select a drive to partition and create a primary DOS partition. Be sure to select the new drive to partition, not the existing drive. Then, still using FDISK, create as many logical drives in the partition as you desire. I recommend a single logical drive that comprises the entire partition.

Procedure:

Formatting, Multiple Hard Drive Systems, or Booting from a Floppy Disk

1. Make the drive and directory containing the FOR-MAT program active.

2. If you want to make the hard disk bootable, enter **FORMAT D:** **/S** at the DOS prompt. Substitute the correct drive ID in the place of D:. If you do not want to make the disk bootable, omit the /S parameter. If the new drive will not be the primary boot disk, you do not need to make it bootable.

3. Follow the FORMAT prompts to complete the for-matting process.

4. After formatting, your new hard disk is ready for use.

Part 2

Adding New Stuff to Your Computer

6

Setting Up Circuit Boards

One of the tasks you'll certainly have to perform at some time in your PC's life is that of configuring a circuit board. The board might be an adapter or a new motherboard, but many of the same techniques and procedures apply to both.

This chapter explains how to configure an adapter or motherboard, and also covers basic concepts about your PC that you'll need to understand to make good decisions about how to configure adapters. In addition, you read about:

- Understanding adapters and other circuit cards
- Precautions to take when handling circuit boards
- Assigning IRQs
- Assigning DMA channels
- Assigning an I/O base address
- Assigning RAM and ROM addresses
- Removal and installation procedures

Using Adapters and Other Circuit Cards

Adapters are the circuit cards that plug into sockets in the PC's motherboard (the main circuit board inside the PC). Cables usually connect to the adapters through the back of the PC's chassis from devices such as the monitor, printer, and mouse. Most of the new devices you add to your PC either will be adapters or will include adapters. Common adapters in a typical PC include the video adapter, I/O (input/output) adapter (to which gadgets such as printers, modems, and mice connect), and the hard disk controller. The basics of knowing how to handle, configure, install, and remove adapters is an important skill.

Figure 6.1 shows a typical adapter that includes an *edge connector* (shown at the bottom of the adapter). An edge connector inserts into the PC's bus, connecting the adapter to the PC. The edge connector is simply a part of the board containing conductive strips called *pins*.

Figure 6.1: A typical adapter for a PC.

The bus slots in a PC come in three different flavors: 8-bit slots use a single connector; 16-bit slots use two connectors in line with one another; and 32-bit slots use three connectors in line with one another. Many PCs have some 8-bit sockets and some 16-bit sockets; others have only 16-bit sockets. A few adapters have a combination of 8-bit, 16-bit, and 32-bit sockets. Figure 6.2 shows the bus slots on a typical 486 motherboard.

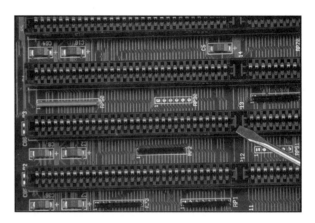

Figure 6.2: Bus slots on a typical 486 motherboard.

An 8-bit card can be installed either in an 8-bit slot or in a 16-bit slot. Some 16-bit cards are designed to operate in 8-bit mode or in 16-bit mode, and these types of adapters can be installed in either an 8-bit or a 16-bit socket. (The 16-bit part of the edge connector isn't inserted into anything if you install the adapter in an 8-bit socket.)

Usually, you want to install a 16-bit card in a 16-bit socket to get the best performance from your card. If you have run out of 16-bit sockets, check the adapter's documentation to see if it can be used in an 8-bit slot, and what the performance penalties will be if you do so. Or, try to move a less important adapter from a 16-bit slot to an 8-bit slot to make room for the new adapter.

 **NOTE**   *32-bit adapters generally can be installed only in a 32-bit socket.*

Jumpers and DIP Switches

Adapters and motherboards often require configuration before you install them in the PC. The configuration process includes setting small switches called *DIP (Dual In-line Package) switches*. Figure 6.3 shows a typical DIP switch.

Figure 6.3: A typical DIP switch on an adapter.

Each individual switch in a DIP has two positions: On and Off. The On position often is marked on the switch by a 1 or the words "On" or "Closed." The Off position often is marked by a 0 or the words "Off" or "Open." Usually, you need to set a selection of switches on the adapter to configure various options.

> **TIP**
>
> Use the tip of a ballpoint pen (or something similar) to flip the little switches into whichever position is required by the device. The manual that comes with the adapter usually includes a table, illustration, or other instructions to tell you which switches to turn on and off for various configurations.

Many adapters also include jumpers. A *jumper* is really nothing more than a rectangular plug that you install on a couple of pins (see fig 6.4). When the jumper is installed on the pins, it makes an electrical connection between the two pins.

To install a jumper, just slide the jumper onto the pins as described in the adapter's installation manual. To remove a jumper, simply slide it off and store it away (you might need it someday). If the jumper is in a crowded location on the adapter, you may need to use a small, flat screwdriver to pry it loose (be careful).

The connectors on which jumpers typically are installed on an adapter come in two configurations: two pins per set or three pins per set. There may be many sets of pins in a row, or there may be only one or two. When the two-pin configuration is used, an option is set by either installing a jumper on the two pins or removing it (see fig. 6.4).

Figure 6.4: A set of jumpers on an adapter, with two-pin and three-pin connectors shown.

When the three-pin configuration is used, the option is set by installing no jumper, by installing a jumper on pins 1 and 2, or by installing a jumper on pins 2 and 3 (see fig. 6.5).

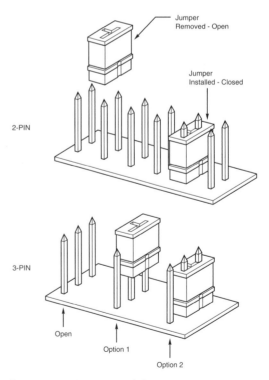

Figure 6.5: Two-pin and three-pin jumper connections.

As with DIPs, the installation manual for a device will provide a table or other information to explain which pins require jumpers to set various options.

Cable Connections

Most adapters require that you connect other devices to them using ribbon cables. Figure 6.6 shows the end of a ribbon cable. *Ribbon cables* are flat, thin cables made up of many insulated wires stuck together side-by-side, forming a sort of ribbon. Sometimes the connectors on either end of a ribbon cable are keyed so they only go into or on their respective connections one way. At other times, you have to keep track of which edge of the cable goes where.

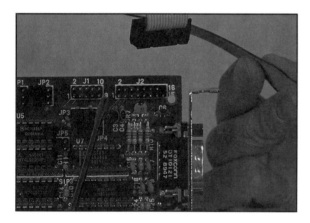

Figure 6.6: The location of pin 1 usually is marked on a connector and on a cable.

NOTE   *Take a look at a ribbon cable and you'll see that the wire on one edge is colored, sometimes faintly, in red or blue (usually it's one of those two colors). The colored stripe indicates the wire that's supposed to connect to pin 1 on the adapter's connector. The cable should be connected so that the edge with the colored stripe hooks up on the pin 1 side of the connector. Connectors on an adapter usually have the number "1" printed on the board to indicate the location of pin 1.*

External connectors that connect to the adapter at the back of the PC are keyed so that they can be inserted in only one way. They almost always include some type of screw to secure the cable to the adapter.

Ribbon cables, though, often are not physically keyed. With ribbon cables, you must pay attention to the location of pin 1 on the connector and match the colored stripe on the ribbon cable with this pin.

Taking Precautions

Adapters, RAM boards, and motherboards all have delicate microchips on them in addition to lots of other electronic components. Many of these devices are sensitive to static electricity. Your body can easily build up a static charge that's strong enough to zap these components and render them useless, often rendering the entire circuit board useless. A few precautions you can take when handling adapters and other circuit boards include:

● *Always* discharge the static from your body before you open a bag containing a circuit board or before you pick up the board. Use an antistatic wrist strap or touch the metal part of the PC's chassis before touching anything else. If the PC is still plugged in, touching the power supply case will discharge your static to ground.

● Handle the boards by the edges whenever possible to avoid touching any of the electronic components on the board.

● Avoid touching the edge connector on a board.

Here are a few tips to keep in mind when working with adapters and circuit cards:

● Occasionally, the pins on an edge connector can become dirty, preventing the pins from making good contact with the bus connector. To clean the pins on an edge connector, rub a rubber eraser over the pins. Use the eraser on a new pencil, for example. Make sure you "erase" both sides of the edge connector, and make sure you do it with the board *out* of the PC. You don't want eraser crumbs floating around in your PC. Brush the eraser crumbs off the board with a small brush. You can buy special wet-wipes that are formulated specially for cleaning edge connectors, but a pencil is a lot cheaper and easier to find.

● Some of the chips on adapters and motherboards are *socketed*: they are installed in a socket instead of being soldered directly to the board. This makes the chips removeable. Unfortunately, the chips sometimes work themselves out of the socket. When you are installing a board, discharge your static, then lay the board on a flat surface and press on the socketed chips to make sure they are fully seated in their sockets. Avoid touching the pins on the chips if possible. Figure 6.7 shows a socketed chip.

Figure 6.7: A socketed chip on an adapter.

IRQ Assignment

Some adapters require an IRQ assignment. IRQ stands for *Interrupt ReQuest line*. When an adapter needs to get the CPU's attention, it signals the CPU using one of the IRQ lines. Each IRQ line is identified by a number. In XT-class systems, the IRQ lines 2 through 7 are user-assignable. In AT-class systems, the IRQ lines 2 through 15 are user-assignable. This means you can configure an adapter to use one of these IRQ lines.

The main point to keep in mind when trying to decide which IRQ to assign to a device that you're installing is that in most PCs, devices can't share the same IRQ line. Each device has to have its own IRQ line. The exceptions to this rule are EISA- and MCA-bus systems, which enable devices to share IRQ lines. The vast majority of systems in use today are ISA-bus systems, which are the type of bus system addressed in this book.

When deciding which IRQ line to assign to a device, keep in mind that many of the IRQ lines already are in use by other devices in your system. Table 6.1 shows the standard IRQ assignments in a typical PC.

Table 6.1	
Typical IRQ Assignments	
IRQ	Device
NMI	Non-Maskable Interrupt, reports parity errors
0	System timer
1	Keyboard
2	EGA/VGA, and cascaded interrupt for second IRQ controller
3	COM2 or COM4
4	COM1 or COM3
5	LPT2 (printer port 2)
6	Floppy disk, or hard disk/floppy disk controller
7	LPT1 (printer port 1)
8	Real-time clock interrupt
9	Software redirected to IRQ2
10	Available
11	Available
12	Available
13	Coprocessor (math chip)
14	Hard disk controller
15	Available, or hard disk controller

Study table 6.1 to determine which interrupts are available in your system. You may need to look through your system manual and the manuals for any devices installed in your system to determine which ones are in use. Keep in mind that some of the IRQ lines are used by system-level devices and you can't change them. IRQ0 and IRQ1 are always off-limits to you. The IRQ lines 6, 8, 13, and 14 also are usually off-limits.

If an IRQ line listed in table 6.1 doesn't have the word "Available" by it, it doesn't necessarily mean that you can't assign it to a device. If you don't have a second LPT port (LPT2), you can use IRQ5. If you're only using one COM port, you probably can use IRQ3.

Use MSD to check your system for used and available IRQs. If MSD describes a device for an IRQ line as "Detected," the IRQ is in use. If MSD describes the device as "Not detected," the IRQ generally is available. Also in MSD, the word "Reserved" for an IRQ generally means the IRQ is available.

After you have identified all of your system's IRQ assignments, write them down in your hardware log so that the next time you need to assign an IRQ, you can just check the log for an available IRQ.

Assigning IRQs on an Adapter

Most adapters that require an IRQ assignment provide jumpers on the adapter, which you use to configure the adapter's assigned IRQ. An increasingly common practice, though, is to assign the IRQ to the adapter with a configuration program that comes with the device. Check your manuals to see which method the adapter uses, then assign an available IRQ to the device using whatever method is required by that particular device.

DMA Assignment

Most devices need to access memory. They do so by going through the central processing unit (CPU). The device makes a request to the CPU, and the CPU writes to memory for the device. The CPU usually has better things to do, though, and making the CPU perform all memory accesses can slow down the system's overall performance, especially with devices like sound cards, which need to write to memory often. In these situations, DMA can come to the rescue.

DMA stands for *Direct Memory Access*. There are a certain number of DMA channels in your PC that some devices can use to write directly to memory, bypassing the CPU. They access memory directly, which is where the term DMA comes from.

Some adapters can be configured to use DMA and improve their performance. As with IRQs, the trick to configuring a device's DMA use is to assign it a DMA channel that isn't used by any other device in the system. You can't share IRQ lines, and you can't share DMA channels. Weird and unpleasant things happen when you try to do so.

So What Channels Can I Use?

An 8-bit, XT-class system has four DMA channels, 0 through 3. A 16-bit, AT-class system has eight DMA channels, 0 through 7. Some of the DMA channels are used by the system, so you have to be careful when assigning DMA channels to a device. Table 6.2 lists the DMA assignments for typical systems.

Table 6.2
DMA Assignments in PCs

DMA Channel	Assignment
0	RAM refresh, XT only; available on AT-class systems
1	Hard disk controller, XT only; available on AT-class systems
2	Floppy controller
3	Available
4	Available (for 16-bit cards only)
5	Available (for 16-bit cards only)
6	Available (for 16-bit cards only)
7	Available (for 16-bit cards only)

Note: AT-class systems include 286, 386, 486, and PS/2 systems.

If you are installing a 16-bit card that can use DMA, try to assign it a DMA channel between 4 and 7. Check the manuals for the devices in your system to determine if any of them use DMA channels, then write down the assignments in your hardware log. If you don't have an available DMA channel, see if you can disable DMA on the adapter you're installing, or on one of the adapters that's already in the system. If you disable DMA for an existing adapter, you can assign the DMA channel it was using to the new adapter.

As with IRQ assignments, DMA channel assignment usually is accomplished by configuring jumpers or DIP switches. A few devices assign DMA by using a software configuration program that comes with the adapter.

I/O Base Address

There is a range of memory addresses in the PC that are allocated for Input/Output (I/O) between various devices in the PC and the CPU. Devices use these addresses to communicate with the CPU, and vice versa. Here's an example: The serial port COM1 usually is assigned the hex addresses 3F8 through 3FF. When data is coming into COM1, the device that's controlling COM1 places the data in those memory addresses. The CPU then reads the data from those memory addresses. As far as the CPU is concerned, the address space between 3F8 and 3FF is the COM port.

When you're configuring an adapter, keep in mind that it may require an I/O address assignment. If it requires an I/O address, you need to assign one to it that isn't in use by any other device. By convention, adapters are supposed to use only the hex addresses 100 through 3FF. If you need to assign an I/O address to an adapter, you'll be working within that range of addresses. Check the adapter's manuals to determine which preset I/O addresses it is designed to use. The default assignment for the adapter will usually work because the adapter's designers thought ahead and picked an I/O address that is considered an "industry standard" for their particular type of device.

To be sure you don't have a conflict, check the devices in your system to determine which ones use I/O addresses and what those I/O addresses are. Write them down in your hardware log, then pick an available I/O address that you can use for your new adapter. Usually, you assign I/O addresses with jumpers or DIP switches on the adapter. The adapter's manual will describe which jumpers or switches to set to assign a particular I/O address to the device.

RAM and ROM Address Assignments

One final consideration when configuring an adapter: does the adapter require a RAM or ROM address assignment, or perhaps both? Adapters that have their own ROM BIOS chips on them generally require you to map a range of memory addresses to the ROM. The reason is that all memory in the PC needs to be mapped to a range of addresses, or the CPU can't access the memory.

A ROM chip, even if it is installed on an adapter, has to have some memory addresses assigned to it or it won't be accessible to the operating system or to the CPU. (Memory mapping is explained in much more detail in Chapter 4). Trying to run some program code that didn't have an assigned memory address would be like trying to find a particular house out of thousands without knowing the house's street address.

Let's take a SCSI host adapter as an example: The SCSI host adapter in one of my systems includes a ROM that by default uses the memory range CA000–CBFFF. That means that the program routines in the adapter's ROM BIOS are mapped to the address range CA000–CBFFF. When those program routines need to be executed, the CPU jumps to that range of memory addresses to execute whatever function happens to be required at the time.

That same SCSI host adapter offers three other address ranges that it can use in the event some other device in my system already uses the range CA000–CBFFF. By setting a few jumpers, I can control which range of memory is assigned to the ROM BIOS on the adapter.

When you're configuring an adapter, check its manuals to determine if it has a ROM BIOS that must be assigned a memory address in the UMA, then assign an available range of memory to the device.

NOTE *If you're using EMM386 or another memory manager to provide program access in the UMA (such as to load device drivers in the UMA), make sure you exclude the range of memory assigned to the adapter from the memory manager's use. This prevents the memory manager from trying to use the same address range for something else.*

In the previous SCSI host adapter example, you would need to exclude the range CA000–CBFFF from the memory manager's use. Refer to Chapter 4, "All You Need To Know about Memory," if you're confused about what you've just read.

What about RAM Address Assignments?

Some devices require a RAM buffer in which to store data. Ethernet network adapters are a good example. Most use a range of memory in the UMA to store information that moves in and out of the network adapter, going to and from the network. So, the adapter needs a unique range of addresses assigned to its use so that nothing else tries to use the same range of memory and corrupts the network data.

When you're configuring an adapter, check its manuals to see if it uses a RAM buffer. If it does use one, you need to identify a unique, unused range of addresses in the UMA for the RAM buffer. Then, configure the adapter to use the range you've identified.

The adapter probably will have three or four different predefined ranges that you can use. As with other settings, the RAM buffer address usually is set with jumpers or DIP switches. Some devices provide a setup program you can use to set the RAM address for the adapter.

If the adapter uses a RAM buffer, make sure you exclude the RAM buffer's address range from use by your UMA memory manager, if you're using one. If you're using EMM386, for example, use the X switch on the EMM386 command line in CONFIG.SYS to exclude the RAM buffer range from EMM386's use.

Removing and Installing Adapters

As you learned earlier in the chapter, being able to remove and install adapters in a PC is a basic skill you need to know. This section includes general procedures for removing and installing adapters.

Procedure:
Removing Adapters

1. Open the PC using the proper opening procedure as a guide.

2. Touch the metal part of the PC's chassis to discharge any static electricity that has built up in your body. Do this often if you're working on a carpeted floor.

3. Locate the adapters. In a desktop system, the adapters will be installed vertically in the PC starting at the left-rear quarter of the case. In a tower case, they are located toward the bottom-rear of the case (viewed upright).

   The following steps explain how you remove the video adapter to examine it:

4. Follow the cable from the monitor to the computer to locate the video adapter.

5. Disconnect the monitor cable from the video adapter. The cable will have either small thumbscrews or regular screws.

   Your video adapter may include a feature connector, which is an edge connector at the top edge of the card. A feature connector is used on some video adapters to connect it to another device inside the PC, such as to a video capture board. If there is a ribbon cable connected to your PC's video adapter, make a note (mental or otherwise) of the location of the colored stripe on the ribbon cable. Then, gently pull the ribbon cable off the adapter.

6. With a screwdriver or nut driver, remove the screw that secures the video adapter to the PC's chassis.

7. Discharge your static again, then grab the adapter with both hands, trying to keep from touching any chips if at all possible. Pull straight up (or out, for tower systems) to remove the adapter from its socket. You will have to wiggle it some along the axis of the connector to get it out. Don't wiggle it from side-to-side or you may break the board or damage the socket.

8. Set the adapter somewhere safe where you won't sit on it, step on it, or otherwise abuse it.

Procedure:
Installing Adapters

1. Set any jumpers or switch settings required on the adapter (these are explained in more detail in later chapters).

2. Locate a free slot in which to install the adapter (see earlier explanation).

3. If a bracket is installed in the chassis covering the hole for the socket you've selected, remove the screw

holding the bracket in place and remove the bracket (see fig. 6.8). Set it aside someplace you'll remember—you may need it to cover another slot's holes.

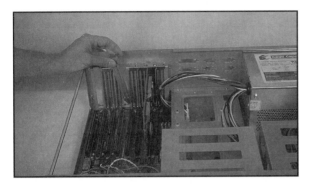

Figure 6.8: A bracket covering the adapter slot at the rear of the PC.

4. Line up the adapter's edge connector with the slot, then slide the adapter firmly into the socket, making sure any connectors that stick out the back of the adapter fit through the hole in the back of the chassis. If you're installing a full-length adapter, read the following note before inserting the adapter.

For full-length adapters only: There are guides for the front end of the adapter mounted near the front of the PC. Make sure you slide the front edge of the adapter into the proper guide (the one that's aligned with the slot in which you're installing the adapter). Figure 6.9 shows some adapter guides.

Figure 6.9: Adapter guides are for full-length adapters only.

5. Check the installation to make sure the adapter is seated securely in its socket, and that you haven't pinched any cables or wires with the adapter.

6. Install a screw in the adapter's bracket to secure it to the PC's chassis.

7. Connect cables to the adapter as required.

7

I/O and Network Adapters

This chapter contains buying and installation tips for I/O adapters and network adapters. It covers the following topics:

- Overview of I/O adapters
- Explanation and procedure for installing new UART chips
- Procedures for installing I/O adapters
- Overview of network adapters
- Procedures for installing network adapters

Finding Out How I/O Adapters Can Help You

I/O adapters (sometimes referred to as multifunction adapters) provide a means for connecting a wide range of devices to the PC. These devices include printers, mice and trackballs, scanners, and modems, just to name a few. I/O adapters generally include COM (serial) ports and LPT (parallel) ports. Most I/O adapters also include at least one game port, to which you can connect a joystick.

Instead of going into detail about parity, stop bits, and all the other technical issues related to I/O adapters, I'm just going to give you a brief overview of COM and LPT ports and explain how you can make your existing I/O adapter perform better.

A Little Bit about COM Ports

A standard PC can contain up to four COM ports, labeled COM1 through COM4. Each port requires an I/O base address and an IRQ line assignment (see Chapter 6, "Setting Up Circuit Boards," for an explanation of these topics). COM ports also are called *serial ports* because data travels through the port one bit at a time, in serial fashion. (For an explanation of bits and bytes, see Chapter 4, "All You Need To Know about Memory.")

The PC does not work with data as a series of bits, however. Instead, it works with *bytes* of data consisting of eight bits. To cram an 8-bit byte through a serial port, the byte must be broken into its individual bits and fed through the serial port one bit at a time. That's where the UART comes in.

UART stands for Universal Asynchronous Receiver Transmitter. The UART is a chip on the I/O adapter that converts parallel bytes coming from the CPU into individual serial bits that can be sent through the COM port. It also converts serial bits (coming in the COM port) back into bytes that can be sent to the CPU. The UART also controls the flow of data in and out of the COM port and the speed at which it occurs. Figure 7.1 shows the UARTs on an I/O adapter.

Many I/O adapters contain 8-bit 8250 UARTs (the number is just a generic part number). Newer adapters contain 16-bit 16450 UARTs instead of the 8250 UARTs. The 16450 provides better performance than the 8250.

Figure 7.1: UART chips on an I/O adapter.

Even better than the 16450 is the 16550 UART. An important addition in the 16550 UART is a 16-byte FIFO (First In First Out) buffer, which the UART can use to buffer data coming and going through the COM port.

This buffering improves overall system performance because the UART can handle more data before it must be serviced by the CPU. The CPU, therefore, can be busy doing something else while the data transfer occurs.

The 16550 is particularly useful in multitasking environments such as Windows, in which you often use the PC for more than one task at a time. The 16550 UARTs also enable much higher data transfer rates than the 8250 and 16450 (important with today's high-speed modems).

NOTE *Your communication software must be written specifically to take advantage of the 16550's FIFO buffer. Most communication programs developed in the last year or so do support the 16550's features.*

If your I/O adapter uses 8250 UARTs, you can't upgrade them without replacing the entire adapter. If your I/O adapter uses 16450 UARTs, however, you can replace them with 16550 UARTs because the two chips are pin-compatible.

The only requirement is that the UART chips be socketed on the adapter rather than permanently soldered onto the board. Later in this chapter you find a procedure that explains how to replace 16450 UARTs with 16550 UARTs.

A Little Bit about LPT Ports

LPT ports get their name from Line PrinTer, indicating that the most common device connected to an LPT port is a printer. LPT ports also are called *parallel* ports because, unlike a serial port, the data travels through a parallel port one byte at a time.

A parallel port includes eight data lines, and each bit of a byte travels through one data line at more or less the same time as the other bits in the byte. A parallel port can transfer data a byte at a time, rather than a bit at a time.

Although the most common use for the PC's LPT port is to connect a printer, you can use other devices to connect to the LPT ports. Special SCSI adapters and network adapters, for example, connect to one of the PC's LPT ports. You use these devices mainly in laptop and notebook PCs.

Configuring an LPT port does not require much effort. LPT ports require only a unique I/O base address and IRQ line assignment.

COM and LPT Ports on an Adapter

Most I/O adapters include two COM ports, a single LPT port, and a game port. Some adapters include other combinations of ports, such as serial-port-only adapters that contain four COM ports and no other ports.

When you need to add another COM or LPT port to your system, you can add another I/O adapter. Sometimes, if you want to add another I/O adapter, you must disable some of the ports on the new adapter so that they don't conflict with the IRQs and I/O base addresses used by other devices in the PC.

You also can disable the ports on an existing adapter in the PC when you're installing a new I/O adapter. You disable the ports, for example, when you're adding a new adapter that includes 16550 UART support which the old adapter doesn't include.

Sometimes, the COM and LPT ports are included on an adapter that performs some other function. Many IDE host adapters include on-board COM and LPT ports. Older video adapters often included an LPT port.

The following procedures cover configuration and installation of I/O-only adapters, but the configuration and installation process for other devices that contain COM and/or LPT ports is much the same.

Installing a New I/O Adapter

The configuration process for an I/O adapter isn't difficult, but it does require a little research. You need to know which I/O base addresses and IRQ lines are available in the PC so that you can assign them to the ports on the adapter.

The first step in installing an I/O adapter is to configure the I/O addresses and IRQ lines it uses. Table 7.1 lists the standard I/O base address and IRQ assignments for serial ports on a PC.

Table 7.1
Standard COM Port I/O Address and IRQ Assignment

COM Port	I/O Base Address	IRQ
COM1	03F8	4
COM2	02F8	3
COM3	03E8	4
COM4	02E8	3

Although you can assign different I/O base addresses and IRQs to your COM ports, most software uses the values shown in table 7.1. Use these default settings to make software setup and use easier.

Procedure:
Setting Addresses and IRQs

1. Based on the ports already installed in the PC and which ports you want to use on the new adapter, decide how you want to use your ports. You have an

existing device that contains two COM ports, for example, and you're adding a new adapter to provide a total of four COM ports.

Each one must have a unique COM port designation. You might want to switch the existing ports from COM1 and COM2 to COM3 and COM4, and assign the COM ports on the new adapter as COM1 and COM2. You also might want to reconfigure your LPT ports, so check them too.

2. After you decide how to configure the ports, check your system logs, manuals, and MSD to determine which IRQ lines are available in the system. If not enough IRQ lines are available, you must disable one of the devices that's using an IRQ line. This device can be a port on an existing device in the system, or it can be one of the ports on the new adapter.

3. If necessary, disable the port with the conflicting IRQ on the device. If you're disabling a port on an existing adapter, you first need to remove the adapter. Then consult the device's manual to determine how to disable it (if you're just taking it out and leaving it out, don't bother hunting for the manuals).

If you're disabling a port on the new adapter, consult the adapter's manual to determine how to disable the port. Usually, you disable the port by changing a few jumpers on the adapter.

4. Configure the port assignments of all the ports that you want to install in the system, including configuring the ports on the new adapter and reconfiguring (if necessary) the ports on an existing adapter, if there is one.

Remember to assign unique port IDs to each port (you can have only one COM2, for example). Usually, you configure ports by setting jumpers on the adapter. Check the adapter's manual to determine how to configure the ports.

5. Configure the I/O base addresses for the ports on the new adapter. You configure base addresses by setting jumpers on the adapter.

6. Check your settings to make sure you don't have any conflicting port IDs, I/O addresses, or IRQs.

Procedure:
Installing the I/O Adapter

1. After you configure the adapter, choose a slot in which to install it. Virtually all stand-alone I/O adapters are 8-bit cards. Other devices that contain I/O ports, such as IDE host adapters, often are 16-bit cards. Install an 8-bit board in an 8-bit or 16-bit slot. Install a 16-bit card in a 16-bit slot.

2. Connect all cables to the adapter as necessary. Consult the adapter's manual to determine where each cable should connect. Remember to verify the orientation of pin 1 on each cable when you install it.

3. Many I/O adapters include cables with port connectors on the end that support the adapter's second COM port or game port. If you're going to use this second port, install the connector in an appropriate slot in the back of the PC (you can tell where it should go because the hole in the back of the PC matches the connector on the cable).

4. Remove the bracket cover for the selected slot; then install the adapter in its slot and secure it with a screw.

Procedure:
Testing

Explanation: I/O adapters seldom include testing and diagnostic software. Either the port works, or it doesn't. To test your new ports, connect a device to each port and verify that the device works. For COM ports, connect a mouse, modem, or other serial device to the port and then verify that the device works properly. For LPT ports, connect a printer to the port and print a small document to test the port.

Upgrading an Existing I/O Adapter

If you use your PC for high-speed data communications, you might want to upgrade the UARTs on your I/O adapter from 16450 UARTs to 16550 UARTs. This change assumes that a) your existing adapter currently uses 16450 UARTs, and b) the existing UARTs are socketed on the adapter. You can't upgrade 8250 UARTs to 16550 UARTs, and you can't replace a 16450 unless it is socketed for removal.

16550 UARTs are relatively inexpensive, costing about $12 per chip. The upgrade process is easy, requiring only a few minutes to remove the 16450 chips and install the 16550 chips.

Procedure:

Replacing the UART

1. Because you're handling chips, use extra care and discharge your static often.

2. Turn off, unplug, and open the PC.

3. Remove the adapter that contains the 16450 UART chips.

4. Use a small, flat-bladed screwdriver to carefully remove the 16450 chips from their sockets (see fig. 7.2).

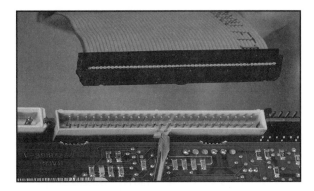

Figure 7.2: Remove the UART carefully by prying up each end with a screwdriver.

5. Discharge your static again. Then, while avoiding touching the pins on the 16550, carefully insert one row of pins into its socket (see fig. 7.3). Rotate the chip down to insert its other row of pins in their sockets. After you verify that the pins are lined up properly, press the chip into place with your thumb.

Figure 7.3: Insert one row of pins and then rotate the chip down to insert the other row of pins.

6. After you install the new 16550 UARTs, reinstall the adapter in the PC.

7. **Windows users:** You need to inform Windows that your COM ports include 16550 UARTs. Edit SYSTEM.INI and, for each COM port that uses a 16550 UART, add an entry in the [386Enh] section similar to the following examples:

```
COM1FIFO=On
COM1Buffer=0
COM2FIFO=On
COM2Buffer=0
```

Replace the number in the COM*x*FIFO and COM*x*Buffer settings with the number of the port that uses a 16550. The COM*x*FIFO setting enables 16550 support for Windows applications, and the COM*x*Buffer setting disables the Windows port buffering in favor of the 16550's internal buffer. If you later remove FIFO support for one of the COM ports, eliminate the COM*x*Buffer setting for the corresponding port to restore its standard communications buffer.

NOTE

Although most Windows INI Boolean settings can use the On, True, or 1 values, a bug exists in the COMxFIFO settings in Windows. You must use On as the value when you want to enable the setting. If you use the value True, the FIFO buffer will not be enabled.

Windows does not provide 16550 UART support to DOS programs that you run under Windows. If you want to take advantage of the 16550s in a DOS program, run the program from the DOS prompt outside of Windows.

You also can use a third-party COM port driver such as TurboCom (Bio-Engineering Research Labs) to provide 16550 support for your DOS programs under Windows.

Installing Network Adapters

Network adapters enable your PC to connect to a network of other computers. If you're installing a network adapter in your PC, you're at least familiar with networking and know how to go about installing your network software, and probably just want some pointers on installing the network adapter.

If you are installing an adapter for a Windows for Workgroups network, I recommend you get a copy of *Inside Windows for Workgroups*, from New Riders Publishing, which covers network topology, terms, and all the features of Windows for Workgroups.

Network adapters are perhaps the most fickle of all adapters because they generally require an I/O base address, IRQ line, RAM buffer, and, sometimes, ROM buffer area. You should not find configuring and installing a network adapter difficult, but you need patience to get all the settings right on the adapter and in your system files.

Some network adapters don't require any hardware configuration, but instead provide a setup program that you can use to define the adapter's settings from software. These adapters are *software-configured*. Adapters that require setting jumpers or DIP switches are *hardware-configured*. Figure 7.4 shows the configuration jumpers on a typical network adapter.

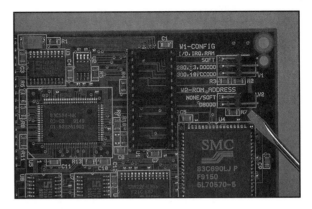

Figure 7.4: Configuration jumpers on a typical network adapter.

Procedure:

Network Adapter Configuration, Hardware-Configured

1. Check the adapter's manual to determine the location on the adapter of the jumpers and/or DIP switches that configure the I/O base address, RAM buffer, use of a boot ROM, boot ROM address, and IRQ.

2. Check your system logs to determine a free I/O base address for the adapter. Choose an I/O base address that no other device in the system uses (the network adapter probably offers only a small selection of addresses from which you can choose).

3. Configure the adapter's I/O base address.

4. Check your system logs to determine a free RAM buffer address for the adapter. Choose an address range in the UMA that no other device or program uses. Check the adapter's manual to determine how large an address range the adapter requires (8K, 16K, and so on).

5. Configure the adapter's RAM base address.

6. Check your system logs (or use MSD) to determine a free IRQ line. Choose an IRQ that no other device in the system uses. If you can't identify a free IRQ, try IRQ2. You might be able to use the IRQ assigned to LPT1 even if you have an LPT1 port in the system because many programs don't use interrupts to communicate with the printer. If possible, though, use a free IRQ.

7. Configure the adapter's IRQ.

8. Determine if you need to use a boot ROM on the adapter. Unless you're booting from a diskless workstation (a PC that doesn't have a disk from which you can boot DOS), you probably don't need to use a boot ROM. The boot ROM enables the workstation to boot DOS from a remote network drive. If your network adapter doesn't require a boot ROM, skip to "Procedure: Installing the Adapter."

9. If your network adapter requires a boot ROM, install the boot ROM, taking care to orient the chip correctly in its socket on the network adapter. Check for the notch on top of the chip and align it in the end of the socket with a corresponding mark, either on the socket or on the board.

10. Determine how large a memory address range the boot ROM requires in the UMA. Then use your system logs to determine an available address range. Configure the adapter to use the desired range. Most adapters enable you to select from only two or three possible address ranges for the boot ROM.

    If another device in the system uses the range you need to assign to the boot ROM, you must reconfigure the other device to use a different UMA address range, making a range available for the network adapter's boot ROM.

Procedure:
Installing the Adapter

1. After you configure the adapter's I/O base address, RAM buffer address range, IRQ, and ROM BIOS address range, choose a bus slot for the adapter. You can install 8-bit adapters in 8-bit or 16-bit bus slots. You must install 16-bit adapters in 16-bit bus slots.

2. Install the adapter in its slot and secure it with a screw.

Procedure:
Installing Cables and Terminators

Explanation: The ways in which you connect the cables to your network adapter vary according to the network topology you're using. Consult the network adapter's manual or your network operating system manual to determine how to connect the cables to your network adapter.

If you're using Thin-Ethernet to connect your workstations together, you must install a terminator at each end of the bus (the first and last workstations on the network). Figure 7.5 shows terminator installation on a network adapter.

Figure 7.5: Installing a terminator on a Thin-Ethernet cable.

If you're using a Thin-Ethernet drop cable to connect to a multiport repeater (which connects to the standard Ethernet backbone cable), you must install a terminator on each workstation at the end of each drop cable. Here's the rule: Each T-connector must have a cable connected to either side, or it must have a terminator on one side and a cable on the other.

Procedure:
Network Adapter Configuration, Software-Configured

1. Verify that you do not need to set any jumper or DIP switch settings on the adapter (check the adapter's manual).

2. Install the adapter in the system.

3. Check your system logs and use MSD (if necessary) to determine a free I/O base address, IRQ line, RAM buffer address range, and ROM BIOS address range (if required) for the adapter. Refer to the section "Procedure: Network Adapter Configuration, Hardware-Configured" if you need more information on checking these items.

4. Run the software setup program that comes with the adapter and configure the settings described in step 3.

Procedure:
Configuring System Software

Explanation: You must configure your UMA memory manager to exclude the range of addresses used by the network adapter to prevent memory conflict with other devices. If you don't exclude the memory, your network adapter does not work properly.

1. Edit CONFIG.SYS using Notepad, Edit, or SysEdit.

2. **EMM386 users:** Locate the EMM386.EXE command line in CONFIG.SYS and add X switches for the appropriate address ranges for your network adapter. The following example excludes the range D800–DBFF for the adapter's ROM and E000–E3FF for the adapter's RAM buffer:

```
DEVICE=C:\DOS\EMM386.EXE X=D800-DBFF
X=E000-E3FF
```

If the memory ranges form a back-to-back range (contiguous range of memory), you can use a single X switch to exclude the entire range.

3. **Third-party memory managers:** Edit your CONFIG.SYS file to add the necessary exclu-sion switches to your memory manager's command line.

4. Save your changes to CONFIG.SYS and then reboot the system.

Procedure:
Testing

Explanation: Network adapters generally include testing software that you can use to test the card. The SMC family of Ethernet adapters, for example, includes software that tests the adapter's I/O port access, LAN address ROM, on-board RAM, RAM buffer area, and other components. You also can use the testing software to generate and receive test messages across the network to test cabling and the capability of the network card to handle network traffic.

Check your network adapter manual to determine what type of testing software is included with your network adapter. Then perform whatever range of diagnostic tests are supported by the testing software for the adapter. If possible, also use the testing software to generate test messages to verify that the network adapter is sending and receiving network packets properly.

Troubleshooting Network Problems

If you're experiencing problems with your newly installed network adapter, you should check a handful of items to troubleshoot the problem. If the diagnostic program locates a problem, it identifies the problem, at least giving you an idea of where to begin looking for a solution. If you forget to exclude the RAM buffer range from use by your memory manager, for example, the diagnostic program probably will fail during the RAM buffer test. If you can't determine the exact cause of the problem, check the following areas:

- **Cabling.** Verify that the cabling is connected properly according to the network topology you're using. If your topology requires terminators, make sure you have installed the terminators in the correct location.

- **Network adapter configuration.** Verify that you have assigned a unique I/O base address, IRQ, RAM buffer, and ROM address range to the adapter. If you assign conflicting settings, the adapter does not work properly.

8

Video Adapters and Monitors

Generally, installing a new video adapter doesn't involve much work, and connecting a new monitor to your PC doesn't take much effort. You should have little trouble with either task. This short chapter covers the following topics:

- Issues to consider when you buy a video adapter
- Video resolution
- Issues to consider when you buy a monitor
- Procedures for configuring a video adapter
- Procedures for adding RAM to a video adapter
- Windows video tips

This chapter first looks at some issues to consider when you're shopping for new video adapters.

Understanding Video Adapters

The *video adapter* is the PC device that actually generates the image you see on the monitor. The video adapter converts the data coming from the CPU into something the monitor can display. The three most important issues related to video adapters are resolution, color, and speed. To understand resolution, you need to understand how an image is displayed on the monitor.

An image on the monitor consists of numerous small dots called *pixels*, which stands for "picture elements." (Actually, pixels are more like short horizontal lines, but dots are a good analogy.) Think of the image as a sand painting—each grain of sand that makes up the painting represents a pixel of a certain color.

Because your monitor is a fixed size, only a fixed amount of space in which to paint the sand painting is available. If your grains of sand are large, the image looks blocky. If the grains are small, the image is more refined.

The smaller the grains, the more grains that can fit in the same amount of space, thus improving the image quality. That's what image resolution is all about—the more pixels, the higher the resolution and the better the image quality.

Higher resolution also means you can display more information on the screen. In Windows, for example, you can display more cells of a spreadsheet, more of a word processing document, or simply more program windows on-screen. Figures 8.1 and 8.2 illustrate the same spreadsheet using two different video resolutions.

Standard Resolutions

The PC industry supports a number of standard video resolutions, each described by the number of horizontal and vertical pixels that make up the display. The following list defines today's most popular video resolutions and includes some recommendations for each:

- **720×350.** This resolution is offered by a Monochrome Graphics Adapter (MGA). MGA adapters are inexpensive and offer a good solution if you don't need color.

- **640×480.** This standard VGA resolution is the minimum I recommend for either DOS or Windows. VGA resolution is acceptable on 14-inch and 15-inch screens.

- **800×600.** An 800×600 resolution is great for Windows because you can display much more data on-screen at one time than you can with a VGA adapter. This resolution works well on all monitor sizes.

- **1024×768.** This resolution is great if you work with drawing programs or want to cram as much data onto the screen at one time as possible. At this resolution, you might find text hard to read on a 14-inch monitor. You should use a 15-inch or larger monitor for this resolution.

- **1280×1024.** This resolution is great for image-processing applications (working with photos, for example), drawing applications, and other applications that require a fine image quality. You should use a 17-inch or larger monitor for this resolution.

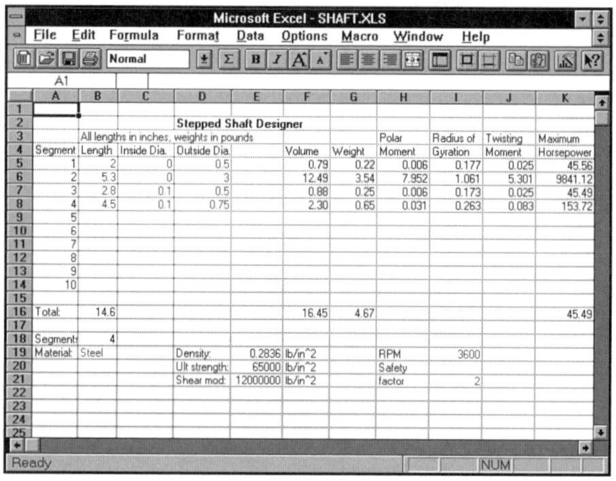

Figure 8.1: An Excel spreadsheet at 640×480 resolution.

Adapters that provide even higher resolutions than those described in the preceding list also are available. These adapters are for special-purpose applications and often are too expensive for the average user (and not particularly useful, either).

Most video adapters support a number of different display modes. An adapter that can display in 1280×1024 also can display using the lower resolution modes described in the list.

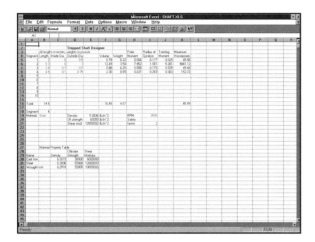

Figure 8.2: The same spreadsheet at 1024×768 resolution.

When you're evaluating a new video adapter, determine whether the adapter uses interlaced display mode or noninterlaced display mode. In *interlaced* mode, the adapter paints every other scan line of the image in the first pass and then paints the other scan lines "in between." A *noninterlaced* adapter paints all scan lines in one pass. A noninterlaced display generates less image flicker and is better for extended use of the PC.

NOTE *Noninterlaced adapters are more expensive than interlaced adapters. Also, some adapters generate a noninterlaced display in some modes but generate an interlaced display in other modes.*

About Color

The number of colors that a video adapter can display also is an important point to consider when you're buying a new adapter. I don't recommend monochrome displays because color enables you to better organize your data. I recommend a 16-color display as a minimum. Also available are adapters that can display 256 colors, 32,000 colors, or even more. The more colors the adapter can display, the better the image quality for images that make extensive use

of color. Usually, these images include digitized photos and computer-generated art or photorealistic images (photo-like images generated by the computer).

If you work only with spreadsheets and word processing documents, you don't need the capability to display a million colors, so pick an adapter that suits the type of work you do (typically, a 16-color or 256-color adapter). Keep in mind that as with resolution, the adapter can use different color modes. An adapter that can display 32,000 colors also offers modes for 256-color and 16-color display.

If you increase the number of colors the adapter can display, you need more memory on the adapter. To display 256 colors, for example, the adapter generally requires at least 512K of video RAM. Increasing the resolution also increases the video RAM requirement.

To display 256 colors at a resolution of 1024×768, the adapter generally requires at least 1M of video RAM. Most adapters sold today provide at least 1M of RAM on the adapter. You should check the standard amount of RAM supplied on the adapter and whether you can add more RAM to increase the capabilities of the adapter.

Getting the Scoop about Monitors

A video adapter basically is useless without a monitor, so it's a sure bet that your PC includes a monitor. If you're shopping for a new monitor, keep the following points in mind:

- **Scan rate/refresh rate.** The monitor must match the capabilities of the video adapter. You can match the scan rate and refresh rates of the monitor to the video adapter, but you might find matching the display resolution easier. Make sure that the monitor you're buying supports the maximum video resolution you use on the video adapter and does so in noninterlaced mode. If you can't afford a noninterlaced display, make sure that the monitor matches the capabilities of the video adapter you use. Ask the salesperson if you're not sure.

- **Interlaced/noninterlaced.** Monitors that support the higher resolution modes using noninterlaced display are more expensive, but a noninterlaced display generates less image flicker and helps keep eyestrain to a minimum with extended use of the PC.

● **Dot pitch.** The smaller the value for the monitor's dot pitch, the better. Look for a monitor with a dot pitch of .28mm or less.

● **Screen.** Look for a monitor with as flat a screen as possible. An antiglare coating on the screen also is a benefit.

WARNING   Monitors generate EMF (electromagnetic frequency) emissions. Extended exposure to EMF emissions might cause cancer and other health side effects. Look for a monitor that meets the Swedish MPR-II specification for reduced emissions, or purchase a filter screen that reduces EMF emissions from the monitor.

Figure 8.3: Installing video DRAM on a video adapter.

Installing a Video Adapter

Video adapters generally require little or no configuration before installation, although a few adapters sometimes require that you set switches on the adapter to control a few options. You also might need to configure one or more switches or jumpers on your system's motherboard. The following procedures explain these tasks.

Procedure:
Installing RAM On Your Video Adapter

1. If your video adapter doesn't have the full amount of RAM possible, and you want to add additional RAM to it, first check the adapter's manual to determine the type of RAM required (usually DRAMs or SIMs).

2. Locate the RAM sockets on the video adapter.

3. **DRAM:** Orient the chip correctly with its socket. Line up the pins on one edge of the DRAM with the socket (see fig. 8.4). Rotate the DRAM down and insert the other row of pins into the socket. After you verify that all pins are aligned properly with the socket, press the chip firmly into place. Repeat this procedure for the other DRAMs.

4. **SIMs:** Determine the correct orientation of the SIM to the socket (check the adapter's manual). Slip the edge connector of the SIM into the socket; then carefully rotate the SIM in the socket until the tabs on each end of the socket snap into place to hold the SIM.

Procedure:
Configuring the Adapter and Motherboard

1. After you install RAM on the adapter (if required), check the adapter's manual to determine whether you need to set any switches or jumpers on the adapter to suit your installation. Set the jumpers or DIP switches as necessary. Check the following section of this chapter for tips on specific video adapters.

2. Check the system manual for your system's motherboard. Determine whether a DIP switch or jumper setting specifies either monochrome or color display. Set the switch or jumper accordingly (many newer motherboards don't have this setting).

Procedure:

Installing the Adapter

1. Choose an appropriate bus slot. You should install 16-bit video adapters in 16-bit bus slots. Some 16-bit adapters function in 8-bit slots, but with a loss of performance. You should install 8-bit video adapters in 8-bit slots, but you can install them in 16-bit slots if no 8-bit slot is available.

2. Install the adapter in the selected slot. Make sure you align the edge connector properly in the slot before you press the adapter into place. With full-length adapters, make sure the adapter is aligned in the correct guide at the front of the PC.

3. Secure the adapter with a screw.

Procedure:

Connecting the Adapter

Explanation: Most video adapters require only that you connect a standard video cable between the adapter and the monitor. Some adapters, however, require special cables. These cables connect the video adapter to other devices in the system by way of the adapter's feature connector.

1. Check the adapter's manual to determine whether the adapter requires special cable connections. If it doesn't require special connections, attach the video cable supplied with the monitor to the rear of the adapter. Secure it in place with the screws provided with the cable. Attach the other end of the cable to the monitor.

2. Some video adapter installations require pass-through cabling. A pass-through cable connects the video adapter to another adapter in the system, and a cable then connects from the secondary adapter to the monitor. These connections usually are required only with video capture boards and other special-purpose video adapters.

Procedure:

Configuring Memory Usage

Explanation: Video adapters require the use of some of the memory in the UMA. If your video adapter uses more memory than a standard EGA or VGA adapter, you should make sure that all the memory that is used by the video adapter is excluded from use by other applications.

1. Check your video adapter's manual to determine the range of memory the adapter uses in the UMA.

2. **EMM386 users:** Edit CONFIG.SYS to make sure that the EMM386.EXE command line includes an X switch to exclude the range of memory used by the video adapter. Refer to Chapter 4, "All You Need To Know about Memory," if you're not sure how to add the proper X switch to the EMM386 command line.

3. **Third-party memory managers:** If you're using a UMA memory manager other than EMM386, check your memory manager's manual to determine how to exclude the video adapter's memory range from the memory manager's use.

4. Save your changes to CONFIG.SYS and reboot the system.

Procedure:

Installing Drivers

Explanation: Video adapters don't require any special device drivers for general operation in the DOS environment. Many adapters do, however, require special drivers for applications, including Windows. The adapter generally comes with one or more disks that contain drivers to support the adapter with various applications.

The software disks provided with some adapters include an installation program that installs the drivers for you automatically. Others require that you use the application's setup or configuration program to install the driver.

1. Check the video adapter's manual and disks to determine which drivers are supplied with the adapter.

2. Decide which applications require the use of a special driver that is included with the adapter (for example, AutoCAD and other CAD programs, and Windows).

3. **Installation program:** If your video adapter software includes an automated installation program, run it to install the drivers for your applications. It may install only some of the drivers, leaving you to install the rest manually.

4. **Application installation:** Install drivers for any applications for which the installation program did not install the drivers. This procedure varies from application to application. Check your programs' manuals to determine how to install the driver. If you don't need to configure Windows for your adapter, this is the last step in the procedure.

5. **Windows:** To install a new driver for Windows, run the Setup program. You can run Setup from DOS by changing to the Windows directory and typing **SETUP**, or you can run Setup in Windows by double-clicking on the Setup icon in the Main program group. The following steps describe Windows-based Setup.

The following steps describe how to install a third-party video driver for Windows. Your video adapter may be compatible with the SuperVGA or other standard drivers supplied with Windows. Third-party drivers generally provide more options for resolution or color support but sometimes do not support all the features included with the standard Windows drivers, such as the use of the mouse in a windowed DOS program.

6. Select the Setup icon from the Main program group.

7. From the **O**ptions menu in the Windows Setup dialog box, select **C**hange System Settings.

8. Click on the **D**isplay drop-down list and then scroll to the bottom of the list to locate the option labeled "Other display (requires disk from OEM)." Select that option.

9. Setup prompts you to insert a disk. Insert the disk supplied with the video adapter that contains the Windows device drivers. Check your video adapter's manual if you're not sure which disk to use. After you insert the disk, click on OK.

10. If Setup displays a list of different video options from which to choose, select the options you want. Then follow the dialog box's directions to install the driver. Setup also might prompt you to insert some of your Windows distribution disks in order to copy font files for the display.

11. Setup prompts you to either continue working with the current setup or restart Windows. You must restart Windows for the new driver to be used.

Testing

The only way to test the video adapter is to start the PC and run your applications. If you turn on the PC and get only a black display, the most likely problem is either that the monitor is turned off, or you have a loose connection between the adapter and the monitor. Check the monitor and the connections first.

If you start Windows and see multiple images on the display, your monitor and adapter aren't using the same video modes. You might be able to set an option (a switch, for example) on the monitor to make it match the video adapter modes. Check the monitor manual and video adapter manual for instructions on how to set options.

The alternative is to switch to a video mode that is supported by both the video adapter and the monitor. Some monitors don't support 800×600 mode with some adapters, for example, but they do support 1024×768 with the same adapter.

If a problem persists in Windows, try running Setup and select either the VGA or Super VGA drivers. If neither of these options works with your video adapter and monitor combination, contact technical support for the video adapter.

Installing a New Monitor

Installing a new monitor is usually just a matter of unpacking the monitor, connecting the power cord, and connecting the video cable between the video adapter and the monitor. Instead of giving you a procedure for installing the monitor, this chapter just gives you some pointers to keep in mind when connecting it.

- **Compatibility.** The monitor must match the video mode that your video adapter uses. If you experience problems, the monitor might be unable to match the video mode being used by the video adapter. Check the manual for the monitor to see whether you can set its switches to make it match the adapter's video mode.

- **Cables.** If you have a tower system and the video cable isn't long enough to reach from the PC to the monitor, you can get a monitor extension cable to double the effective length of the video cable. Also think about getting a monitor power cord that plugs into the back of the PC instead of the wall outlet. A monitor power cord enables you to turn on the monitor automatically when you turn on the PC.

- **EMF filters.** If you're installing an EMF filter on your display, it probably includes a ground cable that plugs into a wall outlet. Make sure you plug it in to ground the filter.

Windows Video Tips

You can use a handful of tips to improve the video performance of Windows and make Windows more usable. The following sections explain these video-related Windows tips.

Optimum Speed and Performance

Because it is a graphical operating environment, Windows relies heavily on the capability of your PC's video adapter. Aside from disk access speed, video speed is one of the most important factors in determining how well a system performs under Windows.

Following is a list of tasks you can do to improve your system's video performance in Windows and troubleshoot video problems in Windows:

- **Use 16-color mode.** The 16-color display mode is generally faster than the 256-color mode (or higher). Use 16-color display mode if you don't use applications that make use of 256-color (or better) capability.

- **Eliminate wallpaper.** Windows wallpaper is a novelty and doesn't add any productivity to your PC or to Windows. Wallpaper takes up valuable memory that your applications can use to better advantage. Unless you've fallen in love with your wallpaper, I suggest that you eliminate it.

- **Use a different resolution.** If you're using a relatively high video resolution and can get by adequately with a lower resolution, switch to the lower resolution. You therefore speed up your PC's video performance under Windows.

- **Troubleshoot.** If strange messages appear on-screen when you try to run Windows, you might have a memory conflict between your video adapter and Windows (or another program). To troubleshoot the problem, try starting Windows by using the WIN /D:X switch. The /D:X switch prevents Windows from using any of the memory in the UMA. If this switch clears up the problem, make sure you exclude *all* the video adapter's memory from use by Windows.

Changing Icon Font

When you're using a high-resolution display on a smaller monitor (14 inch or 15 inch, for example), you might find it difficult to read the descriptions under icons. You can change the font and appearance of the text that Windows uses for icon descriptions by adding a few settings to the WIN.INI file. Following are the settings you can use:

- **IconTitleFaceName.** This setting specifies the name of the font Windows uses for icon text.

- **IconTitleStyle.** This setting specifies whether the font is displayed normal or bold.

- **IconTitleSize.** This setting specifies the size of the font used for icon text.

- **IconTitleWrap.** This setting specifies whether icon descriptions are contained on one line or word-wrap to a total of three lines. Set this setting to 1 to make the titles wrap.

To change the way icon text appears, open Notepad or SysEdit and edit the WIN.INI file. Look for the [Desktop] section and add the settings you like. The following example specifies a 12-point Times New Roman font in bold as the icon text:

```
[Desktop]
IconTitleFaceName=Times New Roman
IconTitleSize=12
IconTitleStyle=1
```

For the change to take effect, you must save the changes to WIN.INI and then restart Windows.

Changing the System Font

In the [boot] section of SYSTEM.INI are three settings that control the font files that Windows uses for various components of the Windows display. The fonts.fon setting specifies the Windows system font. The system font is used for title bar text, menu bar text, and other standard Windows components. If you're using a video resolution that makes it difficult to read the menus in your applications, you can use a larger font.

The system font must be a proportional system font. These files contain SYS in the file name. Examples are VGASYS.FON, 8514SYS.FONT, and so on. If your system is using VGASYS.FON, for example, you can specify the 8514SYS.FON instead and make menu text larger and easier to read. Or you may want to make the text smaller by using a smaller font.

Procedure:

Changing the System Font

1. Decide which font file you want to use. For a listing of fonts, check the Windows distribution disks for any font files containing the string "SYS" and the file extension FO_ or FN_.

2. At the DOS prompt, use the EXPAND command to expand the font file from the Windows disks to the Windows System directory. The following example expands the file 8514SYS.FO_ from the disk in drive A and copies it to the Windows System directory:

```
EXPAND  -R  A:8514FON.FO_  C:\WINDOWS\SYSTEM
```

The -R switch directs EXPAND to rename the file automatically according to its original file name. In the preceding example, EXPAND creates a file called 8514SYS.FON in the Windows System directory.

3. After you expand the font file from the distribution disk to the Windows System directory, edit SYSTEM.INI using Notepad or SysEdit. Look for the fonts.fon= setting in the [boot] section. After the equals sign, specify the name of the font file you want to use. Following is an example using the 8514FON.FON file:

```
fonts.fon=8514SYS.FON
```

4. Save the changes to SYSTEM.INI and restart Windows for the change to take effect.

If you want to change the font used by Notepad, use a different font file for the fixedfon.fon= setting. To change the font used by DOS programs that run in a window, change the oemfonts.fon font setting. Use the same guidelines outlined in the preceding procedure.

9

Mouse-Like Creatures

Primarily because of the phenomenal success of Microsoft Windows, mice and other input devices have grown from being little more than novelty devices to absolute necessities with today's PCs. With that growth has come diversity; you now can buy input devices in many different shapes and styles.

This chapter explains the types of input devices that are available, and offers some tips on buying mice, trackballs, and other input gadgets. The chapter covers the following topics:

- Types of input devices
- Tips for buying a new input gadget
- Procedures for installing a bus-based input device
- Procedures for installing a serial-based input device
- Windows mouse tips

Using Mice, Trackballs, and Other Gadgets

Not too many years ago, the two-button mouse was the only common input device for PCs other than the keyboard. Today, many more options are available, each with its own advantages. The tried-and-true solution, however, is still the mouse.

A Little Background Information

For a long time, the two-button mouse was nearly the only input device you were able to buy for the PC. Then came three-button mice (see fig. 9.1), adding a third button and, at the same time, retaining the same basic method of operation—you push the mouse around on your desktop, and the screen pointer moves on-screen.

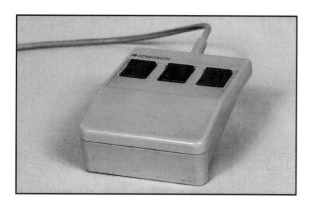

Figure 9.1: A typical three-button mouse.

Unfortunately, most applications (including Windows) make regular use of only one mouse button. Some applications make use of a second button, but no functional standardization exists from one program to the next. And few applications make use of the third mouse button.

Even though applications generally don't use all the mouse buttons, you can use a utility program to make better use of those buttons with your mouse, trackball, or other input devices. One such utility that I use all the time is Whiskers,

from genSoft Development Corporation. Whiskers enables you to create macros, program launchers, and other helpful shortcut tools and assign them to various combinations of mouse buttons and keyboard keys.

Figure 9.2 shows the Whiskers dialog box in which you can program the mouse buttons.

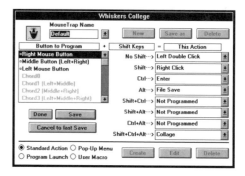

Figure 9.2: You can use Whiskers to assign macros and other shortcuts to your mouse buttons.

Regardless of how many buttons the mouse provides, all mice use much the same technology. As you move the mouse across the desktop, a ball mounted inside the mouse moves. In mechanical and opto-mechanical mice, the ball translates the mouse movement into electrical signals through brushes and contacts or through light-sensitive semiconductors.

Optical mice don't use a ball. Instead, LEDs (light emitting diodes) and light-sensitive transistors detect the mouse's movement over a special mouse pad imprinted with a grid. Although optical mice contain no moving parts and are very accurate, they have the disadvantages of being more expensive and require a dedicated mouse pad.

Trackballs essentially are mice turned upside down. Instead of having a ball mounted inside the mouse that sticks out the bottom of the device, a trackball's ball is mounted on top of the device. Instead of moving the ball indirectly by running the mouse across the desk, you move the trackball's ball with your thumb or finger. Figure 9.3 shows a typical clip-on trackball for a notebook computer. Figure 9.4 shows a desktop trackball.

The main advantage of a trackball over a mouse is that the trackball doesn't require a great deal of desktop space. You can use a trackball in situations where a mouse is nearly impossible to use (such as on an airplane).

Figure 9.3: A clip-on trackball for a notebook computer.

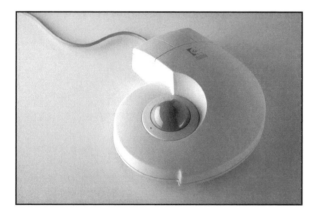

Figure 9.4: A desktop trackball.

Functionally, mice and trackballs are the same, but each has disadvantages where comfort is concerned. Extended use of a mouse can cause a sore wrist, if you have a habit of resting your wrist on the desk while you use the mouse. You can use a wrist pad to help eliminate the problem.

Extended use of a trackball can lead to "trackball thumb," which is pain in the joint that connects your thumb to your hand. Keep your thumb as straight as possible and relaxed while you use the trackball to eliminate this problem.

Here are some points to keep in mind when you're shopping for a mouse or trackball:

- **Resolution.** Check the resolution of the device. Most devices offer anywhere from 200 dpi (dots per inch) to 400 dpi resolution. Higher-resolution devices provide more exact positioning of the pointer but are more expensive. If you work with graphics programs or other programs where exact positioning of the mouse is important, choose a device with a high resolution. Otherwise, a low-resolution device works well.

- **Type.** Unless you need the extra accuracy provided by an optical mouse, an opto-mechanical mouse is a better choice.

- **Drivers.** Make sure the device is supported by the programs you use, including Windows. The mouse might include drivers for programs such as Windows, AutoCAD, and possibly a few others. Instead of providing drivers, many devices are compatible with the Microsoft Mouse and rely on the standard drivers provided by most applications.

- **Buttons.** My input device of choice is a three-button mouse because I use Whiskers to program the buttons. If you want to use a utility like Whiskers, either with a mouse or trackball, get a three-button device. If you just want point-and-click capability without a utility like Whiskers, get a two-button device (or ignore the extra button).

- **Connector.** Make sure the device you buy has the right type of connector for your system, or includes an adapter that enables you to connect it to your system. If you're buying a bus-based device, you don't have to worry about the connector; the device connects to its own bus adapter and has the necessary connector. Many PS/2-style devices (which have a round connector) include an adapter cable that enables you to connect the device to a serial port.

- **Alternatives.** You have a couple of alternatives to mice and trackballs. If you do a great deal of graphics work, either with CAD (computer-aided design) or with paint programs, you might want to consider getting a digitizer (explained in the following section).

Other Input Gadgets

You have a couple of alternatives to the more traditional mice and trackballs. These alternatives include digitizing tablets and touch screens. Digitizers offer much better resolution and more exact positioning than mice and trackballs.

Unlike a mouse or trackball that works by relative positioning of the pointer, digitizing tablets work by absolute positioning of a stylus or puck (much like a mouse) on top of the tablet. As you move the stylus or puck, the exact position of the stylus or puck over a grid of wires in the tablet is recorded.

If you're using graphics programs, a digitizing tablet might be a good option for you to consider. Besides providing higher resolution, a digitizer offers better control of the pointer. You might find drawing with a mouse or trackball almost impossible, but drawing is easy with a digitizer. Pressure-sensitive digitizers are great for paint programs that support them. By varying the pressure of the stylus on the tablet, you can mimic traditional painting methods.

Here are some points to keep in mind when you're looking for a digitizer or touch screen:

- **Price.** Touch screens and digitizers are more expensive (sometimes much more so) than mice and trackballs. If you have the need for a digitizer, the added functionality is worth the extra cost.

- **Connections.** Most touch screens and digitizers connect to one of your PC's serial ports, although a few are bus devices and include their own adapters.

- **Drivers.** Make sure the device you buy includes drivers for the programs with which you plan to use it. As with mice and trackballs, many digitizers are compatible with popular tablets from Hitachi, Hewlett-Packard, and other vendors, and are supported directly by many programs.

- **WinTab Support.** If you plan to use your digitizer with Windows, make sure it includes a Windows driver and can be used as the primary Windows pointing device. Optionally, you might have to use both a mouse and a tablet.

Procedure:

Adding a Bus-Based Mouse or Trackball

Explanation: Installing a bus-based mouse, trackball, or other input device is fairly simple. The procedure includes configuring the bus adapter, installing the adapter, connecting the mouse, and installing software.

1. Using the device's manual as a guide, configure the bus adapter and set the bus adapter to use an available IRQ. Check your system logs and MSD to determine a free IRQ. If necessary, reconfigure other devices to make an IRQ available for the bus adapter.

2. Locate a free bus slot in the PC.

3. Install the bus adapter in the PC and secure the adapter with a screw.

4. Connect the mouse to the bus adapter.

5. Follow the instructions provided in the device's manual to install any necessary device drivers for the device to support your programs.

Procedure:

Adding a Serial Mouse

Explanation: When you're installing a serial mouse, pick a serial (COM) port that does not cause a conflict with your other serial ports. If you have more than two serial ports in an ISA-bus PC, they probably share interrupts. COM1 and COM3 often share IRQ4, whereas COM2 and COM4 often share IRQ3. This IRQ sharing works as long as you don't try to use the two IRQ-sharing ports at the same time.

You probably will use your mouse or other input device most of the time, so you must connect it to a serial port with a unique IRQ, which isn't shared by any other serial ports. If your system has the available IRQs and you can configure your COM ports to use unique IRQs, you should do so.

Depending on your serial port hardware, you might be able to configure COM1 for IRQ4, COM2 for IRQ3, COM3 for IRQ11, and COM4 for IRQ10 (IRQs 10 and 11 are used as examples—you might be able to use other IRQs).

If you can't configure your COM ports to use unique IRQs due to hardware limitations or a lack of available IRQs, attach the mouse to COM2 and disable COM4 (see Chapter 7, "I/O and Network Adapters," for more information about configuring COM ports), or connect the mouse to COM1 and disable COM3. This procedure ensures that the mouse's COM port does not share an IRQ with another device.

1. Determine which COM port you plan to use for the mouse.

2. Reconfigure your COM ports' use of IRQs to accommodate the mouse, if necessary.

3. Connect the mouse to the selected COM port. You might need to use a 9-pin to 25-pin adapter if the selected COM port uses a 25-pin connector. Most I/O adapters come with these port adapters, but you can buy a 9-pin to 25-pin adapter at computer stores, electronics stores, and other places that sell computer hardware.

4. Install any required software or drivers.

Procedure:
Adding a PS/2 Mouse

Explanation: If you're adding a PS/2-style mouse or other input device to a system, the system probably includes a built-in PS/2 mouse connector already. You do not need to add a special bus adapter for the device.

The point to keep in mind is that PS/2-style input devices use an IRQ, just like serial devices. Most systems that contain PS/2-style mouse ports configure the port to use either IRQ10 or IRQ12. If you've been using a mouse with the system until now and are just switching to a new input device, you shouldn't have any problem.

The only situation in which you might have a problem is if you've never used a mouse with the system before, and have another device in the system that is using the IRQ assigned to the mouse port. If that's the case, check your system's use of IRQs to see whether you need to reconfigure the conflicting adapter or the mouse port's IRQ (or both).

1. Check and configure IRQ usage for the mouse port and any conflicting device, if necessary. (See the previous discussion.)

2. Connect the device to the PS/2 mouse port.

3. Install any software or drivers required by the device. Use the device's manual as a guide.

Testing, Tuning, and Troubleshooting

Most input devices include configuration and testing software. The testing software enables you to test whether the device tracks properly across the screen and to test the buttons. If your device included this type of program, use it to test the device.

If you don't have a testing program, you can test the device just as well by using it in your programs. If the device works in one program but not another, you probably need to install a special driver for the program in which it doesn't work.

Check the manuals to determine whether the device came with the necessary driver. If the device does not work in any of your programs, you've probably missed a step in the installation process. Check the following points:

- **Connection.** Make sure you've connected the device to the correct port on the PC.

- **IRQ sharing.** Verify that you haven't assigned an IRQ to the device that is shared by another port or device.

- **Drivers.** To use a mouse or other pointing device in DOS, you need to install a DOS-based driver. To use a pointing device in Windows, you must use the Windows Setup program to install the necessary driver (unless the device's setup program takes care of that step for you). To use the mouse in DOS programs that you run as tasks under Windows, you must load a DOS-based driver before starting Windows.

Many devices also include DOS-based and Windows-based utilities for setting operating parameters of the device. These parameters include the acceleration of the screen pointer relative to movement of the device, specifying which buttons are active, setting the sensitivity of the device, and so on.

Figure 9.5 shows the Windows configuration dialog box for the Microsoft BallPoint trackball, to give you an example of the types of settings you can specify for your device.

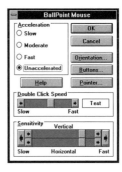

Figure 9.5: The BallPoint Mouse configuration dialog box.

Windows Mouse Tips

Windows includes some standard controls for defining the way your mouse or other input device works. Your device also might include its own configuration utility for Windows (such as the BallPoint utility shown in fig. 9.5).

You can use these configuration utilities to change the sensitivity of the mouse, switch buttons, and set other options. The following sections describe the more common changes you can make to your mouse's configuration.

Swapping Buttons

By default, Windows assigns the left mouse button as the select button. You use the select button whenever you want to select a menu item, icon, or other Windows component from the screen. If you prefer, you can swap this function to the right mouse button rather than the left button. You might want to swap buttons for the following reasons:

- **Relief.** If you use the mouse quite a bit during the day, your wrist can become sore. You can swap mouse buttons and switch to your other hand for a while to rest your right hand (or vice versa).

- **Left-handed.** If you're left-handed, you can swap the left and right mouse buttons to use the mouse with your left hand all the time.

- **Spreadsheet entry.** When you're working with a spreadsheet or other program that requires that you use the numeric keypad on the keyboard, you can control the mouse with your left hand and enter numbers on the keypad with your right hand. This setup eliminates the need to move your hand back and forth continuously between the keypad and the mouse.

Here's how to swap mouse buttons in Windows.

Procedure:
Swapping Mouse Buttons

1. In Windows, open the Control Panel and select the Mouse icon.

2. To set the mouse to use the right button as the select button, check the **S**wap Left/Right Buttons check box. To set the mouse to use the left button as the select button, clear the **S**wap Left/Right Buttons check box.

3. Choose OK and then close the Control Panel.

Controlling Sensitivity

A couple Windows controls change the sensitivity of the mouse. You can change the tracking speed of the mouse as well as the way Windows interprets clicks and double-clicks. If you change tracking speed, you change the mouse's acceleration.

With a fast tracking speed, Windows moves the mouse pointer farther on-screen relative to the movement of the mouse, trackball, or stylus. Tracking speed makes the pointer more sensitive to movement. If you slow down the tracking speed, you make the pointer less sensitive to movement and easier to position.

If you're having trouble getting used to double-clicking the mouse, you can change the amount of time that must pass between two clicks for Windows to interpret the event as a double-click. If you can't click the buttons fast enough, for example, you can increase the time that passes between the two clicks. You therefore can click the buttons more slowly to generate a double-click.

Procedure:
Changing Tracking Speed

1. Open the Windows Control Panel and select the Mouse icon.

2. Use the **M**ouse Tracking Speed slider control to set the sensitivity of the mouse. Slide the control toward the right to increase the sensitivity of the mouse or slide it toward the left to decrease sensitivity.

3. When the mouse sensitivity feels comfortable to you, select the OK button and then close the Control Panel.

Procedure:

Changing Double-Click Speed

1. Open the Windows Control Panel and select the Mouse icon.

2. Use the **D**ouble Click Speed slider control to set double-click sensitivity. Move the control to the right to decrease the amount of time that passes between the two clicks or slide it to the left to increase the amount of time that passes between the two clicks.

3. Double-click on the box with the word Test in it. If Windows recognizes the event as a double-click, the box changes colors. If Windows recognizes the event as a single-click, the box does not change.

4. After you have the double-click speed set the way you want it, choose OK and then close the Control Panel.

Using MouseTrails

If you're interested in a mouse novelty or are using Windows on a notebook or laptop computer, you might want to try MouseTrails. After you turn on MouseTrails in Windows, multiple pointer images appear on-screen. "Ghost" pointers trail the main pointer.

With portable systems (which make it hard for you to find the pointer as it moves), MouseTrails can make it easier for you to locate the pointer because you have a trail of pointers to follow, rather than just a single pointer.

NOTE *Some Windows users refer affectionately to MouseTrails as mouse droppings.*

MouseTrails is supported by only the EGA, VGA, and Super VGA display drivers. If the option for MouseTrails is dimmed in the Mouse dialog box in Control Panel, your display driver doesn't support MouseTrails.

Procedure:

Turning On and Off MouseTrails

1. Open the Windows Control Panel and select the Mouse icon.

2. To turn on MouseTrails, check the Mouse **T**rails check box. To turn off MouseTrails, clear the Mouse **T**rails check box.

3. Choose OK and then close the Control Panel.

Other Mouse Control Settings

You can add a few other settings manually to WIN.INI to control the way the mouse works. These settings are described in the following list. To add these settings, edit WIN.INI using Notepad or SysEdit, and then restart Windows for the changes to take effect.

You can add the following settings to the [Windows] section of WIN.INI:

- **DoubleClickHeight**=*pixels* and **DoubleClickWidth**=*pixels.* Specifies the number of pixels the mouse pointer can move between clicks in a double-click event.

  If you have trouble keeping the mouse still while you double-click, try increasing the value of these two settings. The default for both settings is 4. Odd numbers are rounded to even numbers, so use an even number.

- **MouseTrails**=*number.* When you turn on MouseTrails using the Control Panel, this setting is added automatically to WIN.INI. You can change the value of the setting to change the number of ghost pointers that follow the main pointer. You can specify a number from 1 to 7. If you specify 0, you turn off MouseTrails.

10

Floppy Disk Drives

Although the average floppy drive doesn't use very advanced technology, the floppy drive is still a mainstay in most PCs. Without floppy drives, you can't install software, trade files with other users (unless you're on a network), or back up your files without a tape drive.

This chapter covers configuration and installation of floppy drives, and also provides a little bit of background information about floppy drives. It covers the following topics:

- Floppy disk sizes and disk types
- Floppy disk drive types
- Configuring a floppy drive for installation
- Installing a floppy drive
- Troubleshooting floppy drive problems

Understanding Floppy Drives and Disks

PCs use three different types of floppy disks, as well as three different sizes of floppy drives to go along with those disk types. The oldest format, the 8-inch disk, isn't used much with today's PCs. The two more common sizes are 5 1/4 inch and 3 1/2 inch. Figure 10.1 shows a 3 1/2-inch drive and a 5 1/4-inch drive.

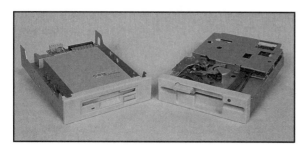

Figure 10.1: 3 1/2-inch and 5 1/4-inch floppy drives.

In addition to these individual drive units, you now can buy *dual-drive units* that combine a 5 1/4-inch drive and a 3 1/2-inch drive in a single unit. With such a unit, you can install two floppy drives in a single drive bay. These drives are great for freeing up a drive bay for a new hard disk or CD-ROM drive. You can replace your existing two floppy drives with a single unit and not lose the advantage of having both floppy formats supported by your system. Figure 10.2 shows a dual floppy drive unit.

Figure 10.2: A dual floppy drive unit.

Floppy Drive Formats

Floppy drives are available in four different formats; two 5 1/4-inch formats and two 3 1/2-inch formats are available. Table 10.1 lists these formats.

Table 10.1
Floppy Drive Formats

Drive Size	Capacity	Disk Designation
5 1/4"	360K	DSDD
5 1/4"	1.2M	DSHD
3 1/2"	720K	DSDD
3 1/2"	1.44M	DSHD

In table 10.1, DSDD stands for double-sided, double-density, and DSHD stands for double-sided, high-density. All the drives store information on both sides of the disk, and that's where the *double-sided* part of the description comes from. *Double-density*, or DD, refers to the way the data is stored on the disk. There once were single density drives, but single density drives are no longer commonly used in PCs. Double-density disks represent the low end in capacity of today's floppy drives.

High-density, or HD, disks can store more information than a DD disk. This is due to a better coating on the surface of the disk. Typically, manufacturers don't go out of their way to manufacture DD or HD disks, though. Instead, they test the disks in the manufacturing process, and if the surface quality is good enough to support HD data storage, the disk is certified as an HD disk. Otherwise, the data is sold as a DD disk.

You also will find disks labeled QD, or *Quad Density*. QD disks can store twice as much data as an HD disk, or about 2.88M in the 3 1/2-inch format. Unfortunately, PCs don't generally support QD disks. You can, however, install a special floppy controller in your system to make your floppy drive capable of reading and writing 2.88M floppy disks.

All high-capacity floppy drives, whether QD or HD, also will read and write lower density drives. You can read a 720K 3 1/2-inch disk in a 1.44M 3 1/2-inch drive, for example.

Floppy Drive Controllers

In some PCs, the floppy drive interface is built onto the motherboard. Most systems, though, include a floppy drive controller. In some cases, the floppy drive controller is a completely separate adapter whose only function is to control the floppy drives.

In other cases, the floppy controller is integrated into one of the system's other adapters. In one of my systems, for example, the floppy controller is contained on the IDE adapter, which also contains the I/O adapter circuitry. On another of my systems, the floppy controller is built onto the SCSI host adapter.

Most floppy controllers support only two floppy drives, but some support up to four drives. You probably won't need more than two floppy drives in your system, so don't worry about rushing out to buy a controller that supports four floppy drives.

Floppy drive controllers are relatively inexpensive. A floppy-only controller sells for about $30. Controllers that integrate hard disk and floppy disk control often sell for more, but you can buy IDE adapters with floppy drive support for about $30 also.

NOTE *If you're having problems with your floppy drive and determine that the controller is the problem, throw away the controller and buy a new one—don't bother trying to have the old one fixed (it would cost more to fix it than to buy a new one).*

The Technical Stuff, Plus Cabling

Like many other devices, floppy drives require an *interrupt request (IRQ)* line. The industry standard for the floppy controller is IRQ6. If you install a new device in the system and your floppy drives suddenly exhibit problems, it may be because you've set the new device to use IRQ6. Don't configure any other device to use IRQ6 unless for some strange reason your PC's floppy drives use a different interrupt.

Floppy controllers also use DMA channel 2, but using this channel presents another possible area for problems. If your system contains another device that is configured to use DMA channel 2, you'll experience problems with your floppy drives. When installing other devices, don't assign DMA channel 2 to the device.

In addition to IRQ and DMA requirements, the floppy controller naturally needs to be connected to the floppy drives in the system. A single cable is used to connect up to two drives to a controller. One end of the cable connects to the controller, and the other end, which has two connectors, connects to the drives. (Standard cabling is covered in more detail in the floppy drive installation procedure.)

The cable might or might not be keyed so that it can be attached in the correct way. If the cable is keyed, the cable connector will have a small plastic tab inside it that aligns with a notch in the edge connector on the floppy drive's circuit board. If the cable isn't keyed, you have to make sure to align pin 1 on the connector with pin 1 on the drive's edge connector. Pin 1 is on the edge of the connector closest to the notch in the board's edge connector.

In addition to these standard two-drive cables, you also can get special cables that enable you to connect two floppy drives and a tape drive to the controller.

Floppy Drive Maintenance

Floppy drives and disks don't fail as often as they used to, partly because the average PC user doesn't use the floppy drives as much as in the past. Floppies are used today primarily for software installation and file backup, two procedures that you probably don't do very often. You can, however, do a few things to keep from having any more floppy drive problems than absolutely necessary.

To Clean, or Not To Clean?

You might be wondering, for instance, if you should clean the floppy drive heads. The heads in a floppy drive actually ride on the surface of the floppy disk (unlike a hard disk, which rides *above* the surface of the disk). Theoretically, the heads can pick up contaminants from the surface of the disk.

If you've ever opened up a floppy disk, though, you've found that the inside of the disk jacket is covered by a soft material that "wipes" the disk clean as it rotates, picking up any contaminants that might be on it. So, any contaminants that end up on the heads usually are airborne, and don't come from the disks themselves. Instead of going through the trouble of tearing open your disks, take a look at figure 10.3, which shows the guts of a couple of floppy disks.

Figure 10.3: The guts of two floppy disks.

You can get special cleaning disks to place in the drive and clean the drive's heads. There are two types: soft cotton disks that you soak with a cleaning solution, and mildly abrasive disks that scrub the heads clean. Unfortunately, the scrubbing kind also wears down the heads, so I don't recommend them.

That brings us back to the question: Should you clean the heads? I never do. In all the years I've been using PCs I've never had to clean the heads on the floppy drive. But if you have a really dusty office environment, work with your windows open a lot, or work outside (taking your notebook out on the deck, for example), you should clean the heads occasionally, perhaps as often as once a month.

In the preceding scenario, cleaning drive heads is important because airborne contaminants such as dust and pollen can build up on the heads even when you're not using the drive. You also should clean the heads if your system begins experiencing problems reading disks in the drive.

NOTE   *If you smoke, for heaven's sake don't do it around your PC! Smoke particles, small though they are, can build up on the heads of the drive and on the surface of your disks. You can always clean the heads, but why make the problem any worse that it would otherwise be?*

Watch the Weather

Floppy drives and disks are somewhat susceptible to temperature fluctuations. Avoid storing your floppy disks in an area where the temperature is hot (like a closed-up car). If you have to leave disks in your car, slide them under the seat where they won't be subjected to direct sunlight. They should be fine.

Also, if you bring your disks inside from a very cold climate, let them warm up to room temperature before you use them. It shouldn't take more than five or ten minutes for them to warm up.

The same temperature problems can apply to a disk drive. If you've just brought your notebook computer in from the cold, let it warm up before you use it. I recommend an hour or more if the computer has been sitting in very cold temperatures for many hours. Such a precaution isn't for the floppy drives, though; it's for the hard disk.

Physical changes caused by temperature variations are much harder on hard disks than on floppy disks. Using the drive when it is very cold can actually damage the disk. At the least, you might have problems reading information from the disk.

Stick a Disk in It

If you're going to be shipping your PC, hauling it somewhere in your car, or checking your notebook on an airplane, insert a disk in the floppy drive and close the floppy drive door (which is automatic on a 3 1/2-inch drive).

A disk in the drive prevents the heads from bouncing around and potentially being knocked out of alignment. Use an old disk, not an important data disk. The drive doors on some drives can be closed without first inserting a disk in the drive. Don't close the drive doors on these drives without a disk in the drive. Doing so can cause the heads to rub together, causing problems with the heads.

Blow Out the Disk

When you're fiddling around inside the PC for one reason or another, it's always a good idea to get rid of any dust that has built up inside the unit. Pull the floppy drives out of the system or insert a disk in them to engage the heads on the disk (to protect the heads from dust), then blow the dust out of the drive. Use a can of compressed air to blow it out if you have one, or just blow it out with your breath. The drives probably will have collected quite a bit of dust, particularly on top.

Adding a Floppy Drive

There really is very little involved in installing a floppy drive, even if you also have to install the floppy controller. There generally are no jumpers or switches to configure on the controller, and only one or two options to set on the drive itself. If you're installing a floppy drive in a system, it's often because you're replacing an existing floppy with a new one, either because you're replacing a defective drive or installing a higher-capacity drive.

Procedure:
Removing a Floppy Drive

Explanation: This is the first step to take if you're replacing an existing drive. If you're installing a new drive, and not replacing one, skip this step.

1. Turn off, unplug, and open the system.

2. Examine the drive to see how it's held in place. Some floppy drives are held in with screws on either side of the drive, while AT-style drives are held in place with small tabs that screw to the chassis in front of the drives. Remove the screws and slide the drive out of the system far enough to allow access to the power and interface cable.

3. Disconnect the power cable from the back of the drive.

4. Disconnect the interface cable from the back of the drive, but keep track of how it's connected to the drive. Check the connector to see if it's keyed. If not, note the location of pin 1 on the cable so that you can reinstall the cable correctly.

5. Carefully slide the drive out of the system, taking care not to catch any drive components on the chassis.

Procedure:
Installing the Controller

Explanation: If you are installing a drive in a system that already contains a floppy controller, either as a stand-alone controller or as part of a hard disk adapter, you can skip this procedure. You don't need to install another controller.

1. Check the manual for your floppy drive controller to determine if the controller requires any configura-

tion. It probably doesn't require any, but you should check to make sure. If the controller requires configuration of IRQ or DMA, assign IRQ6 and DMA2 to the controller.

The assignment of IRQ6 and DMA2 doesn't apply to hard disk host adapters that contain a floppy controller. You might have to assign IRQ and DMA settings to the hard disk portion of the adapter, but you shouldn't use IRQ6 or DMA2 for this. IRQ6 and DMA2 are reserved for the floppy controller portion of the adapter. Check your manuals and Chapter 5, "Hard Disk Tweaking: Cleaning, Packing, and Compressing," for more information on configuring your hard disk adapter.

2. If you're replacing existing floppy controller support, remove the existing floppy controller, or if it is part of an adapter that provides some other function (such as a hard disk adapter), disable the floppy support on the existing adapter.

3. Connect the interface cable(s) to the adapter. Connecting the cables to the controller often is easier to accomplish when the controller is out of the system.

4. Choose an appropriate bus slot in which to install the floppy controller. Use an 8-bit or 16-bit slot for an 8-bit controller, and a 16-bit slot for a 16-bit controller.

5. Secure the controller with a screw.

Drive Termination and Configuration

Floppy drives, like many hard drives, have to be terminated. *Terminating* a floppy drive means that a terminating resistor has to be installed on the last floppy drive on the cable to prevent signal reflection along the cable and potential damage to the controller or drives.

Drives are terminated by resistor packs called *terminating resistors*. Sometimes the resistor pack is in a DIP with pins on either side, and sometimes it's in a SIP with only one row of pins. The resistor pack probably will be identified on the circuit board by the designation RP (Resistor Pack), RA (Resistor Array), or RN (Resistor Network), followed by a number.

Figure 10.4 shows the terminating resistor pack on a 5 1/4-inch floppy drive, along with its drive select jumpers (discussed later).

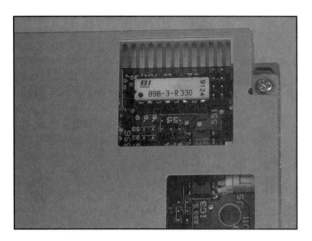

Figure 10.4: The terminating resistor pack and drive select jumpers on a 5 1/4-inch disk drive.

Figure 10.5: Drive select jumpers on a typical 3 1/2-inch drive.

Most 3 1/2-inch floppy drives handle termination without a user-installable terminating resistor, so it's rare that you have to worry about terminating a 3 1/2-inch drive.

In addition to termination, you also need to consider drive select. A *drive select* jumper on the drive determines whether the drive is recognized by the system as drive A or as drive B. Without launching into an unnecessary technical explanation, I'll just say this: both drives can be configured as the second drive.

If your drive labels the jumper positions beginning with DS0, then both the drives should be configured as DS1. If the drive labels the jumper positions beginning with DS1, then the drive should be configured as DS2. Always choose the *second* drive select position, regardless of whether you are installing the drive as drive A or drive B. Figure 10.5 shows the drive select jumpers on a 3 1/2-inch drive.

Why not configure drive A as DS1 and drive B as DS2? Again without going into a technical explanation, I'll keep it simple. If you look at the drive interface cable, you'll notice that some of the wires near the end of the cable, between the two floppy drive connectors, are twisted. The twist in the wire sets up the connection to the two drives so that the system knows which drive is which.

Just remember this rule: drive A always must be the drive to which the twisted wires are connected. In a two-drive system, drive B gets the connector that's in the middle of the cable, and drive A gets the connector that's at the end of the cable.

TIP

Two twists: *There's an exception to the one-twist rule. If the cable has a twist between the controller and the first floppy connector, as well as a second twist between the two first and second floppy connectors, the middle connector is for drive A and the last connector is for drive B. Because the B drive is then at the end of the cable, it must have a terminating resistor, and the terminating resistor must be removed from drive A.*

No twists: *If your floppy interface cable doesn't have any twists in some of the wires, you do need to configure drive A using the second set of jumpers and drive B using the third set of jumpers. On drives with DS0 as the first position, configure drive A as DS1 and drive B as DS2. If labeling starts with DS1, configure the drives as DS2 and DS3.*

Procedure:

Terminating and Configuring the 5 1/4-Inch Drive

1. Examine the back of the drive where the interface cable connects. Look for the terminating resistor and drive select jumpers. The drive select jumpers have the designation DS, followed by a number (such as DS1).

2. Make sure that the drive is configured using the second set of drive select pins. If labeling starts with DS0, install a jumper on DS1. If labeling starts at DS1, install a jumper on DS2. (There should be no other drive select jumpers installed.)

3. If you're installing the drive as drive A, verify that a terminating resistor is in place. If there is no terminating resistor, call the place where you bought the drive (or the manufacturer) and ask for help locating or acquiring the terminating resistor.

   If you're installing the drive as drive B, remove the resistor and store it in a safe place in case you need it in the future. If there are two sets of twists in your interface cable, see the warning in the last section about double-twisted cables. If there are no twists in your interface cable, see the warning about no-twist cables in the previous section.

Procedure:

Configuring the 3 1/2-Inch Drive

1. Examine the back of the drive where the interface cable connects. Look for the terminating resistor and drive select jumpers. The drive select jumpers will have the designation DS, followed by a number (such as DS1).

2. Make sure that the drive is configured using the second set of drive select pins. If labeling starts with DS0, install a jumper on DS1. If labeling starts at DS1, install a jumper on DS2. (There should be no other drive select jumpers installed.)

3. You shouldn't have to worry about terminating the drive, but if you're installing the drive as drive A, consult the drive's manual to see if it mentions termination. If it requires termination, verify that a terminating resistor is installed on the drive.

Procedure:

Installing and Connecting a Drive

Explanation: If you're installing a 5 1/4-inch floppy drive, you probably only have to slide the drive into the chassis and install a few retaining screws. If you're installing it into an AT-style case, you'll need to install plastic slide rails to the sides of the drive. A special mounting bracket assembly is required to install 3 1/2-inch drives in a full-size drive bay (the same bay as for a 5 1/4-inch drive). Often, the 3 1/2-inch drives come with the bracket, but sometimes you have to purchase it separately.

Also, it's usually easiest to attach the power and interface cables before the drive is fully inserted into its drive bay. If the cables are long enough, run them through the drive bay and out the front of the PC so that you can connect the drive before you even begin to install it in the bay.

1. If the drive requires drive rails or a mounting bracket assembly, install the rails or bracket.

2. Carefully slide the drive partially into the selected slot.

3. Connect the power cable to the drive (any of the power cables will work).

4. Connect the interface cable to the drive. If you're installing the drive as drive A, use the last connector on the cable. If you're installing the drive as drive B, use the middle connector on the cable. If the connector isn't keyed for correct insertion, make sure the edge of the cable that's marked with a colored stripe is aligned with the side of the edge connector nearest the slot in the edge connector.

5. Secure the drive with retaining screws on either side, or for AT-style cases, install the retaining clips in front of the drive.

TIP — *Drive A doesn't have to be the topmost floppy drive. You can install drive B on top of A if you like. The only thing that determines which drive is which is the interface cable connection. The last drive on the cable is drive A. This little trick helps prevent someone from booting your PC with a virus-infected disk.*

Procedure:

Testing a Floppy Drive

Explanation: The best way to test a floppy drive is to format a few disks with the floppy drive, store information on the drive, and read that data back into the PC. First, though, you have to configure your PC's CMOS for the correct drive type for the new drive. (The CMOS is a chip the PC uses to store information about the hardware in the system.) To do that, go through the following steps.

1. Start the system and do whatever mumbo-jumbo is required for your system to get into the CMOS setup program.

2. Configure your system's CMOS settings for the correct drive type for the newly installed drive.

3. Save the CMOS changes and reboot the system.

4. Format a disk in the drive using the highest available capacity for the drive. Use the FORMAT command from the DOS command line or File Manager in Windows to format the disk.

5. Open one of your programs, load (or create) a document, then save it on the newly formatted disk.

6. Close the current document and open the copy you just stored on the floppy.

7. If the drive is installed as drive A, create a new emergency boot disk in the drive. Don't omit this step! This is particularly important if you've changed size format or capacity from your previous drive A.

Troubleshooting Floppy Disk Problems

Floppy disk troubles don't happen very often, but when such troubles do occur, you can take a few steps to locate the problem.

If, for example, the problem occurs with only one disk, that means the disk is bad (not the drive). Try running a disk utility (like Norton Disk Doctor) on the disk to recover any data that might be on it. If you can't recover the information, you'll have to throw the disk away. If the problem happens with all or most of your disks, the problem is probably with the drive.

Procedure:

Testing the Drive

1. Try reading a different disk. If the problem persists, continue with the rest of the procedure. If the problem disappears, the first disk you tried might be bad.

2. If the problem occurs with two floppy drives that are connected to the same controller, the problem is the controller or a DMA or IRQ conflict. If only one drive is affected, the drive is the source of the problem. Test both drives to see if they both experience the same problem.

3. Turn off, unplug, and open the system.

4. Check the connections to the drive. Make sure the power connector is securely attached. Verify that the interface cable is connected properly and securely.

5. If you've just installed the drive, check the drive select jumpers and termination again.

6. Retest the drive. If the problem persists, you may have an IRQ or DMA conflict. Check the other devices in your system to make sure none of the devices uses IRQ6 or DMA2. If the floppy drive problem first appeared after you installed a new device, this is a good indication that you may have an IRQ or DMA conflict.

7. If the problem still persists, buy a cleaning disk for the drive (get the type that uses the soft disk and liquid cleaning solution). Follow the directions provided with the cleaning kit to clean the heads of the floppy drive.

8. Test the drive again. If the problem persists, either the drive or the controller probably is bad. If you have an extra floppy controller, or an adapter in the system that currently has a disabled floppy controller built into it, try the other controller.

   If the problem goes away, the floppy controller is causing the problem and needs to be replaced. If you don't have an extra controller but do have access to a spare drive, try the other drive. If the spare drive works, you need to replace the other drive. If the spare drive doesn't work, the problem is the controller.

11

CD-ROM Drives

CD-ROM drives are fast becoming a popular addition to PCs. They offer a cheap and easy means for developers to distribute their applications, and are essential for using multimedia applications on your PC. You even can play audio CDs on your PC if you want to. Given the popularity of CDs, it's a good bet that you'll soon want to add a CD-ROM drive to your system.

This chapter covers some CD-ROM basics and explains how to buy, install, use, and troubleshoot a CD-ROM drive. The chapter covers the following topics:

- Background on CD-ROM technology
- Buying tips for CD-ROM
- Installing a CD-ROM drive
- Setting up your system software for CD-ROM
- Sharing a CD-ROM across a network

Because CD-ROM technology is relatively new to the PC, a little technical background is in order.

Understanding CD-ROM Drives

CD-ROM stands for *Compact Disc Read-Only Memory*. CD-ROM discs and drives used in PCs are a lot like audio CDs and CD drives. The only difference in the discs is the type of information stored on the disc and the way that information is encoded. The only difference in the drives is that CD-ROM drives for PCs generally are a little more ruggedly built to withstand the more exacting requirements of data retrieval. That's the primary reason why PC CD-ROM drives are more expensive than audio CD-ROM drives. Figure 11.1 shows a CD-ROM drive and a data CD.

Figure 11.1: A CD-ROM drive and disc cartridge, and a data CD.

What's so great about CD-ROMs? Primarily, the storage capacity. Each CD can hold 680M of data. As application size steadily increases, many developers are turning to CDs to distribute their software.

Developers are turning to PCs for a couple of reasons. First, duplicating a single CD is much cheaper than duplicating 10 or 12 disks. After you've installed software from a CD, you'll also know why they're great for users—no more swapping disks in and out of the drive during installation.

CD-ROMs also can free up valuable hard disk space. Many applications enable you to leave peripheral files on the CD until you need them. You can leave a large Help file on the disc, for example, then pop the CD into the drive when you need to access the Help file. Clip art and other support files you don't use regularly also can often be left on the CD instead of installed on the hard disk.

The large storage capacity of CDs also is a big asset, bringing the capability to maintain and search large amounts of data very quickly. You can search the entire encyclopedia on CD for the word *freedom*, and almost instantly have a list of all the articles that include that one word.

Can you imagine thumbing through an entire set of hardcover encyclopedia volumes to find all the occurrences of a single word? If you're looking for a piece of information, there is no better way today than to search one of the rapidly growing number of specialty data CDs for it.

What's Available on CD?

You might be amazed at the wide variety of data you can find on CD. Many applications now are available on CD instead of disk, often offering more features and a lower price than their disk-based versions. Microsoft Word on CD, for example, is less expensive than the disk version. It also includes a copy of Microsoft Bookshelf, which gives you the ability to access *Roget's Thesaurus, Bartlett's Familiar Quotations, The Concise Columbia Dictionary of Quotations*, the *World Almanac*, and *The American Heritage Dictionary* right from within Word.

Aside from applications you'll find a wealth of really incredible data, from literary collections to reference works to fact collections on every subject from animals to geopolitical information compiled by the CIA and KGB. If you have a special interest, whether it's Mark Twain or a complete reference to gardening, there's a CD for you. Figure 11.2 shows a clip from Microsoft's Encarta CD, a multimedia encyclopedia.

A good multimedia CD also can give you new ways to learn. You can view how a particular piece of machinery works by watching an animation of the device in action. Clicking on a musical term can give you a musical example of what the term means. If you don't know how to pronounce a word, clicking on the word might cause it to be spoken (assuming you have a sound card in your PC).

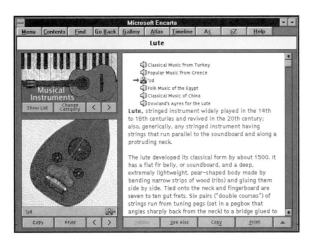

Figure 11.2: A clip from Microsoft's Encarta encyclopedia CD.

The Pros and Cons of CDs

Aside from the fact that you can find a CD title that covers nearly any subject imaginable, CDs offer practical benefits. In addition to providing a quick and easy means to install software and freeing valuable hard disk space, CDs are nearly indestructible. Unlike floppy disks, CDs are not susceptible to damage from dust, dirt, scratches, temperature changes, and magnetic fields.

Currently, CDs also have a few disadvantages. CD-ROM access is relatively slow when compared to hard disk access. A typical CD-ROM drive provides an access time between 265ms (milliseconds) to 300ms or more, which is nearly 20 times as slow as a good hard disk. You also can't save files to a CD, since they are read-only devices. Within a few years, however, writable CDs will be available for the average user, giving you an almost unlimited amount of storage space for your data and applications.

A Buyer's Guide to CD-ROM

You should consider several issues when deciding which CD-ROM drive to buy. Higher-priced units often offer better performance, but you should check the specifications of the drive before deciding which one fits both your use requirements and your budget.

Performance

The first issue to consider when evaluating CD-ROM drives is performance. Average access time is one specification to check. Many drives on the market today offer an access speed of around 300ms. Some offer better access times (indicated by a lower value), and some offer poorer performance—sometimes 600ms or more. Shop for a fast access time (lower numbers), but temper your selection by how much you can afford to spend on the drive.

You also need to check the drive's *data transfer rate*, which is the rate at which the drive can transfer data from the disc to the PC. Most drives today offer a transfer rate of 150 K/sec (kilobytes per second), but some drives offer better transfer rates of 300 K/sec or more. Shop for a drive that gives you the highest possible transfer rate.

Also look for drives that include a built-in disc cache of 64K or more. As it can for a hard disk, a cache on the CD-ROM drive will improve the drive's performance by holding frequently accessed data in memory rather than having to retrieve it from the disc each time it's needed.

Photo CDs

One of the newest additions to CD-ROM technology is the photo CD. Developed by Kodak, *photo CD technology* enables photographs to be scanned and placed on a CD. There's nothing really very novel about the technology—you can scan photos from slides and store them on a writable CD if you have the equipment to do so. Kodak's Photo CD technology simply imposes a proprietary standard format on the discs.

To get a photo CD, you can take your film to a photography shop that has the necessary equipment, and the shop transfers your photos onto CD. Most photo finishing shops that don't have the equipment will send your film to a service bureau that does have the necessary equipment.

When you get the photo CD back, you can load those pictures of Aunt Agnes into Paintbrush on your computer and draw a mustache on her if you want to. Figure 11.3 shows a photo CD image displayed in a Windows application, Collage Complete.

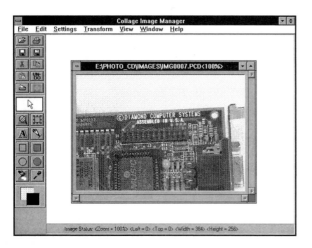

Figure 11.3: A photo CD image displayed in Windows-based Collage Complete.

There are single-session photo CDs and multisession photo CDs. A single-session photo CD has had all its photographic images placed on the CD at the same time (in one recording session). Multisession photo CDs have been recorded in multiple sessions. Some CD-ROM drives are capable of reading only single-session photo CDs, and can read only the first set of images on a multisession CD.

NOTE   If you plan to view only your own photo CDs, a single-session drive may be fine. If you will be swapping photo CDs with other users, shop for a drive that supports multisession photo CDs.

CD-ROM/XA Capability

Also consider whether a drive is XA-compatible. CD-ROM/XA drives offer two benefits: they provide interleaved audio and video, and highly compressed digital audio. The interleaved audio/video capability offers two advantages.

By interleaving the audio and video portions of a video clip, less space is required on the disc to store the clip, making more room available for other data. It also provides faster performance for a more realistic and jitter-free playback. XA's capability to compress digital audio increases its audio storage capacity from the standard 72 minutes in audio CDs to up to 16 hours.

When you're shopping for a CD-ROM drive, look for a drive that not only offers multisession photo CD capability, but also is XA-compatible.

Audio Capability

You probably will want to play audio CDs in your PC at some point. You also want the best possible audio reproduction possible from the drive. Shop for a drive that provides a sampling frequency of 44.1 MHz, which is the sampling rate used in audio CDs.

Multimedia upgrade kits that include a sound card (as well as stand-alone sound cards) generally include software to play audio CDs. Figure 11.4 shows the Pocket CD program that's included with Mediavision's Pro Audio Spectrum card.

Figure 11.4: The Pocket CD program from Mediavision gives you software to play audio CDs on your PC.

Internal or External CD Drives?

CD-ROM drives are available as internal units that mount inside your PC, just like a floppy drive. You also can get external CD-ROM drives that sit on your desk (or on top of your PC) and connect to the back of the PC by an interface cable.

The only benefit internal CD-ROM drives offer over external drives is that they take up less desk space and eliminate one more cable that has to connect to the back of your PC. If you like an uncluttered desk and don't need to move the drive from one system to another, buy an internal drive.

If your system is on a network and you want to be able to access the CD-ROM drive from other nodes on the network, you can do so. If you want the option of being able to move the drive from one system to another, buy an external drive.

Which Interface To Choose?

Some CD-ROM drives use a proprietary data interface and controller to connect the CD-ROM drive to the PC. These proprietary interfaces usually are based on a variation of a standard IDE or SCSI interface. These types of drives naturally include their own controllers.

Other CD-ROM drives use a parallel interface, connecting to the PC through one of its parallel (LPT) ports. CD drives often offer slower performance than other types, primarily because the system's parallel ports are not designed for high-speed data transfer. These types of drives are great, though, for systems that don't offer the possibility of any other type of interface.

Most notebook PCs, for example, don't include built-in SCSI support, and parallel port CD-ROM drives are one solution for these types of systems. You also can buy SCSI adapters that plug into your parallel port, however, so a portable SCSI CD-ROM drive may also be a solution for your notebook PC.

SCSI drives generally are the best choice, although you may have to buy a SCSI host adapter for your system in addition to the CD-ROM drive (read the next section for more information on requirements for a SCSI host adapter). The benefit to the SCSI interface is that you can connect other devices—such as scanners, hard disks, and tape drives—to the same adapter.

Multimedia Kits

A good way to buy a CD-ROM drive is to get it as part of a multimedia upgrade package that includes an audio adapter (a sound card). If you intend to use your CD-ROM drive for audio, either for listening to the audio portion of a multimedia CD or when playing audio CDs in the drive, you'll probably want a sound card.

The only other option (if you want to be able to listen to your CDs) is to plug a set of headphones into the front of the drive. A sound card will give you better sound quality and more options for controlling options like treble, bass, and fade.

There are lots of different multimedia upgrade packages available that include a CD-ROM drive, a sound card, and software. When evaluating a multimedia kit, I recommend

a kit that uses a standard SCSI-2 interface if you plan to connect other SCSI devices to the SCSI host adapter built into the sound card.

If you want to buy a stand-alone SCSI host adapter to get the best possible performance from your SCSI devices, the interface that the sound card uses doesn't matter quite as much, as long as it provides good performance. If the kit includes a SCSI CD-ROM drive, you don't even have to connect it to the sound card if you have a dedicated SCSI host adapter. You can connect it to the host adapter rather than to the sound card.

Adding an Internal CD-ROM Drive

The installation procedure for an internal CD-ROM drive naturally is a little more complex than for an external drive because you have to open the PC to install the drive. (You also might have to open the PC to install an external hard drive, but that's for a different procedure.) Even so, the installation procedure is fairly simple. In fact, it's a lot like the installation procedure for a floppy drive, but with a few extra steps.

Procedure:

Termination and Configuration

1. Set the drive's ID. On SCSI devices, set the SCSI ID for the drive to a higher number than any SCSI hard drives that also are installed in the system. If there are no other SCSI devices in the system, set the drive's ID to 1, leaving ID 0 available for future installation of a hard disk. Make sure to use a unique ID number that isn't shared by any other SCSI device in the system.

   Usually, the SCSI ID is configured by setting DIP switches on the drive. Figure 11.5 shows the SCSI ID configuration switches on the NEC CDR-84 drive.

   If you're installing a parallel-port device, you probably won't need to set a drive ID or other configuration options, but check the drive's manual to be sure. If you're installing a drive that uses a proprietary interface, it's more likely—but not a certainty—that you'll have to set one or more configuration options on the drive. Check the manual to be sure.

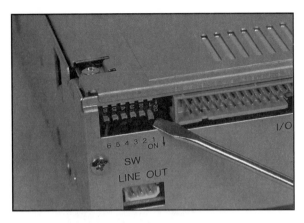

Figure 11.5: The ID configuration switches on the NEC CDR-84 CD-ROM drive.

2. If the drive will be the last device on the bus, it may have to be terminated, which usually involves adding a terminating resistor pack to the drive. Check the drive's manual to determine how to terminate the drive. Some drives, such as the NEC internal drive, require a special terminating adapter that plugs into the drive's data cable.

   If you can't figure out how to terminate the drive, or don't want the added expense of a terminating adapter, consider connecting the drive so that it isn't the last device on the bus (assuming there are other devices on the same bus). The last device currently on the bus probably is already terminated, which solves the problem.

Procedure:
Installing the Drive

1. Turn off, unplug, and open the PC.

2. Choose a drive bay for the CD-ROM drive. If you don't have a drive bay available, you may have to eliminate a floppy drive to install the CD-ROM drive. But first, check your system to see if you can relocate the hard drive to another bay. Many tower systems, for example, include a drive bay at the top of the unit above the bay that normally is used for drive A.

If you can relocate your hard disk and make a bay available for the CD-ROM drive, do that as an alternative to eliminating a floppy drive. Another option is to replace your two floppy drives with a single, dual-drive unit that takes only one drive bay but gives your system a 3 1/2-inch drive and a 5 1/4-inch drive.

3. After checking your drive's configuration, install mounting rails on either side of the drive if your PC's chassis requires them (usually only required on AT-style cases). If there is only enough room in the drive bay for the CD-ROM drive, you don't need the rails. If you need rails and they didn't come with the drive, you can buy a set from a PC component dealer like JDR Microdevices or your local PC shop.

4. Carefully slide the CD-ROM drive into the drive bay (see figure 11.6) until the front of the drive is aligned with the front of the floppy drive(s), then secure the drive in the bay with screws.

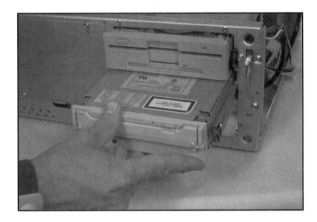

Figure 11.6: Slide the CD-ROM drive into the bay until the front lines up with the floppy drive(s).

Procedure:
Connecting Cables

Explanation: There are either two or three cable connections to make, depending on whether your system contains a sound card. In either situation, you need to connect a power cable to the drive, as well as a data cable. If your system contains a sound card, you also need to make a connection between your CD-ROM drive and the sound card.

It's possible that you might already have run out of power cables if you have two floppy drives, a hard drive, and another device connected to the power supply. If you don't have an available power supply connection for the CD-ROM drive, you can get a power splitter cable that connects to one of your existing power connectors and provides two connectors for the cable harness on which it's installed.

If you need to use one of these power cable splitters, connect it to the power connector for the floppy drive that you use the least, and connect the CD-ROM drive and the floppy drive to the same power cable.

1. Connect a power cable to the CD-ROM drive (see the previous Tip if you don't have an available power cable).

2. Connect the interface cable between the host adapter (or sound card) and the CD-ROM drive. Make sure to align pin 1 on each end of the cable with the proper pin on the CD-ROM drive and on the adapter (see fig. 11.7). You might find it easiest to remove the sound card or host adapter, connect the interface cable to it, and then reinstall the adapter.

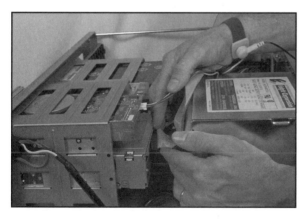

Figure 11.7: Connecting the data interface cable between the CD-ROM drive and the host adapter.

3. If your system contains a sound card, connect the CD-ROM drive to the sound card by the necessary cable (see fig. 11.8). If the cable didn't come as part of a kit, you'll have to buy the cable separately. Check with

the sound card manufacturer or dealer for the right cable. If you don't want to get the cable right away, you can connect a pair of headphones to the front of the CD-ROM drive.

Figure 11.8: Connecting the audio cable between the drive and the sound card.

If you can't see paying extra money for a cable to connect your CD-ROM drive to your sound card, and if you're the adventurous sort, you might be able to make your own cable. The line-out connector on the CD-ROM drive probably will have only three pins—left, right, and ground. If you can locate the right type of connectors at your local electronics supply store, you should be able to put together a cable that will work.

Check the manual for your sound card and for your CD-ROM drive to determine the pin connections for the audio connectors. Then, make a cable that connects the two left outputs to one another, the two right outputs to one another, and the ground pin(s).

After you've finished connecting all of the necessary cables to the drive, skip to the section in this chapter titled "Completing the Installation" to install drivers and test your drive.

Adding an External CD-ROM Drive

The process required to install an external CD-ROM drive is similar, though slightly different, from the procedure for installing an internal drive. Aside from the fact that you don't have to install the drive in one of the PC's drive bays, the connections for the drive are a little different. Even though the drive is external, you still might need to open up the PC. This section covers installation of SCSI-based CD-ROM drives.

The CD-ROM drive requires a connection to whichever device in the PC will be controlling it, whether that device is the sound card or a host adapter. Unless you already have installed the host adapter or sound card and have the necessary connector available at the back of the PC, you'll have to open the PC as part of the installation procedure. SCSI host adapters generally have a connector for external SCSI devices, which sticks out the back of the PC like all the other connectors on the system's adapters.

Many sound cards don't provide the CD-ROM connection on the back of the adapter because the space is taken up by audio connectors. Instead, the CD-ROM data connector is on the adapter, and a short cable connects the adapter to a special bracket that is installed in back of a free bus slot. An external cable then connects the drive to a connector installed on the bracket. This special bracket is supplied with the sound card, not with the CD-ROM drive. Unless the card is supplied in a kit with an external CD-ROM drive, the adapter bracket will be optional.

Procedure:

Termination and Configuration

1. Set the drive's ID. On SCSI devices, set the SCSI ID for the drive to a higher number than any SCSI hard drives that also are installed in the system. If there are no other SCSI devices in the system, set the drive's ID to 1, leaving ID 0 available for future installation of a hard disk. Usually, the SCSI ID is configured by setting DIP switches on the drive.

NOTE *Make sure to use a unique ID number that isn't shared by any other SCSI device in the system.*

2. If the drive will be the last device on the bus, that drive might have to be terminated, which usually involves adding a terminating resistor pack to the drive. Check the drive's manual to determine how to terminate the drive if it isn't already terminated.

   If you have another external SCSI device already attached to the system, and you're adding an external SCSI CD-ROM drive, you can avoid the termination issue altogether by attaching the CD-ROM drive between the PC and the other SCSI device. The CD-ROM then no longer will be the last device on the bus and won't require termination. If the CD-ROM drive is terminated and you install it in the middle of the bus instead of as the last device, you must remove its termination.

Procedure:

Installing and Connecting the Drive

1. Choose a good spot for the CD-ROM drive on your desk or on top of your PC if you have a tower case.

2. Connect the power cord from the back of the CD-ROM drive to an outlet.

3. Connect the interface cable from the drive to the host adapter or special bracket adapter (sound cards only).

4. If your system includes a sound card, connect the audio cable between the CD-ROM drive and the sound card. If you don't have the necessary cable, you can get a small stereo cable and connect one end to the headphone jack of the CD-ROM drive, then connect the other end of the cable to the input jack on the sound card. You also can buy some connectors and make your own cable.

Completing the Installation

The PC's BIOS doesn't include direct support for CD-ROM drives, so your system requires a special CD-ROM driver to enable the CD-ROM drive to communicate with the PC. The required driver will be included with whichever device is controlling the CD-ROM drive, and not with the drive itself.

If you want to connect your CD-ROM drive to a SCSI host adapter, for example, you'll need a CD-ROM device driver specifically written for your SCSI host adapter. Some SCSI host adapter manufacturers include a CD-ROM driver with the adapter, while others make you pay for it as an option. Multimedia kits in which the CD-ROM drive can connect to the sound card include a driver to enable the sound card to control the CD-ROM drive.

Installing the CD-ROM Driver

The procedure you use to install the CD-ROM driver varies according to the type of adapter or sound card you're using, so I can't give you a specific procedure for installing the driver. Instead, check the adapter's manual and disks to determine how to install the driver. Most adapters include an installation program that will install the driver for you automatically.

Installing and Configuring MSCDEX

In addition to the device driver that enables your adapter to control the CD-ROM drive, you also need MSCDEX.EXE, which is the Microsoft CD-ROM extension for DOS. MSCDEX enables DOS to recognize the CD-ROM drive as a logical DOS storage device represented by a drive ID letter, just like a floppy drive or hard drive.

Usually, the CD-ROM or sound card software will include a copy of MSCDEX.EXE, but it might not be the latest revision. MS-DOS 6 includes an update to MSCDEX, so if you've upgraded to the latest copy of DOS, you should have a recent copy of MSCDEX also.

Typically, the installation program for your CD-ROM or sound card software will install MSCDEX for you, but you need to make sure it installs the right copy. Check the copy of MSCDEX provided with your software and the copy provided with MS-DOS. If your DOS copy has a later file date than the one supplied with your CD-ROM software, copy the later copy of MSCDEX to the CD-ROM software disk that contains a copy of MSCDEX. This enables you to let the software install MSCDEX for you and still have the latest version of MSCDEX installed.

Although your CD-ROM software probably will install MSCDEX for you, you might have to install it or change parameters for it manually. MSCDEX can be started from the DOS command line, but usually you should add it to AUTOEXEC.BAT so that it starts automatically whenever you boot the system. Here's the syntax of the MSCDEX command line:

```
MSCDEX.EXE /D:CD_driver_ID /L:drive_ID /M:sector_buffers
```

The CD_driver_ID parameter is taken from the /D parameter specified on the line in CONFIG.SYS that loads your CD-ROM device driver. Here's an example of a line that might appear in CONFIG.SYS (using a Future Domain driver as an example):

```
DEVICE=C:\FDOMAIN\FDCD.SYS /D:MSCD0000
```

The parameter MSCD0000 in the previous example is the logical device name associated with the CD-ROM drive. The line in AUTOEXEC.BAT for MSCDEX would then appear as follows:

```
MSCDEX.EXE /D:MSCD0000 /L:E /M:20
```

What are those other parameters for? The /L parameter specifies that the CD-ROM drive will be recognized as drive E. Specify whichever drive letter you want to use for the CD-ROM drive. The /M:20 parameter specifies 20 sector buffers for the CD-ROM drive, which will improve performance (sort of a disc cache).

The higher the number, the more memory that is used for the buffers. Use 10 or 20 as a rule of thumb. If you want information on MSCDEX's other possible command-line switches, enter **HELP MSCDEX** at the DOS prompt.

Sharing a CD-ROM

If you're on an MS-NET (LAN Manager, NT, or MS-NET compatible) or Windows for Workgroups network and want to share a CD-ROM drive with other users on the network, add the /S switch to the MSCDEX command line on the machine that contains the CD-ROM drive.

The switch is not necessary on the remote nodes that are accessing the CD-ROM drive. If there are no CD-ROM drives installed on the remote nodes, those nodes do not require that MSCDEX be loaded. MSCDEX is required only at the node where the CD-ROM is physically located. It then appears as a logical DOS disk to the other nodes.

Here's an example of the MSCDEX command line to use:

```
MSCDEX.EXE /D:MSCD0000 /L:E /M:20 /S
```

Installing Other Software

After installing your CD-ROM device driver and MSCDEX, you're ready to start using your CD-ROM drive to read data CDs. If you also want to play audio CDs, you need to install some additional software.

If your sound card included an installation program that installed software on your system, the installation program might already have installed the necessary software. Mediavision's software, for example, includes a program for playing audio CDs called Pocket CD, which is installed by the Mediavision setup program.

If you don't have a sound card, or if it didn't include software for playing CDs, you can use the Windows Media Player application to play audio CDs. To use Media Player for audio CDs, though, you first must install the Media Control Interface (MCI) CD Audio driver (covered in the next procedure).

If you want to view photo CDs, your CD-ROM driver must be capable of reading photo CDs (your CD-ROM drive also must be capable of reading photo CDs). In addition, you'll need software to view the images on your PC. Collage Complete, CorelDRAW!, and many other graphics programs include support for photo CD image formats.

Procedure:
Installing the MCI CD Audio Driver

Explanation: The MCI CD Audio driver must be installed for the Windows Media Player to be able to play audio CDs. If you're using a different program to play audio CDs, you might not need the MCI CD Audio driver, depending on how the program accesses the CD-ROM drive.

1. Open the Windows Control Panel and choose the Drivers icon.

2. In the Drivers dialog box, choose **A**dd.

3. From the **L**ist of Drivers, select [MCI] CD Audio, then choose OK.

4. Control Panel will prompt you to insert one of your Windows distribution disks. Insert the requested disk, then choose OK.

5. Control Panel will display an informational dialog box indicating that the driver was installed. Select OK, then choose Close to close the Drivers dialog box. Exit Control Panel.

Testing and Troubleshooting

You should test all the aspects of your CD-ROM drive to make sure all your software is configured properly. You should test the drive's capability to read a data CD, play an audio CD, and, if appropriate, share a CD across the network.

Procedure:
Reading a Data CD

Explanation: Many data CDs include their own viewer/reader programs that display the information contained on the CD. Even so, the data CD still should be recognized by DOS as a logical disk device, which means you should be able to display a directory of the CD.

1. Insert a data CD into the CD-ROM drive.

2. **DOS method:** At the DOS prompt, enter **DIR *E:*,** substituting the correct drive ID letter for your CD-ROM drive in place of the E: in this example. You should see a directory listing of the drive.

3. **Windows method:** In Windows, open File Manager and select the drive icon for the CD-ROM drive. A directory listing should appear for the CD-ROM drive.

4. If you see a directory listing, your CD-ROM drive is working properly. If you don't see a directory listing, or if you receive an error message that the disk does not exist or is not ready, verify that you have inserted

the CD properly. The printed side of the CD faces up, and the data side (with no printing on it) faces down. If the CD is inserted properly and you can't read the CD, verify the installation of your CD-ROM driver and MSCDEX.EXE.

After verifying that you can read the CD's directory structure, follow the directions provided with the CD to install any necessary viewer or application software to enable you to use the CD.

Procedure:
Testing Audio CDs

1. Make sure that your CD-ROM drive is connected to your sound card, or that you have headphones connected to the CD-ROM drive.

2. Place an audio CD in the CD-ROM drive.

3. From the Accessories group in Windows, open the Media Player program.

4. From the **D**evice menu, choose **C**D Audio. The Media Player program window changes to appear as shown in figure 11.9. (If **C**D Audio is not one of the choices in your menu, your driver hasn't been installed correctly.)

Figure 11.9: The Media Player program window configured for CD Audio.

5. If you don't have the **C**D Audio menu option, close the Media Player, erase the file MPLAYER.INI from your Windows directory, and then try running Media Player again.

6. Click on the Play button (the leftmost button in the button bar).

Procedure:
Viewing a Photo CD

1. Insert the photo CD into the CD-ROM drive.

2. Open the program you use to view photo CDs. This program may have been included with your CD-ROM drive, or you might have purchased it separately.

3. Use the commands provided in the program to view the images on the CD. If you receive an error message to the effect that there is no CD in the drive or the drive is not ready, your CD-ROM driver probably is not capable of reading photo CDs. Contact technical support for the CD-ROM manufacturer or the place where you bought the CD-ROM drive.

12

Audio Adapters (You Mean Sound Cards?)

One of the fastest growing markets in PC hardware today is the audio adapter (more commonly known as the sound card). *Sound cards* are adapters that give your PC the capability to play high-fidelity sounds, and they can be used for everything from playing audio CDs to embedding a voice note in a document.

This chapter offers an explanation of some of the things you can do with a sound card, tips on what to look for when shopping for a sound card, and procedures for configuring and installing a sound card. The chapter covers the following topics:

- Uses for a sound card
- Tips for buying a sound card
- Configuring and installing a sound card
- Integrating sound with Windows programs

First, you need some background on what sound cards do and some typical uses for sound cards.

Using Audio Adapters

The speaker in your PC was never intended to reproduce sound with any degree of fidelity. The PC's speaker is good for making beeping noises, but that's about it. The speaker and sound support circuitry can't play back a Bach concerto from CD. Even if you just want to hear the great sound effects from your favorite game, the PC's speaker leaves a lot to be desired.

Sound cards not only enable you to play back audio CDs on your PC, but they also open up a lot of new possibilities for using sound. If you have a sound card, you can do the following:

- Play audio CDs on the PC, enabling you to control contrast, treble, bass, and other parameters, just like a conventional stereo

- Play various types of sound files

- Enjoy realistic sound effects in games and simulation programs

- Digitize and store sounds in files from CD, stereo, microphone, or other audio sources for playback, editing, or use in documents

- Assign sound effects to various Windows events (for example, play an obnoxious noise whenever a warning or error dialog box appears)

- Embed digitized sound clips in documents that you create with Windows programs

- Embed your own digitized voice messages in electronic mail that you send to other people, and play back voice messages received in e-mail from other users (see fig. 12.1)

- Create complex musical compositions with your PC

- Mix and edit sounds and musical compositions

- Experience the full range of sounds and sound effects provided by multimedia CDs and programs

- When combined with a video-grabber board, you can capture and edit video and audio sequences to create your own video presentations

Of all the gadgets that are available for the PC, a sound card probably can add the most enjoyment. But sound cards aren't just for fun; they're great for the business world as well.

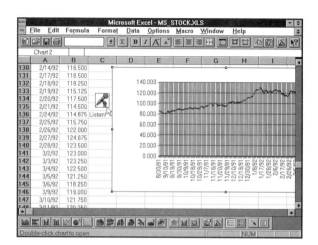

Figure 12.1: A voice annotation embedded in an Excel spreadsheet.

As a matter of fact, the capability to embed a voice annotation in a spreadsheet can be very valuable as a management tool. There's no better way to check a spreadsheet's figures than to have the PC read the numbers back to you as you check them. What's more, sound capability can be a big asset when you're using tutorial and training applications that make use of sound.

Whether you're looking for a little more enjoyment from your PC as you work, or you want to integrate sound into your business documents, a sound card is a good investment.

Shopping for a Sound Card

You need to think about several features when you're considering buying a sound card. Consider not only the technical features of the card, but also whether it includes the right software to fit your needs. The following is a list of features to keep in mind when shopping for a sound card:

- **Support for Windows multimedia extensions.** Make sure the sound card supports the Windows multimedia extensions and works with the sound capabilities built into Windows 3.1. That way, you can take full advantage of sound in Windows, including integrating sound in your Windows documents and using Windows-based multimedia titles.

- **MPC compatibility.** The MPC (Multimedia PC) specifications define the minimum recommended requirements for multimedia hardware. Sound cards that are compliant with the MPC Level 2 standard (currently the latest revision of the standard) support sampling in 8 bits and 16 bits with sample rates of 11KHz, 22KHz, and 44KHz. The card also should support input mixing, MIDI in, MIDI out, and MIDI pass-through, and should use no more than 10 percent of the CPU's time. You don't have to knock yourself out researching all this—hardware meeting MPC requirements is marked with a logo or statement saying so.

- **Compression.** Sound files can be enormous. Shop for a card that supports on-the-fly compression of sound. Look for a compression ratio of at least 3:1 or 4:1.

- **Voice recognition.** Many sound cards support voice recognition, which means you can connect a microphone to the sound card, speak commands into the microphone, and have the sound card recognize and act on those commands. If you're interested in controlling your software with voice commands, look for a sound card that supports voice recognition.

- **Voice synthesis.** This feature enables the sound card to convert text into spoken words. If you want your PC to be able to read your e-mail or other documents to you, look for a sound card that supports voice synthesis.

- **MIDI support.** MIDI (Musical Instrument Digital Interface) is a standard for interfacing electronic instruments such as keyboards to a PC. MIDI sound files store sound as individual notes, rather than as digitized waveforms, saving a tremendous amount of disk space to store sound files. If you want to compose or edit music on your PC, shop for a sound card that includes a MIDI port and can play MIDI files.

- **Maximum number of stereo voices.** The more stereo voices supported by the card, the more complex the MIDI compositions the sound card can render. Think of this as having more musicians in your electronic orchestra.

- **Maximum sample rate.** The sample rate determines the playback quality of a digitized sound. For CD-quality reproduction, shop for a card that supports at least 44KHz sampling.

- **Maximum playback rate.** The higher the playback rate, the better the sound will be. If you want to play audio CDs on your system, shop for a sound card that supports a playback rate of 44KHz or higher.

- **Stereo.** Shop for a sound card that supports stereo playback to get the best possible sound quality.

- **Supports Windows OLE.** If you intend to use sound in your Windows documents, make sure the sound card supports OLE (Object Linking and Embedding).

- **Ad Lib and Sound Blaster compatibility.** If you plan to use your sound card with a wide selection of games, look for a sound card that is compatible with the Ad Lib and Sound Blaster cards. If you're not interested in sound effects for games, this isn't important.

- **Built-in amplifier.** A built-in amplifier on the sound card enables you to use unamplified speakers and deliver more "sound power" to the speakers.

- **CD-ROM interface.** If you buy a multimedia upgrade kit that includes a CD-ROM drive, this isn't as important an issue as if you are buying the CD-ROM separately. If you plan to add other SCSI devices to your system, shop for a sound card that includes a standard SCSI-2 interface. As an alternative, buy a separate SCSI host adapter and use it instead of the sound card to connect your SCSI devices to the PC.

- **Bundled software.** A sound card isn't much good without software to run it. Look for sound cards that include programs for mixing, CD playback, sound recording and playback, and, where applicable, voice recognition and synthesis.

If you can't make sense of the specifications in a sound card's advertisement, call the manufacturer for more information. It's also a good idea to listen to a particular sound card before you buy it. Check out your friends' or business associates' sound cards or shop at a retail dealer where you can listen to the card. Evaluate the sound just as you would when buying a new stereo system.

Sound for Notebooks and Portables

If you want to add sound to your notebook or portable PC, there are some parallel port sound devices you should check out. These devices connect to the PC's parallel port and include audio input and output connections. Two such products are VocalTec's CAT and Logitech's AudioMan. Figure 12.2 shows the Logitech AudioMan.

Figure 12.2: The Logitech AudioMan parallel-port sound adapter.

These devices enable you to continue to use your printer while you play back or record sound. You can connect a set of small speakers to the device or use a set of headphones for playback. The AudioMan includes a built-in microphone, while the CAT uses a plug-in microphone or can use a telephone headset (it includes a standard modular phone jack for plugging in the handset). These devices have the benefit of not requiring configuration for DMA or IRQ settings, so if you've run out of IRQ lines on your desktop PC, these types of sound adapters are an alternative to internal sound cards.

Don't Forget Input and Output

A sound card is absolutely useless if you don't have some type of output device connected to it. At the least, the sound card you buy will have an output jack for a set of headphones.

Using headphones is fine when you're working in an office with someone else, or are using a parallel-port sound adapter connected to your notebook. For the best sound reproduction, though, you may want to connect your sound card to a set of speakers or to a stereo system.

Buying Desktop Speakers

Desktop speakers (also called bookshelf speakers) range from inexpensive to expensive, with price dictating performance up to a point. You can buy a relatively inexpensive set of speakers for about $30, but the sound reproduction won't be as good as with some of the more expensive models. I have a set of Sony SRS-38 speakers that sell for about $60, and which provide a good level of sound quality and volume range.

Some desktop speakers are unamplified, relying on the strength of the signal coming from the sound card to drive the speakers. Others contain their own amplifiers that require battery power or an AC adapter. The Sony speakers that I use are amplified, although they can be used in either amplified or unamplified mode. When amplified, the speakers provide a much broader volume range.

Some of the more expensive speakers also include their own subwoofers, either as separate modules, built into the speaker units, or with all components mounted in an under-the-monitor unit. Whether you buy speakers with these added features depends on the type of fidelity you want from the speakers, but don't expect a speaker system with a subwoofer to necessarily sound better than one without. Test the speakers by listening to them before you buy them.

Look for speakers that are magnetically shielded if you plan to place the speakers next to your monitor. The magnetic field generated by the speakers can affect the display, and the field generated by the monitor can affect the sound quality.

Positioning the Speakers

How you position your speakers relative to your PC and yourself has almost as great an impact on how they sound as how well the speakers are designed. By experimenting with the positioning of your speakers you can potentially coax much better sound from them.

Start with the speakers positioned on your desktop as far apart as possible, and aim the speakers so that their axes converge a few inches in front of you. You also might want to try moving the speakers up to ear level, placing them on a bookshelf on the wall behind your desk or actually mounting them to the wall. Placing the speakers on the wall also will generally improve the speakers' bass output.

Using Your Stereo for Playback

For even better sound control and fidelity, you may want to connect your sound card to a stereo system. This isn't something you'd do if you share an office with someone, but it's great for a home office.

If your stereo has auxiliary jacks, you can connect the sound card to these jacks. The auxiliary jacks probably are RCA-type jacks, while the sound card probably uses a miniature phono-plug, so you need an adapter. You can get the necessary cables and adapters at stereo shops and most stores that sell audio components (like Radio Shack, for example).

Keep in mind that your sound card probably uses a single stereo output jack, with output lines for both left and right channels. Your stereo probably uses separate left and right inputs, so shop for a Y-cable that has a stereo connector at one end and two individual channel connectors at the other end. If you're not sure what to get, tell the salesperson you need the cables and adapters necessary to go from a single stereo mini-jack to separate left and right auxiliary jacks on your stereo.

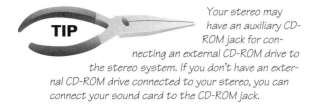

TIP Your stereo may have an auxiliary CD-ROM jack for connecting an external CD-ROM drive to the stereo system. If you don't have an external CD-ROM drive connected to your stereo, you can connect your sound card to the CD-ROM jack.

If there are no auxiliary jacks (common with less expensive, single-unit stereo systems), you still should be able to connect the sound card to the stereo system, but it requires a little more work. Check the components in your stereo system to determine how they connect to the system's amplifier.

In particular, check the connections from the turntable and/or tape deck. Either one probably will be connected inside the system by RCA connectors (which simplify the assembly process when the unit is manufactured). You'll probably have to open the system in order to check it, so make sure you turn it off and unplug it before doing so.

If either component connects to the amplifier with RCA plugs, you can disconnect the component, install splitter cables (Y-cables) in the line, then reconnect it. You then can connect your sound card to these splitter cables.

When you're using the sound card connected to the stereo system in this way, the stereo device selection will have to be set to the device to which the Y-cables are connected. If you have the Y-cables connected between the turntable and the amplifier, for example, select the turntable on the front panel of the stereo system whenever you want to use your sound card.

Input to the Sound Card

If you will be using your sound card to digitize or mix voice annotation or music, you need to connect one or more input devices to the sound card. In the case of voice annotation, you need to connect a microphone to the sound card. The sound card will provide a microphone input jack. Check the sound card's manual to determine which type of microphone is best.

If you will be capturing audio from a CD-ROM drive, you need a connection between the sound card and the CD-ROM drive. Check the card's manual to determine where its line-in connectors are located. There may be only one, or there may be two. Generally, the line-in connectors are located on the board rather than on the connector bracket that attaches at the back of the PC's chassis (where the MIDI connector and output jacks usually are located).

If there is a primary line-in and an auxiliary line-in connector on the sound card, the CD-ROM drive should be connected to the primary line-in connector. You can connect other devices (including a second CD-ROM drive) to the auxiliary input, but you may have to make a cable for it.

Adding a Sound Card

Like many devices, sound cards require a free IRQ, and usually, a free DMA channel. In addition to configuring these options on the card, you also might need to make speaker and CD-ROM connections when installing a sound card. Then, finish the installation by installing any required drivers and other software to enable you to use the card.

Procedure:
Adapter Configuration and Installation

1. Use MSD and your system logs to determine a free IRQ and DMA for your sound card. You may need to shuffle the IRQ and DMA settings for other devices to allocate settings for your sound card.

2. Turn off and open the system.

3. Configure the sound card's IRQ line. Make sure you assign an IRQ to the card that isn't used by any other device. If necessary, you may have to disable an unused COM port. An alternative is to use the same IRQ allocated to LPT1 or LPT2, although you may experience problems using the sound card while printing, and possibly at other times as well. If you have no other options, however, sharing an LPT port IRQ with the sound card is worth trying. Most sound cards provide jumpers or switches on the card to set the IRQ, but some use a configuration program instead.

4. Configure the sound card's DMA channel, making sure to assign a DMA channel that isn't used by any other device in the system. You may have to assign a DMA channel from a specific range of channels in order to use all the capabilities of your sound card. Read the section in the sound card's manual carefully to see if this is the case. As with IRQ settings, most sound cards use jumpers or switches to set the DMA channel, but some use a configuration program instead.

5. Depending on where the connectors are located on your sound card, it may be easier to connect the cables to it before installing the card in the PC. Examine the card to locate any connectors you will be using. If you think it will be easier to connect the cables now, skip forward to the procedure on connecting cables to the card, then return to this procedure.

6. Locate an appropriate slot for the adapter. Choose an 8-bit slot or 16-bit slot for an 8-bit adapter, and choose a 16-bit slot for a 16-bit adapter.

7. Carefully install the sound card in the slot, securing it with a screw.

Procedure:
Connecting Cables

Explanation: The number of connections you need to make to your sound card depends on the optional equipment you'll be using with the sound card. Adding a CD-ROM may require connecting the drive to the sound card's CD-ROM port. Adding speakers and a microphone or connecting the sound card to your stereo are other possibilities.

1. **CD-ROM drives:** Unless you're using a separate SCSI host adapter for the CD-ROM drive, connect the interface cable of the CD-ROM drive to the sound card's interface connector. Connect the cable from the line-out connector on the CD-ROM drive to the primary line-in connector on the sound card. Optionally, connect the CD-ROM drive to the sound card's stereo line-in connector (there might be a stereo line-in connection on the card itself, as well as a stereo line-in connector at the back of the sound card). See figures 12.3 and 12.4.

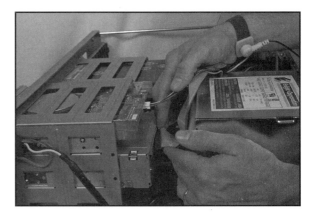

Figure 12.3: Connect the CD-ROM drive to the card's interface connector.

2. **Microphone:** Connect the microphone to the sound card's microphone line-in at the back of the adapter (probably a monaural, rather than stereo, connection).

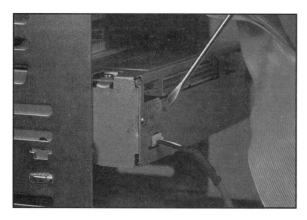

Figure 12.4: Connect the audio cable from the line-out connector on the CD-ROM to the line-in connector on the sound card.

3. **Speaker output:** Connect the speakers to the sound card's stereo line-out connector (see fig. 12.5). Most desktop speakers require a single stereo cable connection between the sound card and one speaker, and another stereo line connection between the two speakers. Set up the speakers as described in the section "Positioning the Speakers" earlier in this chapter.

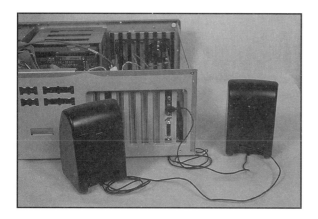

Figure 12.5: Connect the speakers to one another and to the sound card.

4. **Stereo system output:** If you want to connect the sound card to your stereo system instead of to bookshelf speakers, read the section earlier in this chapter titled "Using Your Stereo for Playback." Then,

with the stereo turned off, make a connection from your sound card's stereo line-out connection to the auxiliary input on your stereo (or to the Y adapters you have installed between one of the stereo system's components and its amplifier).

5. **Auxiliary input:** If you have other, non-MIDI devices to connect to the sound card, make a connection between the device and the sound card's auxiliary line-in connector.

Completing the Installation

If you are using the sound card to drive a CD-ROM drive, you need to install a CD-ROM driver for the card. The driver will be included with the sound card if you purchased the CD-ROM drive and sound card as a multimedia kit. If you purchased the sound card and CD-ROM drive separately, you may have to buy the driver and cable kit separately.

The software for your sound card probably includes an installation program that will install the driver for you. If not, you'll have to install the driver manually by adding an entry for the driver to CONFIG.SYS and copying the driver file to the appropriate directory. In addition to this CD-ROM driver, you need to install MSCDEX.EXE. Read Chapter 11, "CD-ROM Drives," for more information on installing and configuring your CD-ROM drive and MSCDEX.

In addition to installing a CD-ROM driver and MSCDEX, you also need to install the software included with your sound card that enables you to use the card. These applications typically include a sound mixer, recorder, CD playback, and possibly other programs. The installation process for your sound card might also install one or more drivers for Windows. Otherwise, the manual may direct you to install the drivers yourself using the Windows Control Panel.

Procedure:

Installing Device Drivers for Windows

Explanation: If you will be using your sound card in Windows, you will have to install some sound drivers with

Control Panel, unless the software installation program for the sound card takes care of this step for you.

1. In Windows, open the Control Panel and choose the Drivers icon.

2. In the **D**rivers dialog box, choose the **A**dd button.

3. From the Add dialog box, choose the driver required by your sound card. Check the manual to determine which drivers to install. It's probable that your sound card disks include updated drivers. Choose the option titled Unlisted or Updated Driver to install drivers from your sound card disks. You might need to install more than one driver, which will require that you repeat this step for each driver.

4. When you have finished installing all of the necessary drivers, close the Drivers dialog box and close Control Panel. Then, restart Windows.

You can assign sounds to various events so that when the event occurs, the assigned sound plays on your sound card. This is covered in the next section, "Integrating Sound with Windows."

Integrating Sound with Windows

There are a number of ways you can integrate sound with the Windows environment and with Windows programs. Some are purely for fun, while others apply to the everyday use of your PC for business. This section covers ways you can use sound in Windows, starting with assigning sounds to general Windows events.

Assigning Sounds to Windows Events

There are a number of standard events that occur in Windows. These events include starting and exiting Windows, various types of dialog boxes opening, and more. By default, you can assign sounds to seven standard Windows events through the Windows Control Panel. You can assign the TADA.WAV file ("Tah Dah!"), for example, to play when Windows starts.

Your sound card may include software that enables you to assign sounds to other Windows events. There also are some third-party programs that enable you to assign sounds to other Windows events not supported through the standard Control Panel.

Procedure:

Assigning Sounds to Windows Events

1. In Windows, open the Control Panel and choose the Sound icon.

2. Verify that the **En**able System Sounds check box is checked.

3. In the Sound dialog box, select the event from the **E**vents list to which you want to assign a WAV file.

4. In the **F**ile list, select the WAV file you want to assign to the event. If you want to listen to a WAV file before you assign it, click on the **T**est button. Whichever WAV file is selected will be played.

5. Repeat steps 3 and 4 for any other events to which you want to assign sounds.

6. Click on the OK button to store your selections.

*If the selections in the **E**vents and **F**iles lists are dimmed, your sound drivers are not properly installed. Windows is not recognizing that you have a valid sound device installed in the system. Run through your driver installation steps again to make sure the drivers are properly installed, and make sure you restart Windows after installing the drivers for the changes to take effect.*

Using Sound in Documents

If your sound card supports Windows 3.1's OLE, you can embed sound objects in your Windows documents—you can embed a voice notation in a Word or Excel document, for example. Someone else who views the document can double-click on the object to hear your note played back (assuming there's a sound card in his system). Or, you may want to embed a short voice note in an e-mail message.

Procedure:

Recording and Embedding a Sound Object in a Document

Explanation: The steps in this procedure are geared toward Word for Windows, but the general procedure applies to most applications that support OLE. The only differences will be in menu names and options—some programs may use slightly different menu names and commands, but the general procedure still is the same.

1. From the application's **I**nsert menu, choose **O**bject. The Object dialog box appears, as shown in figure 12.6.

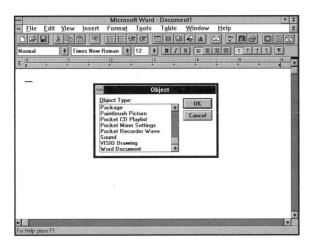

Figure 12.6: The Object dialog box in Word for Windows.

2. Scroll through the list of objects in the Object dialog box and locate the Sound entry.

3. Click on the Sound entry, then choose the OK button. The Sound Recorder appears on the desktop.

4. When you are ready to record your note, click on the microphone button. The screen pointer changes to an hourglass as the Sound Recorder sets up the recording.

5. When the arrow pointer reappears, the Sound Recorder is recording. Speak your message into the microphone, then click on the Stop button when you are finished. (The Stop button has a solid rectangle on it.)

6. From the Sound Recorder's **F**ile menu, choose E**x**it. Sound Recorder asks whether you want to update the object in the document. Choose **Y**es to embed the sound in the document.

Procedure:

Embedding an Existing Sound File in a Document

Explanation: Use this procedure if you want to embed an existing WAV file in a document.

1. Open the document in which you want to embed the file and position the cursor where you want the sound file to be inserted.

2. Open File Manager and locate the WAV file to be inserted.

3. Drag the file from File Manager to the document and release the mouse button. A Sound Recorder icon will appear in the document with the title of the WAV file listed underneath it. If you don't want to change the text under the icon, skip the remaining steps.

4. To edit the description under the WAV file object, click once on the object's icon. Then from the **E**dit menu, choose Package **O**bject. This opens the Object Packager.

5. From the Object Packager's **E**dit menu, choose La**b**el, then type the label you want to appear under the icon. Click on the OK button when you've finished editing the label.

6. From the Object Packager's **F**ile menu, choose E**x**it. Click on **Y**es when you're prompted to update the document.

There are a number of other ways to embed a sound object in a document. If you're interested in learning more about OLE, pick up a copy of *Maximizing Windows 3.1*, from New Riders Publishing.

Embedding a Voice Note in an Electronic-Mail Message

If you want to embed a sound recording in an e-mail message, you first need to record the message in a WAV file using the Sound Recorder or the recording program that is included with your sound card. You then attach the WAV file to the message, just as you would attach any other binary file to a text message.

With most mail programs, you begin by composing the text of the note, if any. A short explanation of what the voice message is about might be useful. Then, position the cursor where you want the voice note object to be inserted in the message. Next, choose the mail program's Attach menu, or whatever menu option is required in the program to attach a file to a message.

When you're sending voice notes to other users, remember that the recipient must have a sound card in her system in order to play back the recorded note.

13

Printers

If there is one piece of hardware that causes the most aggravation to the average user, it's the printer. Often the printer is one of the simplest devices connected to the PC, but it also is the one item that most often fails to work.

I hate to break it to you this way, but it's probably not the printer's fault—the problem often stems from user error. The printer might be connected improperly, it might be using the wrong driver, or you just might be trying to access it incorrectly from your program.

This chapter helps you get your printer working, whether it's brand-new or has been connected to your system for a while (and whether you caused the problem or not). You'll also find a buyer's guide to printers in this chapter, along with the following topics:

- Understanding the different types of printers
- Tips for buying a new printer
- Some background on LPT ports
- Installing printers and printer drivers
- Tips for using a printer in Windows

Understanding Printers

Printers are a lot better (in terms of speed and quality) than they were ten years ago, but in many respects, printers are still the same as they were back then. The technology has improved, but it hasn't altered radically. Even so, there are some new types of printers available, and one of them might fit your needs and your budget. The next section takes a look at the types of printers commonly used with PCs today.

Types of Printers

Five basic types of printers are available, each offering its own advantages and filling a particular printer market niche:

- **Dot-matrix.** These printers use an array of impact pins to drive small dots of ink onto the paper. Dot-matrix printers use ribbon cassettes, much like conventional typewriters.

- **Laser.** Laser printers use a technology similar to that employed in photocopiers to "draw" the page. Even though laser printers require toner cartridge replacement, which is more expensive than the print supply replacement costs for other types of printers, laser printers produce some of the best quality output.

- **Inkjet.** Inkjet printers use various methods for essentially spraying a jet of ink onto the paper. Inkjet printers produce very good quality output and sell for substantially less than laser printers.

- **Color PostScript dye sublimation.** These are relatively new to the market, and still expensive. They are capable of producing near-photographic quality images in color, but it's a sure bet that you won't be willing to spend the $7,000 to $10,000 for one.

- **Monster machines.** A new trend is the all-in-one machine, comprising a laser printer, photocopier, fax, and scanner in one device. These devices are naturally more expensive than a typical printer, with prices around $3,500 for a black-and-white system.

A Brief Buyer's Guide to Printers

If you are shopping for a new printer, first decide what you need to produce with the printer rather than what you want to produce with it. It's nice to have a printer that can render scanned photographs with great quality, but is it really necessary?

If the paper documents you generate are for home or internal use only, a dot-matrix printer is the way to go. Although dot-matrix printers are noisier than other types of printers (and usually slower), they also are a lot cheaper and have a lower per-page operating cost.

Dot-matrix printers also are a good choice for making draft copies of documents, freeing your laser printer for more important printing jobs (only an issue in an office environment where many users share printers).

If you generate letters and other documents that consist primarily of text and don't mix a lot of graphics and text, consider an inkjet printer. You'll get outstanding quality for about $350 to $400, and replacement costs for the inkjet cartridges are very reasonable. For a price premium, you can get a color inkjet printer, but don't buy one just because it prints in color. If you don't have a real need to print in color, buy a standard, black-only inkjet.

For the best quality, particularly when mixing text and graphics in your document, consider a laser printer. Although more expensive, laser printers have a distinct edge over inkjet printers. When quality output is important and you are trying to present a professional image, a laser printer is a must.

Buying Tips for Dot-Matrix Printers

The chief advantage to dot-matrix printers is their cost. The number of pins in the print head defines, to some degree, the quality of the printer's output and its cost; 9-pin printers sell in the price range of $100 to $200, and 24-pin printers sell in the range of $200 to $400. You also can buy 18-pin printers.

Here are some issues to consider and technical points to evaluate when shopping for a dot-matrix printer:

- **Multipart forms.** If you work with multipart forms, the only type of printer that will print on your forms is a dot-matrix printer.

- **Wide carriage support.** If you find that you need to print documents that are wider than a standard 8 1/2-inch page, a dot-matrix printer is one of the few options available for wide-carriage printing.

- **Operating cost.** The amount that it costs to generate a page depends on the cost of the printer's ribbon and how long it will last. Dot-matrix printers generally have an operating cost ranging from less than half a cent per page to about 1.5 cents per page.

- **Number of pins.** For the best print quality, choose an 18-pin or a 24-pin printer. If you need to save as much money as possible, choose a 9-pin printer. Generally, the more pins the printer has, the finer the printed image will be.

- **Text speed.** Check the printer's characters per second rating. Dot-matrix printers generally have two speeds; one for draft printing and a slower speed for quality printing. Look for a draft print speed of at least 120cps (characters per second), but keep in mind that you can buy printers with draft speeds of up to around 280cps. Quality output will generally be around half the speed of draft output, but might be somewhat slower than that.

- **Graphics speed.** If you plan to print a lot of graphics, check the printer's graphics printing speed. Most printers support anywhere from 0.5 pages per minute to more than 2 pages per minute.

- **Graphics resolution.** The graphics resolution of the printer is measured in *dots per inch*, or *dpi*. The lowest resolution you will find is around 120×144, with the high end of resolution around 360×360. If graphics quality is important, pick a printer with a higher resolution value.

- **Paper handling.** Shop for a printer that includes both friction and tractor feed, and which also offers automatic feeding of cut sheets (which may be included as a cost option).

Buying Tips for Inkjet Printers

Today's inkjet printers are a good alternative to dot-matrix printers. Inkjet printers are much quieter and offer better output quality for both text and graphics. Here are some points to consider when shopping for an inkjet printer:

- **Resolution.** Inkjet printers typically have a resolution of around 300 dpi, which is comparable to lower-end laser printers. Even at the same resolution, an inkjet printer can't match the quality of a laser printer because the ink tends to spread slightly on the paper, adding a touch of fuzziness to the text that doesn't happen with laser printers.

- **Operating costs.** With an inkjet printer, you can expect to spend from 4 cents per page to 6 cents per page for plain black-on-white text. Color inkjet printers are more expensive to operate, running anywhere from 50 cents to 75 cents per page.

- **Ink smudging.** Many inkjet printers use water-soluble ink, so you can expect a little smudging in some situations. The oil on your fingertips, for example, can smudge the ink if you don't let the ink dry completely before picking up the page.

- **Text speed.** Draft and quality text speeds are slower on inkjet printers than on dot-matrix printers. Expect about 70 cps in draft mode and 80 cps in quality mode.

- **Graphics speed.** Graphics print speed typically is better on inkjet printers than on dot-matrix printers. Expect from 1.4 to 1.9 pages per minute.

Buying Tips for Laser Printers

When quality output is essential, your best choice is a laser printer. Laser printers also are best for printing graphics, particularly when the graphics are embedded on a page with text. There are lots of options to consider when buying a laser printer.

If you're buying a laser printer for your use only, for instance, you can save money by buying a personal laser printer (which generally means that the printer is a little slower than some of the other printers available). If you're buying a printer to share with other users, printing speed and connection options (such as network connections) become more important.

Here are some issues and features to consider when shopping for a laser printer:

- **Resolution.** Most mainstream laser printers offer 300 dpi resolution. Newer designs double that resolution to 600 dpi, but for a higher price. For an extra cost, you can add enhancements to some laser printers to boost the resolution to 800 dpi or 1200 dpi, depending on the model.

● **Resolution enhancement.** Almost as important as overall resolution is whether the printer uses any sort of resolution enhancement. Many manufacturers use different technologies to improve output, including varying the size and placement of the dots that make up an image or character. Shop for a laser printer that offers some type of resolution enhancement technology.

● **Printer engine.** Although you might think all laser printers are designed differently from the ground up, it's not the case. Many laser printers are based on the same internal print engine as other brands. Canon and Hewlett-Packard laser printers use Canon's printer engines, as do many other manufacturer's laser printers. Just because a printer is manufactured by a particular company doesn't mean it isn't similar in quality and design to another company's printer.

● **Speed.** Expect a text print speed of 4 pages per minute (ppm) with personal laser printers, and 8 ppm for higher-end printers. For shared laser printers (printers on a network, for example), shop for a printer with 12 ppm rate or better. Graphics print speed varies, but shop for a printer that can do at least 1.8 to 2.5 ppm.

● **PCL 5.** PCL stands for Printer Control Language, and is a page-description and printer control language developed by Hewlett-Packard. PCL 5 support can enable a printer to print 600-dpi text and graphics without requiring PostScript support.

● **PostScript.** PostScript is a printer control language that has been around for quite some time. Many printers support PostScript directly, while others support it with optional cartridges or boards that are installed in the printer. Like PCL 5, PostScript provides improved resolution.

● **Printer connections.** Some laser printers provide only a parallel port, while others include a parallel port and a serial port. Some network printers are available with Ethernet or token-ring connections, making it possible to connect them directly to the network just like a PC.

● **Printer enhancements.** You can get a number of enhancements for many laser printers, including

PostScript support, additional memory, and resolution enhancement. Put as much memory in the printer as you can afford. If you need high-quality output, consider a PostScript cartridge if the printer doesn't support PCL 5.

Adding a Printer

There really isn't much to installing a printer. The physical connections are simple. What often trips up most users is installing and configuring the printer driver and setting options to control the port to which it's connected. This section on installing a printer wouldn't be complete without a quick discussion of ports and drivers.

About LPT and COM Ports

Printers are most commonly connected to the PC's parallel ports. Parallel ports are also called *LPT ports*, an acronym for Line PrinTer. A typical PC can have up to three physical LPT ports: LPT1, LPT2, and LPT3. (Many network operating systems support additional logical LPT ports, such as LPT4, LPT5, and so on.) LPT1 also is recognized by the system as PRN.

In older PCs, LPT ports usually were located on the graphics adapter. Most PCs today incorporate the LPT ports on separate I/O adapters or on a multifunction host adapter that might include an IDE host adapter, floppy controller, two COM ports, and one LPT port in a single adapter. The LPT port connector is a 25-pin female connector (male connectors have exposed pins and female connectors do not).

Usually, you don't have to set any special parameters to make your printer work with a particular LPT port. Just connect the printer and specify in your program which port is to be used. You can specify some settings for both DOS and Windows, however, if you're experiencing certain problems with your printer. Here's a list of the settings you can control for an LPT port:

● **Device Not Selected.** You can set this value in Windows to specify the amount of time (in seconds) that Windows should wait for the printer to come on-line and get ready to print. If the printer doesn't become available in the specified amount of time, Windows displays an error message. Setting the Device Not

Selected value to a higher number is useful if your printer requires a long setup or warmup time, or is located elsewhere on a network (and may be in use by another node).

● **Retry.** This setting, which can be set in DOS or in Windows, specifies the length of time in seconds for which the system will attempt to retransmit data to the printer when the printer's buffer is full or the printer is not ready to accept more data (if it is downloading fonts, for example). When the time limit expires, the printer *times out.* A setting of 45 seconds usually is sufficient for a non-PostScript printer, although 90 seconds is more appropriate for a PostScript printer (which often has a longer setup time).

Specifying values for these settings is explained in more detail later in this chapter. Figure 13.1 shows the dialog box in Windows that you can use to set LPT port options.

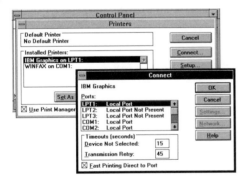

Figure 13.1: The Connect dialog box in Windows enables you to specify LPT port parameters.

Some printers can be connected to one of the PC's COM ports. Depending on the system and on the printer, connecting the printer to a serial port can sometimes speed up printing by increasing the speed at which the data travels to the printer from the PC. Another advantage to serial port connection is that the cable can be up to 50 feet in length, compared to the parallel port's 10 feet.

Configuring a COM port for a printer requires setting more options than for an LPT port because you have to specify the baud rate, number of data bits and stop bits, and other settings. Here's a listing of the COM port settings you might have to set for a printer:

● **Baud rate.** This is the rate at which the information is sent through the port.

● **Data bits.** Without launching into a long technical explanation, I'll just explain that this is the number of bits in each byte of data sent to the printer that actually represents data. The printer probably will use either seven or eight data bits (with eight being most likely).

● **Stop bits.** Stop bits are added to a data stream to indicate the end of a data byte. The most common setting for a printer is 1 stop bit.

● **Parity.** Specifies whether parity checking is used (and what type) to identify transmission errors. Settings are Even, Odd, and None. Most printers require None for this setting.

Often, you can hook up your printer to the selected COM port and specify which port to use, and the printer will work because the program or operating environment takes care of setting the port parameters for you. Sometimes, however, you have to set the parameters. Figure 13.2 shows the dialog box used in Windows to specify COM port settings.

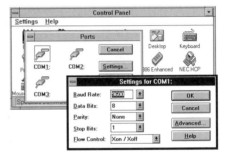

Figure 13.2: The Settings dialog box in Windows enables you to specify COM port settings.

For reasonably hassle-free printer connection, use the LPT port if one is available. If you don't have a free LPT port but do have a free COM port, or you need to use a printer cable longer than ten feet, use the COM port connection if your printer provides one.

Why Do You Need a Driver?

The PC can perform some low-level access of the printer without any other special software. A good way to test whether your printer is working, for example, is to print a copy of a directory listing from DOS with the DIR command. I'll explain how to do that in the testing and troubleshooting section.

One printer is as different from another as apples from oranges, so to take advantage of all the features a printer has to offer, a program needs a software driver that gives it access to those features.

Here's a simple example about how a software driver works: Let's say that you have a document that contains some bold text. The printer has no way of knowing that the document contains bold text, so the program has to be capable of telling the printer, at the appropriate point, to begin printing in bold. After the printer has finished printing the bold text, the program needs to tell the printer to switch back to normal text. The program does this with special control codes that it sends to the printer.

Literally hundreds of different kinds of printers are available, and not all of them use the same codes for all their features. Instead of building into a program all the codes necessary to support all the different types of printers, programmers use a printer driver as an intermediary between the program and the printer. The driver takes care of sending the proper codes to the printer when necessary.

Figure 13.3 shows the Printers dialog box in Windows, which you use to install and configure printer drivers.

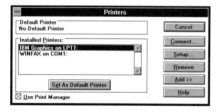

Figure 13.3: The Printers dialog box in Windows enables you to install and configure a printer driver.

Of all the printer problems I've helped people solve over the years, driver problems are the most common. If you use the wrong driver for a printer, the printer either will not work at all or will print garbage on the page along with your document (sometimes all you get is the garbage).

When you are setting up a printer, it is important to install the correct printer driver. DOS programs generally include printer drivers as part of the application package. Windows programs, however, rely on Windows to supply the printer driver.

If you are installing a new printer and want to print from a DOS program, you have to use the DOS application's installation program to install a printer driver for your new printer. If you're installing a new printer to use in Windows, you need to use the Windows Control Panel to install a printer driver. These steps are covered in more detail in upcoming procedures.

If you can't locate a driver specifically for your printer, you might be able to use a driver for a different printer. Many printers emulate some of the more popular printer models; lots of dot-matrix printers will emulate one of the IBM graphics printers, and many laser printers emulate the HP line of laser printers.

If you can't find a driver for your printer, check your printer manual to see if it is compatible with another brand and model, or if it can be configured to be compatible by setting a few switches on the printer. Set up the printer for this compatible mode, then use the printer driver for the printer being emulated by your printer.

Procedure:

Setting Up and Connecting Your Printer

Explanation: This procedure explains how to set up a printer and connect it to your system.

1. Unpack the printer, then check for packing materials inside the printer and remove them. Also check for parts that might have been taped for shipment.

2. Follow the directions provided with the printer to set it up, including installing any paper cartridges, paper feed attachments, or other options. For laser printers, you'll need to install a toner cartridge. Before you install the toner cartridge, shake it from side to side to evenly distribute the toner. Follow the directions provided with the printer to install the cartridge.

3. For parallel printers, connect a parallel printer cable between one of the PC's LPT ports and the parallel port on the printer.

   For serial printers, connect a serial cable between the printer and one of the PC's COM ports. You might need a 25-pin to 9-pin adapter to connect the cable to the PC if the COM port to which you're connecting the printer uses a 9-pin connector.

4. Connect the power cord, plug it in, and turn on the printer.

Procedure:
Adding Printer Drivers to Your System

Explanation: Before you can use the printer, you have to set it up and configure it in your software. You'll have to install a separate printer driver in each DOS program in which you plan to use the printer, even if you will be using those DOS programs under Windows.

If you'll be using the printer for Windows programs, you need only install a single printer driver for the Windows environment. Your Windows programs will use that single printer driver—you do not have to install a separate driver for each Windows program. See the following steps.

1. If you have DOS programs already installed, start the DOS program. Select the menu option in the program that enables you to select a specific printer. It should be in a menu associated with printing, setup, or options. Check your program's manual if you're not sure which menu option to select.

   After you find and select the correct menu option, the program should give you a list of printers from which to choose. Select the printer description that matches your printer (or that is compatible with your printer). Follow any other directions provided in your program manual to configure the printer's options, including specifying to which port the printer is connected. Repeat this step for every DOS program in which you plan to use the printer (it will be different in each program).

2. If you do not have DOS programs installed, run the installation program for the DOS application. Part of the installation process probably will include selecting a printer driver to install. Select the appropriate driver and let the installation program install it.

   If the installation program doesn't prompt you to install a printer driver, you'll need to run the setup procedure described in step 1. Remember to set options for the printer in your program, including specifying the port to which the printer is connected.

Installation for Windows is much more "cut and dried" than it is for DOS programs. The remaining steps explain how to install and configure a printer driver for Windows.

1. Start Windows and open the Control Panel, then choose the Printers icon. The Printers dialog box will open (see fig. 13.4).

2. From the Printers dialog box, click on the **A**dd button. The dialog box expands to show a list of printers (see fig. 13.4).

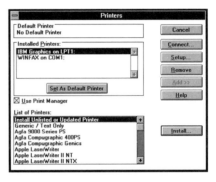

Figure 13.4: The Printers dialog box in the Control Panel showing a list of printers.

3. Scroll through the list of printers provided in the Printers dialog box to locate your printer. If you can't find a listing specifically for your printer, look for a selection that is compatible with your printer (check your printer manual for a list of compatible printers). If your printer included a disk with Windows drivers on it, select the option labeled "Install Unlisted or Updated Printer."

4. After selecting your printer, click on the **I**nstall button. Windows probably will prompt you to insert one of your Windows disks; insert the requested disk and click on the OK button.

5. After Windows has installed the driver for your printer, select the printer driver's description in the Installed **P**rinters list, then click on the **C**onnect button.

6. In the Connect dialog box, select the port to which the printer is connected, then click on the OK button.

7. Next, click on the **S**etup button to configure the printer driver's options. This might include specifying printing resolution, paper selection, amount of memory in the printer, and other settings. Figure 13.5 shows the setup dialog box for an HP LaserJet IIIP.

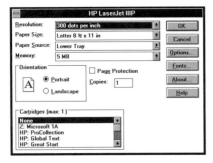

Figure 13.5: A typical setup dialog box for an HP laser printer.

8. When you've finished setting printer options, click on OK to close the setup dialog box. Click on the Close button to close the Printers dialog box, then close the Control Panel.

Testing

Before trying to print from a program to a new printer, it's a good idea to try printing a sheet from the DOS prompt, just to make sure the printer is working. If you later try to print from a program and the printer doesn't work properly, you'll know that the problem is with the program or printer driver, and not with the printer.

Procedure:

Printing from the DOS Prompt

Explanation: This procedure explains how to copy the output of the DIR command to the printer by redirecting its output to the device LPT1:. If your printer is connected to LPT2 or LPT3, specify the appropriate port in the following procedure.

1. Make sure the printer is connected to the PC and turned on. Then verify that the printer is on-line (there should be an indicator light of some kind on the printer to indicate when it is on-line).

2. At the DOS prompt, enter **DIR > LPT1:**.

The printer should generate a listing of the current directory, just as you would otherwise see on the display. If you don't get an output of the DIR command on the printer, check the connections to the printer, verify your printer driver selection and port setting, see that the printer is on-line, and then try again.

Printing from a DOS Program

The procedure for printing from a DOS program varies from one DOS program to another—there is no standardization. If you are not familiar with how to print from your DOS program, look for a Print or Output command (or something similar). If you can't get the printer to work from the DOS program, but it does work from the DOS command prompt (see the previous procedure), recheck your printer driver installation and configuration. In particular, make sure you have specified the correct port for the driver and correct options for the printer.

Procedure:

Printing from a Windows Program

Explanation: This procedure explains how to print from a Windows program. Because Windows applications are similar in design, this generic procedure covers virtually all Windows programs.

1. Open the program and load or create the document that you want to print.

2. From the program's **F**ile menu, choose **P**rint Setup and select the printer driver for your printer. You should not have to configure it if you did so when you installed the printer driver. You'll only need to change the printer's configuration when you want to use a different resolution, paper source, or other options for a particular print job.

3. After selecting the printer, open the **F**ile menu and choose the **P**rint command. Depending on the program, the document can be sent to the printer immediately (or to Print Manager), or the program can display a dialog box prompting you for various options to print the document. If it displays a dialog box, specify whatever options are necessary for the current document (such as which pages to print), then click on OK to print the document.

Enhancing a Laser Printer

You can do several things to improve the performance and quality of your laser printer. One of the best things you can do is to add memory to the printer. Adding memory enables the printer to hold more text, use more fonts, and store complex pages of graphics. It can speed up printing, particularly when you are using downloaded fonts.

Procedure:
Adding Memory

Explanation: Most laser printers accept special memory cards to enable you to expand the amount of memory in the printer. Others provide SIMM sockets in the printer for installing memory. Check your printer manual or your printer vendor to determine which type of memory you need to install in your printer. The following steps are for an HP IIIP printer, but the process is similar for other HP printers (and also for other brands).

1. Disconnect the power and interface cables from the rear of the printer. Do not open the memory board bag until directed to do so.

2. Loosen the screws holding the rear access panel (see fig. 13.6).

3. Remove the screws that hold the interface plate in place, then gently pull off the interface plate (see fig. 13.7).

4. Before opening the bag containing the memory board, touch the surface of the bag or any metal part of the printer to drain the static from your body.

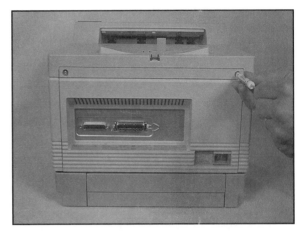

Figure 13.6: Loosen the rear access panel screws.

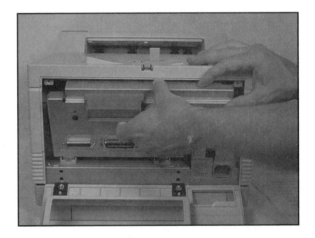

Figure 13.7: Gently remove the interface plate.

5. Look inside the board slots to find the connector that will connect the memory card to the printer. Orient the board in the slot so that the connector on the board lines up with the connector in the printer.

6. Press the board firmly into place (see fig. 13.8).

7. Replace the interface plate, making sure it aligns properly with the connectors in the printer. Secure it with its screws.

8. Close and secure the rear access panel.

Figure 13.8: Press the memory board firmly into place.

9. Connect the printer and turn it on. Check the status display during the self test to make sure that the display registers the correct amount of memory. If the printer generates an error message, check your memory board installation again.

Adding Cartridges to Your Printer

Another good way to enhance your laser printer's capabilities is to install optional cartridges in the printer. Typically, these cartridges simply slide into a socket in the body of the printer, and don't require any additional setup process.

You can get cartridges with different fonts, which enable the printer to print these fonts without having to download them from the PC—thus saving time. This also gives you access to more fonts from DOS programs that don't support TrueType fonts, which are used in Windows. After you have installed a font cartridge, you need to configure your printer driver's options to include the font cartridge.

You also can install PostScript cartridges in your laser printer. Adding a PostScript cartridge will give your printer improved resolution and a wider selection of fonts, but you need to use a PostScript driver for the printer.

Another option to look for are GDI cartridges or enhancement products for your laser printer if you use Windows. *GDI* stands for Graphics Device Interface, which is the

standard set of routines that Windows uses to display graphics. By adding GDI support to your printer, you can increase its speed considerably.

Troubleshooting Printers

If your printer stops working (or never started working), the problem might be as simple as a loose or incorrectly connected cable. More often, though, the problem is that you selected the wrong printer driver or configured the driver to use the wrong port. Use the following steps to troubleshoot your printer problem:

1. Make sure the printer is plugged in and connected to the PC, verifying that it is connected to the correct port. Next, make sure that the printer is turned on and is on-line. If the printer doesn't register as on-line, that means that the printer won't work. Look for the on-line button, and press it to put the printer on-line. Make sure there is paper in the printer.

2. Try printing a directory listing to the printer by entering **DIR > LPT1:** at the DOS prompt (change the port specification if you're using a different port).

3. If you get the DIR output on your printer, go on to step 4. If the printer doesn't work and you have verified all the connections, call technical support at the place where you bought the printer.

4. Verify that you have installed the correct printer driver for your printer and that you have configured it properly. For DOS programs, driver installation and configuration is done through the application. For Windows programs, driver installation and configuration is done through the Windows Control Panel. Make sure that you have configured the driver for the correct printer port.

5. If the printer works, but the output is garbled in some way, recheck your printer driver configuration. If the printer doesn't print, and you are using the printer in Windows, open the Control Panel and choose the Printers icon. Select the printer driver for your printer, then choose the **C**onnect button. Double the settings for **D**evice Not Selected and **T**ransmission Retry, then close the Control Panel. Try printing again.

Improving Your Printer's Performance

You can do a few things to improve printer performance in Windows, and most of the changes are accomplished with just a few settings in a dialog box. One change you can make is to disable the Print Manager.

Disabling Print Manager

By default, Windows processes all printing through a program called the Print Manager. Print Manager is a *print spooler*, which means that it takes over the task of sending the document to the printer, making it possible for you to continue using your program even while a document is printing.

Normally, I recommend that you use Print Manager because it enables you to continue to work while your documents are printing. If you generally do not work while the printer is going, though, you can speed up printing a little by turning off Print Manager. Turning off Print Manager also saves disk space.

When you print a document in Windows, Print Manager intercepts the document and creates printer files on the disk, each containing a page of the document. Print Manager then begins sending the pages to the printer, which frees the program so that you can use it while Print Manager prints.

To disable Print Manager, open the Control Panel and select the Printers icon. In the Printers dialog box, clear the **U**se Print Manager check box to bypass the Print Manager when you print.

Using Fast Printing Direct to Port

By default, Windows bypasses printer interrupts for printing, instead sending the data directly to the printer port. This can improve printing speed, but it sometimes can cause problems with some programs. For best performance, use the Fast Printing Direct to Port option. If you have problems printing from a particular Windows program, try disabling this option. Use the following steps to enable or disable direct printing:

1. In Windows, open the Control Panel.

2. Select the printer driver for which you want to enable or disable direct-to-port printing, then click on the **C**onnect button.

3. To disable direct-to-port printing and use standard DOS interrupt services to print, clear the **F**ast Printing Direct to Port check box. To enable direct-to-port printing, check the **F**ast Printing Direct to Port check box.

4. Click on OK, then click on the Close button to close the Printers dialog box.

Using Multiple Configurations

If you switch printer configurations often, such as changing from Portrait mode to Landscape mode or using different font options, reconfiguring the printer driver each time can be a nuisance. You can get around the need to reconfigure the printer driver each time you use it by using multiple printer driver configurations.

To store multiple configurations, create a port entry in WIN.INI for each configuration, and give it a name that describes the printer configuration. This multiple configuration is placed in the [ports] section of WIN.INI and might have entries that look like LPTI.Portrait=, LPTI.Landscape=, and LPTI.Font_cartridge=.

The part of the port description to the left of the period specifies the physical printer port, and can be LPT1, LPT2, LPT3, and so on, depending on the port to which the printer is connected. The part of the port description to the right of the period just helps you keep track of how a driver is configured. You can use any description, but you can't use spaces. Use the underscore (_) or dash (-) characters instead. Make sure that you include an equal sign (=) at the end of the description. Each entry that you create later is associated with a particular printer configuration.

After you create the port entries, you can configure multiple instances of the same printer driver for each of the port entries. Whenever you need a particular configuration, you just use the P**r**int Setup command in the program's **F**ile menu to choose the configuration you need.

Procedure:

Creating and Using Multiple Printer Configurations

Explanation: This procedure explains how to create multiple printer configurations to use in Windows. Besides creating some new printer port definitions in SYSTEM.INI, you also must install multiple instances of the driver for the appropriate printer.

1. Open SysEdit or Notepad and load the file WIN.INI from the Windows directory.

2. Add whatever port entries you want to the [ports] section. Remember to preface each entry by a valid port ID such as LPT1, then follow it with a period and a description of how the driver associated with the entry will be configured. End the line with an equal sign. Here are some examples:

   ```
   LPT1.Portrait=
   LPT1.Landscape=
   LPT1.Top_Tray=
   LPT1.Envelope_Tray=
   LPT1.FineDither=
   ```

3. Save the changes to WIN.INI.

4. In Control Panel, choose the Printers icon.

5. Choose the **A**dd button in the Printers dialog box to display the list of printer drivers, then select the driver for your printer. Click on the **I**nstall button to install the driver.

6. Click on the **I**nstall button once for each of the port entries you have added to WIN.INI (one for each configuration you want to maintain). Each time you click on the **I**nstall button, a new instance of the driver appears in the Installed **P**rinters list.

7. In the Installed **P**rinters list, choose the first of the duplicate printer driver entries, then click on the **C**onnect button.

8. In the Connect dialog box, select one of the port entries you created in step 2, then click on OK.

9. With the same driver still selected, click on the **S**etup button and set the options for the printer driver. When you are finished setting options, click on OK.

10. Repeat step 9 for the other port entries, configuring each one as required. When all of the driver instances are configured, click on the Close button, then close the Control Panel.

11. To use a particular driver configuration, open the document you want to print. From the program's **F**ile menu, choose Print **S**etup. Choose the appropriate driver, then print the document.

If you are using an HP PCL 5 driver, such as the one that ships with Windows 3.1 for the HP IIIP, you won't be able to store multiple configurations. This driver file has the file name HPPCL5A.DRV. You need to get an updated driver, HPPCL5MS.DRV, from the Microsoft BBS or from someone who has a copy (it ships with Windows for Workgroups, also).

TIP

To make Windows install the driver for you, first use the **R**emove button in the Printers dialog box to remove all of the instances of the HP driver. Then erase the file HPPCL5A.DRV from your Windows System directory. Next, copy the unexpanded file HPPCL5MS.DR_ from the distribution disk to your hard disk and rename it HPPCL5A.DR_.

Use the Control Panel to install the printer driver again, but when prompted to insert the disk containing the HPPCL5A.DRV driver, enter the drive and directory containing the file you just copied to your system.

After installing the new driver, you should be able to maintain multiple printer configurations for the HP PCL printers.

14

Tape Drives

The most important maintenance task that you can perform on your PC is to back up your system's hard disk on a regular basis, particularly if you use it for business. If something happens to your hard disk, you literally could be out of business. At the very least, losing some of your files is an inconvenience you can avoid by backing up your system.

One of the easiest ways to back up your system is to use a tape drive, copying your files from the hard disk to magnetic tape. This chapter explains the different options for connecting a tape drive to your PC, and covers the following topics:

- Buyer's guide to tape drives
- Configuring and installing tape drives
- Tips for backing up your system

Buyer's Guide to Tape Drives

Tape backup has long been the method of choice for backing up computers—mainframe systems have used reel-to-reel tape storage since their inception. Until rewritable CD-ROMs become common, tape backup will remain one of the best alternatives for backing up your data.

TIP

If your PC is on a network, another option is to back up your files to a network hard disk. Just remember that if that network hard disk fails, your backups will be gone. Although tape is slower, it's usually more secure. The exception is if your backup hard disk is mirrored by another drive, meaning there are two disks in the remote system, each identical to the other. If one disk fails, the other still is available, along with your backup files.

A tape backup system copies your files onto tape, much like when you copy music onto a cassette tape. Backing up to tape is more convenient than backing up to floppy disk because a single tape can hold much more than a floppy. Depending on the tape format, a single tape can hold from 40M to over 5G (gigabytes) of information. No matter how large the capacity of your hard disk, it's possible to back up your entire disk to a single tape.

Tape Formats

Different tape formats are available, including 9-track reel-to-reel tape, 1/4-inch cartridge tape, and 4mm and 8mm digital audio tape (DAT).

The 1/4-inch tape format is used in tape drives that support the QIC-40 and QIC-80 data formats, which are common tape drive data formats. QIC-80 provides higher capacity than QIC-40 format, and is the most common format used. These types of tape drives can store from 120M to over 300M per tape, depending on the tape drive.

Another format is *DAT*, which stands for Digital Audio Tape. DAT tape drives have a much higher capacity and are capable of storing 1G, 2G, or more depending on the tape drive. As you might expect, DAT tape drives are much more expensive than QIC-80 format tape drives.

Tape Drive Interfaces

Most QIC-80 format tape drives use one of two methods of connecting to the PC. The most common and least expensive method is to connect the tape drive to the PC's floppy disk controller. This type of configuration is convenient, because it doesn't require an additional controller just for the tape drive. These types of tape drives provide a data transfer rate of around 3.5M per minute.

Some manufacturers improve the tape system's performance by adding a dedicated controller for the tape drive. The tape drive connects to this special controller instead of the floppy controller, providing faster performance and quicker backup. These types of tape drives provide a transfer rate of about 7M per minute.

Tape drives also are available with IDE interfaces. These tape drives connect to the same IDE host adapter to which the PC's IDE hard disk(s) connect. IDE tape drives are more expensive than floppy controller or dedicated controller tape drives, but they provide better performance, providing a transfer rate of about 10M per minute.

The other option for tape drive interface is SCSI, which is most commonly used with DAT tape drives. The SCSI interface offers the advantage of portability between different types of systems (such as the Macintosh and PC) in addition to high transfer rates of 10M per minute or more.

Here are some shopping tips to help you decide which type of tape drive is right for you:

- **QIC-80.** If you want to save as much money as possible, consider a QIC-80 format tape drive that connects to your floppy disk controller.

- **Dedicated controller.** If your system doesn't include an IDE host adapter and you've decided to buy a QIC-80 format tape drive, see if the manufacturer sells a dedicated controller for the tape drive. You can double the transfer rate of the drive with a dedicated controller, cutting backup and restore time roughly in half. If backup speed isn't a big consideration, skip the dedicated controller. You don't need the extra expense or complexity caused by adding yet another device to your PC.

- **IDE in the system.** If your system contains an IDE host adapter, consider buying an IDE tape drive. You'll get about 10M per minute performance without the hassle of adding a dedicated controller. These tape drives currently cost more, but if you're interested in backup speed, they're worth the difference.

- **SCSI in the system.** If your system contains a SCSI host adapter, you might want to think about getting a SCSI-based tape drive. SCSI is most often used in the more expensive DAT tape drives, but this may change if tape drive manufacturers feel the market is picking up for lower-capacity SCSI tape drives.

- **Capacity.** Shop for a tape drive with a capacity equal to or greater than the total size of your hard disk, including all logical drives on the disk. This enables you to back up the entire disk onto a single tape. Although it isn't necessary to use a single tape, it's more convenient. If cost is a concern, look for a tape drive with a capacity of at least one-half of the total capacity of the disk. This will enable you to back up the disk onto two tapes.

- **Format.** The choice between QIC-80 format and DAT format boils down to two main considerations: price and disk size. If you need to back up a large capacity disk (1G or more), shop for a DAT drive. For backing up smaller capacity drives, DAT isn't yet cost effective. Another advantage to DAT is in file access time—often, you can retrieve a file from a DAT tape in a matter of seconds, whereas it would take considerably longer with a QIC-80 format tape.

- **Cables.** If you're getting a tape drive that connects to your PC's floppy controller and you have two floppy drives in the system, make sure you tell the salesperson that when you buy the tape drive. You need either a special interface cable with three drive connectors, or a floppy controller that supports more than two floppy drives.

If your floppy controller supports more than two floppy drives, you can connect a standard floppy cable from the secondary floppy connector on the controller to the tape drive.

TIP *Don't buy a new floppy controller if yours doesn't support more than two floppy drives—buy the correct interface cable, instead.*

Internal or External Tape Drive?

When shopping for a tape drive, you also must decide whether to buy an internal tape drive or an external drive. External tape drives make sense only when you need to back up multiple PCs that are not on a peer-to-peer network. On a peer-to-peer network, the disk resources at each node (workstation) can potentially be accessed from any other node. This means that you can back up someone else's hard disk on a remote node onto the tape drive installed in your PC.

Even when the situation described above holds true, external tape drives aren't always the answer. Each PC being backed up needs to provide an interface to the tape drive. This means that each system needs an external SCSI, IDE, or floppy port.

When you're dealing with only a few PCs, it's not too expensive to add an interface for the tape drive in the form of a host adapter or optional external connector bracket. When you're dealing with a larger number of PCs, it makes more sense to back up to a single internal tape drive. Later in this chapter you will find some tips on backing up across the network.

Adding Internal Tape Drives

Installing an internal tape backup system is a lot like installing a floppy disk or CD-ROM drive. The procedure varies depending on the type of interface used by the drive. One of the easiest types to install is a QIC-80 format drive that connects to the PC's floppy controller.

Adding a Floppy Controller Tape Drive

Essentially, installing this type of tape drive is no different than installing a floppy drive. All you have to do is install the drive in the PC and connect a cable from it to the floppy controller, and you're done. There might be some added steps, though, depending on the type of cable you're using and the number of drives installed in the PC.

Procedure:

Installing the Tape Drive

Explanation: This procedure covers installation of the tape drive into the system unit.

1. Turn off the system and open it.

2. Locate an available drive bay. If you do not have any available drive bays that are accessible from the front of the PC, you might need to move a hard disk to an internal drive bay, making its bay available for the tape drive.

3. If you're installing the tape drive in an IBM AT, you will need to add drive rails to each side of the tape drive. If the rails didn't come with the tape drive, you can buy a set from a computer dealer.

4. Slide the tape drive into the drive bay, align the front of the drive with the front of the floppy drive(s), and secure it with screws (see fig. 14.1).

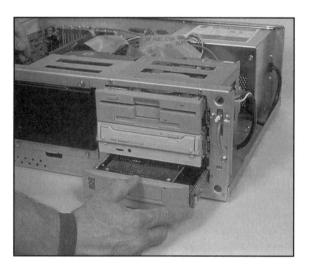

Figure 14.1: Install the tape drive in one of the available drive bays.

Procedure:

Connecting Cables

Explanation: After installing the drive, you need to connect the power cable and interface cable to it. This procedure covers those steps.

1. Locate a free power cable and connect it to the tape drive. If you don't have a free power cable, get a power cable splitter and connect it to the same cable as your system's floppy drive B (or drive A), then connect the other end to the tape drive (see fig. 14.2).

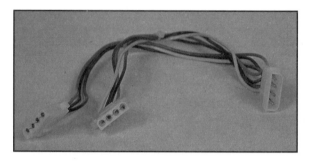

Figure 14.2: A power splitter cable used to connect two devices to the same power wire assembly.

2. **Single floppy drive systems.** The cable you need has three connectors on it—one for the floppy controller connection, one for drive A, and one for the tape drive (or drive B). The drive connector at the end of the cable must be connected to drive A. The drive connector in the middle of the cable connects to the tape drive. If the cable connector isn't keyed, make sure that pin 1 on the cable is oriented closest to the notch in the drive's edge connector.

3. **Dual floppy drive systems, controller supports maximum of two floppy drives.** The cable you need has four connectors on it—one for the floppy controller connection, two for the floppy drives, and a fourth for the tape drive. These are special cables, so you might need to buy one separately if the drive doesn't include it.

Check the cable; it will have either one twist in it between the last two connectors, or it will have two twists—one between the second and third connectors, and another between the third and fourth connectors.

If your cable has one twist, the first two connectors are for drive B and the tape drive, and the connector at the end of the cable is for drive A. If your cable has two twists, the first one (nearest the controller) is for drive B or the tape drive, the middle connector is for drive A, and the connector at the end is for drive B or the tape drive. It doesn't matter which connector goes to drive B or to the tape drive, as long as you don't use the drive A connector for either one (see fig. 14.3).

Figure 14.3: Attach a connector to the drive. Use a connector that doesn't have a twist between it and the previous connector or controller.

4. **Dual floppy drive systems, controller supports more than two floppy drives.** You need two standard floppy cables. The first cable will connect the two floppy drives to the controller, and the other cable will connect the tape drive to the controller. When connecting the tape drive to the controller, use the connector that has the twist in the cable (probably the connector at the end of the cable).

Procedure:
Adding an IDE Tape Drive

Explanation: Adding an IDE-based tape drive is very similar to adding a floppy controller tape drive. If you're adding an IDE tape drive to a system with a single IDE hard disk, you should have no problems at all. If, however, you already have two IDE hard disks in the system, you need to see if your IDE host adapter will support more than two drives (most don't). If yours supports only two drives, you'll have to buy another IDE host adapter for your system to support the tape drive and the hard disks. Check with the dealer from whom you're buying the tape drive to make sure you get the right type of host adapter for your system.

The following steps explain how to add an IDE tape drive:

1. Verify that the tape drive is configured as a slave unit. The master/slave status will be set by jumpers or DIP switches on the drive. The default status for the tape drive should be slave, but check it anyway and set it if necessary. If you find no reference to slave/master settings in the drive's manual, just install it. It probably is configured properly.

2. Install the drive in an available drive bay (see fig. 14.1), sliding it in to align with the floppy drive(s).

3. Attach the extra connector on the IDE cable to the pins on the back of the tape drive, making sure to align pin 1 on the cable with pin 1 on the drive. The socket on the drive may be keyed so that you can insert the connector only in the correct orientation.

4. Attach a free power connector to the back of the tape drive. Use a splitter adapter if you don't have any more power connectors available, and attach the splitter to the power cable that is hooked up to a floppy drive or CD-ROM drive.

Procedure:
Adding a SCSI Tape Drive

Explanation: When you install a SCSI tape drive, you have to set the SCSI ID on the tape drive to a unique ID number. When you're deciding which ID to assign to the tape drive, remember that no two SCSI devices can share the same ID. Also, most manufacturers recommend that you assign SCSI ID 7 to the tape drive, but check the tape drive's manual to be sure. Also, before buying the tape drive, check with your SCSI host adapter's vendor to make sure the tape drive will be supported by your host adapter.

1. On the tape drive, configure the tape drive's bus ID number by setting jumpers or DIP switches on the drive. Check your manual to determine where the configuration jumpers/switches are located.

2. Install the tape drive in an available drive bay, aligning the front of the tape drive with the front of the floppy drive(s).

3. Attach a power cable to the tape drive. If you don't have any available power cables, attach a splitter cable to a floppy drive or CD-ROM, and attach the other end to the tape drive.

Using a Backup Strategy

Backing up your files is just like insurance—you never need it until some kind of disaster strikes. If your hard disk fails or you do something dumb (such as accidentally delete your disk's partition), having a backup of the file system just might mean the difference between keeping your business going or going under. At the very least, having a backup will eliminate hours, if not weeks, of restoring your data.

You are the only one who can decide how often your system needs to be backed up. It really depends on how much data you're willing to lose, and how much time you're willing to spend re-creating that lost data.

If you're backing up a home computer, once a week might be enough (or even once a month) if you make backup copies of your documents on floppy when you create them. If you rely on your PC in your business, however, you probably should back up the system once a day.

Programs Versus Documents

It isn't as necessary to back up your programs as it is to back up your documents. You can reinstall your programs if something happens to them, but it's easier and quicker to restore them from tape. I suggest backing up your programs once, then adding to tape any new programs that you install later.

You don't need to back up your programs every time you back up your system. Having your programs and documents on different disks (or at the very least in different directories) helps here. You can just select a disk or directory and back it up without having to sort out document files from program files.

Full and Incremental Backup

A *full backup* is a complete backup of every file in the selected disk or directory. You should make a full backup of your programs and documents right after you install your tape drive, backing up all of the directories on each logical hard disk.

An *incremental backup* takes advantage of a file's archive bit to determine if it has changed since the last backup was performed. When you use your backup program to back up files, the program sets the archive attribute to indicate that the file has been backed up. If the file is later changed, the archive bit changes. When you run an incremental backup, the backup software backs up only those files that have changed since the last backup.

Personally, I think full backups are better from a management point of view. It can be tough hunting through one or more tapes to make sure you have the latest copy of a file. If you perform a full backup each time you back up the system and date the tape, you'll know exactly where to find the most up-to-date copy of a file—just look on the latest tape.

Tape Tips

Imagine this scenario: You have only one tape that you use to back up your system. At the moment, it has an old backup of your files on it. You stick the tape in the tape drive and start a backup. A few minutes into the process, something drastic happens—the hard disk suddenly dies.

"No problem," you say. You'll just reformat the disk and restore your files from the tape. But wait a minute…it never finished backing up, and you've just lost your files on the tape, too, because the tape header has been overwritten by the aborted backup. Hmm…you shouldn't have used that tape.

It would be extremely expensive and a waste of tape to use a new tape every time you make a backup, but you should never use your latest backup tape to make a new backup. Ideally, you should use three tape sets for the most security. Assume that you back up your system every day. Today is Wednesday, and it's time to back up the system. Use the tape from Friday's backup and leave Monday's and Tuesday's backups alone. On Thursday, you can use Monday's tape to make a new backup. Having two unaltered backup tapes ensures that you have a secure tape and a redundant tape in the event something happens to one of them.

If you are using a QIC-80 format tape without a dedicated tape controller, you'll have to format the tape before you perform a backup. Formatting a tape takes as much time as backing up files to the entire tape. You might want to pay the price premium for preformatted tapes. If you're using a dedicated tape controller, you can format and back up in the same process.

Using Unattended Backups

If you're backing up your home computer, waiting while the system is backing up is not a big deal—you surely can find something to do around the house while the system is being backed up. Take a nap on the couch if nothing else.

If you're backing up the PC at the office, you can't just flop onto the couch for a little siesta. You probably don't want to tie up your system during the day, and you have better things to do than stick around after quitting time to back up your system. You should make use of *unattended backups*.

Many tape backup programs enable you to define which disk, directories, or files are to be backed up, then enable you to schedule the backup to occur at a specific time. The backup program wakes up when it's time to perform the backup, and handles the task unattended. This is particularly useful when backing up a disk that is shared with other users on a network. You can schedule the backup to occur in the wee hours of the morning when no one is using the system.

NOTE Do you remember that I recommended a tape drive with a capacity equal to or greater than the capacity of your hard disk? One reason for that is that you can back up the entire disk unattended—you don't have to be around to switch tapes when the first one is full. Just stick a tape in the drive, schedule the backup, and leave the system until tomorrow.

Unattended Windows Backups

If your Windows-based tape backup program doesn't enable you to schedule a backup for a later time, but it does enable you predefine the set of files to be backed up, you might still be able to schedule an unattended backup. A number of software developers have Windows scheduling utilities that enable you to schedule events.

The event might be a dialog box message to make a phone call or pick up some milk on the way home, or it might actually start a program running, such as your backup program. PowerLauncher, from hDC, is an example of a Windows utility suite that includes a scheduler.

Backing Up Your Network Workstations

Tape drives are not recognized by DOS or Windows as a logical drive with a drive letter. Typically, the tape drive is recognized "transparently" by the tape backup software. This means that you can't directly access a tape drive connected to a remote node on the network.

You can't tell the computer to "take these files and put them on the tape drive over there," because the system's reply would be "what tape drive?". If it doesn't have a drive ID, your node won't know that a tape drive exists on the other node. Even so, backing up files across the network isn't as difficult as it might seem.

Backing Up on a Dedicated Network

A *dedicated network* is one in which all of the workstations access a common server node. They are called dedicated networks because the servers typically are dedicated to serving only as servers—they often can't be used as workstations at the same time.

On a dedicated network, you can't sit down at a particular node and access all the other nodes on the network. You can access only the server. Even the server can't access the files on other nodes. If that's the case, how do you back up all of the disks on the network?

One of the simplest methods from a management point of view is to have the users' data stored on the server, rather than on the users' workstations. You then can back up those directories on the server's tape drive. Sometimes it's not convenient or even possible to have everyone's data on the server, so you have two other options: move an external tape drive from node to node or have the users save critical files on the server where they can be backed up.

You'll have to evaluate your situation to decide how to proceed. You may decide that it's worth buying a new high-capacity hard disk for the server to provide enough storage space for your users' files. This will save you the trouble of moving the tape drive from node to node to back them up.

Backing Up on a Peer-to-Peer Network

On a peer-to-peer network, any node on the network has the potential to be a server while still acting as a workstation. Someone can be accessing your disk from another node, for example, at the same time you're using it. This also means that you have the potential to access everyone else's disks from your node. Windows for Workgroups is a good example of a peer-to-peer network.

You can use the same method to back up a peer-to-peer network that is used to back up a dedicated network—you can have the users copy their files to a common shared server, then back the files up from the server. But because potentially you can access all of the workstations from the server, there is another option.

In that option, you can connect to each of the other nodes from the server and back up their hard disks across the network. Each of the remote nodes will appear as a logical disk on the node containing the tape drive, and backing them up is virtually the same as backing up a local logical drive.

To access the files on the other nodes, the directories containing the files must be shared. Your users probably won't want to share their data directories, so see if your network operating system enables you to create *hidden shares*. These are shared directories that don't appear in resource lists, but are available if you know they're there. With Windows for Workgroups, adding a $ character before the share name hides the shared resource.

15

Modems and Fax-Modems

You can access a wealth of information by using your computer. Information services such as CompuServe, Prodigy, America Online, and many others offer a wide range of services, including on-line references and databases, travel and weather services, technical help, and much more. You can bank from the comfort of your home with your PC and pay your bills electronically. You can log on to electronic bulletin board services (BBSs) and download games, shareware, and other useful files. Or, you can just connect to a friend's computer to share files. Whatever the case, you need a modem. If you also want to send and receive faxes on your PC, you need a fax-modem.

This chapter offers tips for buying, installing, and using a modem or fax-modem. The sections and topics covered in this chapter include the following:

- An overview of how modems and fax-modems work
- A buyer's guide to modems and fax-modems
- Configuring and installing an internal modem or fax-modem
- Connecting an external modem
- Setting COM port parameters
- Troubleshooting modem problems
- Windows communications

First, you need some background information about modems and fax-modems.

Modems, Fax-Modems, and Communications Software

The word *modem* is an acronym for MODulator DEModulator, which is exactly what a modem does: modulates and demodulates. Unless you're a techno-geek, that doesn't make sense, so here's a better explanation: A modem's main function is to convert serial data coming from one computer into a signal that can be transmitted across a phone line to another computer. Modems also convert data coming down the phone line into a format your PC can use. So, a modem serves as a translator that enables your computer to communicate with other computers over a phone line.

The computer at the other end of the line doesn't have to be a PC, but it does need to have a modem. The other computer can be any type of personal computer (a Mac or Amiga, for example), and it also can be a mainframe computer operated by a big information service such as CompuServe. For the most part, it doesn't matter what type of computer is at the other end of the phone line; the modem makes it possible for your PC to communicate with it.

Communications Software

A modem can't magically communicate with other computers without some software. You need communications software to control the modem and provide support for functions such as *file transfer*, which enables you to send and receive files. Most modems are sold with communications software, but you also can buy communications software separately if you want more capabilities, such as support for a wider range of file transfer protocols, support for Windows, and so on. If you're a Windows user, you already have a communications program. Terminal, included with Windows, is one such program (see fig. 15.1).

A communications program like Terminal enables you to control the speed at which the modem operates, specify the methods it uses to communicate with the other computer and transfer files, store phone numbers for other computers or services that you call, and more. Many com-munications programs also include their own macro programming languages or macro recording features, which enable you to create scripts or macros for calling and logging on to various systems.

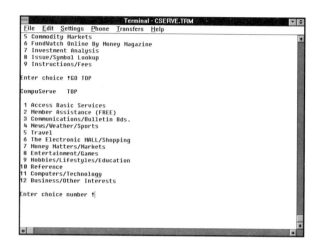

Figure 15.1: Terminal is a communications program that's included with Windows. Here, it's connected to CompuServe.

Fax-Modems and Fax Software

A fax-modem serves the same function as a modem, but it also has the capability of sending and receiving facsimiles (faxes). You don't need both a modem and a fax-modem because the fax-modem can do everything a standard modem can do.

If you have a fax-modem, other people can send faxes to you. The faxes are stored as files in your PC after your system receives them. You also can use a fax-modem to fax documents to other people if the recipient has a fax machine or fax-modem.

Unlike a fax machine, fax-modems don't print your fax as soon as it's received. Instead, a fax management program running on your PC (see fig. 15.2) directs the modem to answer the phone line when it rings. It then receives the fax transmission and stores it in a file. You then can use the fax program to view the fax on your PC, just as you view other kinds of documents. If you need to print the fax on paper, you can use the program to send the fax to the printer.

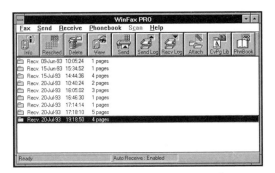

Figure 15.2: WinFax PRO is a fax program that runs under Windows.

You also can send faxes with a fax-modem. You create a fax file, then the fax program calls the recipient's fax machine or fax-modem and transmits the fax. After the fax transmission is complete, the fax-modem hangs up the phone line. In most Windows-based fax programs, the fax software acts like a printer driver. If you want to fax a document, you open the document (in Word, for example), select the fax printer driver, then print the document. The fax program intercepts the fax print job and directs it to the fax-modem.

The disadvantage of a fax-modem is that you can't use it to directly fax paper documents—there's no way to stuff the paper into the fax-modem the way you can with a fax machine. Instead, you have to scan the document into your PC as a file with a hand scanner or page scanner, modify the document (if necessary), then fax it.

Many fax programs support scanners directly, providing you with an easy way to scan a paper document into your PC in the right file format for your fax program. After the document is scanned into the PC, you can edit it before you fax it.

Fax programs also enable you to view and print faxes. Most fax programs include tools with which to annotate a fax. If you receive a fax that you need to fill out and return, you can add text and graphics to the received fax, then fax it back. Figure 15.3 shows the annotation tools provided by WinFax PRO.

Some fax programs also provide special fax cover sheets that you can include with any fax you send. Figure 15.4 shows a cover sheet supplied by WinFax PRO.

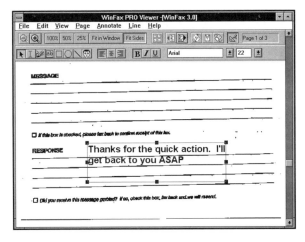

Figure 15.3: Like many fax programs, WinFax PRO enables you to add notes and graphics to a fax.

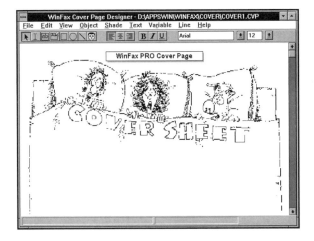

Figure 15.4: One of WinFax PRO's many cover sheet designs.

Many fax programs also can convert a received fax into text with a fairly high degree of success. This means you can convert a fax to a text document, then load the document into your word processor for editing.

Modem Buyer's Guide

Modems and fax-modems are fairly standardized today, so you don't have to worry much about compatibility with your system. There are some issues to consider when you're shopping for a modem—some practical and some technical. The first question you need to ask is whether you need a modem or a fax-modem.

Do You Need a Modem or a Fax-Modem?

If you don't have need or want to send or receive faxes, or if you prefer to use a dedicated fax machine, you can save a few dollars by buying a modem that doesn't support faxing. The price difference isn't very significant, though, so you might want to buy a fax-modem anyway. If you decide later you need or want to send and receive faxes with your PC, you don't have to buy a new fax-modem and until then, you can use just the communications capabilities of the fax-modem.

One of the primary advantages of a fax-modem over a dedicated fax machine is that the fax-modem cuts down on the amount of paper you need. A dedicated fax machine prints every page it receives. The fax management software you use with a fax-modem stores the fax as a file on your PC's hard disk. You only print it when you need a paper copy of the fax. Until then, you can view the fax on your PC without printing it.

Another major advantage of a fax-modem over a dedicated fax machine is that you can convert the fax file into a text file. To achieve the same result with a fax machine, you need a scanner to scan the document into the PC and a separate program to perform the conversion.

Speed, Speed, Speed!

The speed at which a modem or fax-modem works is its most important technical aspect. Modem speed is particularly important when you are connecting to an on-line information service that charges you for connect time by the minute. Speed also is important if you don't have a local access number for your information service and have to make a long-distance call to connect to it.

Modem speed is measured in *baud*. I won't give you a long technical explanation of what baud rate means—it really isn't that important. All you need to understand is that the higher the baud rate, the faster the modem, and the more money you save on connect time and phone charges.

Currently, the fastest mass-market modems operate at 14,400 baud (often referred to as 14.4K). Other common top speeds are 9600 baud and 2400 baud. If you're shopping for a modem (or your main concern in a fax-modem is its data communications speed), buy one that supports at least 9600 baud for data communications. If you can afford the extra expense, buy a modem that supports 14,400 baud. Although 2400-baud modems still are available, I don't recommend them. You recover the price difference between a 2400-baud modem and a 9600-baud modem in a few hours' use.

Fax-modems have two speed designations: one for data communications and another for the fax speed. There are three main speed combinations: 2400/9600, 9600/9600, and 14,400/14,400, where the first number indicates data speed and the second number indicates fax speed.

If you do not intend to ever use your fax-modem for data communications, only for faxing, a 2400/9600 unit is fine. If you plan to use it for data communications, buy one that has a data speed of at least 9600 baud. If you can afford the premium, buy a unit that supports a 14,400 data rate.

Supported Standards

The different aspects of data communications have a number of standards. First, make sure the modem you buy supports the Hayes command set. This ensures compatibility with nearly every data communications program sold today.

Buy a unit that supports both MNP-5 and V.42bis data-compression standards, as well as V.32 and V.42 error correction. Support for these standards ensures that the modem can take advantage of standard data-compression and error-correction methods to improve overall performance and accuracy. I won't explain what the numbers and standards define—that's more techno-geek information than you really need to know to use the modem.

For fax-modems, seek compatibility with Group III, Class 1 and Class 2 fax devices.

Internal, External, or PCMCIA?

I prefer external modems, mainly because I can move them from one PC to another. I've invested in only one 14.4K modem, and I can move it between my systems just by moving a few cable connections. Not to mention that I can use the external modem with my notebook PC.

If you have only one PC, or want to use the modem in only one PC, you can save a little money by buying an internal unit. Internal modems are adapter cards that are installed in one of the PC's bus slots like any other adapter. As an example of the price difference, Viva's 14.4K internal fax-modem sells for about $230. Viva's external 14.4K fax-modem, which offers the same features, sells for about $270. An internal modem has the additional advantage of not cluttering your desk with yet another piece of equipment.

If you are shopping for a modem or fax-modem for your PC, consider buying a PCMCIA modem. PCMCIA adapters are small credit-card sized adapters that you can install in a notebook's PCMCIA slot. PCMCIA modems offer the advantage of small size—you don't have to carry around a bulky external modem when you take your notebook PC on a trip. Figure 15.5 shows a typical PCMCIA modem.

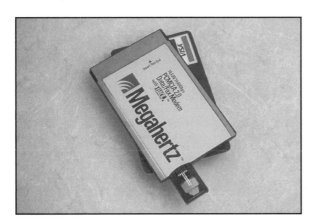

Figure 15.5: A typical PCMCIA modem.

When you shop for a modem for your notebook PC, check to make sure your notebook has a PCMCIA slot. Some notebooks force you to buy internal modems specifically designed for the specific brand and model. If your PC has at least one PCMCIA slot, though, you can use a standard PCMCIA modem.

Line-Sharing Hardware

If you use only one phone line for voice, data, and fax, you should consider some additional hardware that eliminates some of the hassle of juggling three (or more) devices on a single phone line.

Some internal fax-modems, such as Intel's SatisFAXtion 400, include built-in line sharing. When a call comes in, this type of fax-modem can answer the call and listen for a special tone that indicates the call is an incoming fax. If the fax-modem doesn't detect the tone, it passes the call to the phone as a voice call.

If your modem doesn't include built-in line sharing, you can buy an external line-sharing switch that performs the same function. There are two types of line-sharing switches. The first type doesn't answer the incoming call, but rather passively monitors the phone line after it has been answered by using your handset or your answering machine. If the switch detects a fax tone, it takes over the line and receives the fax. If it doesn't detect the tone, the call is handled normally.

The other kind of line-sharing switch actively answers the call. If it doesn't detect a fax tone or a special fax-transfer number on the sender's phone pad, the line-sharing switch rings the call through to the telephone and/or answering machine. Both types of switches work well.

16550 UARTs

Chapter 7, "I/O and Network Adapters," explains UARTs, but here's a quick summary, because the topic relates to buying a modem. UART stands for Universal Asynchronous Receiver Transmitter. COM port circuitry includes a UART to handle the transmission and reception of data through the COM port.

Internal modems, because they include all the circuitry that makes up a COM port, include UARTs. Chapter 7 explains that a 16550 UART offers better performance than a 16450 UART because of the 16550's on-board buffer. If you're buying a 14.4K internal modem, shop for one that uses 16550 UARTs instead of the 16450 UARTs. If you are buying an external modem and your I/O card uses 16450 UARTs, you might consider replacing the 16450 UARTs on the I/O card with 16550 UARTs. Chapter 7 explains the procedure.

Adding an Internal Modem/Fax-Modem

Internal modems and fax-modems use a serial port (COM port) connection to tie into your PC. If you install an external modem, it connects to one of your PC's external COM port connectors. If you install an internal modem, though, the modem contains serial port circuitry, and you have to configure the modem to use one of the system's COM port IDs.

Your system probably has at least two COM ports in it, and possibly four. When you install an internal modem, you have to make sure it doesn't conflict with an existing COM port in the system. You might configure the modem as COM2, for example, which means you have to disable the existing COM2 in the PC. The serial port circuitry on the modem essentially becomes a COM2 dedicated only to use of the modem.

TIP

Keep this in mind when you set up your modem: COM1 and COM3 share the same interrupt on a standard ISA bus system. COM2 and COM4 also share an interrupt. You can use a device on COM1 for a while, then use another device on COM3, but you can't use the two devices at the same time because of interrupt conflict.

The exception to this rule is a mouse. If you have a mouse on COM1, you can't use COM3 at all because the mouse causes problems. If your mouse is on COM2, you can't use COM4 at all. And, you can't use the mouse on COM3 or COM4. If you use a serial mouse with your PC, you should install it on COM1, configure the modem for COM2 or COM4, and not use COM3 at all. Or, you can use your mouse on COM2, install the modem on COM1 or COM3, and not use COM4 at all.

If you're not sure how to disable a COM port so that you can assign it to the modem, refer to Chapter 7.

Procedure:
Configuring the Modem

1. Decide which COM port you're going to assign to the modem. Choose a port that doesn't share an interrupt with your mouse.

2. Turn off, unplug, and open the system.

3. Discharge your static, then configure the modem to use the selected COM port. Check the manual to determine which jumpers or DIP switches to set on the modem to assign it to the selected COM port. Typically, internal modems let you select from pre-defined options. These options associate a particular IRQ and I/O base address with the selected COM port, and you can't change the IRQ or base I/O address. When you select COM1, for example, the modem automatically uses IRQ4 and I/O base address 03F8h. So, you may have to adjust the IRQ and I/O base address settings for your other COM ports. Unless you changed the settings for your other COM ports from their original settings, however, it's unlikely that you'll have to make any changes to them.

4. Install the modem in an appropriate bus slot. Use an 8-bit slot or 16-bit slot for an 8-bit card, and use a 16-bit slot for a 16-bit card. Secure the modem to the chassis with a screw.

Procedure:
Connecting Cables

Explanation: Your modem has two RJ11 phone jacks, just like the ones you probably have on your modular phone connectors on your wall or on the back or bottom of your telephone set. One jack is marked *Line* and the other is marked *Phone* (or something similar). If you are using only the modem on the phone line and nothing else, connection is simple: you just connect a phone cable (supplied with the modem) from your phone jack on the wall to the *Line* connector on the modem.

If you have a phone, answering machine, or other phone gadgets on the same line as the modem, the connections are a little more complicated. The devices will be *daisy-chained* together on the phone line, with the phone being the last device on the chain. The phone is last because it has only one jack; the other devices have two jacks. Use the following steps to hook up a modem, answering machine, and phone on the same line without using a line-sharing switch. Figure 15.6 illustrates the connections.

Figure 15.6: Cable connections for an internal modem, answering machine, and phone.

NOTE

If you're using a line-sharing switch, skip this procedure and refer to "Connecting to a Line-Sharing Switch," which follows this section.

1. Connect a phone cord from your wall phone outlet to the *Line* connector on the modem.

2. Connect a phone cord from the *Phone* jack on the modem to the *Line* jack on the answering machine. If you don't have an answering machine, connect the cord from the *Phone* jack on the modem to the telephone, and skip step 3.

3. Connect a phone cord from the *Phone* jack on the answering machine to the telephone.

Procedure:
Connecting to a Line-Sharing Switch

Explanation: If you're using a line-sharing switch, the connections are a bit more straightforward. Instead of daisy-chaining the devices together, everything connects to the line-sharing switch.

1. Connect a phone cord from the wall connector to the *Line* jack on the switch.

2. **Fax-modem:** Connect a phone cord from the *Line* jack on the fax-modem to the *Fax* jack on the switch. If you have a dedicated fax machine, use step 3 instead.

3. **Dedicated fax machine:** If you have a dedicated fax machine instead of a fax-modem, connect a cord from the *Line* jack on the fax machine to the *Fax* jack on the switch. Then, connect a cord from the *Line* jack on the modem to the *Modem* or *Aux* jack on the switch.

4. Connect a phone cord from the *Line* jack on the answering machine to the *Answering machine* jack on the switch.

5. Connect a phone cord from the phone to the *Phone* jack on the switch.

Adding an External Modem/Fax-Modem

Installing an external modem is a lot easier than installing an internal modem. You don't have to configure the modem at all; just connect it. But you do have to decide which COM port to use.

Choose a COM port that doesn't share an interrupt with a serial mouse, if your system uses a serial mouse. If you install the modem on a COM port that shares an interrupt with a device other than a serial mouse, make sure the other device won't be used when you use the modem. If you have a fax-modem, you should use a COM port that doesn't share an interrupt with any other device, because you have no way of knowing if you'll be using that other device when a fax call comes in. You don't have to disable the port that shares an interrupt with your fax-modem port; just don't use the other port at all.

Procedure:
Installing/Connecting the Modem

1. Connect the modem's power cord to the modem, but leave the modem turned off.

2. Connect a serial cable between the modem's serial connector and the COM port connector you selected on your PC.

3. Follow the steps in the previous procedures "Connecting Cables" or "Connecting to a Line-Sharing Switch" to connect the phone lines to the modem. Use figure 15.7 as a guide.

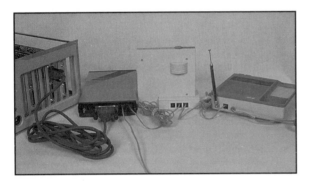

Figure 15.7: Cable connections for an external modem, answering machine, and phone.

Completing the Installation

After you set up your modem and other phone equipment, you might need to install some software before you can use the modem. There usually are no drivers to install or changes to make in CONFIG.SYS or AUTOEXEC.BAT, but some fax-modems require a special device driver. Also, DOS-based fax receive programs often work as a TSR that installs via AUTOEXEC.BAT. Fortunately, the software installation routine for the communications/fax software you've chosen should take care of these items for you.

If you install a data-only modem, or don't intend to use the fax capability of a fax-modem, you don't need any drivers to use the modem. Just install your data communications software, configure it for your brand and model of modem, and start using the modem. If your software doesn't recognize your particular brand and model of modem, look for a setting that specifies "Hayes-compatible."

Troubleshooting

If you have trouble with your modem or fax-modem, check the following basic items:

● **COM port assignment.** Make sure you are not using a COM port assignment already in use. If you install an internal modem as COM2, for example, make sure you don't have another COM2 on your I/O card. Disable the extra COM port if there is one.

● **Sharing interrupts.** Make sure your modem is using a COM port that isn't sharing an IRQ line with any other device.

● **Software setup.** Make sure your software is configured for the same COM port to which the modem is connected. If the software thinks the modem is on COM1 when it's really on COM2, it doesn't work.

● **Connections.** Check your connections again to make sure the phone line is connected properly. With external modems, make sure the power cord is connected and the modem is turned on.

● **Modem lights.** If you have an external modem, it should have a light labeled MR, which stands for Modem Ready. If this light isn't on, turn the modem off, wait about five seconds, then turn it on again. If the MR light still doesn't come on, your modem might be defective. Call for technical support.

● **Software problems.** The problem might not be with your modem at all. It might be with your communications or fax software instead. Verify your program settings and, if necessary, call for technical support on the software.

Procedure:
Testing the Modem with Windows Terminal

Explanation: If you're having problems with your modem and you have Windows on your system, you can use Windows Terminal to verify that the PC is communicating with the modem. Terminal is included with Windows, so there's nothing else you need to buy to do the test.

The following procedure relies on the standard Hayes AT modem command set to send a few common commands to the modem. Your modem probably uses the Hayes command set, but there isn't a sure guarantee. If the following procedure doesn't produce the correct results, you could have one of two problems: your modem doesn't support the Hayes AT command set (unlikely), or your modem isn't working due to a loose or incorrect connection or some other malfunction.

1. In Windows, open the Accessories group, then launch Terminal.

2. From the **S**ettings menu in Terminal, choose **C**ommunications. The Communications dialog box appears (see fig. 15.8).

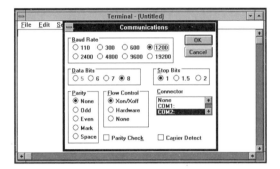

Figure 15.8: Use the Communications dialog box in Terminal to specify the COM port used by the modem.

3. Select the appropriate data baud rate for your modem in the **B**aud Rate group box.

4. In the **C**onnector list box, choose the COM port to which your modem is connected (or to which it is assigned if it's an internal modem).

5. Choose OK to close the Communications dialog box.

6. From the **S**ettings menu, choose Terminal **P**references. The Terminal Preferences dialog box appears (see fig. 15.9).

7. In the Terminal Modes group box, check the Local **E**cho check box.

8. In the CR -> CR/LF group box, check the **O**utbound check box, then choose OK.

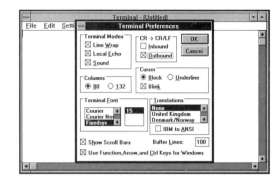

Figure 15.9: Set Local Echo and Outbound options in the Terminal Preferences dialog box.

9. Type **AT** at the keyboard. These characters should appear in the Terminal window. After you press Enter, you should receive the message OK below the AT command. If you don't receive the OK response, continue with step 10. If you do receive an OK response, your PC apparently is communicating with your modem. Check the settings in your communications or fax software.

10. Type **ATQ0V1** and press Enter. The AT gets the modem's attention, Q0 enables display of result codes, and V1 directs the modem to use verbal result codes rather than numeric codes. After entering the command sequence and pressing Enter, type **AT** again and press Enter. You should get an OK result code. If you don't get a return code, your PC isn't communicating with your modem. If you do get some type of return code from the modem, even if it isn't OK, you know the PC at least is communicating with the modem.

Windows Communication Tips

You can add a handful of settings to SYSTEM.INI to eliminate problems or improve data communications under Windows. The following is a list of the settings with a description of how to use each one. If you add any of these settings, place them in the [386Enh] section.

- **COMBoostTime=*milliseconds*.** This setting specifies the amount of time in milliseconds that a virtual machine (a DOS session under Windows, for example) has to process a COM interrupt. You can increase this number if your communications program loses characters (missing characters when downloading e-mail or a text file, for example). The default value for this setting is 2.

- **COM*x*FIFO=*On* or *Off*** (where *x* is a number from 1 to 4, indicating the COM port). If set to On, Windows applications can use the FIFO buffer on your COM port's 16550 UART. Windows 3.1 doesn't support the 16550's FIFO buffer for DOS applications, but your DOS program may support the FIFO buffer if you run it outside of Windows. There's a bug in Windows 3.1 relating to this setting: you can't use the values True or False as you can with other Boolean variables (On/True/1 or Off/False/0). To disable the FIFO buffer, set COM*x*FIFO to Off or 2. To enable it, set COM*x*FIFO=On. If you use the FIFO buffer, disable Windows' normal COM port buffer with the setting COM*x*Buffer=0 (substitute the appropriate COM port number in place of the *x* variable).

- **COM*x*Buffer=*number*.** This setting specifies the size of the buffer that Windows uses to handle text transfers. If you lose text characters during a high-speed communications session, you can increase the size of the buffer and possibly eliminate the problem, although increasing the buffer size can slow down performance. This setting has to be set in conjunction with the setting COM*x*Protocol, described next.

- **COM*x*Protocol=XOFF or blank** (no entry). If you're performing binary transfers with your application, you should leave the setting out altogether, which is the same as setting it to blank (no entry). If you're losing text characters during a communications session, and not performing binary transfers, set COM*x*Protocol=XOFF for the appropriate port and increase the value of COM*x*Buffer.

16

Motherboards

Does your PC not perform up to speed anymore? Are you lusting after the latest 486 or Pentium technology? The solution to your problem might be as simple as a board swap: the ultimate upgrade is to replace your system's motherboard. You can switch your current board for one with the latest and fastest processor. Contrary to what you might think, replacing a motherboard is easy. This chapter explains everything you need to know to replace your system's motherboard, including the following topics:

- Choosing a new motherboard
- Removing your existing motherboard
- Configuring and setting up your new motherboard
- Installing the motherboard and testing your system

A Buyer's Guide to Motherboards

The heart of your PC is the CPU, which resides on the motherboard. The CPU handles most of the processing that occurs in your system, and without it, you would have no PC (figure 16.1 shows the CPU in a 486SX system). Sometimes the CPU is inseparable from the motherboard—you simply cannot pull out the CPU chip and replace it with one that is more powerful.

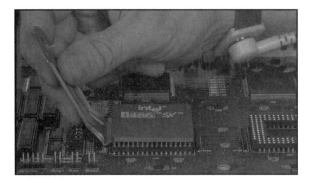

Figure 16.1: The CPU in a 486-SX PC (being removed).

The exception to this is the wave of new 486-based motherboards that can be upgraded merely by replacing the CPU with a faster or more powerful model. For most systems—including all 386 and earlier systems, as well as some 486 systems—the only viable option for upgrading your system is to replace the motherboard.

That's what this chapter is all about. Chapter 17, "Add-In Chips," covers improvements you can make to your PC by changing the CPU or adding a math coprocessor.

CPU Type

One of the first questions you should ask yourself when you shop for a new motherboard is "What CPU do I want?" You probably want the best performance possible from your PC, so choose the most powerful system you can afford, but temper your selection with a dose of reality.

If you use your system for word processing, playing games, or other tasks that don't take a lot of CPU horsepower, you don't need a new Pentium motherboard. You might not need a 486 system, either. If you're upgrading your 8088 or 286 system, a 386SX system probably is fine and certainly costs considerably less than more powerful boards.

If you use your system for more demanding applications, use Windows, plan to run Windows NT, or use multimedia titles on your PC, buy a 486 motherboard. If you need the fastest possible system, consider a Pentium-based motherboard. You're going to pay a premium price for it though, so make sure you really need that much power before investing.

DX, SX, or DX2?

After you decide which CPU you want, you need to decide whether to buy a DX or SX version. The 386-SX CPU uses a 32-bit internal bus, but only a 16-bit external bus. The 386-DX uses a 32-bit internal and external bus. This means that a 386-DX chip outperforms a 386-SX chip of the same speed. Neither the DX nor the SX versions have built-in math coprocessors. Currently, 386-SX motherboards are about $80 cheaper than 386-DX motherboards. If you decide that a 386 system is right for you and you can afford the extra $80, buy a 386-DX motherboard.

The 486-SX CPU basically began life as an accident. Intel Corporation, which designs and manufactures the chip, had problems with the built-in math coprocessors in many of their 486-DX chips. Rather than throw out the chips, Intel disabled the internal math coprocessors and marketed the CPU as the 486-SX. It offers the same capability as a 486-DX chip of the same speed, minus the internal math coprocessor. The 486-SX was a success because of the lower price, so Intel continues to sell the chip, although the chips are now specifically manufactured without the math coprocessor circuitry. Both the 486-DX and 486-SX CPUs use a full 32-bit internal and external bus.

Whether you decide on a 486-DX or a 486-SX system depends on whether you need a math coprocessor for your programs. Some programs, such as AutoCAD, require a math coprocessor. Other programs take advantage of the math coprocessor if it's available. (Windows itself does not use the coprocessor, although many Windows programs do.) If you need a math coprocessor, now or in the future, buy a 486-DX motherboard. If you don't need the math coprocessor and want to save a few dollars, buy a 486-SX motherboard.

If you have a 486-SX system running at up to 25MHz and want to upgrade it to a full DX system, complete with math coprocessor, you don't have to replace the motherboard. Just replace the 486-SX with a 487-SX. Chapter 17 explains what the 487 is and how to install one.

The 486-DX2 is essentially the same as the 486-DX except that it's twice as fast. The DX chips are available in 25MHz and 33MHz versions, whereas the DX2 chips are available in 50MHz and 66MHz versions. If you want the most possible speed from your system without buying a Pentium motherboard, buy a 486-DX2 motherboard.

If you have a 486-DX system now and want to upgrade to 50MHz or 66MHz, you don't have to replace the motherboard. Instead, you can replace the CPU. See Chapter 17.

Speed

The speed at which the CPU runs on your new motherboard is almost as important as the type of CPU you choose. Common CPU speeds today are 25MHz, 33MHz, 50MHz, and 66MHz. Choose the highest speed you can afford, but keep in mind that speed isn't the only issue. A 33MHz 486 CPU outperforms a 33MHz 386 CPU by a factor of over 2:1. After you decide which CPU is right for you, *then* decide how much you're willing to spend for the extra speed.

Bus Type

There are five choices today for bus types in a PC:

- **ISA (Industry Standard Architecture).** The ISA bus is by far the most common bus in use today. The main advantage of the ISA bus is that most adapter vendors design their products for the ISA bus, which makes a wide range of special-purpose adapters available.

- **EISA (Enhanced Industry Standard Architecture).** The EISA bus is an extension of the ISA bus. You can

install standard ISA bus adapters in these systems, but EISA-specific adapters provide improved performance. Although EISA is a technical success, it hasn't been a great commercial success so far.

- **MCA (Micro Channel Architecture).** The MCA bus is a proprietary bus developed by IBM. The MCA bus, like the EISA bus, offers better performance than the more common ISA bus. The disadvantage is that adapters must be designed for the MCA bus. Because the MCA bus has not been a big commercial success, the choices for MCA adapters are limited.

- **VESA Local Bus.** This is an ISA bus system with one or more local bus connectors on the motherboard. In a local bus system, some devices can communicate directly with the CPU rather than go through the PC's normal bus. Local bus video adapters and hard disk host adapters are the most common local bus devices, and they offer significant speed improvements over similar ISA bus adapters.

- **PCI Local Bus.** This is a new bus standard that retains compatibility with ISA bus devices but also offers the performance benefits of a 64-bit local bus. Although the PCI local bus is relatively new, it promises to be a success in high-end systems such as those based on Pentium technology.

Which bus should you choose? I don't recommend MCA systems because they aren't compatible with ISA-bus devices. I don't recommend EISA systems because they lack a broad selection of EISA-specific adapters. This leaves ISA, VESA, and PCI as options.

If you want to save as much money as possible, consider an ISA-bus motherboard but keep in mind that a similar VESA local bus motherboard costs only about $50 more (according to today's prices). So, you might want to spend the extra few dollars for a VESA local bus motherboard, even if you don't plan to buy local bus video or hard disk adapters until later. Neither PCI local bus motherboards nor PCI-based adapters are readily available, but keep them in mind if you shop for a Pentium motherboard.

Memory Capacity and Type

Most of the aftermarket motherboards available today provide for at least 16M of RAM on the motherboard and many allow for up to 32M or even 64M on the motherboard.

Because of that, memory capacity isn't something to worry much about—the motherboard you select should support as much memory as you want to use throughout the life of the system. Avoid buying a motherboard that uses a proprietary 32-bit memory card instead of providing sockets on the motherboard for RAM, unless the memory card allows for at least 32M of RAM.

Form Factor

Most aftermarket motherboards are designed to conform to the mini-AT size form factor (13¼ inches × 8¾ inches)—that is, fit into a minicase, XT-size case, or full-size case. If you install your motherboard in a full-size case, you don't need to worry about the motherboard's size. If you plan to install it in a minicase or XT-size case, make sure the motherboard you select will fit.

Repair or Replace?

If you replace the motherboard because you think it's defective, check the board carefully to see if you can determine what is wrong. If you see physical damage, such as scorched components, a crack in the board, a damaged conductive trace, or some other obvious problem, your CPU might still be good. Unfortunately, you have no way to test the CPU except to install it in the motherboard of another system. If you don't have that option, you still might want to keep the CPU and replace only the board. Because the CPU is by far the most expensive component on the board, you can save quite a bit on the replacement cost.

Many vendors now are buying motherboards without CPUs installed, because CPU prices often fluctuate. The vendors then buy CPUs when the prices are lower, which gives them a better profit margin and enables them to sell the boards at a lower cost. If you replace the motherboard because it's defective and you know that the CPU is good, see if you can order a replacement motherboard without a CPU. Chapter 17 explains how to remove and replace a CPU.

Procedure:
Removing a Motherboard

Explanation: Unless you're putting together a new system, the first step to installing a new motherboard is to remove the old one. You might think it's a hard task, but it's not. It should take you only a few minutes to remove the board.

1. Before you remove your motherboard, make sure you know the required CMOS settings. If necessary, run the CMOS setup program for your system and write down the settings for the hard drive. See Chapter 22, "The Computer Starts, But Doesn't Boot," for an explanation of the CMOS chip and the system configuration program.

2. Turn off, unplug, and open the system.

3. Discharge your static, then disconnect and remove all the adapters from the system. If you're afraid you might forget which cables connect to which adap-ters, label the cables that you remove from each adapter. Use a stick-on label (disk labels work well) or mark right on the cable with a marker.

4. Label the cables that run from the PC's front panel to the motherboard (speaker, keylock, turbo, and other cables), then disconnect them from the motherboard.

5. There should be six or eight screws that hold the motherboard in place. Remove these screws and set them aside—you will need them to install the new motherboard.

6. After removing the retaining screws, carefully remove the board from the PC. Slide it out to the left (with the bus slots away from you) and up. With some cases, you might need to remove part of the chassis to make board removal easier, but this usually isn't a problem.

7. If the old motherboard has nylon or brass spacers mounted on the back of it, remove the spacers to use with the new motherboard.

8. Set the motherboard aside. After you install the new motherboard, repackage the old motherboard in the new motherboard's antistatic bag and box for safekeeping.

If your old motherboard is good, you might be able to sell it. If not, you might at least be able to remove the CPU and math coprocessor (if it has one) and sell them.

Installing a Motherboard

Installing a new motherboard is easy, and shouldn't take much more than a half hour. The only real variation in installation procedures from one board to another are due to the type of stand-offs used in the chassis to mount the motherboard in place. Some chassis use nylon or brass spacers that slide into slots in the chassis to hold the motherboard in place. Others use small hex-shaped threaded stand-offs that screw into the bottom of the chassis, and the motherboard then mounts onto these stand-offs with screws. Either way, screws are used to mount the motherboard to the chassis to keep it in place.

In addition to installing the motherboard in the chassis, you also must install memory on the board, set a few jumpers or DIP switches on the board to specify operating parameters for the board, and connect the front-panel cables to the motherboard.

Procedure:

Configuring the Motherboard

TIP *Because motherboards are relatively expensive compared to some of the other components in your system and contain lots of chips, you should take special care to prevent damaging the motherboard with static discharge. Invest the $5 or $6 that an antistatic wrist strap will cost, and use it when you install the motherboard.*

1. Discharge your static.

2. Open the motherboard's box and remove the motherboard from its static-free bag. Handle the board by its edges and avoid touching any of the chips on it. Avoid touching the back of the board whenever possible—not only can you discharge static through the pin leads that stick out the back of the board, but the leads are sharp.

3. Set the motherboard on a flat surface so that you can begin setting options on the motherboard.

4. **Cache memory:** If your new motherboard contains cache RAM (see fig. 16.2) and you're increasing the amount of cache RAM, you need to remove the existing cache RAM chips and install higher-capacity chips. Check your manual to make sure you have the right type of memory chips, then install them using

the techniques described in Chapter 4, "All You Need To Know about Memory." If you change the amount of cache RAM on the motherboard, you probably need to change jumper or DIP switch settings on the motherboard to accommodate the new amount of cache RAM. Check the motherboard's manual to determine which settings to use.

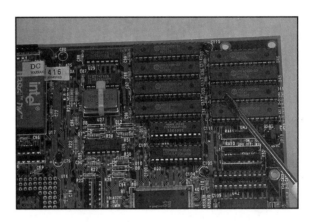

Figure 16.2: Cache RAM installed on a motherboard.

5. **RAM:** Using the procedures in Chapter 4 as a guide, install RAM on the motherboard. Some motherboards don't require any jumper or DIP switch settings to define the amount of memory installed, while others do require you to set switches or jumpers. Check the motherboard's manual to determine if you need to set switches or jumpers to specify the amount of RAM installed on the board.

6. **Video:** Some motherboards require a jumper or switch setting to define whether the system uses a color video adapter or monochrome video adapter. Check your manual to see if your motherboard requires this setting, then set it accordingly.

7. **386s and math coprocessors:** If you install a math coprocessor on a 386 motherboard, you might need to set a jumper or switch on the motherboard to indicate that the math coprocessor is installed. Check your motherboard manual to be sure.

Attaching Hardware

Depending on your system's chassis design, you might have to install nylon or brass spacers on the motherboard (see fig. 16.3). These spacers slide into slots in the chassis and support the motherboard in the chassis. Even when spacers are used, the motherboard still requires screws to hold it in place.

Figure 16.3: Attaching a spacer to the back of the motherboard.

Hold the motherboard in position in the chassis to determine which mounting holes require spacers. Then install the spacers in the required holes. Brass spacers are attached to the board with screws, while nylon spacers clip into the holes.

Procedure:

Installing the Motherboard

1. With the bus slots oriented toward the back of the PC, slide the motherboard into place in the chassis. If you install the motherboard in a tower system, you might have to remove the bottom part of the chassis to make it possible to slide the motherboard into place. The bottom of the chassis should be held in place by a few screws. With other chassis designs, it's sometimes necessary to remove the hard drive and its support structure to install the motherboard.

In most systems, though, you can slide the motherboard into place without any problems (see fig. 16.4). Be careful not to catch any of the motherboard's components on the chassis when you are sliding it into place.

Figure 16.4: Slide the motherboard into position.

2. If your chassis uses spacers to support the motherboard, lower the motherboard so the spacers fit into their sockets, then slide the motherboard toward the right (desktop case) or top (tower case) into its final position. Line up the mounting holes with the threaded studs in the chassis.

3. Secure the motherboard with the screws provided with your chassis (see fig. 16.5). Many systems include paper washers to install between the screw and the motherboard. If you have these washers, use them.

Procedure:

Connecting Cables

1. Verify that the PC's power supply is unplugged.

2. Connect the P8 connector from the power supply to the rear power connection on the motherboard (see fig. 16.6). Connect the P9 connector from the power supply to the forward power connection on the motherboard.

Figure 16.5: Secure the motherboard to the chassis with screws.

Figure 16.6: Connecting the power supply to the motherboard.

3. Attach the front-panel cables from the PC's front panel to the motherboard, using the motherboard's manual as a guide to locating the correct pins and orienting the connectors properly (see fig. 16.7). You might also need to consult the manual that came with the chassis (if you bought the case separately) to determine the correct orientation of the wires to the connectors on the motherboard. Red generally indicates a positive polarity (+), and black usually, but not always, indicates a ground.

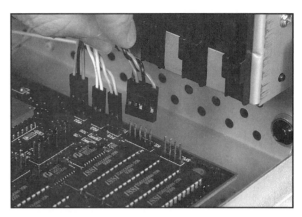

Figure 16.7: Connect the front-panel wires to the motherboard.

The front panel connections usually include: turbo switch, turbo LED, keylock, speaker, reset, and hard disk LED. The hard disk LED connects to the PC's hard disk controller or host adapter. If you have a sound card in the system, the speaker cable usually connects to the sound card. If you don't have a sound card, the speaker cable connects to the motherboard.

4. Connect the backup battery to the battery connector on the motherboard, and be careful to connect the red wire to the plus (+) side of the connector. Check your motherboard manual for the correct orientation if you're not sure.

5. Check your connections one last time, making sure that all the wires are connected properly. Also check your RAM and other option switches or jumper settings.

Completing the Installation

After you install the motherboard, you're ready to begin putting the system back together and get it running. The first step is to install the system's adapters. I recommend installing only the minimum number of adapters to get the system up and running. These include the video adapter, hard disk controller or host adapter, and the I/O adapter if it is separate from the hard disk host adapter. Install only a minimum number of adapters to make it easier to determine if the board is working properly—so you don't mistake a sound card problem for a motherboard problem, for example.

Procedure:

Installing Adapters and Connecting Peripherals

1. Install the system's video adapter and connect it to the monitor.

2. Install the system's hard disk controller or host adapter and connect the hard drives and floppy drives (install the floppy drive controller if it's separate from the hard disk adapter).

3. Install the I/O adapter (if it is separate from the hard disk adapter). Connect the mouse if you have a serial mouse.

4. If you use a bus mouse, install the mouse bus card and attach the mouse.

5. Check your adapter installation to make sure all the adapters are secured with a screw and that all cable connections are correct.

You're now ready for a smoke test—if you turn it on and it doesn't smoke, you did something right.

Procedure:

System CMOS Configuration

Explanation: After you install the necessary adapters, you are ready to turn the system on and see if it works. The first task to perform is setting the system's CMOS parameters. A CMOS chip is used to store information about your system, such as the type of hard disk, the types of floppy drives, the amount of RAM installed, and other options. The CMOS chip and system configuration program are explained in Chapter 22, but the following procedure should give you enough information to get started.

1. Check your motherboard's manual to determine how to access the system configuration program to configure settings in the CMOS chip. In many systems, you press the Del key while the system boots. With other systems, you have to press a combination of keys after the system boots.

2. Plug in the monitor and PC, then turn on both devices.

3. The system performs a POST (Power-On Self Test). Listen for any repeated beeps and look for any error messages displayed on the monitor. During the start-up process, watch for a message that tells you how to run the system's configuration program. If your system requires that you press a key during boot to enter the system setup program, watch for the prompt that tells you to press the necessary key to start the configuration program.

4. In the CMOS setup program, set the options for floppy drive(s), hard drive(s), RAM, and any other options you need for your system.

5. Save the settings and reboot the system.

After you reboot the system, run some software to make sure your new motherboard is working. If you can successfully boot to the DOS prompt, you should have no problems with your other software.

Your new motherboard probably includes an advanced setup menu that you can use to set options such as video shadowing, ROM shadowing, memory interleave, and more. Check your motherboard's manual for an explanation of how to set these options for your motherboard.

17

Add-In Chips

Although replacing the motherboard is a good way to improve your PC's performance, it's not always the best solution. Instead, you may be able to add a math coprocessor or new CPU to your PC. This chapter explains the options for adding math coprocessors and new CPUs to 386 and 486 systems. It covers the following topics:

- Understanding math coprocessors and options
- CPU upgrade options for 486-SX and 486-DX systems
- Installing 387-compatible and Weitek math coprocessors
- Installing 487-SX and OverDrive CPU upgrades

Math Coprocessors

A math coprocessor handles one task: math operations. Although the PC can perform the same math calculations as the math coprocessor, the PC has to do it in software. The math coprocessor instead works in hardware, which is faster. Some programs require a math coprocessor, others will use one if one is available, and other programs do not use a math coprocessor at all (although the math coprocessor doesn't interfere with the program in any way).

In 386 systems, the math coprocessor is a separate chip from the CPU, and is called a 387. In 486 systems (with the exception of the 486-SX), the math coprocessor is built into the CPU. Most 386 and 486 systems also can use an external math coprocessor designed and manufactured by Weitek. The Weitek line of math coprocessors offers better performance for some programs than a typical Intel-compatible math coprocessor. A program has to be written specifically to take advantage of the Weitek math coprocessor.

By adding a math coprocessor to your system, you can speed up the performance of any of your applications that are written to use one. Most popular spreadsheet, graphics, CAD, and database programs support a math coprocessor. If you use an application that deals with numbers or graphics, you may be able to speed it up by adding a math coprocessor to your system.

TIP

Before buying a math coprocessor to add to your system, check your program manuals to make sure your programs will use it.

If you have a 386 system and you're thinking about buying a math coprocessor for it, keep the following points in mind:

● You won't be replacing the 386 CPU. The 387 math coprocessor is an addition to the system, not a replacement for your 386 CPU.

● The speed of the math coprocessor must match the speed of the CPU (or exceed it). If you have a 25MHz 386 system, buy a 25MHz 387 or compatible math coprocessor.

● Intel is not the only manufacturer of math coprocessors. Cyrix and IIT manufacture math coprocessors that are compatible with the 387.

If you have a 486-DX system, you already have a math coprocessor built into the 486 CPU, but you may want to add a Weitek 4167 to your system to improve the performance of programs that support the Weitek math coprocessor. Check with your program manuals to see if your programs support the Weitek chip.

If you have a 486-SX system, you can replace the CPU with a chip Intel has dubbed the 487. The 487, unlike the 387, is not just a math coprocessor chip. The 487 is a 486 CPU with an integrated math coprocessor. In some systems (those without a 487-SX upgrade socket), you have to remove the 486 CPU and replace it with the 487 CPU. In systems with a 487 upgrade socket, the original CPU remains in the system and the 487 is installed in the extra socket.

Adding an 80387-Compatible Math Coprocessor

The two most important points when installing a math coprocessor are these: take care not to zap the chip with static electricity, and make sure you orient the chip correctly in its socket before trying to press it into place. The math chip has a dot in one corner to indicate the location of pin 1 on the chip. The socket will have a notch in one corner or a dot or other indicator painted on the motherboard to indicate the location of pin 1. Make sure you align pin 1 on the chip with pin 1 on the socket.

Some systems use sockets called LIF (Low Insertion Force) or ZIF (Zero Insertion Force) sockets. With these sockets, the chip isn't pressed into place and held by the friction of the pins in the socket. Instead, a screw or lever holds the chip in place.

Procedure:
Installing the Chip

1. Turn off, unplug, and open the system.

2. Discharge your static.

3. Remove the math chip from its package, being careful not to touch the pins if possible. Handle the chip by its edges to reduce the danger of static damage.

4. Examine the pins for damage and gently straighten any that are bent (see fig. 17.1).

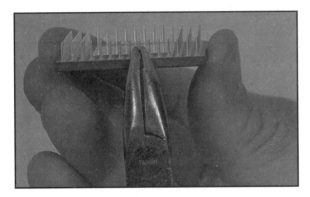

Figure 17.1: Check the pins and straighten any that are bent.

5. Locate the socket for the math chip and determine the correct orientation of the chip in the socket. Match the dot on top of the chip with the notch or dot on the socket or motherboard.

6. Lower the chip into place in the socket, making sure all the pins are aligned in their holes.

TIP *Before pressing the chip into place, make sure the mother-board is well supported under the socket. If the motherboard is out of the system, place it on a flat, stable surface. Avoid bending the motherboard when you press the chip into place; you could damage the motherboard.*

7. Press the chip firmly into place as shown in figure 17.2. (If your system uses a ZIF or LIF socket, you only need to place the chip in the socket and secure it with the hex screw or lever.)

8. Check your motherboard manual for a jumper or DIP switch setting that informs the PC that a math coprocessor is installed. Most 386 systems require this setting on the motherboard. Set it accordingly.

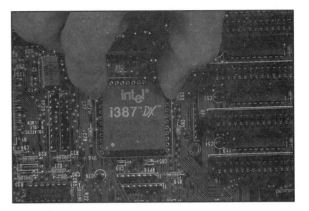

Figure 17.2: Installing the 387 chip in its socket.

Procedure:
Testing the Chip

1. Turn on the PC.

2. While the PC is booting, look for any error messages on the display.

3. If your math chip includes a diagnostic disk, the disk will contain a program to test the math chip. Run the diagnostic program.

4. If you don't have a diagnostic program for your math chip, enter your system's CMOS configuration setup program. You should see an indication in the basic configuration screen that the math chip is installed. If the program indicates that the math chip is not installed, turn off the system. Recheck your installation steps and verify that the chip is installed correctly in the socket.

Adding a Weitek Math Coprocessor

The Weitek math coprocessor is installed in the system's optional math chip socket, just like the 387-compatible math chips. Some systems will recognize the Weitek chip automatically after it is installed, but others require that you run a program called 67SETUP.EXE that comes with the Weitek chip in order for the chip to be recognized by the system. This program has to be run every time you want to use the chip, so you should add the program to your AUTOEXEC.BAT file.

Procedure:
Installing the Chip

1. Turn off, unplug, and open the system.

2. Discharge your static.

3. Remove the math chip from its package, being careful not to touch the pins if possible. Handle the chip by its edges to reduce the danger of static damage.

4. Examine the pins for damage and gently straighten any that are bent (see fig. 17.1).

5. Locate the socket for the math chip and determine the correct orientation of the chip in the socket. Match the dot on top of the chip with the notch or dot on the socket or motherboard.

6. Lower the chip into place in the socket, making sure all the pins are aligned in their holes (see fig. 17.3).

Figure 17.3: Installing the 4167 Weitek math coprocessor.

TIP   Before pressing the chip into place, make sure the motherboard is well supported under the socket. If the motherboard is out of the system, place it on a flat, stable surface. Avoid bending the motherboard when you press the chip into place; you could damage the motherboard.

7. Press the chip firmly into place.

8. Check your motherboard manual for a jumper or DIP switch setting that informs the PC that a math coprocessor is installed. The jumper or switch setting is not specific to the Weitek chip—it applies to all math chips.

Procedure:
Testing the Chip

1. Turn on the PC.

2. While the PC is booting, watch for any error messages on the display.

3. Run the program 67TEST.EXE that comes with the Weitek chip. This will check for the presence of the Weitek chip and run tests to ensure that it's working properly. If the system fails to detect the Weitek chip, run the program 67SETUP.EXE that comes with the chip. Then, run 67TEST.EXE again. If the diagnostic program still fails, check your installation again. Make sure the chip is aligned correctly in the socket.

Upgrading a 486-SX to a 487-SX (486-DX) System

The method you use to install a 487-SX in your PC depends on the design of your motherboard. Some 486-SX systems include a separate socket for the 487-SX chip. In systems that don't include a separate 487-SX socket, you have to remove the existing 486-SX CPU and replace it with the 487-SX CPU.

Procedure:

Removing the Existing CPU

Explanation: Use this procedure if your motherboard doesn't include a separate 487-SX socket. The 487-SX includes a special tool for removing the 486-SX chip from its socket.

1. Turn off, unplug, and open the system.

2. Locate the 486-SX chip. You can't miss it—it's the biggest chip on the board and has 486-SX written on it.

3. Discharge your static.

4. With the chip removal tool provided with the 487-SX, gently remove the 486-SX CPU (see fig. 17.4). Alternate from side to side of the chip to extract it evenly. Be careful not to damage any components that might be located around the CPU socket.

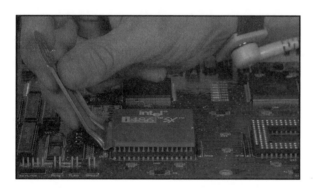

Figure 17.4: Remove the 486-SX CPU with the chip removal tool provided in the 487-SX package.

5. Set the 486-CPU in the plastic box that came with the 487-SX (the same box that held the removal tool).

Procedure:

Installing the 487

1. Discharge your static again, then remove the 487-SX from its package.

2. Align the dot on the chip with the notch or indicator on the motherboard, then lower the chip into place (see fig. 17.5).

Figure 17.5: Installing the 487-SX CPU in the CPU socket.

 **TIP**
Before pressing the chip into place, make sure the mother-board is well supported under the socket. If the motherboard is out of the system, place it on a flat, stable surface. Avoid bending the motherboard when you press the chip into place, because you could damage the motherboard.

3. Press the chip firmly into place.

4. Check your motherboard manual to see if there is a jumper or DIP switch setting required on the motherboard to configure it for a math coprocessor. Set it accordingly.

Upgrading Your 486 CPU

If you have a 486 system, you might have a couple of options for upgrading your CPU depending on the design of your system's motherboard. Many 486-DX systems include a socket called an OverDrive socket that will accommodate one of Intel's OverDrive processors. These processors operate at twice the normal internal clock speed, enabling you to switch from a 25MHz system to a 50MHz system, or from a 33MHz system to a 66MHz system. They are the same as the 486-DX2 CPUs.

Although many systems include the OverDrive socket, other systems require you to remove the existing 486-DX CPU and replace it with the OverDrive chip. There are two different versions of the OverDrive chips to support these two system configurations. Check your system's manual and your motherboard to determine which type of Over Drive chip you need. If necessary, contact the PC's manufacturer to be sure you can install an OverDrive chip in your system.

The performance improvement you get by switching to an OverDrive processor depends on the types of programs you run on your PC, but you may get as much as a 70 percent increase in performance over your existing 486-DX CPU.

Procedure:
Removing the Existing CPU (No Overdrive Socket)

1. Turn off, unplug, and open the system.

2. Locate the 486-DX CPU—it's the largest chip on the board and has 486 written on it.

3. Discharge your static.

4. With the chip removal tool provided with the OverDrive processor, gently remove the existing 486-DX from its socket. Alternate from side to side of the chip to extract it evenly and avoid bending the pins. Be careful not to damage any components surrounding the 486 socket.

5. Place the 486-DX chip in the plastic box provided with the OverDrive processor (the same box that held the removal tool).

Procedure:
Installing the OverDrive CPU

1. Discharge your static, then remove the OverDrive processor from its package.

2. **Systems with an OverDrive socket:** Install the OverDrive chip in the special OverDrive socket, taking care to correctly align the dot on the top of the chip with the notch or other pin 1 indicator on the motherboard.

3. **Systems without an OverDrive socket:** Install the OverDrive chip in the main CPU socket, taking care to correctly align the dot on top of the chip with the notch or other pin 1 indicator on the motherboard (see fig. 17.6).

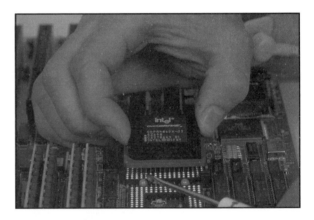

Figure 17.6: Installing the OverDrive processor in the CPU socket.

TIP You may find it easiest in some systems to remove the motherboard in order to install the OverDrive chip.

The OverDrive chip comes with diagnostic and testing software. If your system boots without any errors, however, the chip is working properly. Even so, you may want to run the demo program on the disk to test the system's speed.

18

Power Supplies

There are two reasons to replace your power supply: a) it has failed, or b) it doesn't supply enough watts to power all the devices in your PC. If you think your power supply may have failed, there are a few simple procedures to go through to test it. If you need to replace your power supply because it has failed or it doesn't have a high enough rating for your system, you'll have no problem doing so—that's an easy procedure, also.

This chapter covers the following topics relating to power supplies:

- Testing a power supply
- Buying a power supply
- Replacing a power supply
- Protecting your PC from spikes and surges

Power Supplies and Power Protection

The power supply in your PC is a switching power supply, which means it converts alternating current (AC) to direct current (DC). The CPU needs 5 volts (5V) to operate, and peripherals generally use 12V for motors and 5V for electronics. (The low-power SL series of processors, such as the 486-SL, use only 3.3V.) So, the PC's power supply puts out 5V and 12V.

The power supply connects to the motherboard using two connectors, labeled P8 and P9. P8 connects to the set of power connector pins toward the back of the PC, and P9 connects to the set of pins in front of P8. PC power supplies usually have four sets of power cable assemblies for connecting to peripherals. These cable assemblies have four wires: two ground wires (black), a +5V line (red), and a +12V line (yellow).

The capacity of the power supply is rated in watts. The higher the wattage, the more power it can put out and the more devices it can power. One reason to replace the power supply is to increase the amount of available power for lots of peripherals.

Most desktop systems sold today have at least a 200-watt (200W) power supply. Tower systems typically have 250W to 300W power supplies. If yours is an older system, its power supply may have a rating as low as 150W.

If you're trying to power a hard drive, a CD-ROM, a couple of floppy drives, a tape drive, an internal modem, and lots of other gadgets, your power may not be up to the task. A power supply with a capacity that's too low to drive all the devices in your system can lead to intermittent problems in the PC, including disk access errors and other problems. If you have a power supply of less than 200W and are trying to power much more than a hard drive and a floppy drive, you might consider upgrading to a 200W or 250W power supply.

Power Protection and Power Supply Repair

The other reason to replace your power supply is if it has failed. The most common reason for a power supply to fail is a surge or spike on the line. A *spike* is an overvoltage of less than a millisecond, and a *surge* is an overvoltage of a few milliseconds or longer (even seconds). Sometimes these power problems are caused by lightning, but more often they're caused by common fluctuations in the power supply coming from the power company or by other appliances on the same circuit cutting on and off.

If your power supply does fail, you can't repair it. You have to replace it. The only exception is if the fan fails and the rest of the power supply still works. You can replace the fan, but I'm not going to tell you how, because it's possible to get shocked by your power supply even when it's turned off and unplugged. I don't want to get sued because you got fried, so just replace the power supply unless you really know what you're doing.

Can you protect your power supply and the rest of your PC from damage by power surges and spikes? To some degree, yes. You can plug your PC and peripherals into a surge suppressor. Woods Wire Products makes a line of suppressors that include connections for your phone lines. These help protect your phone, modem, and other devices that are connected to your phone line.

Recently, I had one of my systems connected to a surge suppressor, but didn't have the phone lines connected. We had a lightning strike nearby and my phone hold switch got fried. Everything else that was connected to the surge suppressor was fine.

Most household surge suppressors do a good job up to a point, but they can't handle very large spikes. A spike needs only a few milliseconds to destroy your PC, and many surge suppressors can't damp the spike that fast. For everyday surges and spikes, though, they're a good idea.

Here are some tips for avoiding power problems with your PC:

● **Check your outlet.** Use an AC line tester to make sure the hot, neutral, and ground lines are connected properly. If the outlet is wired incorrectly, you have not only the potential for damage to the PC, but also a significant shock hazard. Figure 18.1 shows a typical AC circuit tester.

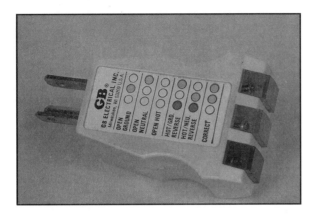

Figure 18.1: A typical AC circuit tester.

● **Isolate the PC on the circuit.** If possible, your PC should be the only device on the circuit. If nothing else, avoid plugging the PC into an outlet on the same circuit as equipment with large motors (washers, refrigerators, and so on), copiers or laser printers, and resistance-heating appliances (heaters, coffee makers, and the like).

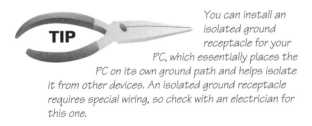

TIP *You can install an isolated ground receptacle for your PC, which essentially places the PC on its own ground path and helps isolate it from other devices. An isolated ground receptacle requires special wiring, so check with an electrician for this one.*

● **Use a surge suppressor.** These won't catch all the surges and spikes, but they're effective in a lot of cases.

● **Grounding.** Make sure your PC and other devices are grounded through the outlet. It's a good idea to have all your PC devices share a common ground to prevent signal problems between them. You can accomplish this by connecting all the devices to the same outlet (just don't overdo it).

● **Put a knot in your power cords.** This is a weird one, but it works. If you take a lightning strike, the surge will burn out the cord instead of your PC.

● **Keep the power supply clean.** You occasionally should remove the dust from your PC. After unplugging and opening the PC, use a brush to remove the dust from the PC's vent holes. As you brush off the dust, suck it up with a vacuum cleaner. Also, clean the fan blades from the back of your PC (see fig. 18.2).

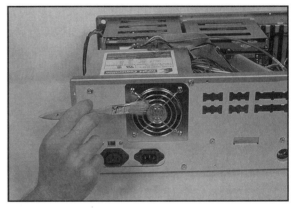

Figure 18.2: Keep the power supply free of dust build-up.

If you think your power supply may be bad, read Chapter 21, "The Computer Won't Start," which contains procedures for checking your power supply. If your power supply turns out to be bad, you need to remove it and replace it with a new one.

Procedure:

Removing a Power Supply

1. Turn off, unplug, and open the PC.

2. Disconnect the power supply from the motherboard. Pull up the connectors, then tilt them away from the power supply to disconnect them from the motherboard connectors.

3. Disconnect the power supply from the peripherals such as the hard disk and floppy drives.

4. Locate the four screws at the back of the PC that hold the power supply in place and remove them (see fig. 18.3).

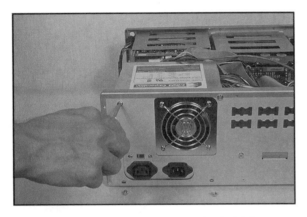

Figure 18.3: Remove the screws that hold the power supply in place.

5. **Desktop case:** Slide the power supply toward the front of the PC to disengage the holding tabs on the bottom of the power supply, then lift the power supply clear of the chassis.

6. **Tower case:** Disconnect the power cord from the front panel switch. Remove the power supply from the chassis.

Procedure:

Installing a Power Supply

1. **Desktop case:** Place the power supply in the PC, then slide it back into position with the rear of the power supply lined up with the mounting holes in the back of the chassis (see fig. 18.4). Make sure there are no cables stuck underneath the power supply. Attach the power supply to the chassis with four screws.

2. **Tower case:** Position the power supply in place, making sure there are no cables caught between the power supply and the chassis. Screw the power supply to the chassis with four screws.

Figure 18.4: Installing the power supply in a desktop chassis.

3. Reconnect all the peripherals to the power supply.

4. Connect P8 from the power supply to the rear power connector on the PC's motherboard (see figure 18.5).

Figure 18.5: Connecting the power cables to the motherboard.

5. Connect P9 from the power supply to the forward power connector on the PC's motherboard.

6. **Tower case only:** Connect the power cable from the power supply to the front panel.

7. Check your connections.

8. Make sure the system is turned off, then plug in the PC. Turn it on to test the system.

19

That Stupid Keyboard Problem

Of all the devices inside of or attached to the PC, the keyboard is the one that suffers the most from continued use. I've never had a motherboard, hard drive, or floppy drive fail, but I've gone through a couple of keyboards. They literally take a pounding every time they're used. They're also susceptible to dust, dirt, hair, and other junk that collects under the keys, preventing them from working properly. Then, there is the problem of the errant drink. A spilled cup of coffee or cola can do a lot of damage to your keyboard.

This short chapter covers a few of the maintenance procedures you can perform on your keyboard, including the following:

- Fixing a key that won't work
- Cleaning up the keyboard after a spill

Problem: Keys Don't Work on Keyboard

Occasionally, one or more of the keys on your keyboard will quit working. Sometimes the hardware actually wears out, requiring you to replace the keyboard. More often that not, however, something has deposited itself between the key actuator and the contacts. I have to clean my keyboard about once every two months to remove the built-up dust, hair, and other junk that somehow finds its way into the keyboard and under the keys.

Generally, all you have to do to fix this problem is to open the keyboard and brush the junk out of it. There are a million little screws to take out (okay, only about 20 or so), but there's nothing difficult about opening the keyboard and cleaning it.

Procedure:
Clean Keyboard

1. Turn off the PC and unplug the keyboard.

2. Turn over the keyboard, then remove the screws that hold the bottom and top of the case together.

3. Remove the case bottom to expose the keyboard printed circuit board, then remove all the little screws that hold the circuit board to the key assembly (see fig. 19.1).

Figure 19.1: Remove the screws that hold the printed circuit board to the key assembly.

4. Turn over the printed circuit card to expose the contacts. Clean them with a brush (see fig. 19.2) or compressed air. If they're really dirty and have gunk built up on them, you also can clean them with a soft cloth dipped in alcohol.

Figure 19.2: Clean the contacts on the printed circuit card.

5. Reinstall the printed circuit board on the key assembly, then reinstall all of the screws.

6. Reinstall the whole assembly in the case, taking care to position the cable and the choke (the little round thing around the cable) correctly in the case before screwing the case back together.

7. Plug in the keyboard and turn on your PC to test the keys. If one or more keys still don't work, replace the keyboard.

Problem: Liquid Spilled on Keyboard

The worst thing you can do to your keyboard is spill a drink on it. If the drink is a straight shot of tequila, it probably won't do a lot of damage. If the drink is a diet cola, you may be able to clean the keyboard sufficiently to use it again. If the drink has a lot of sugar in it (like a regular cola), you're probably going to have to throw the keyboard away and buy a new one—sugar wreaks havoc on electronics.

If you've spilled water, coffee, or tea on the keyboard, unplug it immediately. Open it up using the previous procedure as a guide and dry it out. It's a good idea to wipe the printed circuit board with a soft cloth dipped in alcohol to help prevent oxidation. This also is important with a coffee spill to remove any residue, particularly if you use cream or sugar in your coffee.

If you've spilled a diet cola of some kind on the keyboard, open it and clean it out with alcohol. Make sure you let the keyboard dry for an hour or so before trying to use it again. This will ensure that the remaining liquid has evaporated.

If you've spilled a regular cola or some other kind of drink that has a lot of sugar in it, your keyboard might be a total loss. If you can't stand the idea of spending money for a new keyboard or you can't wait for the new keyboard to show up, try cleaning the old one anyway. The spill may not be as bad as it looks—the amount of liquid that actually made it into the keyboard's guts may be minimal.

In the case of a spill like this, open the keyboard and clean it with a liberal dose of alcohol. Use cotton-tipped swabs to clean out the crevices. You may have to pop the keys off the key assembly to clean under them.

Before popping off any keys, check underneath them for little springy wires. The Enter key and the space bar usually have them, as do a few other keys. Avoid removing these keys, because getting the little wires inserted properly can be difficult.

After you've cleaned the keyboard, let it sit for an hour or so to dry out. Check it again to see if you missed any gunk. Clean it again if you did. Then, put it back together and keep your fingers crossed while you try it out.

Remember, the best way to get around a keyboard problem is to not let it happen at all. Keep liquids away from your keyboard whenever possible.

Part 3

Healing Your Computer

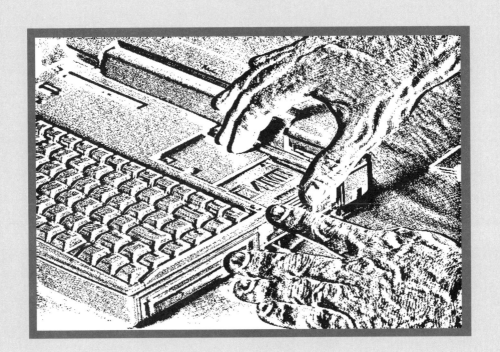

20

The Zen of Troubleshooting

Sooner or later, something is going to go *blooey* in your PC, leaving you with two options: pack it up and take it to someone to fix it for you, or fix it yourself. Should you try to fix it yourself? You bet! Why pay someone $100 or more to fix something you may be able to easily fix yourself? It may require something as simple as changing a few entries in one of your configuration files.

This chapter will help you get your feet wet and give you some general tips for troubleshooting problems that crop up on your PC. Following chapters cover specific problems. This chapter covers these general topics:

- General suggestions from a voice of experience
- How to perform a single-step boot to isolate a problem
- What a clean boot is and why to try it
- Using a minimal configuration
- Using a boot disk
- Tips for isolating a problem

Wait! Before you start monkeying around and trying to find the root of your PC's evil, check to see whether you have run out of disk space. Issue the DIR command at the DOS prompt and read the amount of free space it reports. If your system is low on disk space, that could be the problem. Clean out your old files (refer to Chapter 5 for advice), and then try your program again to see whether the problem is gone.

First, a few words of wisdom.

Murphy's Law and PCs

Murphy's Law doesn't apply to PCs. At least, it doesn't apply directly. (In case you've been living in a vacuum, Murphy's Law states that if something can go wrong, it will.) Instead, PCs are subject to Boyce's Corollary to Murphy's Law, which is this:

> Your PC will continue to work just fine until you start fiddling with it and screw it up.

PC hardware degrades over time, so it's possible, but uncommon, for something in the PC to actually break down. Instead, the most common cause of problems on a PC by far is someone (usually you) making a change to the system that just doesn't compute. Maybe you added a new piece of hardware and didn't get the settings right. Maybe you fiddled and tweaked your configuration files once too often. Maybe your three-year-old with the magic touch has touched your PC once too often. Or, maybe you just don't live right and things are catching up with you.

Whatever the cause of your PC's problem, there are some general things you can do to help isolate the cause and fix the problem. More about those in a minute. First, some things to keep in mind while you're gnashing your teeth over the fact that your PC is bent on not doing its thing:

- It's probably something that you did to the PC that caused the problem. If you did it, you can undo it.

- If the problem is caused by a hardware failure, you probably can undo that, too.

- There may be more than one thing wrong. Don't assume that because you find and fix one problem that another won't rear its ugly head.

- You're smarter than the machine. You *will* find the cause.

- You should follow some specific steps religiously when troubleshooting a problem.

That last suggestion is one of the most important, and it has to do with using logs.

Using Your Logs and Backups

I'm going to sound like a broken record, but here goes: whatever is wrong with your PC probably was caused by something you did. Did you do any of the following?

- Install a new piece of hardware in the PC

- Change a setting (however minor) in CONFIG.SYS, AUTOEXEC.BAT, WIN.INI, or SYSTEM.INI

- Install some new software

- Let someone else use (or even touch) your system

- Run SysEdit

Any one of the things in the previous list could have altered your configuration files, either by design or by accident. Have you done any of those things, or have you done anything besides just use your PC? If so, the first step you might want to take is to check your system logs to determine what was last changed in the system.

Checking Your System Logs

If you have faithfully been noting system changes to hardware and software in your logs, the change that is causing your problem will be in the log. (Unless a piece of hardware has broken down.) It's likely—but not a certainty—that the last thing you changed is what's causing the problem. It could be that something you changed a few days or months ago didn't cause a problem until you tried doing something you haven't done before. Maybe you're trying to run a program that isn't compatible with a change you made a month ago, for example, and this is the first time you have tried to run it since making the change.

Check your logs for the last change you made to the system. Use that as a guide to begin searching for the problem.

Trying a Backup

You learned in Chapter 3 that you always should make a backup copy of CONFIG.SYS, AUTOEXEC.BAT, and your Windows INI files. You have been doing that, haven't you?

If you have been making a backup copy each time you make a change, open the backup copy and compare it with your current copy of the file. If you have installed some new software, it's very possible that the installation process automatically changed some settings in one of the files. If so, the new settings might be the cause of the problem.

Procedure:
Comparing Working and Backup Files for Differences

Following is a quick way to find out if your working copy and your backup copy are the same:

1. If you're running Windows, exit Windows.

2. At the DOS prompt, enter **FC *file1 file2***, where *file1* and *file2* are the names of the files you want to compare. To compare, for example, a backup copy of CONFIG.SYS (called CONFIG.BAK) with the working copy of CONFIG.SYS, which is located in the root directory of drive C, you use this command:

   ```
   FC C:\BACKUP\CONFIG.BAK C:\CONFIG.SYS
   ```

   If the files are identical, you see the message FC: no differences encountered. If there are differences, FC lists the differing lines from each file, which will help you locate the change. If the files are radically different, FC displays an error message telling you that the files are too different.

If the files are different, determine why they're different. Did you add something to one of the files? Did a program that you installed make a modification to one of the files? Whatever is the case, the difference in the files should be your first approach to troubleshooting. If you can't deter-

mine the problem from just looking at the files, try the procedure in the next section.

Procedure:
Restoring Configuration Files

1. Copy the file to a new file. For example, copy CONFIG.SYS to CONFIG.NEW.

2. Copy the backup file you have made previously to replace the current working file. For example, copy CONFIG.BAK to CONFIG.SYS.

3. If you are restoring CONFIG.SYS or AUTOEXEC.BAT, reboot the system. If you are restoring SYSTEM.INI or WIN.INI, restart Windows.

4. If the problem goes away, you have located the problem: one of the changes in the file was causing the problem. Examine the file (such as CONFIG.NEW), locate the line that's different, and begin researching why it's causing the problem. Use FC to locate the different line(s) in the file.

5. If the problem doesn't go away, restore the file. For example, copy CONFIG.NEW back to CONFIG.SYS. You need to look elsewhere for the problem. Read the other sections of this chapter for troubleshooting techniques.

When Windows Won't Start

When Windows won't start, usually it's caused by a Windows driver problem, although memory and disk problems also can keep Windows from running properly. Windows recognizes two optional command-line switches that provide a means for troubleshooting a problem that is preventing Windows from running at all or from running correctly. These *debug switches* are entered on the DOS command line with the WIN command when starting Windows. The first of these two switches is the /B switch.

Troubleshooting Windows with the BOOTLOG.TXT File

If you're having a problem getting Windows to run, you can cause Windows to generate a log file when it attempts to start. The log file, called BOOTLOG.TXT, contains messages that indicate when the various parts of Windows are being loaded and whether they are successfully initiated. Reviewing the boot log will help you determine, at least in general, when the problem is occurring and which Windows component is causing the problem. If, for example, the video driver never finishes initializing, it might indicate a problem with the video driver.

To generate a boot log file when you start Windows, enter the following command on the DOS command line:

```
WIN /B
```

As Windows is booting, it creates the file BOOTLOG.TXT in the Windows directory. Here's a sample from a typical BOOTLOG.TXT file:

```
[boot]
LoadStart = system.drv
LoadSuccess = system.drv
LoadStart = keyboard.drv
LoadSuccess = keyboard.drv
LoadStart = mouse.drv
LoadSuccess = mouse.drv
LoadStart = vga.drv
LoadSuccess = vga.drv
LoadStart = mmsound.drv
LoadSuccess = mmsound.drv
LoadStart = comm.drv
LoadSuccess = comm.drv
LoadStart = vgasys.fon
LoadSuccess = vgasys.fon
LoadStart = vgaoem.fon
LoadSuccess = vgaoem.fon
LoadStart = GDI.EXE
LoadStart = FONTS.FON
LoadSuccess = FONTS.FON
LoadStart = vgafix.fon
LoadSuccess = vgafix.fon
LoadStart = OEMFONTS.FON
LoadSuccess = OEMFONTS.FON
LoadSuccess = GDI.EXE
LoadStart = USER.EXE
INIT=Keyboard
```

```
INITDONE=Keyboard
INIT=Mouse
STATUS=No mouse driver installed
INITDONE=Mouse
INIT=DisplayLoadStart = DISPLAY.drv
LoadSuccess = DISPLAY.drv
INITDONE=Display
INIT=Display Resources
INITDONE=Display Resources
INIT=Fonts
INITDONE=Fonts
INIT=Lang Driver
INITDONE=Lang Driver
LoadSuccess = USER.EXE
LoadStart = setup.exe
LoadStart = LZEXPAND.DLL
LoadSuccess = LZEXPAND.DLL
LoadStart = VER.DLL
LoadSuccess = VER.DLL
LoadSuccess = setup.exe
INIT=Final USER
INITDONE=Final USER
INIT=Installable Drivers
INITDONE=Installable Drivers
```

If a driver is missing a LoadSuccess statement, it may mean that the driver file has been corrupted. Run Setup and reinstall the driver, if possible. If no INIT statement exists for a module or driver, it may indicate a hardware problem.

Windows is particularly sensitive to display and font problems. If the video driver isn't compatible with the video adapter you're using, Windows may fail to start. Using the wrong type of font also will cause problems.

To troubleshoot the problem, use the procedure in the following section.

Procedure:

Reinstalling Video Drivers in Windows

1. From the DOS prompt outside of Windows, change to the Windows directory (by entering **CD \WINDOWS**, for example).

2. Enter **SETUP**.

3. Select the Display option, and press Enter.

4. From the list of display drivers provided by Setup, choose the same driver you currently are using. If you're using a third-party device driver, choose the option Other, and insert the disk containing the driver when prompted to do so.

5. Setup prompts you to specify whether you want to use the current version of the driver or install a new copy. Choose the option to install a new copy.

   Setup reinstalls the font files required by the selected video driver in addition to the video driver itself.

6. After you have exited Setup, try starting Windows again.

7. If Windows still doesn't start, run Setup again and install the standard VGA driver (assuming that your system is VGA-compatible). If you still can't start Windows, your problem lies elsewhere.

Using the /D Debug Switch To Troubleshoot Windows

In addition to the /B switch, Windows supports one other debug switch that provides four options that control the way Windows starts and runs. The /D switch, which is added to the WIN command line to start Windows, supports these options:

- **/D:F.** This option turns off 32-bit disk access. If you have been experiencing problems with file access and you're currently using FastDisk (32-bit disk access), you may want to try this switch. This is equivalent to specifying the setting 32BitDiskAccess=Off in the [386Enh] section of SYSTEM.INI.

- **/D:S.** This option prevents Windows from using the UMA address range F000–FFFF (1M), and is equivalent to the setting SystemROMBreakPoint=False in the [386Enh] section of SYSTEM.INI.

- **/D:X.** Prevents Windows from using any of the UMA address space from A000 through FFFF, and is equivalent to the setting EMMExclude=A000-FFFF in the [386Enh] section of SYSTEM.INI. This switch is particularly useful when troubleshooting a problem with a device driver or device that uses a memory range in the UMA.

- **/D:V.** Specifies that hard disk interrupts will be handled by the system's ROM BIOS, not by the virtual device driver that Windows otherwise would use in Enhanced mode. This switch is equivalent to the setting VirtualHDIRQ=False in the [386Enh] section of SYSTEM.INI. If you have a SCSI hard drive, you may need to use the setting VirtualHDIRQ=False in order for the drive to work properly. You can use the /D:V switch when starting Windows to test this.

If you're having a problem starting Windows, try each of the switches by entering them on the command line to start Windows. Following is an example with the /D:F switch:

```
WIN /D:F
```

If Windows starts and runs successfully after using one of the switches, you have narrowed down the problem. If the /D:V switch clears up the problem, add (or edit) the setting VirtualHDIRQ=False in the [386Enh] section of SYSTEM.INI. If /D:X clears up the problem, you have a memory conflict. Read Chapter 4, "All You Need To Know about Memory," if you're not familiar with memory terms and concepts, and then refer to the section on memory conflicts in Chapter 24, "Healing Your Hard Disk," to solve your memory conflict.

If the /D:F switch clears up the problem, you can't use 32-bit disk access with your hard disk. Add the setting 32bitDiskAccess=False in the [386Enh] section of SYSTEM.INI. If the /D:S switch clears up the problem, add the setting SystemROMBreakPoint=False to the [386Enh] section of SYSTEM.INI.

Using a Single-Step Boot

If you suspect that the problem with the system may be caused by a driver or other setting in CONFIG.SYS, you can perform a single-step boot if you're using MS-DOS 6 (this capability doesn't exist in earlier versions of MS-DOS). Even if you have no clue whatsoever what's wrong, a single-step boot is worth a try.

In a *single-step boot*, you can selectively execute each line in CONFIG.SYS. After all the lines in CONFIG.SYS have been processed (either executed or ignored), you have the option of processing AUTOEXEC.BAT. If you choose to process AUTOEXEC.BAT, all the lines in the file are executed—you cannot single-step through AUTOEXEC.BAT.

Procedure:
Single-Step Boot

Explanation: To perform a single-step boot, follow this procedure:

1. Press Ctrl-Alt-Del, or press the reset button on your PC.

2. Watch for the message `Starting MS-DOS....` While the message is displayed, press F8.

3. If you use a multi-boot configuration menu, the menu is displayed. Choose the option under which you have been experiencing the problem.

4. The system will prompt you by displaying, one at a time, each line in CONFIG.SYS that normally would be processed according to the boot configuration you're using. Read each line, and then press Y to process it.

5. If the problem appears (an error message, for example), you probably have located the problem. The line in CONFIG.SYS last processed probably is generating the error or is related to the problem. After the system boots, examine the line to determine what may be causing the problem. If the system will not boot, refer to the next section on performing a clean boot.

6. If the problem doesn't appear when any of the CONFIG.SYS entries are processed, process AUTOEXEC.BAT. While AUTOEXEC.BAT is being processed, watch for the error or problem to appear. If it appears, note the entry in AUTOEXEC.BAT that apparently caused it.

If you need to pause execution of AUTOEXEC.BAT to read a message or just keep track of what's going on, press Ctrl-S to stop execution. To start it again, press the space bar.

What you do from this point depends on the error or problem. If an error is generated by HIMEM.SYS or EMM386.EXE, you probably have a memory problem or a problem with your PC's extended CMOS setup. If the problem is caused by a device driver, your problem may be with the command-line switches used on the device driver entry, or it could be due to a hardware conflict.

If you get an error similar to `EMM386 exception error` or `Bad fault in MS-DOS extender`, see whether someone has switched the speed on your PC. (Did someone punch the turbo button, for example? I spent all day tracking down that problem.).

Procedure:
Bypassing an Entry in CONFIG.SYS

Explanation: If you have been having a problem running Windows or running a particular application and an error appears when the system processes CONFIG.SYS, follow this procedure to see whether you can get the problem to go away:

1. Press Ctrl-Alt-Del, or press the Reset button on your PC.

2. Watch for the message `Starting MS-DOS...` to appear on your display. While the message is displayed, press F8.

3. Process all the lines in CONFIG.SYS *except* the one that generates the error message or appears to be causing the problem. Respond to this line by pressing N to not process it.

4. Process AUTOEXEC.BAT.

5. After the system has booted, attempt to run the program that was experiencing the problem (or start Windows if you experienced the problem in Windows).

If the problem goes away (you can successfully run the program), you have located the problem. Based on what the error or entry is, begin troubleshooting the problem. This procedure doesn't apply to Windows users if HIMEM.SYS is generating an error message. You need HIMEM to run Windows (or a third-party memory manager that's compatible with Windows).

Isolating CONFIG.SYS and AUTOEXEC.BAT Entries without MS-DOS 6

If you're using a version of DOS other than MS-DOS 6, you can't perform a single-step boot as described previously. With a bit of trouble, you still can isolate the problem. The following sections contain procedures that will help you isolate a problem in CONFIG.SYS or AUTOEXEC.BAT.

Procedure:
Isolating Entries in CONFIG.SYS

1. Edit CONFIG.SYS and comment all but the first line. To comment a line in CONFIG.SYS, place a semicolon at the beginning of the line.

2. Reboot the system to see whether the problem or error occurs.

3. If the problem or error doesn't occur, edit CONFIG.SYS again and remove the comment from the next line (remove the semicolon).

4. Reboot the system to see whether the problem or error occurs.

5. If the problem or error doesn't occur, repeat steps 3 and 4, rebooting the system each time, until you have located the line that's causing the error or problem, or have removed the comments from each line and not found a recognizable problem.

Procedure:
Isolating Entries in AUTOEXEC.BAT

Explanation: The entries in AUTOEXEC.BAT can be processed either at boot time as part of AUTOEXEC.BAT, or can be entered one at a time from the DOS command line after the system has booted. The easiest way to isolate and test entries in AUTOEXEC.BAT is to process the entries a line at a time.

1. Print a copy of your AUTOEXEC.BAT file. You can load it into Edit or Notepad to print it. If you can't print it, write each of the lines in the file on a piece of paper and keep it handy.

NOTE *You can get a copy of AUTOEXEC.BAT if you have problems printing it from Edit or Notepad (assuming your printer works). At the DOS prompt, enter* **COPY C:\AUTOEXEC.BAT PRN.** *This command copies AUTOEXEC.BAT to the printer (LPT1).*

2. If you are using MS-DOS 6, reboot the PC and press F8 when the message Starting MS-DOS appears. This causes a single-step boot. Process all lines in CONFIG.SYS. When prompted to specify whether to process AUTOEXEC.BAT, press N.

3. If you are running a version of DOS other than MS-DOS 6, rename AUTOEXEC.BAT to AUTOEXEC.TST, and then reboot the system.

4. One at a time, enter on the DOS command lines the lines from AUTOEXEC.BAT. Watch the display after entering each command to determine whether any of the entries in AUTOEXEC.BAT is generating an error message or causing a problem. As you type each line, verify that you have entered it correctly.

Performing a Clean Boot

You may run across the situation that your PC will not boot at all because of a problem with CONFIG.SYS. You should be able to single-step through CONFIG.SYS as described earlier, but you may prefer to perform a clean boot. The term *clean boot* means to boot the system without processing CONFIG.SYS and AUTOEXEC.BAT. A clean boot is particularly useful when a combination of entries in CONFIG.SYS and/or AUTOEXEC.BAT is causing the problem.

Procedure:

Performing a Clean Boot

1. Press Ctrl-Alt-Del, or press the Reset button on your PC.

2. Watch for the message Starting MS-DOS..., and while the message is displayed, press F5.

3. When the DOS prompt appears (if it does), try executing the program that's been giving you problems.

NOTE

Sorry, but you can't run Windows after you have performed a clean boot—Windows requires HIMEM.SYS or a compatible extended memory manager in order to run. (You can run Windows 3.0 in real mode without HIMEM.SYS.) Your solution is to use a minimal configuration for troubleshooting. That topic is covered in the next section.

With a clean boot, no applications will be running and no device drivers will be in memory after the boot. HIMEM.SYS, EMM386.EXE, SMARTDRV.EXE, and any other device drivers you normally use, for example, will not be available. Following are some points to keep in mind when you're working from a clean boot:

- **No PATH.** Because AUTOEXEC.BAT hasn't been processed, your system PATH variable will not be set. If you try to start a program that has worked before and receive the error message Bad command or file name, it's probably because COMMAND.COM can't find the program you're trying to execute. You probably have an entry for the program's directory in the PATH statement in AUTOEXEC.BAT. Because the path hasn't been set, COMMAND.COM is looking only in the current directory for the program. Use the CD command to change to the directory containing the program, or set a minimal path manually with the PATH command.

- **No memory managers.** Neither HIMEM.SYS nor EMM386.EXE will be running. (If you're using a third-party memory manager, it will not be running, either.) If you have an application that requires extended memory (like Windows), you cannot run the program. Try a minimal configuration instead of a clean boot.

- **No device drivers.** Devices that require a driver, such as your mouse and CD-ROM drive, will not work when you try to use them. They need their device drivers to do their thing.

- **Nothing in the UMA.** Without a memory manager to manage the UMA, all of DOS will be loaded into conventional memory. If you load device drivers from the DOS command line, they will be installed in conventional memory.

Using a Minimal Configuration

If you're trying to troubleshoot a problem in Windows or a problem in a program that requires a memory manager or device driver, you should try a minimal configuration instead of a clean boot. A *minimal configuration* means that the system is booted with only the very minimum device drivers and other settings required to test the program with which you're having problems.

To boot with a minimal configuration, you need to edit CONFIG.SYS and AUTOEXEC.BAT and comment everything that isn't absolutely necessary. Following is a suggested CONFIG.SYS file to use for troubleshooting:

```
; This is a minimal CONFIG.SYS file
DEVICE=C:\DOS\HIMEM.SYS
FILES=20
BUFFERS=10
SHELL=C:\DOS\COMMAND.COM /P
```

You don't need to actually create a new, minimal CONFIG.SYS file. Just place a semicolon at the beginning of each line, except the lines shown in the previous example.

Next, turn your attention to AUTOEXEC.BAT. Following is a suggested AUTOEXEC.BAT for troubleshooting:

```
PROMPT=$P$G
PATH=C:\DOS;C:\WINDOWS;C:\
REM   Change the previous line according to your
REM   system's configuration, but only include the
REM   root directory, DOS directory, and Windows
REM   directory on the path.
```

As with CONFIG.SYS, you don't need to create a new AUTOEXEC.BAT file. Just add REM statements in front of each line, except for those lines shown in the previous example.

After you have "minimized" CONFIG.SYS and AUTOEXEC.BAT, reboot the system and start troubleshooting.

System Won't Boot? Use a Boot Disk!

If you've fiddled and gnashed your teeth and can't get the PC to boot, it's time to try booting from your emergency boot disk. It's such a simple procedure that it hardly rates a section of its own. Nevertheless, here it is:

Procedure:
Using a Boot Disk

1. Dig your emergency boot disk out of the desk drawer, closet, or wherever you've stashed it.

2. Place the disk in drive A.

3. Press the PC's reset button (or turn your PC off, wait about five seconds, and turn it on again).

If you didn't make an emergency boot disk, read Chapter 2, "Basic Stuff To Get Started," again as a penance. Then, find a friend who is using the same version of DOS and ask him to please, please, please make one for you.

Checking the Hardware

If fiddling with your configuration files doesn't solve your PC problem, and you have tried backup copies of your configuration files without any success, it's time to start checking hardware. The following chapters have procedures that will help you troubleshoot specific problems with the PC. If you know you're having a problem with a specific piece of hardware, turn to the chapter in the book that covers that particular type of item. Read through the configuration and troubleshooting sections to see whether you can locate the problem.

Following are some steps you can take to troubleshoot general hardware problems:

- **Check cables.** Cables can come loose, so check the connectors to make sure that they're securely seated. Check power cables and interface cables on the item that seems to be giving you trouble.

- **Seat adapters.** If you're experiencing a problem with an adapter, it may be because the adapter isn't firmly seated in its socket. Installing a screw in the adapter's bracket usually prevents this problem. To seat the adapter, push firmly on it, pressing it down securely into its bus socket.

- **Seat chips.** Because of minute vibration and the expansion and contraction caused by heating and cooling, chips can work their way out of their sockets, causing problems. If you're having a problem with an adapter, remove the adapter and place it on a flat, antistatic surface. Then, discharge your static, and press firmly on all of the socketed chips on the adapter to make sure that they are seated in their sockets. If you're having a general problem with the system, discharge your static and reseat the chips on the PC's motherboard.

Hardware troubleshooting is covered in more detail in other chapters.

21

The Computer Won't Start

It's likely that your PC will at least try to start, even if you're experiencing problems with it. This chapter, though, covers problems that prevent your PC from starting at all. This is the chapter to turn to when you press the switch to turn on your PC and nothing happens.

This chapter covers these types of problems:

- Bad and loose cables
- Bad power source
- Power supply problems
- Bad motherboard

Potential Problems

You've just flipped the big red switch or pushed the power button on your PC, and it's still lifeless. It's not even making feeble whirring or humming noises. Obviously, something is wrong. It may be a simple problem, like a loose cable, or it may be something harder to fix, like a bad power supply. Whatever the problem, there are some general procedures to follow to find out what's wrong with your system.

If the problem is a loose or bad cable, you can get the PC up and running again quickly with little or no expense. If the problem is a failed power supply, you must replace the power supply. But isn't there a fuse inside the power supply, you ask? Yes, there is. Why not try replacing it?

Inside a PC's power supply are large capacitors that condition the power generated by the power supply (they're the big round things in fig. 21.1). A *capacitor* stores electrical energy and is, in some ways, a little like a battery. With a very high-capacity capacitor (say that three times, quickly), there is a potential for a substantial shock from the capacitor, even when the power supply isn't connected to the wall outlet. Why am I telling you not to try replacing the fuse in the power supply? To be honest, I don't want you to get shocked and sue me for telling you it's okay to do it. I've worked inside a PC's power supply and lived to tell about it, but I don't recommend that you do it. If the power supply isn't generating power and you have determined that everything else is working properly, replace the power supply—don't try to fix it.

Figure 21.1: The inside of a typical PC power supply.

Another reason not to try to repair the power supply is that whatever blew the fuse may have zapped some other components in the power supply. Although you might get it working again, it may be operating outside its designed limits and could fry something in your PC.

Now, to work! Let's find out why your PC isn't humming and whirring like it should be.

Is It Making Any Noises?

When you turn on your PC, does it make any noises? Specifically, is the fan on the power supply running? If the fan is running, you know that at least the power supply is getting electricity from the wall outlet and there's no need to test the outlet.

If your PC is plugged in correctly and the fan still isn't running, it can be an indication that the PC isn't getting AC from the wall outlet, due either to a loose connection, a bad cable, a tripped circuit breaker, or a bad outlet. But, it's also possible that whatever zapped your PC also got the fan. The power supply may be getting electricity, but the fan may be burned out and some other problem may be preventing the PC from running.

If the fan in your PC's power supply is burned out but the power supply still functions normally, it is theoretically possible to replace the fan. However, you should just bite the bullet and buy a new power supply because of the shock hazards involved with working inside a power supply.

If the fan isn't running, the first thing you should check is whether the PC is plugged in. Maybe you have knocked the power cord out of the outlet by accident.

Checking Cables and Power Source

As with any troubleshooting operation, you should check the most likely things first, along with those things that are easiest to fix. The first thing to check when your PC doesn't run is the power cable.

Procedure:
Checking the Cable

1. Check the PC's power cord at the wall or floor outlet. Is it plugged in securely? Jiggle it in the outlet to make sure. If the plug seems loose, you may need a new outlet—more on that later.

2. After checking the outlet connection, check the power connection at the back of the PC. Make sure that the cord is securely plugged into the system.

3. Next, check to make sure that the power cord for the monitor is plugged in.

4. Try turning on the PC again.

If the PC still doesn't start, you may have a bad cable. Before going to the trouble of checking the cable, however, you should check the outlet.

Procedure:
Checking the Outlet

1. If you have an AC outlet tester (you can get one at a hardware store for a few dollars), plug it into the outlet to see whether the outlet is working. Figure 21.2 shows a typical AC tester. Circuit testers verify not only that you're getting AC current at the outlet, but that the circuit is connected properly and that it is grounded.

2. If you don't have an outlet tester, plug in a lamp or other gadget to see whether you're getting electricity at the outlet.

3. If the tester indicates that there's a problem with the outlet (such as no current), check the circuit breaker for that circuit.

4. If the circuit breaker is tripped, look for a reason why it's tripped. Do you have too many gadgets plugged into that circuit?

5. If the circuit breaker isn't tripped, you may have a bad wall socket. Check it again, and if it still doesn't work right, call an electrician.

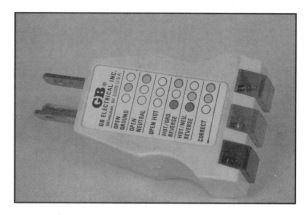

Figure 21.2: A typical AC circuit tester.

If you still can't find the problem, you should check the power cord to see whether it's good.

Procedure:
Testing the Power Cord

1. If you have a spare power cord, plug it in to the PC and see whether the system will start.

2. If you don't have a spare power cord, use a multimeter to test the cable (see fig. 21.3). Unplug the cord from the computer, and then plug it into the wall outlet and set your multimeter to test AC voltage. Taking care not to touch the metal part of the multimeter's probes (you'll get zapped if you do), carefully insert the probes into each of the holes in the computer end of the power cord. If your meter reads in the neighborhood of 110 volts, your cord is good. If you're not reading any voltage, either you don't have the multimeter connected properly or the cord is bad.

3. If your multimeter will not check for AC current, you can test the cord's continuity. Remove the power cord from the wall and from the computer. Set the meter to test for resistance. The meter settings for resistance are marked with an R and a number. Use the lowest-numbered setting.

   Place one of the test probes on one of the cord's prongs, insert the other probe into the other end of the cord (see fig. 21.4), and wiggle it around to get a good connection. Resistance on the meter should reduce to 0. If it doesn't, your power cord is bad. (Remember to check the ground, as well as the neutral and hot lines—the ground is the round pole.) If the cord is bad, buy another one from your local computer store. You also might be able to find one at a discount chain store, such as Wal-Mart or K-Mart.

Figure 21.3: Testing the power cord with a multimeter.

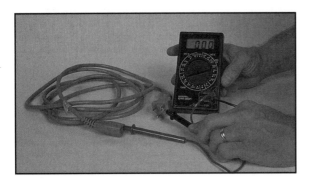

Figure 21.4: Testing the power cord for continuity.

If both the power cord and the receptacle are good, the source of your troubles probably is the PC's power supply. The next step is to open the PC and check the power connections to the motherboard.

Procedure:

Checking the Motherboard Connections

Explanation: If you have checked the power cord and receptacle and both seem to be working properly, the next step is to check the connections from the PC's power supply to the motherboard.

1. Unplug the system from the wall!

2. Open the PC and locate the power supply. It's the big silver box, usually located in the rear-right in a desktop system and the rear-top in a tower system.

3. Locate the two wiring assemblies that connect the power supply to the motherboard.

4. Make sure that the plugs at the end of the two wiring assemblies that connect to the motherboard are securely connected to the motherboard. (These two connectors should be labeled P8 and P9.)

If the plugs are securely connected to the motherboard, the problem may be a failed power supply. That's what you should check next.

Checking the Power Supply

If you have checked the outlet, the power cord, and the connections to the motherboard, you next need to check the power supply. You need a multimeter to test it. You should be able to find one at a hardware store, electronics store, or discount chain. The analog-type multimeters that have a meter display cost around $12. A digital type, which I prefer, costs around $25. It's a good investment, because you can use the multimeter to test batteries and other gadgets around the house as well as your PC.

Multimeters are designed to measure DC voltage (such as that from batteries), AC voltage (what you get at a wall outlet), amps (the rate at which electrical current flows), and resistance to the flow of current. When you test the wall outlet, you're testing AC (alternating current) voltage. The PC runs on DC (direct current), so the power supply converts AC to DC.

To test the power supply, turn on the PC and check for the proper DC voltages at the power supply's connectors. If you're reading the right voltages, the power supply is good. If you're reading no voltages, the power supply is bad, and it's time to replace it. Reading anything other than the correct voltages also indicates that the power supply is flaky and needs to be replaced.

WARNING

Some power supplies must have a load on them (be connected to something) when they are switched on or they might explode. Others simply will not work if there isn't a load connected to them, while still others will work just fine without being connected to anything. To be safe, never turn on a power supply if it isn't connected to the motherboard by connectors P8 and P9.

Procedure:

Testing the Power Supply

Explanation: You're going to test the voltage coming from the PC's power supply by touching the probes of your multimeter to the wires on one of the peripheral power connectors, such as the one going to the power supply to your hard drive.

1. Make sure that the PC's power switch is off, but leave the PC connected to the wall outlet.

2. Open the system unit.

3. Set your multimeter to read DC voltage in the next range higher than 12 volts (such as 20V, for example).

4. Use a free peripheral power plug for your test. If there are no free peripheral power plugs, such as those that connect to the hard disk and floppy disk drive, disconnect one of the power connectors from the floppy drive or hard drive.

5. Turn on the PC.

6. Insert the black probe of the multimeter into the power connector on one of the black wires (these are ground wires). It doesn't matter which one you choose.

7. Touch the red multimeter probe to the yellow wire on the power connector. The multimeter should read +12V.

8. Touch the red multimeter probe to the red wire on the power connector. The multimeter should read +5V.

If you get a reading of 0V on either of the lines, your power supply needs to be replaced. If you get a voltage reading that varies significantly from the expected amount, either the power supply has become unreliable or something is wrong with your motherboard. Whatever the case, you should check the power supply connections to the motherboard next.

Procedure:

Checking the Motherboard Power Connections

Explanation: There are two wiring assemblies that run from the power supply to the motherboard. One is labeled P8, and the other is labeled P9. P8 is always located nearer the back of the PC (toward the keyboard connector, for example), and P9 is located toward the front of the PC, relative to P8.

If you have checked the voltage at one of the peripheral power connectors and read a voltage of 0, there's no need to check any further. Your power supply needs to be replaced because it's not putting out any power. If you get a voltage reading, either the correct +5V or +12V reading or some off-reading, you next need to check the power going to the motherboard.

1. Set the multimeter to measure DC volts at the next highest setting above 12V.

2. With the PC's power cord plugged in and the power switch turned on, carefully insert the black multimeter probe into plug P8 on one of the black wires (see fig. 21.5).

3. Carefully insert the red multimeter probe into P8 at the red wire. You should get a reading of +5V.

4. After checking the red wire, carefully insert the red probe into P8 at the yellow wire. You should get a reading of +12V.

Figure 21.5: Testing motherboard power connections at P8 and P9.

5. After checking the yellow wire, check the blue one. You should get a reading of –12V.

6. After checking the blue wire on P8, check the wires on P9. Remove the black probe from P8 and connect it to one of the black wires on P9. Then, with the red probe, test the white wire. You should get a reading of –5V.

7. Finally, check each of the red wires on P9 with the red probe. You should get a reading of +5V on each one.

Did each of the wires test within 10 percent or so of the norm? If so, your power supply is good and the problem is in your motherboard somewhere. If you didn't get any voltage readings, the power supply is bad. You need to get a new one. See Chapter 17, "Add-In Chips," for procedures on replacing the power supply.

22

The Computer Starts, But Doesn't Boot

If your PC tries to start when you turn it on (you hear the usual hums and whirs from your PC), but the PC doesn't boot, take heart—your problem likely is a fairly simple one. The system might even be giving you a hint in the form of an error message, telling you what is wrong.

Many problems of this type are caused by software configuration errors or other simple causes, such as a non-bootable disk in drive A or a loose cable. Often, you can get the system running properly again just by reconnecting the loose cable, making a simple change to a configuration file, or resetting the system configuration settings.

This chapter covers the types of problems that can prevent your PC from booting successfully. Following is a brief list of the topics in this chapter:

- An overview of the boot process and potential problems
- Problems with the monitor and display cables
- The system keeps rebooting by itself
- Common boot errors
- CMOS configuration error messages

NOTE

This chapter covers only a few of the more common disk-related problems that prevent the system from booting. Many other problems are covered in Chapter 23, "The System Runs, But Not Without Complaining." If you don't find a procedure or problem description in this chapter that fits your situation, refer to Chapter 23 for help.

Before you read through a bunch of material on the boot process, you should try a couple of things first if your system seems to be running but the display is black. If you get an error message when the system tries to boot, skip to the section "Understanding the Boot Process" later in this chapter. If the display is black, read the next section.

Problem:
The Screen Is Black

You may feel really stupid after running through these procedures, but you might be able to get your PC running again with just a jiggle on a cable. If your PC is making the usual noises and sounds that seem to indicate it's trying to run, but you don't see anything at all on the display, do these things:

Procedure:
Checking the Monitor

1. Make sure that the monitor is plugged into the back of the monitor and to the wall outlet or to the back of the PC.

2. Make sure that the monitor switch is turned on.

3. Make sure that the contrast and brightness knobs are not adjusted all the way down.

I have spent a few minutes cussing at the display, only to find that someone (surely not me) had fiddled with the brightness adjustment and turned it all the way down. So if that's your problem, don't feel bad—you're in good company.

If the problem was that you hadn't turned on the monitor, here's a suggestion: Buy one of the monitor power cords that plugs into the back of the PC instead of an AC outlet.

Then, leave the monitor turned on all the time. Because it's plugged into the PC, the monitor will switch on when you turn on the PC, and switch off when you turn off the PC. Figure 22.1 shows a monitor power cable that plugs into the back of the PC.

Figure 22.1: A monitor power cord that plugs into the back of the PC.

Procedure:
Checking
the Video Cables

Explanation: If you have checked the monitor and still don't have anything on the display, check the video cables:

1. Verify that the video cable is securely attached to the back of the monitor.

2. Verify that the video cable is securely attached to the video adapter at the rear of the PC.

3. If you have a special-purpose video adapter in your PC in addition to a VGA or Super VGA card, there may be a pass-through cable that connects the two. Follow the video cable from the monitor to the PC. Is there another cable coming out of that same adapter and connecting to another adapter (or not connecting at all)? Check the connection or hook it back up, whichever is appropriate.

Hopefully, that cleared up your problem.

If you're getting error messages, the problem is not your monitor. In order to troubleshoot a problem that's happening when the system attempts to boot, you need to understand the process that occurs when the system boots.

Understanding the Boot Process

When you first turn on the PC, a few diagnostic routines contained in the PC's ROMs are executed. These diagnostics are collectively called the *POST*, which stands for Power-On Self Test. You're probably familiar with at least part of the POST—the memory status message that appears when the system is booting is part of the POST.

After the POST has checked the system, one of three things happens. If a major error occurs during the POST, the system halts and displays an error message. You then have to correct the problem and reboot the system. If a minor error occurs during the POST, the system displays an error message but continues to boot. A keyboard error is a good example of this type of error. The PC can boot without a keyboard, but it tells you there's a problem in case you're expecting to use the keyboard. The third possibility is that everything checks out just fine during the POST, and the system continues a normal boot process.

After the POST executes, the BIOS is loaded. The BIOS determines whether there is a floppy drive and a hard drive in the system (if you watch your drive lights when the system boots, you will see the floppy lights come on briefly, and then the hard disk light).

If a floppy disk is in drive A and the drive door is closed, the BIOS attempts to read the first sector on the floppy disk, which is side 0, cylinder 0, sector 1. This is where the BIOS expects to find the floppy disk's boot record. The *boot record* tells the BIOS where to jump on the disk to locate the bootstrap program. The *bootstrap program* is a small program that loads the rest of the operating system.

If the disk in drive A isn't bootable (it's a regular data floppy, for example), you receive the error message Non-system disk or disk error. *You must replace the floppy disk with one that's bootable or open the drive door so that the system can boot from the hard drive.*

If the disk is one that you have gotten from someone else, there is a chance that your PC has just been infected by a virus. Check the section later in this chapter that describes what to do when the Non-system disk or disk error *message appears.*

If there isn't a disk in drive A and there's a hard drive in the system, the BIOS reads the first sector of the hard disk, which is side 0, cylinder 0, sector 1. This sector is called the *master boot sector*. It contains the master boot record and the partition table, which together tell the BIOS where to locate the boot record and bootstrap program.

The main point to understand is that if there's a disk in drive A, the system tries to boot from it. If there is no disk in drive A, the PC tries to boot from the hard drive.

When the bootstrap program executes, it looks for the hidden system files IO.SYS and MSDOS.SYS on the same drive from which the boot record was read. IO.SYS extends and updates functions in the BIOS, and MSDOS.SYS forms the low-level portion of DOS (called the DOS *kernel*). After these hidden system files are located and loaded, the DOS kernel takes over and executes CONFIG.SYS and AUTOEXEC.BAT. After CONFIG.SYS and AUTOEXEC.BAT have been processed, the DOS kernel executes COMMAND.COM. COMMAND.COM is the command processor for DOS, and is what generates the DOS prompt (such as the C:> prompt).

What Can Go Wrong, Murphy?

There are simple things that can be causing your problem. A common problem is that you have left a non-bootable disk in drive A. The BIOS does not attempt to bypass the floppy and check the hard drive for an operating system if a disk is in drive A.

The PC's inability to boot also might be caused by a problem with the hard drive, dead batteries (I'll explain that one later), or configuration errors. Whatever the cause, the PC probably will generate an error message to let you know what's wrong. Most of the rest of this chapter is separated into sections according to the error message that appears when the system tries to boot.

I Hope You Have Those Backups

Before going on to the troubleshooting sections, I have to reemphasize the importance of backups. Some of the problems described in this chapter can be corrected only by reformatting the hard disk when all other options have failed. If you have a recent backup of your system, that's no big deal. It's a little inconvenient and time-consuming, but not a major problem. If you don't have a current backup or don't have a backup at all, you may be up the proverbial tributary with no feasible means of locomotion. You're going to lose some data, and you're not going to like it one bit.

Always back up your data! If you don't have a tape drive, back up your data documents onto floppy disk. MS-DOS 6 users can use Microsoft Backup or a third-party utility—like Norton Backup, Central Point Backup, and so on—to do this. If you're not using MS-DOS 6, you will need a third-party utility.

At the very least, always save an extra copy of your document files onto floppy whenever you finish editing them. You can reinstall your applications if necessary, but it's unlikely you will be able to re-create all your document files without a tremendous amount of work. I doubt you will even be able to do it.

Back up, back up, back up. Then, back up some more.

Error: General failure error reading drive C:

This error usually is caused by the inability of the BIOS to read the information in the master boot sector on the hard drive. There are a handful of potential causes. A virus might have infected the system and corrupted the data in your master boot sector so badly that the system can't read it. Other causes include damage to the master boot sector from general wear and tear, and dropping the disk while it was running (a severe bump to a desktop or tower system, or actually dropping a notebook or other portable PC) and accidentally performing a low-level format of the disk.

If the problem is a toasted master boot record caused by wear and tear or a virus, you may be able to use the FDISK.EXE program that comes with DOS to repair the damage. The following procedure applies to users of MS-DOS 5 and MS-DOS 6.

WARNING *The FDISK command can wipe out everything on your hard disk. I mean it; I'm not kidding. You could lose everything in less than a second if you start fiddling with FDISK and don't know what you're doing. If you're at work, will the higher-up muckety-mucks like it if you blow away your hard disk? Will you be in the unemployment office tomorrow?*

The following procedure uses a special switch with the FDISK command that is perfectly harmless, even on a good disk. As long as you include the /MBR switch on the FDISK command line, you're safe.

Procedure:

Re-Creating the Master Boot Record

1. Dig out your emergency boot disk, insert it into drive A, and reboot the PC.

2. After DOS boots, locate the program FDISK.EXE on the emergency disk.

3. At the DOS prompt, type **FDISK /MBR** and press Enter. If you mistakenly entered just **FDISK** and are now looking at the FDISK program menu, press Esc immediately to get out of FDISK. If you have entered the FDISK /MBR command correctly, you don't see anything happen. FDISK re-creates the master boot record and returns you to the DOS prompt.

4. Remove the floppy disk from drive A and reboot the system.

If the system boots successfully after you complete the previous procedure, you should run a virus check on the system and on any floppy disks you have used recently. This might help you determine whether the hard disk's master boot record was toasted by a virus, or it might tell you absolutely nothing if the hard disk's master boot record was the only thing infected by the virus.

If you're using MS-DOS 6, use the MSAV.EXE or MWAV.EXE programs that come with it to scan the disk (the former is DOS-based and the latter is Windows-based). If you're using a version of DOS other than MS-DOS 6, you need to use a third-party utility, such as Norton Anti-Virus, McAffee's Virus Scan (a shareware program), or Central Point Tools.

Regardless of whether you find signs of a virus, you should perform a backup of your hard disk. At the very least, back up all your document files. The best course of action to take is to back up the entire drive, including your applications. If your problem was caused by a defective or soon-to-be defective drive, it's absolutely essential that you make and keep current backups.

Error: Bad or missing command interpreter

This error is caused by the DOS kernel being unable to locate or read COMMAND.COM. Occasionally it's due to a COMMAND.COM file that has become corrupted. Usually, though, the problem is that DOS just can't find COMMAND.COM. Following is a list of potential causes of this error message, along with solutions to the problem:

● You booted from a floppy disk and now have a different floppy disk in drive A. Place the correct floppy disk in drive A, and then reboot the system.

● Someone (possibly you) has inadvertently copied an older version of COMMAND.COM into the root directory, replacing the correct version with the older version. Boot from your emergency boot disk and copy COMMAND.COM from the floppy to the hard drive.

If you forgot to create an emergency boot disk when you last upgraded your version of DOS, boot using the emergency disk that you do have. Locate COMMAND.COM on your DOS distribution disks (the original disks for your new version of DOS) and copy it to the root directory of the hard drive. Then, remove all disks from the floppy drives and reboot the PC.

● You were logged onto the network and were using a network copy of COMMAND.COM, and have now logged off of the network. DOS no longer can find COMMAND.COM, because it's located on the network. Reboot the system and make sure that you're logged onto the network. Consult your network administrator if you continue to have the problem.

● COMMAND.COM may be corrupted or occupying a sector that has gone belly-up. Reboot from your emergency boot disk, and then copy COMMAND.COM from the boot disk to the root directory of the hard disk.

● You erased COMMAND.COM. Reboot from your emergency boot disk, and then copy COMMAND.COM from the boot disk into the root directory of the hard disk.

● You are booting from a floppy disk that was formatted with the FORMAT /S command, but the floppy doesn't contain a copy of COMMAND.COM. Place a copy of COMMAND.COM on the disk.

TIP

The copy of COMMAND.COM that you place in the root directory of the hard disk must be from the same version of MS-DOS as installed on your hard disk (as in the DOS directory). Also, your CONFIG.SYS file may contain a SHELL= statement that specifies the location of COMMAND.COM. As long as there is a valid copy of COMMAND.COM in the root directory, your system will boot.

If you have a SHELL= statement that specifies a location for COMMAND.COM other than the root directory, copy COMMAND.COM from your emergency boot disk to the directory specified by the SHELL= statement. You then can erase the copy from the root directory (just don't change the SHELL= setting).

Error: Invalid COMMAND.COM

This error generally means that DOS is trying to read a version of COMMAND.COM other than what it expects. Maybe you have accidentally copied an older version of COMMAND.COM to replace your working copy. Whatever the cause, restoring COMMAND.COM should be simple:

1. Boot from your emergency floppy disk.

2. Copy COMMAND.COM from the boot floppy to the appropriate directory of the hard disk (the root directory will work).

3. Remove the boot floppy disk from drive A, and then reboot the system.

Error: Cannot load COMMAND, system halted

This error sometimes occurs when you've just exited from a program. The resident portion of COMMAND.COM (which is always in memory) can't locate the non-resident portion of COMMAND.COM on the disk. You may be able to fix the problem simply by rebooting the system. Try that first, and if it doesn't work, use the procedure in the section for the error Invalid COMMAND.COM.

Error: Non-system disk or disk error

By far, the most common cause of this problem is that you have a non-bootable disk in drive A. The other possible cause is a missing IO.SYS or MSDOS.SYS file. If you have a floppy disk in drive A and it's one of your own, you probably have nothing to worry about. All you need to do is remove the disk (or just open the door if it's a 5 1/4-inch disk) and then press any key to let the system boot from the hard drive.

If the disk in drive A was put there by someone else or it's a disk you received from someone else, your PC may just have been infected by a virus. Booting from a virus-infected disk generally infects your hard disk; it doesn't matter whether your PC actually booted DOS or not. If the floppy was infected and the PC tried to boot from it, your PC is infected. Use the following procedure immediately.

Procedure:
Checking for Virus Infection

Explanation: If you have tried to boot the PC with a suspect floppy disk in drive A, use this procedure to make sure that your PC hasn't been infected by a virus:

1. Locate your emergency boot disk, but don't put it into drive A yet.

2. Verify that the emergency disk is write-protected. If it's a 5 1/4-inch disk, it should have a write-protect tab (a piece of opaque tape) covering the notch on

the right edge of the floppy disk. 5 1/4-inch disks usually come with a set of labels and write-protect tabs (look in the box the disks came in).

If it's a 3 1/2-inch disk, the moveable tab in the left corner of the disk (looking at the disk as if you're going to insert it in the drive) should be pushed down to cover the hole. If there's no tab to push, someone has removed it. Place a piece of opaque tape or a write-protect tab from a 5 1/4-inch disk over the slot (a piece of a disk label works well).

3. Remove the floppy from drive A and set it aside where you can keep track of it.

4. Insert the write-protected emergency boot floppy in drive A and reboot the system.

5. Run MSAV.EXE, MWAV.EXE, or your favorite third-party anti-virus utility to test the PC for viruses. Eradicate the virus(es). If your PC has become infected by a boot-sector virus (very common among viruses), run FDISK /MBR to re-create the master boot record, which will get rid of the virus.

6. Remove the floppy disk from drive A and reboot the system.

Procedure:
Restoring the System Files (IO.SYS or MSDOS.SYS Missing)

Explanation: If you get the Non-system disk or disk error message when there is no floppy in drive A, something might have happened to the system files on your hard disk. Use the following procedure to restore the system files to your hard disk:

1. Boot from your emergency boot disk.

2. At the DOS prompt, type **SYS C:** and then press Enter. The SYS command transfers the system files IO.SYS, MS-DOS.SYS, and COMMAND.COM to your hard drive.

3. Remove the floppy from drive A, and then reboot the PC.

You also might want to run a virus check after the system boots. The question you should ask yourself is, "What happened to those files, anyway?" A virus could have ruined them or you may have erased them accidentally. It's unlikely you erased them, because they are hidden system files and can't be erased unless you purposely change the file attributes of the files before you erase them.

Error: File allocation table bad

If you receive this error message, it means that something has happened to the data table on the disk that DOS uses to keep track of where files are located. Refer to Chapter 23 for help fixing the problem.

Error: Configuration too large for memory

This error locks up your system, and it's caused by screwy settings on the EMM386.EXE command line in CONFIG.SYS. If you're using MS-DOS 6, you can reboot the system, bypass CONFIG.SYS, make the necessary changes to CONFIG.SYS, and then reboot the file. If you're using a version of MS-DOS other than version 6, you must boot from an emergency floppy disk to fix the problem.

Procedure:
MS-DOS 6 Users Only

1. Press Ctrl-Alt-Del to initiate a reboot, and watch for the Starting MS-DOS message.

2. While the message is displayed, press F5 to bypass CONFIG.SYS and AUTOEXEC.BAT (perform a clean boot).

3. At the DOS prompt, enter **DOS\EDIT\CONFIG.SYS**, substituting the appropriate directory if DOS is not located in the directory \DOS.

4. Verify the settings for EMM386.EXE (it's probably a strange combination of the X and I switches). If you need help with the settings, refer to Chapter 4, "All You Need To Know about Memory." If you can't figure out the settings, comment the line and add a

new line below it that loads EMM386.EXE without any switches at all.

5. Save the changes you have made to CONFIG.SYS.

6. Reboot the system.

Procedure:
Users with MS-DOS Versions Other than 6

1. Boot from your emergency boot disk.

2. Make drive C active by entering **C:** at the DOS prompt.

3. At the DOS prompt, enter **DOS\EDIT\CONFIG.SYS**, substituting the appropriate directory if DOS is not located in the directory \DOS.

4. Verify the settings for EMM386.EXE (it's probably a strange combination of the X and I switches). If you need help with the settings, refer to Chapter 4. If you can't figure out the settings, comment the line and add a new line below it that loads EMM386.EXE without any switches at all.

5. Save the changes you have made to CONFIG.SYS.

6. Reboot the system.

For users of any version of MS-DOS: If you change the switches and still get the same error message when the system tries to boot, remove all switches from the EMM386.EXE command line and then reboot the system. If you have a network card or other adapter requiring that a range of memory be excluded from use in the UMA, add X switches to the EMM386 command line only for those devices. MS-DOS 6 users then can run MemMaker to reoptimize memory for Windows.

Understanding CMOS

CMOS is an acronym for Complementary Metal Oxide Semiconductor. It refers to the type of semiconductor chip that stores configuration information in a typical PC. The term *CMOS* has nothing to do with the function of the chip in the PC. It refers only to the way the chip is designed and manufactured.

What does the chip do in the PC? It stores information about your system's configuration, including the types of floppy and hard drives that are installed, the amount of memory in the system, the current date and time, and other system-level information. That information enables the system to keep track of the hardware configuration even when the PC has been turned off. But how does it keep that information even when it's turned off?

A CMOS chip can retain its data with a very small amount of electrical charge. That's why that particular type of chip is used to store the PC's configuration data. When you turn off the PC, batteries in the PC feed a little bit of electricity to the CMOS chip to enable it to retain its configuration information. The PC's batteries may be four AA batteries that you can replace, a rechargeable battery that you can unplug and replace, or a rechargeable battery that's built onto the motherboard.

What Can Go Wrong Again, Murphy?

As long as the CMOS chip gets its necessary dose of electricity, it will retain its information correctly until you change it. If the batteries in the PC go bad, your system's configuration information can be lost. Also, you might make a change to the CMOS settings by running your PC's system setup program (not to be confused with DOS or Windows Setup programs). Problems also can arise if you install or reconfigure some equipment in the PC and don't make a necessary change to the CMOS configuration to account for the change.

Running Your System's Setup Program

PCs include a system configuration setup program to enable you to change settings in the CMOS chip. You need to run this program whenever you replace the batteries in the PC or change the hardware configuration in a way that requires a change in the CMOS chip.

PCs don't have a common method for starting the system configuration setup program. On some, you press the Del key while the system is booting. Others require that you press Ctrl-Alt-Esc. Still others require that you perform an arcane start-up ritual, while yet others require that you run the program from disk.

To find out how to run your PC's system configuration setup program, consult your system manual. It will tell you how to start and use it. (Setup programs are designed to be easy to use, at least for setting basic system configuration options, so you shouldn't need any help using it—just follow the instructions and prompts provided by the program.)

Error: CMOS display type mismatch

This error occurs when the type of video adapter in your system doesn't match the type stored in the PC's system configuration information. Have you changed video adapters?

Procedure:
Resetting Display Type

1. Reboot the system and do whatever your PC requires to start its setup program.

2. Using the system setup program, specify the correct type of display for your PC.

3. Save the CMOS settings and reboot the PC.

Error: CMOS memory size mismatch

This error is generated when the configuration information that's stored in the CMOS for the amount of memory in the system doesn't match the amount of memory that's actually *in* the PC. Did you add some memory to the system or take some out to change the total amount of RAM in the system? If so, you need to reset the amount of memory in the CMOS settings.

Procedure:
Resetting Memory Capacity

1. Reboot the system and start the PC's system configuration setup program.

2. Respecify the correct amount of RAM in the CMOS settings.

3. Resave the new CMOS settings and reboot the system.

Error: CMOS battery state low

This error is just what you think it is—the backup batteries in your system are about shot. You need to replace the batteries.

Procedure:

Replacing the Backup Batteries

1. Unplug the system and open it.

2. Discharge yourself, and then look for a battery pack that's connected to the motherboard by a couple of wires.

3. If you find the battery pack, note the location of the red wire on the connector so that you can plug it back in the same way later. Write it down if you're liable to forget it.

   If you can't find anything that looks remotely like a battery pack, your PC's backup battery may be built onto the motherboard. All the ones I've seen are soldered onto the motherboard, so you cannot replace it (at least not very easily). Call the place where you purchased the PC and describe your problem to them. Their technical support people can tell you how to proceed.

4. If the battery pack already is disconnected, the batteries are probably good, but something (like moving the system) has caused the plug to come loose. Reconnect it and go on to step 7. If the pack *is* connected, disconnect it and go on to step 5.

5. Remove the battery pack. If it contains replaceable batteries, replace them with the same type. If the battery pack is sealed, it's a rechargeable battery that has gone bad. You must get one of the same type. If you can't find one locally, leave the battery out

and put the system back together. Run the CMOS setup program to reset your system's options, and then leave the system turned on until your new battery pack arrives. Otherwise, you must run the setup program each time you turn on the PC.

6. When you have the new battery pack or fresh batteries, replace the pack in the computer and reconnect the plug. If you have lost your note or can't remember how to connect it, check your system's manual. It should have a section that describes the motherboard connectors.

7. After replacing the batteries, run the system's configuration setup program and restore all the settings. You may have to dig out the papers that came with your hard disk to determine which settings to use for it. If you can't find the right settings, call the place where you purchased the hard drive (or the PC—they came as a unit) and ask for help.

8. After restoring the CMOS settings, save the settings and reboot the system.

Error: CMOS checksum failure

This error is caused by corrupted data in the CMOS chip. It may be something as simple as a bad battery or loose battery connection. Use the procedure "Replacing the Backup Batteries," described previously. If the problem persists after you have replaced the batteries, call the place where you purchased the PC. The CMOS chip may be bad, and you may have to replace the motherboard. But check with their technical support department before you do something that drastic.

Error: CMOS system options not set

You've lost your CMOS settings or they have been corrupted. Run the system's configuration setup program and reset them. If the problem persists, try changing batteries as described in the "Replacing the Backup Batteries" procedure earlier.

Error: CMOS time & date not set

For some reason, your system has lost its time and date settings. Run the system's configuration setup program and set the correct date and time. If the problem persists, try changing batteries as described in the "Replacing the Backup Batteries" procedure earlier in this chapter.

Problem: System Reboots by Itself

This one is most irritating. You're trying to start a program or start Windows and suddenly the system reboots on its own. You didn't even come near the Ctrl-Alt-Del keys or the reset button. Many times this is caused by a memory conflict or a bad setting in the system's extended CMOS settings.

One example of this problem is the time someone had switched my system from 25MHz to 8MHz speed by pressing the turbo switch. The extended memory settings in the CMOS weren't compatible with the 8MHz bus speed because of timing problems. Putting the PC back in turbo mode solved the problem.

Procedure:
Overcoming Auto-Reboot

1. Turn the system off, let it sit for a minute or so, and then turn it back on. Try to start the program that caused the reboot. If the problem goes away, chalk it up to gremlins and be happy.

2. If the problem persists, make sure that you (or someone else) hasn't accidentally switched the system's bus speed by pressing the turbo switch. If the speed has been changed, change it back to its original speed and reboot the PC.

3. If changing bus speed didn't work, you may have a memory conflict. Refer to Chapters 4 and 24, "Healing Your Hard Disk," for memory troubleshooting procedures.

4. If you're still having no luck, call the place where you purchased the PC and let the technical support department figure out what went wrong.

23

The System Runs, But Not Without Complaining

Previous chapters have covered problems that prevent the PC from starting or booting. This chapter covers problems that don't prevent the PC from booting, but that generate error messages. Most of the problems in this chapter are minor and are caused by a loose keyboard cable, software configuration error, PATH problem, or something equally easy to fix. Instead of giving you a list of the topics in this chapter, I'll give you a list of the error messages covered:

- Access denied

- Write protect error writing drive *x* Abort, retry, fail?

- Display adapter failed; using alternate *or* Display switch not set properly

- Divide overflow

- Not ready reading drive *x* Abort, retry, ignore, fail?

- Insufficient memory *or* Not enough memory

- Incorrect DOS version

- Bad command or file name

- Out of environment space

- Specified memory ranges overlap

- Keyboard failure

There are plenty of error messages that can appear on your system. The errors covered in this chapter are some of the more common ones, but are by no means the only ones that might pop up when you least expect it. Due to differences in BIOS manufacturers, some of the errors covered in this chapter may be worded differently. You should be able to identify the error, though.

Error: Access denied

This error pops up when you try to access a file that is read-only. This means that the file's read-only attribute has been turned on. A read-only file behaves just as its name implies: it can be read, but you can't erase it or change it (write to it).

The file very likely is read-only for a reason. I'm about to tell you how to turn off the read-only attribute, but I want you to be aware that you might be about to erase or write to a file that you shouldn't be messing with. Make sure that you know exactly what the file is for and why it is read-only before performing the following procedure.

WARNING

If the file in question is located on a network drive, don't change its attributes! (You probably won't be able to do it anyway, but don't try.) Your network administrator has made the file read-only so that people like you can't mess with it. If you really think you need to do something to the file, have a chat with your network administrator.

Procedure:

Changing a Read-Only Attribute, DOS Method

1. At the DOS prompt, change to the directory in which the read-only file is located (use the CD command).

2. At the DOS prompt, enter **ATTRIB -R** *filename*, where *filename* is the name of the file from which you want to remove the read-only attribute.

Procedure:

Changing a Read-Only Attribute, Windows Method

1. In Windows, open File Manager and display the drive and directory containing the read-only file.

2. Select the read-only file.

3. From the **F**ile menu, choose **P**roperties (or just press Alt-Enter). The Properties dialog box shown in figure 23.1 appears.

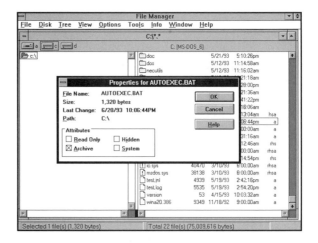

Figure 23.1: The Properties dialog box enables you to change a file's attributes.

4. Clear the **R**ead Only check box, and then click on OK.

5. Exit File Manager.

Error: Write protect error writing drive *x* Abort, retry, fail?

This error pops up when you try to write to a disk that is write-protected. This includes when you try to erase a file from a write-protected disk. The question you should ask is,

"Did I write-protect that disk for a reason?" Are you really sure that you want to modify the files on the disk?

If so, you need to remove the write-protection from the disk. On a 5 1/4-inch disk, an adhesive tab covers the notch in the side of the disk. Removing the tab enables you to write to the disk. If it's a 3 1/2-inch disk, a moveable plastic tab is in the bottom left corner of the disk (looking at the disk as if you were inserting it into the PC). Sliding the tab to cover the hole removes write-protection from the disk.

If there is no tab on the 5 1/4-inch disk or the tab on the 3 1/2-inch disk already covers the write-protect hole, there may be a problem with your floppy drive. Call the place where you purchased the PC and discuss the problem with their technical support people. If the drive turns out to be bad, don't bother trying to fix it. Replace it instead.

Error: Display adapter failed; using alternate or Display switch not set properly

These errors generally are caused by having the color/mono selection jumper set incorrectly on the motherboard. These errors occur only after you have installed a video adapter and changed (or not changed) the jumper to match your video configuration. Locate your system manual and find the section that describes the mother board jumper and switch settings. Locate the one that specifies the color/mono option and set it correctly. (Use the usual care by unplugging the system, discharging your static, and so on).

Error: Divide overflow

This error is a software error and typically is caused by a bug in the program you're running or a weird incompatibility between the program and DOS. Try rebooting the PC.

If the problem disappears, don't worry about it. The moon must be full or something

If the problem persists, call the developer of the program that's causing the error to appear. You probably have found a bug in the program.

Error: Not ready reading drive *x* Abort, retry, ignore, fail?

This error usually is caused by an open floppy drive door (5 1/4-inch disk) or no disk being inserted in the drive (3 1/2-inch disk). Make sure that the disk is properly inserted in the drive and the drive door is latched. Then, press R to retry reading the disk.

If you have simply entered the wrong disk ID (such as specifying drive B when you really wanted to read drive A), press A to abort. If the system keeps trying to read the disk, giving you the Abort, Retry, Ignore, Fail? message again, press F, then specify drive C as the current drive.

If you get this error message even after properly inserting the floppy disk, you may have a problem with the drive or the drive cables. Check the cables to make sure that they're properly seated. If you still can't get it to work, call the place where you purchased the PC. You may have to replace the drive.

Error: Insufficient memory or Not enough memory

This is not really an error message in the sense that it doesn't indicate a problem with your PC. It just means that you have run out of enough available memory to run your program. If you have other programs running (including memory-resident programs that are loaded by CONFIG.SYS or AUTOEXEC.BAT), terminate those programs and try again. Occasionally, you will have to reboot the PC. The best solution to this problem is to add more memory to the PC.

Error: Incorrect DOS version

This error means that you have tried to run a program that isn't compatible with the version of DOS you're using. Often, this happens if you try to run a DOS program that was included with your previous version of DOS.

MS-DOS 6 users: Are you lamenting the loss of a few of the files that formerly were included with MS-DOS 5 and now are no longer included with MS-DOS 6? If so, you may be trying to use a copy of the program that was included with MS-DOS 5.

Although there is a workaround to get it to function properly, you should log onto the Microsoft BBS at 206-936-6735 and locate the MS-DOS supplementary files, which are located on the BBS. These are copies of your "missing" DOS programs that have been marked to work with MS-DOS 6.

Procedure:
Checking the Default Version Table

Explanation: If you're working with a third-party DOS program that is generating the Incorrect DOS version error message, you can use the SETVER.EXE command included with DOS to "fool" the program into thinking it's running under the earlier, compatible version of DOS. The first thing you should do is check the default version table to see if your program is listed in it.

1. At the DOS prompt, enter **SETVER ¦ MORE**.

2. Examine the version table to determine whether your program is listed in it.

If your program is listed in the default version table, all you need to do is install the SETVER device driver. If your program isn't listed, you also need to add an entry in the version table for the program.

Procedure:
Installing the SETVER Device Driver

Explanation: To use SETVER, either with an entry in the default version table or with an entry you add yourself, you first need to install the device driver with an entry in CONFIG.SYS.

1. Use your favorite method for editing CONFIG.SYS, and add the following line to file (specify the correct location for your DOS files):

    `DEVICE=C:\DOS\SETVER.EXE`

2. Save the changes to CONFIG.SYS and reboot the system.

Procedure:
Adding an Entry to the Version Table

1. If Windows is running, exit Windows.

2. At the DOS prompt, enter **SETVER** *program.exe x.xx*, where *program.exe* is the name of your program and *x.xx* is the version of DOS with which the program is compatible. Here's an example:

    `SETVER FIDDLE.EXE 5.0`

3. Start your program to make sure that it works properly.

Procedure:
Deleting an Entry from the Version Table

Explanation: Use this procedure to remove an entry from the version table.

1. If Windows is running, exit Windows.

2. At the DOS prompt, enter **SETVER** *program.exe* / **DELETE**, where *program.exe* is the name of the program you want to remove from the version list.

Error: Bad command or file name

This is an easy one. This error is generated by COMMAND.COM when you have entered the name of a program at the DOS prompt and COMMAND.COM can't find it. There are a few possibilities:

- The file doesn't exist. If the program you're trying to start doesn't exist on the disk, no amount of fiddling will make it run.

- You may be typing the name of a file that doesn't have a COM, EXE, or BAT file extension. The file must be one of these three types of files in order for COMMAND.COM to be able to run it.

- The file is not in the current directory or on the PATH. COMMAND.COM first looks in the current directory for the file, then looks in each of the directories on the PATH for the file. When it finds a file with a matching name, it tries to run it. Either use the CD command to change to the directory containing the file or add the program's directory to the PATH.

Error: Out of environment space

This error is generated when all the environment space in which DOS stores environment variables is being used. This can happen if you set a large number of environment variables or use a long PATH. There are two solutions: decrease the number of variables or shorten the PATH, or increase the amount of memory allocated for environment space. The latter method usually is the most useful, so that's the one I'll explain how to accomplish.

Procedure:
Increasing DOS Environment Size

1. If Windows is running, exit Windows.

2. Use your favorite method to edit CONFIG.SYS.

3. Hunt through CONFIG.SYS for a SHELL= statement. If you have a SHELL= statement, you need to edit the setting. If there is no SHELL= statement, you need to create one.

4. If you don't have a SHELL= statement, add one similar to the following, substituting the correct location for your COMMAND.COM file:

   ```
   SHELL=C:\DOS\COMMAND.COM /E:512 /P
   ```

   The /E:512 sets the environment size to 512 bytes (the default is 256 bytes). If you need a larger environment, specify a larger number. You shouldn't need anything over about 1,024 bytes. Make sure that you include the /P switch, or COMMAND.COM will not remain in memory.

5. If you had an existing SHELL= statement, edit the /E:*nnnn* parameter. If there is no /E:*nnnn* parameter, add one of the appropriate size.

6. Save the changes you have made to CONFIG.SYS, and then reboot the system.

Error: Specified memory ranges overlap

This error is generated when you specify memory ranges to include or exclude on the EMM386.EXE command line in CONFIG.SYS, and the switches specify ranges of memory that overlap one another. If the memory ranges overlap, you should be able to specify a single switch that covers the full range of memory specified by the existing switches. Edit CONFIG.SYS and change the entries on the EMM386.EXE command line accordingly.

Error: Keyboard failure

If you receive a keyboard error, it may mean that your keyboard is not securely plugged into the system.

1. Check the connection at the back of the system where the keyboard plugs into the motherboard, and then reboot the system to see whether the problem goes away.

2. If the problem persists and you're using a keyboard extension cable, disconnect the keyboard extension cable and connect the keyboard directly to the PC. Reboot to see whether the problem goes away.

3. If the problem persists, you may have a bad keyboard. If you can find a spare keyboard, try it.

 **NOTE**   *Most keyboards have DIP switches on the bottom that enable you to configure the keyboard for use on an XT or AT (see figure 23.2). If you're installing a new keyboard and get a keyboard message, check to make sure that these switches are set properly.*

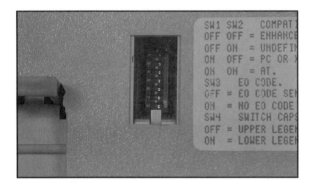

Figure 23.2: Keyboard configuration DIP switches on the bottom of the keyboard.

24

Healing Your Hard Disk

This is the chapter to turn to when your hard disk suddenly doesn't seem to work. Maybe you have tried to boot your system and it won't come up. If you haven't yet checked Chapter 22, "The Computer Starts, But Doesn't Boot," do so. It offers solutions to boot problems that may correct your problem. If you have been through Chapter 22 already and still can't get your hard disk to work, you have come to the right chapter.

This chapter explains hard disks in a little more detail than previous chapters. It covers these topics:

- General technical information about hard drives
- Recovering from specific errors
- Using CHKDSK to fix file problems
- Sending your drive to get fixed (or have data recovered)

First, you need to know about hard disk utility software.

Disk Utility Programs

Many different utility programs are available that enable you to fine-tune the performance of your hard disk and recover the disk when it suffers a catastrophe of one sort or another. Although you can perform some hard disk troubleshooting and repair without these utilities, having them makes it possible to recover the drive when you otherwise wouldn't be able to so with just DOS tools.

I've used three different hard disk recovery utilities over the years: Norton Utilities (Symantec), PC Tools (Central Point Software), and SpinRite (Gibson Research). All of them worked well. There are other utilities that I've never had the opportunity to use, but which also do a good job. If you're having a problem with your hard drive, I recommend that you purchase a copy of one of these hard disk utilities. If you don't have one, go out and get a copy before you run through the rest of this chapter. If you're interested in the disk utilities included with DOS, read the sections on CHKDSK and FDISK later in this chapter.

Now, let's dig into that hard drive stuff.

A Little Technical Stuff

Unfortunately, you need to understand some technical things about your system's hard disk in order to troubleshoot and fix problems with it. I promise to keep the technical jargon and the interesting but seldom-useful information to a bare minimum.

Cylinders, Tracks, and Sectors

Instead of containing a single disk like a floppy drive, a hard disk consists of multiple platters (disks) all spinning together on a common spindle. Each of the platters is magnetically formatted into circular rings called *tracks*. Tracks are further divided into segments called *sectors*. A sector is the smallest unit of storage space on a disk. The corresponding tracks on the disk's platters form a *cylinder*. Figure 24.1 illustrates cylinders, tracks, and sectors. Essentially, all the tracks and sectors do is break the data space on the disk into manageable, logical chunks.

Clusters

DOS allocates disk space in clusters. A *cluster* is a group of sectors on the disk. The number of sectors in a cluster varies according to drive type. Table 24.1 shows cluster and sector relationships for common PC drive types. When DOS needs to store a file on disk, it doesn't do it on a sector-by-sector basis. Instead, DOS allocates enough clusters to contain the file.

Table 24.1
Cluster and Sector Relationships

Type of Disk	Cluster Size (in bytes)	Sectors per Cluster
3 1/2-inch floppy	1,024	2
1.2M floppy	512	1
0 to 15M partition*	4,096	8
16 to 128M partition*	2,048	4
128 to 256M partition*	4,096	8
256 to 512M partition*	8,192	16
512M to 1G partition*	16,384	32

*Also applies to similarly sized disks consisting of a single partition.

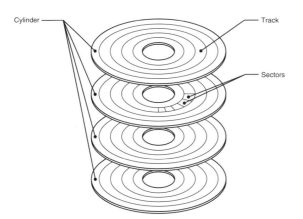

Figure 24.1: Cylinders, tracks, and sectors on a disk.

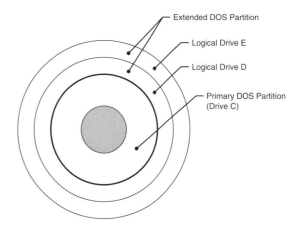

Figure 24.2: A primary DOS partition and extended DOS partition on a disk, with logical drives.

Partitions

A hard disk is partitioned into different data areas. A *partition* is a group of clusters on the disk that have been allocated on the disk as being a unique storage area. Partitions are just a way to group clusters into logical collective units so that the clusters can be collectively recognized as a logical drive represented by a drive letter, such as C.

A hard disk can have up to four partitions, but DOS hard disks generally have only one or two. All DOS hard disks must have a primary DOS partition. Logical drive C is located in the primary DOS partition. A DOS hard drive also can have an extended DOS partition. The extended DOS partition can contain a single logical drive, just like the primary DOS partition, or it can contain multiple logical drives. You can, for example, create an extended DOS partition that will contain drives D, E, and F (or more). Figure 24.2 illustrates partitions on a disk.

The Partition Table

In the first sector of the hard drive (cylinder 0, track 0, sector 1) is the master boot record. The master boot record contains, among other things, the disk's partition table. The partition table stores information about which clusters make up the different partitions on the disk, which operating system controls each partition, and which partition is active. The active partition is the one the system will try to boot from when you turn on the PC.

Here's a brief overview of what happens when a DOS system boots.

After the BIOS performs hardware tests on the system, it looks on the hard disk for the master boot record (MBR). It reads the MBR to determine which partition is active. Because this is a DOS system, the primary DOS partition is active. The BIOS then uses information contained in the MBR to locate and read the DOS boot record, which contains basic information about the hard drive, such as size, cluster size, number of sectors, and other information. Then, the BIOS turns over execution to the bootstrap program, which also is located in the DOS boot record. The bootstrap program then begins loading the DOS files IO.SYS, MSDOS.SYS, and COMMAND.COM.

FATs and Directories

A DOS partition contains a data table called the *File Allocation Table*, or FAT. (Actually, there are two FATs; there is a primary FAT and a backup FAT that's used in the event the primary FAT becomes corrupted.) The

FAT contains an entry for every cluster on the disk. DOS uses the FAT to keep track of which clusters are allocated to which files on the disk. The FAT is the key that enables DOS to locate, read, and write files on a disk.

A FAT cluster entry can contain any one of the entries listed in table 24.2.

Table 24.2

Possible FAT Cluster Entries

Entry	Meaning
0	Cluster is available
BAD	Cluster contains bad sector and can't be used
Reserved	Cluster has been set aside for use only by DOS
EOF	Marks the last cluster in a file
### (numbers)	Number identifying the next cluster in the file

The FAT isn't much good by itself. DOS uses the root directory table in conjunction with the FAT to locate a file. The root directory table contains the name of the files in the root directory and the starting cluster number of the file.

Here's how the two tables work together: Assume that you use the TYPE command to direct DOS to display the contents of a text file in your root directory. DOS looks in the root directory table and finds that the file starts at cluster 200. DOS then reads the data in cluster 200. Next, DOS reads the entry in the FAT for cluster 200. The entry tells DOS that the next cluster of this file is located in cluster 201. So, DOS reads the data contained in cluster 201. Then, DOS reads the FAT entry for cluster 201 to see where to go next. This entry tells DOS that the next cluster for the file is cluster 322 (the file is fragmented). DOS reads the data from cluster 322, and then reads the cluster entry in the FAT for cluster 322. The FAT entry for cluster 322 contains EOF, which tells DOS that 322 is the end of the file. So, DOS quits looking for any more data.

NOTE *The root directory table also contains entries for any subdirectories directly under the root directory. Subdirectory entries in the root directory table reference the starting cluster of the*

subdirectory's file list (which usually takes only one cluster to store). The subdirectory cluster contains a list of the files in the subdirectory and their starting clusters. DOS then uses the FAT to locate files in subdirectories in the same way it locates root directory files.

What's All That Information Good For?

Now that you know all about tracks, sectors, clusters, FATs, and all the other technical stuff you have just read, what good is that information? Most of it was background information that enabled you to understand how DOS uses the FAT and to understand what is contained in the master boot record. When something happens to the disk, it usually involves the master boot record or the FAT. Understanding what those things are and how they're used by DOS will help you troubleshoot and fix problems that arise with them.

Now that you have some background information under your belt, you're ready to solve some specific problems.

Specific Errors

Usually, your PC generates an error message when the hard drive isn't working properly. The message probably will be a bit cryptic, but at least it gives you a general idea of what's wrong.

Error: General error reading drive C:

This error typically is caused by the BIOS not being able to read the information in the hard drive's master boot record. Chapter 22 has a procedure to re-create the master boot record using the FDISK command. Turn to Chapter 22 to perform this procedure. If you re-create the master boot record and still can't get the drive to work, or you are unable to re-create the master boot record, use a disk utility, such as Norton Disk Doctor or Central Point's DiskFix, to try to recover the disk. Use the disk utility to perform a surface analysis of the disk.

If the problem persists even after you have attempted to re-create the master boot record and tried a disk recovery utility, your disk's boot sector (0,0,1) may be bad. If so, you won't be able to recover the disk yourself. You may be able to send it to a data service bureau and recover the data (some service bureaus are listed near the end of this chapter).

Error: `File allocation table bad`

If this error appears, it means that something sinister has happened to your disk's primary FAT. Unfortunately, DOS won't automatically use the backup FAT and keep working. It's possible to use the DOS DEBUG program to copy the backup FAT and replace the damaged primary FAT, but the process is incredibly cryptic. Instead, use your favorite disk utility (Norton or Central Point, for example) to re-create the FAT.

A bad FAT may be an indication that the drive is about to go bad. After you recover the disk by re-creating the FAT, back up the entire disk, reformat it, and restore your files on it. Be vigilant about backing up your data.

Error: `HDD controller failure`

This error generally indicates that your hard disk controller has failed, but it can be caused by other problems. Use the following procedure to troubleshoot the problem.

Procedure:

Troubleshooting the Disk Controller

1. Turn off and open the system.

2. Verify that the hard disk controller is firmly seated in its bus socket.

3. Verify that the interface cables are connected properly and securely to the hard disk.

4. Try to boot the system and access the drive.

5. If the problem persists, turn off the system. Then, check for other adapters in the system that may share a ROM BIOS address with the disk controller or host adapter (you might have just installed a new adapter, for example, and it is conflicting with the disk controller). If you locate such a device, remove it and retest the system to see whether you can access the hard drive.

6. If the problem persists, try a new hard disk controller or host adapter. Try to acquire the same brand and model of controller as the original. Using the same brand and model is not as important with SCSI and IDE drives as it is with other types of hard drives.

Error: `Hard disk failure (or 1701)`

If you receive the numeric error `1701` or `Hard disk failure` during boot, the disk controller is having trouble communicating with the hard drive. Often, this error is caused by a loose connection between the controller or host adapter and the drive.

Procedure:

Checking Hard Disk Connection and Configuration

1. Turn off, unplug, and open the system.

2. Verify that the power cable to the hard drive is securely attached.

3. Check the connection of data cables to the hard drive to verify that they are installed correctly (check for pin 1 orientation).

4. Verify that the drive select jumper is set properly on the drive (refer to Chapter 5, "Hard Disk Tweaking: Cleaning, Packing, and Compressing," for more information on hard disk installation).

5. Plug in the system and turn it on to see whether the problem is solved.

6. If the error still occurs, you may have a bad controller or bad disk drive. If you have access to another controller or host adapter, try it. If the problem persists, contact the technical support department at the place where you purchased the hard drive (or PC).

Error: Hard disk read failure — Strike F1 to retry boot

This error has a number of possible causes, from loose connections to a bad disk.

1. Press F1 to retry the boot. If it works, run a disk recovery utility on the drive to see whether you can locate the cause of the problem.

2. If the utility doesn't locate the problem, or pressing F1 doesn't work, turn off, unplug, and open the PC.

3. Verify that the power cable to the hard drive is securely attached.

4. Check the connection of data cables to the hard drive to verify that they are installed correctly (check for pin 1 orientation).

5. Verify that the drive select jumper is set properly on the drive (refer to Chapter 5 for more information on hard disk installation).

6. Plug in the system and turn it on to see whether the problem is solved.

7. If the problem persists, the problem may be an unreadable master boot record. Turn to Chapter 22 and perform the procedure "Re-Creating the Master Boot Record," and then reboot the system.

8. If the problem persists *and you have a backup of the drive*, reformat the drive by entering **FORMAT C: /U /S** at the DOS prompt. After the drive is formatted, restore your files and try booting the system again from the hard drive.

9. If you don't have a backup of the drive, don't format it. Instead, try a disk recovery utility on the drive. If that isn't successful, contact technical support at the place where you purchased the drive (or PC).

10. If you are unable to format the disk *and you have a backup of the drive*, use FDISK to delete the existing partition(s) on the drive. Then, use FDISK to create new partition information. Reformat the drive as described in step 8. Restore your files, and then try to boot from the drive.

11. If you're still unable to access the disk, either the disk or the controller is bad.

Other Errors

If your hard disk is generating errors other than those described, follow the next set of steps to attempt to diagnose the problem.

Procedure:

General Drive Troubleshooting

1. Open the system and check the disk connections.

2. Check the drive select jumper for correct drive selection.

3. Verify that the adapter is seated in its socket.

4. Run a disk recovery utility on the drive.

5. Re-create the master boot record if step 4 doesn't solve the problem.

6. Contact technical support for help.

Using CHKDSK

CHKDSK is a program that comes with DOS. CHKDSK, instead of checking your disk, is designed to check the FAT and fix problems that may occur with the FAT. CHKDSK is a good tool to use often for routine maintenance of your PC's file system.

You will recall from earlier in the chapter that the FAT stores entries about each of the clusters on the disk. The FAT serves as a one-way linked list that DOS uses to locate the clusters that make up a file. The entries in the FAT for a particular file form a chain, because DOS follows the chain of entries until it has located all the parts of the file.

But, what happens when a cluster entry is somehow damaged? You end up with lost chains. The chain of entries is broken, DOS can no longer follow the chain, and part of the file is lost.

You can use CHKDSK to recover these lost clusters. CHKDSK can either convert the lost cluster chains to files so that you can use them, or it can mark the clusters in the FAT as being available, making more free space available on the disk.

TIP

Never run CHKDSK inside of Windows. Always run it from the DOS prompt outside of Windows.

Procedure:
Running CHKDSK to Fix Disk Errors

1. If Windows is running, exit Windows.

2. At the DOS prompt, enter **CHKDSK /F**.

3. If CHKDSK reports that there are lost clusters and asks whether you want to convert them to files, these are your options: If you want to review the files, answer Yes. CHKDSK will convert the lost cluster chains to files in the root directory of the disk with the file names FILE*nnnn*.CHK, where *nnnn* is a number. You then can view the contents of the files to see whether you need them. If you don't want to view the files, answer No when CHKDSK prompts you about converting the clusters to files.

NOTE

The files created by CHKDSK /F from lost cluster chains retain their original file formats. You may need to use different applications to view the files. To view a recovered Excel file, for example, you need to use Excel.

CHKDSK may also report that you have cross-linked files on the disk. *Cross-linked files* are multiple files or directory entries that use the same disk space. As in the physical world, no two things can occupy the same space, so one of the cross-linked files is corrupted.

CHKDSK won't recover cross-linked files—it just tells you they exist. Here's how to unlink them:

Procedure:
Eliminating Cross-Linked Files

1. Copy the cross-linked files to a new directory, creating new, unlinked copies of the files.

2. Examine the files to see which one is corrupted. If it's a document file, you might be able to restore the file opening it in its parent application and adding the missing data. EXE and COM files that become cross-linked and corrupted should be restored from the original copies on the program's distribution disks.

Seeking Professional Help

If you've have tried to fix a hard drive problem yourself and have contacted technical support, but still can't get the drive working, you might be able to send the drive to a data service bureau to have the files recovered from the disk. The cost of these services varies from bureau to bureau, and also depends on the severity of your disk problem (the more trouble it is to get the data off, the more you're going to pay).

Table 24.3 lists some data service bureaus that perform hard disk recovery for a fee.

Table 24.3

Data Recovery Service Bureaus

Company	Location	Phone Number
CNS, Inc.	Denvile, NJ	201-625-4056
Data Retrieval Services	Clearwater, FL	813-461-5900
Disk Drive Repair, Inc.	Seattle, WA	206-575-3181
Disktec	Houston, TX	713-681-4691
Drive Repair Serv	San Leandro, CA	510-430-0595
Electric Renaissance	Roselle, NJ	908-417-9090
FRS, Inc.	Sacramento, CA	916-928-1107
Hard Drive Associates (HDA)	Portland, OR	503-233-2821
Magnetic Data	Eden Prairie, MN	800-634-8355
Sleepy Hollow	Woodland, CA	916-668-5637
OnTrack Data Recovery, Inc.	Eden Prairie, MN	800-872-2599
Randomex, Inc.	Signal Hill, CA	310-595-8301
Resource Dynamics	Dallas, TX	214-733-6886
Total Peripheral Repair (TPR)	San Diego, CA	619-552-2293
Valtron Technologies, Inc.	Valencia, CA	805-257-0333

25

Healing a Memory Problem

By far one of the most aggravating problems that can crop up in a PC is a memory error. When it occurs, the problem often is sporadic, coming and going without rhyme or reason. Fortunately, memory problems don't crop up very often. When they occur on your PC, however, you can use the procedures provided in this chapter to find the problem and cure it.

This chapter covers the following topics:

- Memory problems

- Memory banks and memory arrangement

- Memory-testing procedures

Overview of Memory Problems

Problems caused by a memory failure just don't crop up very often in a PC. In the last 10 to 12 years, I have seen one PC generate an error message caused by a chip that went bad. That's 1 PC out of about 200 with which I have dealt. A 1/2 percent failure rate in 10 years leaves me fairly confident that you will not experience memory failures very often.

When you do experience a memory error or problem with your PC, however, the cause might not even be a bad chip or memory module. It could just be that a chip or module is loose in its socket. Because such simple-to-fix problems are the most common, they are the ones this chapter covers.

When a memory error occurs, you might receive an error message. Sometimes the memory error can help you find the memory chip or module that's experiencing the problem. Often, though, the memory error does not reference the correct memory and does not help you identify the problem. So I am foregoing a discussion of memory error messages and concentrating on the procedures that you follow with or without an error message. If your system manual includes a list of memory error messages and solutions, however, you still might want to try the manual's suggested solution first.

Before you begin, you need to understand the way memory is organized on the motherboard or memory adapter.

Understanding Memory Banks

Memory is arranged on a motherboard in banks. The banks are identified on the board by a painted rectangle surrounding each bank. A typical 386 or 486 motherboard includes 2 banks, Bank 0 and Bank 1, and each consists of 4 system sockets, for a total of 8 sockets. Some 386 and 486 systems include 16 SIM sockets—4 sockets per bank for a total of 4 banks. Typical 286 and prior systems use 4 rows of DRAM sockets (2 rows per bank, and still a total of 2 banks). Some 286 systems use SIMs or SIPs rather than DRAM chips, and their memory is organized similar to typical 386 and 486 systems. Figure 25.1 shows the memory banks on a typical 486 motherboard.

Figure 25.1: The memory banks on a typical 486 motherboard.

Why am I telling you about memory banks? I'm describing them because there are a few important points to remember when installing memory. If you just installed new memory and are having a problem, the cause might be the way the memory in each bank is installed. Following are some points to check:

- **Do memory speeds match in each bank?** All the memory in a bank must be of equal speed. You can install memory of different speeds in a PC, but all the SIMs, SIPs, or DRAMs in a bank must have the same speed.

- **Are the banks filled properly?** When you install memory, the banks must be filled in specific ways according to the amount of RAM you're installing and the design of the motherboard. Check your system manual to determine whether you filled the banks properly.

- **Did you set the proper switches?** When you change the amount of memory in the system, you usually have to change jumper or switch settings on the motherboard according to the amount of memory that is installed on the motherboard.

Whether you just installed new memory or your memory problem seems to have cropped up from nowhere, you can follow several procedures to try to eliminate the problem. First, however, a few words of caution:

 **WARNING** *Memory chips are very vulnerable to damage by static electricity. To avoid any more damage to your system's memory than it has suffered already, be extra cautious about discharging the static from your*

body before touching any chips or memory modules. Avoid touching the chips themselves if you can help it, and try to touch only the chip's casing and not any conductive pins, on the chip or on a SIM or SIP. Keep a hand on the chassis whenever you can to provide an easy path to ground for any nasty static in your body.

Procedure:
Check Memory Seating

Explanation: Memory errors or problems often are caused by poor contact between the memory chip or module and its socket. DRAMs and other types of chips have a tendency to wiggle out of their sockets over time due to vibration and changes in temperature. You also could have installed a chip improperly.

1. Turn off, unplug, and open the system.

2. Discharge yourself (do this often throughout the procedure).

3. Find your system's memory (refer to Chapter 4, "All You Need To Know about Memory", if you're not familiar with where you can find it and what it looks like).

4. **For DRAMs:** After you discharge again, examine each of the DRAMs to verify that the pins on each of the chips are inserted into their sockets properly. Look for pins that are bent under the chip or are outside the socket. If you find any pins out of their sockets, remove the chip, straighten the pins, and reinstall the chip, and make sure you get all the pins in their sockets.

5. **For DRAMs:** After you verify that all the pins are properly installed, press down firmly on the top of each chip to ensure that each one is seated in its socket (see fig. 25.2).

6. **For SIMs and SIPs:** Verify that each memory module is seated in its socket securely. For SIPs, verify that no pins are bent and that all pins are inserted in their sockets correctly. For SIMs, verify that the tabs for each socket are holding the SIM securely in the socket (see fig. 25.3).

7. Plug in the system and turn it on to test it. If the problem disappears, close the system—the problem is solved. If the problem persists, continue with the next troubleshooting procedure.

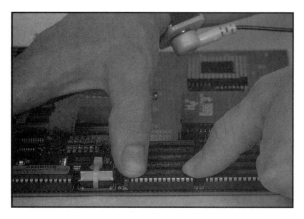

Figure 25.2: Seating a memory chip in its socket.

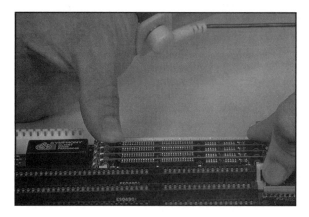

Figure 25.3: Checking socket seating of a SIM.

Procedure:
Rearrange Memory

Explanation: You might be able to eliminate the problem by rearranging the memory in the system. Just the act of removing the memory and reinstalling it sometimes fixes the problem (due to a loose or dirty contact).

1. Turn off and unplug the system. Remember to discharge your static often throughout this procedure.

2. In systems with DRAMs on the motherboard, you may need to remove the motherboard in order to remove the DRAMs. If the memory with which you are working is installed on an adapter, remove the

adapter. In systems with SIMs or SIPs, you should be able to remove the memory without removing the motherboard. For SIMs/SIPs on an adapter, remove the adapter before trying to remove the memory modules.

3. If all the memory in your PC is the same capacity, swap the memory from one bank with the memory in the other. If you have different-capacity memory in each bank, check your system manual to determine whether you can swap capacities between banks. If you can, you probably should reset some jumpers or DIP switches on the motherboard. (The system manual explains these settings.)

   If you can't swap memory, skip the rest of this procedure and go to the next procedure.

4. After you reinstall the system's memory, plug in and turn on the system to test it.

Procedure:

Minimize and Substitute Memory

Explanation: This procedure essentially is a trial-and-error process of elimination to determine which chips or modules are causing the problem. You begin by removing all the system's memory, and then reinstall it in minimal amounts and test the installation. If the installed memory functions properly, install more and test it again. If you have a bad memory chip or module, you eventually will narrow down the possibilities regarding which chip or module is causing the problem.

1. Turn off and unplug the system. Discharge your static often.

2. Refer to your system manual for the minimum RAM you can install in the system.

3. Install the minimum RAM, filling up the first bank. Remember to configure the motherboard's jumpers or DIP switches to specify the amount of memory installed.

4. Turn on the system and access its system setup configuration program (CMOS setup). In the CMOS setup, specify the amount of memory installed in the system, save the changes, and then reboot the system.

5. After the system reboots, test it to see if it functions properly. If you receive a memory size mismatch or memory-related CMOS error, you probably have not configured the system properly for the amount of memory you have. Check your settings and try again.

6. If you do not receive a CMOS or mismatch error but still experience the problem, remove the memory from the system and set it aside. You already might have found the bad memory. Replace it with an equal amount of other memory, such as another set of SIMs, and turn on the system to see if it works.

7. If, after swapping memory, you still experience the problem, you may have a problem with the motherboard or memory card. Stop now and call the technical support department where you purchased the PC, explain the troubleshooting process you have used, and ask for assistance in locating the problem.

8. If the system functions normally after you install the first set of memory chips, SIMs, or SIPs, in Bank 0, turn off and unplug the system, and then install another set of memory in Bank 1. Reconfigure the board's jumpers/DIP switches, reconfigure CMOS setup, and then reboot and test the system. If the system malfunctions, you have narrowed down the potential cause of the problem.

   At this point, you can begin extensive swapping of the memory in and out of the system to identify the chip or module causing the problem; however, this will take a lot of time. Instead, I recommend that you remove the memory from the bank causing the problem and take it to your favorite PC fix-it shop. Have the memory tested there, and then replace the faulty chip or module.

Procedure:

Clean Pins

Explanation: The pins that connect the DRAM or SIM/SIP in their sockets can become oxidized or just dirty from crud floating around in the air in your office. A dirty contact causes problems, often intermittently. If your system uses DRAMs, I feel sorry for you. You probably will need to remove the motherboard to remove the DRAMs. If you work with a memory adapter, you're lucky—the adapter is easy to remove. Removing SIMs or SIPs from a system seldom requires removing the motherboard. If you're working with SIMs/SIPs on an adapter, however, you need to remove the adapter.

1. Turn off and unplug the system.

2. Discharge your static, and if necessary, remove the motherboard or adapter that contains the memory.

3. **For DRAMs:** Carefully remove one row of DRAM chips (read the procedure, "Removing DRAMs," in Chapter 4 if you're not sure how to remove them). Apply some isopropyl alcohol to a soft cotton cloth, and then wipe the pins on each DRAM. Reinstall the chips, and then repeat the procedure for the other rows of chips. Use a dry cotton cloth to wipe away any excess alcohol from the chips.

4. **For SIMs:** Carefully remove the SIMs from one bank. Clean the pins on the SIM module's edge connector with a clean rubber eraser (see fig. 25.4). Rub the eraser over the pins to remove any oxidation or residue. Perform this cleaning procedure away from the PC so you don't get any eraser crumbs inside the PC or on the adapter.

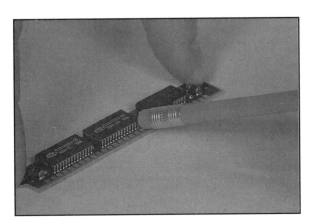

Figure 25.4: Cleaning the edge-connector pins on a SIM.

5. **For SIPs:** Carefully remove the SIPs from one bank. Clean the pins on the SIPs with a soft cotton cloth dipped in isopropyl alcohol. Remove any excess alcohol with a dry cotton cloth.

6. Replace the memory in the bank and repeat the process for the other bank(s).

7. Let the system sit for a few minutes to allow any remaining alcohol to evaporate.

8. Plug in the system and turn it on to test the system.

Procedure:
Seek Help

This procedure doesn't require a set of steps—just an explanation. If you have followed the procedures to this point and still experience memory problems, I suggest you call the technical support department at the place in which you purchased the PC and ask for help troubleshooting your memory problem. Let *them* figure out what the memory error messages, if any, are trying to tell you.

If you can't resolve the problem through technical support, I suggest you take your PC to your favorite computer technician/fix-it shop so that they can check the PC's memory. You could spend days trying to troubleshoot the problem and never find it. If you haven't solved the problem by now, turn it over to a professional to solve.

If you just can't stand the idea of taking your PC to someone else to fix, and if you have the money to spend on some additional memory, try the following procedure. (If you haven't located the problem yet, you probably need some new memory anyway—the memory you purchase for the next procedure will not go to waste.)

Procedure:
Replace Memory

Explanation: If you're willing to spend some time coaxing your PC back to health, you can begin swapping out your PC's memory with new memory that you know is good (at least, you have to assume that new memory you just purchased is good). In this procedure, you selectively replace memory until you eliminate the bad chip or module.

1. Read through your system manual to determine which type of memory to buy for your system. If your system contains DRAMs, buy enough DRAMs to replace one row of chips. If your system uses SIMs or SIPs, buy one SIM or SIP (whichever is used by your system).

2. After buying the new memory, leave it in the packaging until you're ready to install it. (Remember to discharge your static often during this procedure.)

3. **For DRAMs:** After discharging your static, remove one row of DRAMs from their sockets and set them aside where they will not get mixed up with your new DRAMs.

   Install the new DRAMs in place of the one(s) you removed.

   Plug in and turn on the system to test it.

   If the problem goes away, package the old DRAMs and a) throw them away; b) stick them on a shelf for testing at a later date; or c) take them to a PC fix-it shop to be tested.

   If the problem persists, remove the new DRAMs and set them aside. Reinstall the old DRAMs in the first row, then remove the DRAMs from the second row and set them aside. Install the new DRAMs in the second row and retest the system. If the problem persists, repeat this step until you have replaced each row with the new DRAMs and tested the system each time. If the problem still persists, the problem is probably in the motherboard or memory card. Call for help or have the PC serviced by a technician.

4. **For SIMs:** Remove the first SIM from Bank 0 and set it aside. Install the new SIM in its place, and then turn on and test the system. Continue swapping the new SIM for an old one in each bank until you have swapped and tested each SIM. When you do not experience the problem, you have located the bad SIM. Make a tie-clasp out of it. If the problem persists, the trouble must be in the motherboard or memory card. Call for help or have the system serviced.

5. **For SIPs:** Follow the process described in step 4.

The type of trial-and-error testing described in this procedure can take quite a bit of time, but is worthwhile if you're trying to avoid paying for a service call.

26

You Installed a New Gadget, and Everything Went Blooey!

You just installed a wonderful new gadget in your PC, and now nothing is working right or you're getting weird error messages or flaky behavior from the computer. This chapter should help you figure out what is wrong. It covers the following topics:

- Checking adapter installation
- Checking connections
- Checking software configuration options
- Checking for DMA and IRQ conflicts
- Checking for memory conflicts
- What to do when it still won't work after all your fiddling

If you just installed an adapter, the first thing you need to check is the adapter's installation.

Procedure:

Check Adapter Installation

1. Read the installation manual for the adapter cover-to-cover and take the time to understand what you're reading. You might find the answer to your problem in the manual.

2. Check the installation steps for the adapter. Did you omit a step?

3. Examine the adapter to ensure that it is installed in the correct type of bus slot. If a 16-bit bus slot is required and you installed it in an 8-bit bus slot, move it to a 16-bit slot.

4. Be sure that the adapter is fully seated in its adapter socket and that a retaining screw is holding it in place.

If you find any problems in any of the preceding steps, reboot the system and see if the problem is gone.

Procedure:

Check Device Installation

Explanation: If you installed a device other than an adapter, such as a tape drive, CD-ROM drive, or other device, you should check the installation of the device.

1. Read the installation manual for the device cover-to-cover and take the time to understand what you're reading. You might find the answer to your problem in the manual.

2. Check the installation steps for the device. Did you omit any steps?

3. If you find any problems in step 1 or 2 and correct them, reboot the system to see if the problem is gone.

Procedure:

Check Connections, Adapters, and Devices

Explanation: If you can't locate the problem, it's time to check the connections. A cable might be connected incorrectly or just loose.

For adapters and devices other than adapters:

1. Verify the installation with the Check Device Installation procedure if you haven't already done so.

2. If you install a device that requires a power connection cable, check the cable. All the power cables coming out of the power supply are the same. If you see more than one power connection cable, try a different one. Otherwise, just make sure the connection is secure. Check the cables for all other devices in the system to ensure that you haven't knocked something loose while working inside the PC.

3. If the device requires interface connections to an adapter or another device, check the installation steps to make sure you installed the interface cable(s) properly. Verify that pin 1 on each cable is oriented properly on the connector. Also, check the cable connections of other devices in the system to make sure you didn't knock something loose.

For adapters only:

4. Verify the adapter installation with the Check Adapter Installation procedure if you haven't already done so.

5. Make sure that the interface cables to the adapter are attached securely. Verify that pin 1 on each cable is oriented correctly on the adapter's connector.

6. Reboot the system to see if the problem is fixed.

Procedure:

Check Software

Explanation: If your problem persists after checking the installation of the device and/or adapter, the next step you take should be to check the software installation steps required for your device. Simply read through the installation instructions for the device's software again and see if you missed any steps. Then run the installation routine again, verifying your selections as you go.

Problem: Possible DMA or IRQ Conflict

In Chapter 6, "Setting Up Circuit Boards," you learned about DMA channels and IRQ lines. If you didn't read Chapter 6, you should do so. It describes areas of potential conflict between the new adapter or device you have just installed and the rest of the system.

After you've read Chapter 6, you'll understand that the device you just installed could have a DMA or IRQ conflict with another device in the system. It might not conflict with another adapter, but it might conflict with a board-level device (a device built into the motherboard's circuitry). Two devices can't share the same DMA channel, and unless your system is an EISA- or MCA-bus system, you can't assign the same IRQ line to two devices.

NOTE *You can use the same IRQ for two devices in an ISA-bus system. You just can't use them simultaneously. COM1 and COM3 might be sharing an IRQ, for example, but you can't use them at the same time. Attempting to share IRQ lines like this is only marginally useful, so avoid it if you can.*

The way to eliminate a DMA or IRQ conflict is no secret. You simply need to check the devices in the system to verify that no two are using the same DMA channel or IRQ line.

Procedure:

Check DMA

1. Locate your system manual to determine the available DMA channels. In general, unless your system is an XT-class system, only DMA channel 2 will be used (by the floppy controller). If yours is an XT, DMA channels 0 and 1 also will be in use.

2. Check your hardware logs to determine which other devices in the system are using a DMA channel. To determine which DMA channels you can use for your adapter, compare this with the list of available DMA channels you identified in step 1.

3. If your adapter's DMA usage is set in hardware, remove the adapter from the system and assign to it a new DMA channel. (For 16-bit devices, always try to use DMA channels 4 through 7 whenever they are available.) See step 4 if you can't locate a free DMA channel. If your adapter's DMA usage is set in software through a configuration program, run the program and assign a new DMA channel to the adapter.

   If you removed the adapter from the system, re-install and reconnect it. Turn on and test the system to verify that the problem is gone.

4. If you can't locate a free DMA channel, determine which DMA-using devices in the system can have the use of DMA disabled. Decide which of the devices will cause the least drop in overall system performance if its DMA use is disabled. (Disabling a device's use of DMA generally causes a drop in the device's performance, often affecting the system's overall performance.)

   Disable the DMA capability of the selected device, and then assign the resulting free DMA channel to your adapter. If you decide that the new adapter is the best candidate for DMA disabling, disable its use of DMA.

If changing DMA channels does not clear up the problem, check the device's IRQ line, if applicable.

Procedure:

Check IRQ

1. Consult your system manual to determine which IRQ lines are available.

2. Check your hardware logs to determine which other devices in the system are using an IRQ line. Compare this with the list of available IRQ lines you identified in step 1 to determine which IRQs you can choose for your adapter. You also should use MSD to check IRQ usage in the system.

   If you locate an affable IRQ line, continue with step 3a. If you can't locate an available IRQ line, skip to step 3b.

3a. **Free IRQ identified:** If the adapter's IRQ is set in hardware, remove the adapter and reconfigure it to use the available interrupt. (If you're not sure how to set the interrupt, refer to Chapter 6.) Reinstall the adapter and test the system. If the adapter's IRQ is set using a configuration program, run the program, set the IRQ, and then test the system.

3b. **No free IRQ:** If no free IRQ is available, consider one of the following options:

   ● **Eliminate an LPT port.** If your system includes more than one LPT port, ask yourself "Do I really need both ports?" If not, disable LPT2. If you're not sure how to do this, check the manual for the adapter that contains LPT2 (or the system manual). You should be able to disable LPT2 by setting jumpers or DIP switches on the adapter. After you disable LPT2, assign the IRQ it was using to the new adapter.

   ● **Eliminate a COM port.** Your system probably contains more than one COM port, each of which uses a different IRQ. If the system contains more COM ports than you need, disable one and assign its IRQ to the new adapter. Check the manual for the adapter that contains the COM ports (or the system manual) to determine which jumpers or switches to set to disable the port.

   ● **Eliminate a device.** If you can't disable an LPT or a COM port, consider eliminating a device from the system. You might have a device in the PC that you don't use often enough to warrant keeping it, or you might be able to move it to another system (if you have more than one).

Memory Conflicts

Another common problem when installing a new adapter is a memory conflict. Memory conflicts occur when two devices attempt to use the same area of the UMA, and are common with devices such as video adapters, network adapters, and other adapters that require a RAM buffer in the UMA or that include an on-board BIOS mapped to a range of memory in the UMA.

If the new adapter or device you just installed uses a RAM buffer in the UMA, use the following procedures to troubleshoot the adapter's installation.

Procedure:

Verify RAM Buffer and Memory Exclusion

Explanation: After you configure the adapter the first time, you might forget to exclude its RAM buffer from use by your PC's UMA memory manager. Or, you might exclude the wrong range of memory. This procedure helps you verify that you set the memory exclusion properly.

1. Turn off, unplug, and open the system.

2. Remove the adapter from the PC.

   Steps 3 and 4 are optional. If you're sure of the RAM buffer range you specified for the adapter, skip to step 5. If you're not sure which RAM buffer range you assigned to the adapter, follow steps 3 and 4.

3. Remove the adapter from the system. Then, using the adapter's manual as a guide, verify the RAM buffer range you have assigned to the adapter.

4. Reinstall the adapter.

5. **For EMM386 users:** Edit CONFIG.SYS and look for the line that loads EMM386.EXE. Verify that you have an X switch on the EMM386 command line for the range of memory used by the adapter. If the adapter uses the range D000 through D7FF, for example, the EMM386 command line should look similar to the following example:

   ```
   DEVICE=C:\DOS\EMM386.EXE X=D000-D7FF
   ```

   If other adapters in the system that require a RAM buffer or include a BIOS mapped to a range of addresses in the UMA exist, you might see other X switches on the command line.

6. **For a third-party memory manager:** If you're using a third-party memory manager rather than EMM386, add the switches necessary to the memory manager's command line to exclude the range of RAM used by the adapter.

7. Save the changes to CONFIG.SYS, if any, and return to the DOS prompt.

If the line in CONFIG.SYS for EMM386 already includes the correct X switch (or your third-party memory manager included the correct switch), you probably have two devices trying to use the same RAM address range. See the following procedure, "Resolve UMA Conflicts."

If you had to add the correct exclusion option, reboot the system and test the adapter. If the problem persists, then you also should follow the procedure "Resolve UMA Conflicts."

Procedure:
Resolve UMA Conflicts

Explanation: If you checked the memory manager's line in CONFIG.SYS and the correct range of memory already is excluded for your adapter, but you're still having the problem, another device in your system probably is trying to use the same range of RAM as the adapter you just installed. If you add the correct setting and reboot to test the system and it still isn't working properly, this also could be the problem. This procedure helps you verify that no two devices are trying to use the same UMA range.

1. To determine which devices are using a range of RAM in the UMA (check for devices that require a RAM buffer or include their own BIOS), check your system's hardware logs and the manuals for each device that uses a range of RAM in the UMA. If the information isn't in your hardware logs, you need to open the system, remove all the devices that are using RAM in the UMA, and verify their settings.

2. Write down the ranges of memory used by each device and verify that no two devices are using the same range of memory.

3. Adjust the ranges as necessary to eliminate the overlapping memory use. If you don't have enough space in the UMA, try to disable on your system video BIOS shadowing or system ROM shadowing. This creates more available memory in the UMA (because the video or system BIOS isn't using the area), but slows down the system's performance. Depending on how you use your system, the difference in performance may be noticeable.

4. Reinstall all adapters and retest the system.

Procedure:
Check for I/O Base Address Conflicts

Explanation: If the adapter uses an I/O base address, you might have assigned the adapter an I/O address that another is using. This procedure helps you check the I/O address assignment.

1. Check your hardware logs to determine which devices are using an I/O base address and which addresses they are using.

2. Check your new adapter to determine which I/O base address it is using.

3. If the adapter's I/O base address conflicts with another device, check the adapter's manual to determine which other I/O base addresses it supports.

4. Choose an available I/O base address and reconfigure the adapter.

5. Reinstall the adapter and retest the system.

Problem: It Still Doesn't Work

If you verify that the new adapter isn't using an I/O base address, IRQ line, DMA channel, or RAM address that conflicts with another device, the adapter itself might be defective or you might simply be overlooking an option or step required by your adapter. If you can't locate the problem, contact the adapter manufacturer's technical support department so that they can help you troubleshoot the installation. If they can't help you get it up and running, the adapter may be defective and you will need to replace it with a new one.

27

Give Up and Call for Help

If you've been through the procedures in this book that you think should have fixed the problem, and the problem still won't go away, it's time to call in the experts. This chapter suggests some guidelines to use for deciding who to call, getting in touch with the right people, and getting your problem solved. It covers the following topics:

- Who to call

- Phone numbers for Microsoft Technical Support

- Tips for calling

- What to expect when you do call

Does Anyone Ever Read the Manual?

Yeah, but sometimes you would get more out of it by whacking yourself over the head with it. At least it would feel good when you stop. If you have never thumbed through the manual before, try to find it. Try to stay awake while you read it.

At least if you call for help and are asked if you have read the manual you can say, "Of course. It doesn't seem to cover my problem." If you hear silence, it's because they're amazed that you read the manual. They didn't really *expect* you to have read it.

Maybe you searched and said "Enough is enough!" Or, maybe you just don't want to waste your time fiddling around when you don't have a clue about what to do. Why should you? Why not call someone who knows the answer or knows enough to find the answer quickly? I do it all the time. I have enough to do in a day without spending hours tracking down some stupid little problem that I probably caused myself. So, I call someone else and let *him* do the thinking and figuring.

Should I Call the Place Where I Bought the Computer?

That depends on a few things. If any of the following apply, I'd begin by calling the place where you bought the computer:

- *You bought it from a local computer store, and the people there are nice and seem to know what they're doing.* Someone might even come over and fix the problem for you (you don't have to give them bagels or anything, unless you want to).

- *You're pretty sure that you are having a hardware problem.* The place where you bought the computer might need to send you some replacement parts. When the parts show up, call them back again to get help putting in the new stuff. If you bought a piece of equipment from someone else, call *them* when you have a problem with that particular equipment. Don't call the place where you bought the computer.

- *You bought the computer from a mail-order place and they have a toll-free technical support number.* Even if they can't help you and tell you to call someone else, your call to them doesn't cost a thing.

- *You don't know who else to call.* Okay, if the folks from whom you bought the computer can't help you, they should at least be able to steer you to someone who can.

Excessive Finger Pointing

Remember to stand up for yourself if you have to. Sometimes the hardware place will claim it's a software problem. When you call the software place, they tell you it's a hardware problem. You can spend all day in the phone shuffle. Be nice, but tell them you have been shuffled back and forth. The following is a couple of suggestions:

- *Talking to the hardware place:* "Thanks, but I already called (the software company). They assured me it's a hardware problem. Maybe I need a replacement." You always can make unhappy noises about sending the whole thing back if it's still under warranty. That should get them to try a little harder to fix your problem. If they can't figure it out, it really could be a software problem.

- *Talking to the software place:* "I called (the hardware place) and all the hardware checks out fine. They assured me it is a software problem. Maybe your program doesn't support the hardware I have." They hate to admit that their program will not run on your hardware, and try harder to get it to work.

TIP

The more you can narrow the problem down, the better. Ask them what you want to know—they are there to serve you. Just be polite, and try to be in front of the computer when you call.

Can I Call Microsoft?

You bet you can! If you're having a problem with Windows or a Microsoft program, such as Word for Windows or Excel, it's a good idea to call Microsoft for help. The call is

going to cost you (it's not toll-free), so you still might want to call the place where you bought the computer. Try this:

- *If the place you bought the computer has a toll-free technical support line, call them first.* If they can't answer your question, you still can call Microsoft. You haven't lost anything by trying.

- *Call Microsoft if you can't get an answer from the place you bought the computer, or if you just want to go directly to the "experts."* The people who staff the technical support phones at Microsoft are really nice and usually can fix your problem in a few minutes.

Now, you have decided you want to call Microsoft. What's the number? Here are a few:

- **Windows:** 206-637-7098

- **Word for Windows:** 206-462-9673

- **Excel:** 206-635-7070

- **Everything else:** 206-454-2030

- **Sales:** 800-426-9400 or 800-227-4679

- **Bill Gates:** 206-882-8080. Ask for Bill, but don't hold your breath . . .

Can I Call Someone Else?

If you're having problems with a program published by someone other than Microsoft, don't call Microsoft. Call the place that publishes the program. Find the program's manual and look through it to find the technical support number.

If you don't find anything that gives you a number specifically for technical support, call the company's main number. You then should be transferred to tech support or given the number. If they don't have a technical support department, pack up the software, take or send it back where you got it, and get a refund. They don't need your business badly enough.

What To Know before You Call

You should know a few things before you call for help. If you don't know these things off the top of your head, make a list and keep it handy when you call.

- What type of PC (brand and CPU type) are you using?

- What version of DOS are you using? To find out, type **VER** at the DOS prompt.

- What version of Windows are you using? To find out, select the **H**elp menu in Program Manager, and then choose **A**bout. You can do the same thing in File Manager and all the programs in the Accessories group (and just about any of the programs that come with Windows).

- What is the problem? You should be able to describe the problem in a few specifics. Don't say, "Well, it's not working." Tell them *what* isn't working. Don't worry if you don't use the correct technical terms.

- Does the problem happen every time you try to make it happen?

- Do you get any error messages? Write them down so that you can repeat them to the technician.

- If it seems to be a problem with a peripheral, such as a CD-ROM drive or an optional card, you should know the name and model number of the card or peripheral. It's in the manuals for the equipment.

Where To Sit When You Call

It's best to have a phone right beside the computer. The technician probably will want you to poke and prod a few things while you're on the phone. If you have a cordless phone, you're in good shape. If you don't have a phone nearby, have a pen and paper handy so that you can write down instructions.

If you have to do a lot of running back and forth between the phone and computer, the technician might give you a list of things to try, ask you to hang up, try the things on the list, and then call back if they don't work. Another solution is to have someone else talk to the technician while you fiddle with the computer. Because this could get to be like a Laurel and Hardy movie, consider buying a longer cord for your phone.

NOTE

Better yet, get a headset phone. I bought one at Radio Shack for about $50. It leaves my hands free so I can type and use the mouse without getting a neck-ache. I use it all the time, and it was tax-deductible.

How To Ask Your Questions

- Even if you aren't asked, give the technician your first name. You seem more friendly that way, and might make a new friend. Microsoft technicians usually ask you who you are so they don't have to say "Hey you."

- Try to describe the problem in one sentence that is something like this: "When I move the mouse, the pointer on the screen jumps all around." Tell them what you're doing, and what happens when you do it.

- If you can't describe the problem in one or two sentences, write down a description of what happens in a step-by-step fashion, and then place the call. This way, you don't have to interrupt the technician five minutes down the road to say, "Oh, I forgot to tell you that the computer also belches foul-smelling green smoke when I turn it on."

- If you have an answering machine that can record calls, you might want to turn it on and record the conversation with the technician. If you have to hang up and try something the technician suggested, you can listen to the tape if you forget the finer points of what it was you were supposed to do.

Some Things They Might Ask You To Do

If the technician could sit down at your computer and pound on the keys or mouse, she probably could find and fix the problem in a few minutes. You might, however, be 3,000 miles away, so you have to be the ears, eyes, and hands for the technician. So, you probably will be asked to do some or all of the following.

Reproduce (No, Not That)

No, you don't have to clear off your desk for this one. The technician might ask you if the problem occurs all the time. In other words, can you *reproduce the error* or weird behavior by going through a set of steps? "I choose this from the menu, choose this option, and then choose OK, and a full eclipse of the sun happens and I grow really thick hair on my butt. It happens every time."

If the problem happens consistently, write down the steps leading up to the problem. The technician then can follow your steps to see if the same thing happens on her machine. If it does, you probably have a bug in the program (which software companies affectionately refer to as "undocumented features"). If the technician can't duplicate the error, at least you have provided the technician with a better idea of what you are doing when the problem happens.

Repeat an Error Message

If you're lucky, the problem you are experiencing generates some kind of error message. In Windows, these error messages usually show up in a dialog box with an exclamation mark. `This program has generated an error and will self-destruct in 30 seconds. Press OK to blow up the system now, or Cancel to let it die on its own.` The messages usually don't make that much sense to the average user. Sometimes the message will say something like "The application caused a general protection fault in module something-or-other" or "This application has violated system integrity".

The main thing is that when the error happens, write down what the error message says. Then, you can repeat it word-for-word to the technician. Microsoft keeps a database of errors and what can cause them, so this makes it easier for the technician to find out what might be wrong.

Describe Your System

This doesn't mean you need to tell the technician, "It's about two feet wide, eight inches high, has a lot of coffee stains on the keyboard, and there's a big scratch across the serial number." And, she probably will not be interested to learn that you saved fifty bucks on shipping by driving 300 miles in your '68 VW van to pick it up yourself.

The technician needs to get an idea of what your system contains to be able to determine what might be causing the problem. Following are some intimate secrets you might be asked to divulge:

- Computer brand and model
- CPU type (286, 386, 486)
- Type of video card (the monitor usually doesn't matter)
- Type of mouse you're using and whether it's a bus mouse (uses its own card and probably has a round connector) or serial mouse (uses a 9-pin or 25-pin D-shaped connector)
- Type of floppy drives you have (5 1/4-inch 1.2M or 3 1/2-inch 1.44M)
- Brand and model number of the hard drive
- Type of hard drive interface (IDE, SCSI, and ESDI are the most common these days)
- Other equipment that might be installed on the system, such as tape drives, CD-ROM drives, fax or modem cards, network cards, sound cards, and stuff like that
- The IRQs used by some of your equipment
- Which area of memory a card uses

Tell Them What's In Some Files

No, you will not have to tell them about the secret stuff you have been collecting about the neighbors for the CIA. Be prepared to open and describe the contents of CONFIG.SYS, AUTOEXEC.BAT, WIN.INI, and SYSTEM.INI. Because the technician probably also will ask you to use MSD to check out your hardware, I recommend using MSD to view the files. If you need to actually edit the files, you need to use EDIT, SysEdit, or Notepad because MSD doesn't enable you to edit the system configuration files.

Reboot or Restart the System

After you are at the DOS prompt, the technician might ask you to reboot the computer or restart Windows—and sometimes both. If something is really hosed, the computer might not reboot when you press Ctrl-Alt-Del. Instead, you might have to press the reset button on the front of the computer. You should have one somewhere. If you can't find the reset button, turn off the computer and let it sit for about five seconds. Then, turn it on again.

Send Money

If you bought your computer from a mail-order place, and you're talking to a technician from there, you might be asked to buy a replacement component. This usually is how it works:

1. The technician, after much fiddling and fooling around over the phone, decides that you have a severely messed-up gadget in the computer.

2. If it's under warranty, the company generally sends you a replacement part for free. But, they have no way to be sure that you'll send the old one back when you get the new one. So, they ask you to buy a new one, and then recredit you when you send in the old one. (Credit cards are handy here.) They charge a new one to your card, and then credit your card when the old one comes in.

3. The technician will give you an RMA or RA number that stands for Return to Manufacturer Authorization or just Return Authorization. *Write the number down and don't lose it!* You will need to write the RMA number on the outside of the box when you send the old part back. If there's no RMA number on the box, they will not accept the box and you will not get credit for it. If you lose the RMA number, call the place back and ask them to look it up for you.

4. If the part is no longer under warranty, you still need to buy the new one, but you won't get credit for the old one. You don't have to send it back. Use it for a nifty, high-tech paperweight, doorstop, or coffee table conversation piece.

5. When the new part shows up, call the technical support department again to get help to install it. You usually need just a Phillips screwdriver. Remember to unplug the computer before opening it up.

This type of arrangement is pretty common. Using a credit card to buy the replacement gives you a little more leverage should the replacement part "disappear" in the mail. You can call the credit card company and put a hold on the transaction until the whole mess is settled.

Part 4

Appendix

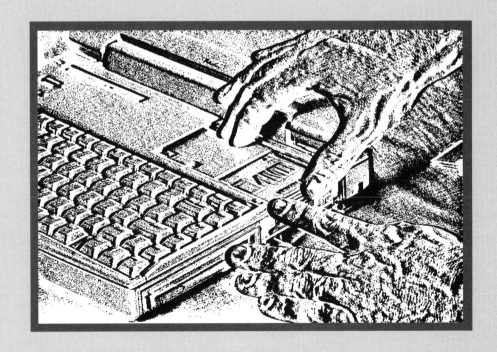

System Log Sheets

This appendix contains log sheets you can use to keep track of your system hardware, including IRQ, DMA, and base I/O address assignments. You also should keep track of changes you make to your system's software configuration. Use comments in your system and Windows configuration files when you make changes to them. Note other changes in this appendix.

IRQ Assignments

IRQ	Common Function/Assignment	Use on This System
NMI	Non-maskable interrupt	Reports parity errors
0	System timer	System timer
1	Keyboard	Keyboard
2	Cascade input to 2nd interrupt handler	
3	COM2, COM4	
4	COM1, COM3	
5	LPT2	
6	Floppy disk	
7	LPT1	
8	Real-time clock interrupt	
9	Software redirected to interrupt OAh	
10	Available	
11	Available	
12	Available	
13	Coprocessor	
14	Hard disk controller	
15	Available	

Common Base I/O Address Assignments

Base I/O Address	Common Device/Assignment	This System
1F0–1F8	Hard disk	
200–207	Game I/O adapter	
278–27F	LPT2	
2E8–2EF	COM4	
2F8–2FF	COM2	
300–31F	Prototype or network card	
360–363	PC network low address	
368–36B	PC network high address	
378–37F	LPT1	
380–38F	SDLC, Bysynchronous	

Base I/O Address	Common Device/Assignment	This System
3A0–3AF	Bysynchronous (primary)	
3B0–3BF	Monochrome display adapter	
3C0–3CF	EGA/VGA	
3D0–3DF	CGA/MCGA	
3E8–3EF	COM3	
3F0–3F7	Floppy controller	
3F8–3FF	COM1	

UMA Memory Range Assignments

Memory Range	Common Assignment	This System
A000–AFFF	EGA, VGA	
B000–B7FF	MDA, Hercules, VGA	
B800–BFFF	EGA, VGA, CGA, Hercules	
C000–CBFF	8514/A, VGA, EGA	
CC00–CFFF		
D000–D3FF		
D400–D7FF		
D800–DBFF		
DC00–DFFF		
E000–E3FF		
E400–37FF		

continues

Memory Range	Common Assignment	This System
E800–EBFF		
EC00–EFFF		
F000–F3FF		
F400–F7FF		
F800–FBFF		
FC00–FFFF		

DMA Channel Assignments

DMA Channel	Common Assignment	This System
0	RAM refresh (XT only)	
1	Hard disk (XT only)	
2	Floppy controller	
3	Available	
4	Available	
5	Available	
6	Available	
7	Available	

Notes

Notes

Index

C

cables

CD-ROM connections, 148-149

checking, 231

connecting, 89-90

checking connections, 266

floppy controller tape drives, 180-181

hardware-configured network adapters, 115-116

motherboard, 200-202

sound card, 160-161

floppy disks, 135

modem, connecting, 190-191

monitor power, 236

power, checking, 227

ribbon cables, 102

splitter (Y-cables), 159

tape drive, 179

video, checking, 236-237

cache RAM, 60-61, 199

caching disk controllers, 61

Cannot load COMMAND, system halted error message, 240

cartridges, laser printer, 174

CAT sound adapter (VocalTec), 158

CD-ROM discs, *see* **CDs**

CD-ROM drives, 30, 144

audio CDs, testing, 153

cables, connecting, 148-149

data CDs, reading, 152-153

external, configuring/installing, 150

installing, 151

interfaces, 147

internal, configuring/installing, 147-149

internal versus external, 146

multimedia kit, 147

performance, 145

photo CDs, viewing, 145-146, 153

purchasing considerations, 145-147

sharing on networks, 151-152

sound cards, 157-160

types, 151

CD-ROM/XA drives, 146

CDs (compact discs)

audio

playing, 146, 152

testing, 153

benefits/detriments, 145

data, reading, 152-153

data availability, 144-145

features, 144

multimedia, 144

photo, viewing, 153

Central Point Backup utility, 238

Central Point Tools utility, 238

central processing units, *see* **CPUs**

channels, DMA

assignments, 282

configuring, 159-160

conflicts, eliminating, 267

child windows, SysEdit program, 9

chips

CMOS, 241-242

data corruption, 243

settings, 202, 243

DRAM, replacing, 264

faulty, identifying, 262

seating, 227

SIM (single in-line module)

edge-connector pins, cleaning, 263

installing, 67-69, 120

pin installation, verifying, 261

removing, 67-69

replacing, 264

SIP (single in-line package)

installing, 69

pins, 261-263

removing, 69

CHKDSK command, 73, 256-257

choke, repositioning, 214

Q

QIC-40 format tape drives, 178
QIC-80 format tape drives, 178
quad density (QD) floppy disks, 134
quoted strings, 45

R

RAM (random-access memory), 29, 54
  address assignments, 105-106
  cache, 199
  installing
    on motherboards, 199
    video adapters, 120
  mapping ROM, 57
RAM buffers, disabling, 268-269
Randomex, Inc., 258
read-only files, accessing, 246
read-only memory, *see* **ROM**
real mode, 80
rebooting, 275
  automatic, overcoming, 244
recording sound objects
  embedding sound in e-mail messages,
    164
  Word for Windows, 163
records
  boot, 237
  master boot, re-creating, 238-239
refresh rates, 119
relationships, sector/cluster, 253
REM command, 34
removing
  adapters, 106
  DRAM (dynamic RAM) chips, 66
  floppy disk drives, 137
  jumpers, 101
  SIMs (single in-line modules), 67-69
  SIPs (single in-line packages), 69

replacement components,
  purchasing, 275-276
resolution
  dot-matrix printers, 167
  inkjet printers, 167
  laser printers, 167
  mouse, 127
  video, 118-119, 123
Resource Dynamics, 258
[restrictions] section (PROGMAN.INI
  file), 49
ribbon cables, 102
RJ11 phone jacks, 190
RLL (Run Length Limited) hard disk
  subsystem, 82
RMA/RA numbers, 275
ROM (read-only memory), 30, 54
  address assignments, 105-106
  mapping into RAM, 57
root directory tables, 254
Run Length Limited (RLL) hard disk
  subsystem, 82

S

sample rates, sound card, 157
SatisFAXtion 400 (Intel) fax-modem, 189
scan rates, 119
scanners, fax program support, 187
ScreenLines=*integer* **setting (SYSTEM.INI**
  file), 47
screens
  black, 236
  selecting, 120
SCSI (Small Computer System Interface)
  hard disk, 178-179
  address assignments, 105
  disks, 82
    configuring, 87-89
    host adapter, configuring,
      91-92

Keeping Your PC Alive
REGISTRATION CARD

Fill out this card to receive information about future New Riders titles!

Name _____ **Title** _____

Company _____

Address _____

City/State/ZIP _____

I bought this book because: _____

_____

I purchased this book from:

☐ A bookstore (Name _____)

☐ A software or electronics store (Name _____)

☐ A mail order (Name of catalog _____)

I purchase this many computer books each year:

☐ 1–4   ☐ 5 or more

I currently use these applications: _____

_____

_____

_____

I found these chapters to be the most informative: _____

_____

I found these chapters to be the least informative: _____

_____

Additional comments: _____

_____

☐ I would like to see my name in print! You may use my name and quote me in future New Riders products and promotions. My daytime phone number is: _____

New Riders Publishing 201 West 103rd Street • Indianapolis, Indiana 46290 USA

- Fold Here -

PLACE
STAMP
HERE

New Riders Publishing
201 West 103rd Street
Indianapolis, Indiana 46290
USA

WANT MORE INFORMATION?

CHECK OUT THESE RELATED TITLES:

	QTY	PRICE	TOTAL

PCs for Non-Nerds. This lighthearted reference presents information in an easy-to-read, entertaining manner. Provides quick, easy-to-find, no-nonsense answers to questions everyone asks. A great book for the "non-nerd" who wants to learn about personal computers. ISBN: 1-56205-150-4.

   ____ $18.95   _____

A Guide to CD-ROM. This is the complete guide to selecting, installing, and using CD-ROMs in business and at home! Learn how CD-ROMs work and what to look for when purchasing a CD-ROM drive. This title also covers where to get CD-ROM titles for any use—from research to games! You'll also learn how to install and share CD-ROMs on networks and workstations. ISBN: 1-56205-090-7.

   ____ $29.95   _____

OS/2 for Non-Nerds. Even non-technical people can learn how to use OS/2 like a professional with this book. Clear and concise explanations are provided without long-winded, technical discussions. Information is easy to find with the convenient bulleted lists and tables. ISBN: 1-56205-153-9.

   ____ $18.95   _____

Windows for Non-Nerds. *Windows for Non-Nerds* is written with busy people in mind. With this book, it is extremely easy to find solutions to common Windows problems. Contains only useful information that is of interest to readers and is free of techno-babble and lengthy, technical discussions. Important information is listed in tables or bulleted lists that make it easy to find what you are looking for. ISBN: 1-56205-152-0.

   ____ $18.95   _____

Name _____

Company _____

Address _____

City _____ State ____ ZIP _____

Phone _____ Fax _____

☐ Check Enclosed ☐ VISA ☐ MasterCard

Card # _____ Exp. Date _____

Signature _____

Prices are subject to change. Call for availability and pricing information on latest editions.

Subtotal   _____

Shipping   _____

$4.00 for the first book and $1.75 for each additional book.

Total   _____
Indiana residents add 5% sales tax.

New Riders Publishing 201 West 103rd Street • Indianapolis, Indiana 46290 USA

Orders/Customer Service: 1-800-541-6789
Fax: 1-800-581-4670

NETWORKING TITLES

#1 Bestseller!

INSIDE NOVELL NETWARE, SPECIAL EDITION

DEBRA NIEDERMILLER-CHAFFINS & BRIAN L. CHAFFINS

This best-selling tutorial and reference has been updated and made even better!

NetWare 2.2 & 3.11

ISBN: 1-56205-096-6

$34.95 USA

MAXIMIZING NOVELL NETWARE

JOHN JERNEY & ELNA TYMES

Complete coverage of Novell's flagship product…for NetWare system administrators!

NetWare 3.11

ISBN: 1-56205-095-8

$39.95 USA

NETWARE: THE PROFESSIONAL REFERENCE, SECOND EDITION

KARANJIT SIYAN

This updated version for professional NetWare administrators and technicians provides the most comprehensive reference available for this phenomenal network system.

NetWare 2.2 & 3.11

ISBN: 1-56205-158-X

$42.95 USA

NETWARE 4: PLANNING AND IMPLEMENTATION

SUNIL PADIYAR

A guide to planning, installing, and managing a NetWare 4.0 network that serves your company's best objectives.

NetWare 4.0

ISBN: 1-56205-159-8

$27.95 USA

To Order, Call 1-800-428-5331

OPERATING SYSTEMS

INSIDE MS-DOS 6

MARK MINASI

A complete tutorial and reference!

MS-DOS 6
ISBN: 1-56205-132-6
$39.95 USA

DOS FOR NON-NERDS

MICHAEL GROH

Understanding this popular operating system is easy with this humorous, step-by-step tutorial.

Through DOS 6.0
ISBN: 1-56205-151-2
$18.95 USA

INSIDE SCO UNIX

STEVE GLINES, PETER SPICER, BEN HUNSBERGER, & KAREN WHITE

Everything users need to know to use the UNIX operating system for everyday tasks.

**SCO Xenix 286, SCO Xenix 386,
SCO UNIX/System V 386**
ISBN: 1-56205-028-1
$29.95 USA

INSIDE SOLARIS SunOS

KARLA SAARI KITALONG,
STEVEN R. LEE, & PAUL MARZIN

Comprehensive tutorial and reference to SunOS!

**SunOS, Sun's version of UNIX for the
SPARC workstation, version 2.0**
ISBN: 1-56205-032-X
$29.95 USA